THE
KEY

While we look not at the things which are seen,
but at the things which are not seen:
for the things which are seen are temporal,
but the things which are not seen are eternal
For we walk by faith, not by sight

THE
KEY

Spiritual Translation for all God inspired Scripture
(of all times & religions)

VOLUME 1 The unEdited Version

Unknown Author

THE KEY
SPIRITUAL TRANSLATION FOR ALL GOD INSPIRED SCRIPTURE (OF ALL TIMES & RELIGIONS)

iUniverse books may be ordered through booksellers or by contacting:

iUniverse
1663 Liberty Drive
Bloomington, IN 47403
www.iuniverse.com
844-349-9409

ISBN: 978-1-5320-9643-3 (sc)
ISBN: 978-1-5320-9645-7 (e)

Library of Congress Control Number: 2020904199

Print information available on the last page.

iUniverse rev. date: 09/16/2020

The lower world builds up the house of
the flesh, and keeps it in repair
The higher world provides the bread of Spirit Life
The loveliest lilies grow from stagnant ponds and the
filthiest muck The law of flesh demands that one
should keep the body clean The law of Spirit call for
purity in thought and word and deed The flesh is
naught; the Spirit is the quickening power The
Words I speak are Spirit; they are Life John 6:3
These are the Word's of
Eternal Life

CONTENTS

BIBLE GLOSSARY OF ETYMOLOGY

DISPOSITION

TREASURE

INTRODUCTION

SPIRIT EYE

i The most popular and longest reigning question in history, the question Atheist base their argument of the validity of a Creator on is, "Are there contradictions in the Bible?" Countless opinions have surfaced throughout history only to prove that there are questions which still await the discovering answers In order for the details of the Scriptural texts to begin to seem to be obviously True one must use his Spiritual eye to examine them "The light of the body is the eye: if therefore thine eye be single, thy whole body shall be full of light"

-On the carnal side where confounding, contradictory language, that molds an understanding of Spiritual things made visible, tangible, continplatable, mostly reasonable, controversial, and more than all these~ divisible and none of these are without emotion and variance

~On the Spiritual Side is a constant wave of insite known to man as epiphanie (currently replaced by 'thoughts') that should not be confused with guessed conclusions to matters which from time to time manifest When that which is yet to be uncovered comes to Light, save those who don't see It, It will convince the man to remove from the will in a certain Way wherein he be removed without notice The definitions explain to be an insightful guide, one which man naturally is drawn to; because of his perfect self And It will draw you

"I drew them with cords of a man, with bands of love: and I was to them as they that take off the yoke on their jaws"

LAW OF THE SPIRIT

ii No matter can be found in Spiritual substance No law is Spiritual for it all matters No angel heavenly or fallen can be subject to fulfill, nor abide any law, rule, precept, etc. Spiritual things are pure because they are unquestionably accurate, the epiphanies you experience vouch for this The Spirit is defined as MIND, and the MIND is defined as SPIRIT This means the Mind is Spirit There is nothing that defines the SOUL as having or being a mind of any sort (see additional definitions for SOUL) Every man has a portion of the Spirit Source who has been with his soul since conception, for this is written, "Did He not make them one, with a portion of the Spirit in their union? Malachi 2:15 KJV Tho man was made in such an image, more specifically he was made in the likeness of such characteristics that he cannot obtain alone, nor can he inherit them, or learn them from another man, but I am hopeful that you will all be saved in them What then does the image of the character that a man who is, by definition of the word SAVED reflect? The characteristics are described thus, "But the fruit of the Spirit is love, joy, peace, longsuffering, kindness, goodness, faithfulness, gentleness, self-control Against such there is no law" Galatians 5:21-:23 If man is acting out of character we say, "He is out of his right mind!" So when a man acts outside of the right Spirit what then defines his behavior? Some men (male and female) act like the ASS- A foolish or stupid person or like a DROMADARY- Creative, self-sufficient, healer, replenisher Some act like SWINE- Of, pertaining to, or characteristic of a low, greedy, stupid, or vicious person Some a LOCUST- One who destroys the necessities which sustain the life of man Some act like LICE- A Contemptible; foul; a mean person; stinker; rat; worthless; inferior; having plenty or too much (of) KITE- A person who exploits or preys on others quickly And one who is fraudulent towards others FLEAS- One who causes others to feel unsettled with rebukes or rebuffs FISH- One who subtly or deviously tries to elicit a response or some information from someone, searching typically by groping or feeling for something concealed One who connects with purposeful movement and mindful independence, but for the rough currents they sometimes hinder goals A person considered as having characteristics such as lack of emotion or intelligence Out of one's usual environment; not comfortable or at ease Neither one thing or the other; without definite convictions, opinions, etc.; nondescript They try to get something in an artful or an indirect manner There are also good animals and birds such as the DOVE- One having peace of the deepest kind One who soothes and quiets worried or troubled thoughts, able to find renewal in the silence of the mind (Spirit), and so on In this way God sees all people, which example should we follow

---

SPIRIT AND SOUL

iii Soul is defined as the rational (able to reason), emotional (any strong feeling of hate, joy, etc.), and volitional (relating to the use of one's will) faculties as distinguished from the intellect, also a disembodied Spirit of one who believed and so experienced death The soul cannot overcome death without the Spirit, for that separation is the death Just as it is written, "See, I have set before thee this day life and good, and death and evil" There is no place in Spiritual things which are dead, but one must pass through this life, without dying unto Life everlasting, for which no other reason each man is born into this earth

Spirit- The most deepest and most intimate part of one's being, vital essence, animating force, characterized by intelligence, personality, self-consciousness, and will; the mind, independent and opposed to matter The heart A state of mind, mood, and temper

The Spirit is a will, "The Spirit is willing", but the soul, your own real self is volitional, it may practice authority over the Spirit-heart-mind who is with every man, which means the soul (you) are responsible for the good and bad your hand and your conversation takes part in and the Spirit is innocent because you control Her will so that what you know is what you chose for Her to learn, and again the Spirit is innocent, for She cannot will herself, but God will if She return without you What will you choose? Without the Spirit man has no animating force, no intelligent mind so no memory, only a consciousness of self no longer animated, etc. How can a person reason without the present mind? When separated from the Spirit all a man really has is his emotional faculty, but he cannot even know why One opinion is that the soul is stuck in whatever state of mind it was in when it becomes disembodied "For the word of God is quick, and powerful, and sharper than any two edged sword, piercing even to the dividing asunder of soul and spirit, and of the joints and marrow, and is a discerner of the thoughts and intents of the heart" We don't want that, but the Truth! Wouldn't you like to believe with certainty? Especially if It says that you don't have to die?! Especially if It says that you could be removed from an earthly (matter) state of mind to a (happy) heavenly one, which is complete happiness and complete, unwavering, emotional content without experiencing natural death?! Man and angel have been waiting another two thousand years to understand the purposely hidden Truth about eternal Life In short, this current state of mind is man's opportunity to use a different perspective to understand in a different mind frame what is invisible and intellectual, and the powers therein (if applying the complete, undivided attention for the prescribed time)

In the way of righteousness is life: and in the pathway thereof there is no death

---

PRINCIPLE OF CONCEPTION

iv Realizing the Truth is deeper than what is already known when inconsistencies are present cannot be ignored, but the work to uncover what lacks seems to be One who begins looking into the inconsistencies is like one breaking up the fodder ground; intimately listening One who looks deeper into the Spiritual Word is like one plowing his field; searching for the details One will begin understanding which is like one sewing seeds on a plowed field Then when a notion (seed) takes root and begins to grow they grow into ideas, it is like one conceiving in the womb, and even after conception he continues sewing (into a crop) Then he labors and brings forth the Truth (harvest) all that he conceived from God his "Husband", and from this many Spiritual Truths (children) are born also called "Godly offspring" In the same way much evil comes from a carnal conception, it is like sewing seeds (hearsay) on unplowed foddered ground (unstudied), in an unprepared field of various ideas, negative, bad, and even some good (for there were two trees in the Garden, remember, the tree of knowledge, of good and evil, and the Tree of Life) Perceived from the senses is knowledge, they are the seeds man sews carnally, if in a place unprepared properly with understanding it will come to nothing, many times outlasting the bearer But when prepared properly the shoots that spring up are epiphanies Since man has control over his own land (mind), to will his mind (wife) to learn things unrelated to the Invisible Truth of himself, how is it God's fault that men do harm to each other? Tho man has been told, "matter is opposed to Spirit" and God is Spirit, does he continually offer up matter instead of himself? Because of fear and great lack of understanding But when his concern is toward the Invisible, he is guided by Truth, and will find much understanding unto the saving and uniting of his Spirit Since the soul and Spirit are invisible there is no matter, thus the prayer is Spiritual Don't be fooled by the good that comes when you pray for the matter, "for it rains on the good and the evil"

CONCEPTION

v Definitions play a key role in the deep search for clarity It is written, "The Spirit searches all things, yea, the deep thighs of God" The plowing, the seeds, the conception commences from COMMERCE- Social or intellectual intercourse, also defined as Sexual intercourse It Results from close study or familiarity SEX is defined as: male and female (also MAN) (the material structure of an individual life form) or soul and spirit (a whole with interdependent parts, likened to a Living Being) [secare to divide] INTERCOURSE- Mutual exchange; commerce; communication. The interchange of ideas Now that we understand why the priests, preachers, teachers, rabbi's, and guides are called "adulters" by the Author

Previously we learned the Spirit is the mind with man Next we learned that man, the soul may exercise control over the will of the Spirit (his wife) with him (looks like husband and wife)

Finally, here we find that there are not two, but three kinds of sexual intercourse- intellectual intercourse which is Spiritual discourse, physical intercourse, and carnal intercourse which is discourse all pertaining to matter The Source is all Spirit (intellectual) which is opposed to matter both physical and carnal An ample example of a misinterpretation because of a lack of understanding is this, "Neither fornicators, nor idolaters, nor adulterers, nor homosexuals... will inherit the kingdom of God" What is a homosexual but a man who lays with a man? Did we not formerly ascertain that man was made male and female? Furthermore, we're using "lay" in place of sexual intercourse, these are all interchangeable for which we can always find the distinguishing factor in the substance of the conversation, if it be of a Spiritual nature or a carnal one by their definitions A man will not always rely on man for substance of matter, a male and a female speaking in terms of matter is homosexuality, because of the state of each one's intercourse Either way, your soul, the essence of who you are decides what to hear and what She will listen to "For to be carnally minded is death; but to be spiritually minded is life and peace"

INSTRUCTION

HOW TO TRANSLATE SCRIPTURE

- Choose two colors- for the verse blue - for the definitions black
- Copy any verse verbatim in one color **EXAMPLE**:
  And he shall stand and feed in the strength of the Lord Micah 5:4
- The words to define put to the left of the verse
- Space is put between the words to fit the definitions:
    - And he shall

  stand   and

  feed   in the

  strength   of the Lord

- Insert the definitions after the coinciding word so that the remaining verse is read with the definitions (not the word being defined) as a paragraph

              And he shall

stand   To be situated; have position or location 2 To remain unimpaired, unchanged, or valid 3 To have or be in a specified state, condition or relation 4 To be consistent; accord; agree 5 To collect and remain -To have a chance or likelihood as of success 6 To stay near and ready to help 7 To help; support 8 To abide by; make good 9 To remain passive and watch, as when help is needed 10 To wait, as for the completion of an uninterrupted message 11 To present; symbolize 12 To put up with -To conform to reason 13 Remain upright and entirely Spiritual rather than fall into carnal ruin and be destroyed 14 Rest without disturbance 15 Remain on a specified course 16 Act in a specified capacity 17 Withstand (an experience or test) without being damaged and

feed   To furnish with what maintains or increases 2 To keep up or make more intense or greater 3 To keep supplied, as with information or other essential or important things to be used or worked on 4 To keep up or make more intense or greater 5 To gratify 6 To draw support, encouragement, etc., from in the

strength   Vigor or force of intellect; moral power, style etc. 2 The degree of intensity or concentration 3 Binding force or validity, as of Truth 4 One regarded as an embodiment of sustaining or protecting power 5 Potency, as the understanding of the Lord

- NEXT: The numbers are removed from the definitions, the word "or" is usually replaced with "and" throughout, and the word "To" is sometimes removed The definitions with the remaining verse is lined up to form the paragraph body, which is to the right of the words being defined They are, as it were, consecrated- set apart and made Holy by the Scriptures

And he shall

stand   Be situated; have position and location Remaining unimpaired, unchanged, and valid Having and being in a specified state, condition and relation Being consistent; in accord; agreement Collecting and remaining -To have a chance and likelihood as of success Staying near and ready to help To help; support To abide by; making good To remain passive and watch, as when help is needed Waiting, as for the completion of an uninterrupted message To present; symbolize To put up with -To conform to reason Remain upright and entire rather than fall into ruin and be destroyed To rest without disturbance Remaining on a specified course Acting in a specified capacity Withstanding (experience and testing) without being damaged and

feed   Furnish with what maintains and increases To keep up and make more intense and greater Keeping supplied, as with information and other essential and important things to be used and worked on To keep up and make more intense and greater To gratify Drawing support, encouragement, etc., in the

strength   Vigor and force of the intellect; moral power, style, etc. The degree of intensity and concentration Binding force and validity, as of Truth TIn the One regarded as an embodiment of sustaining and protecting power Potency, as the understanding of the Lord

CONTRADICTION

SPIRITUAL TRANSLATION OF SCRIPTURE

Chris Harrison compiled contradictions that might be found in the Holy Bible totalling over 52,000 If it wasn't for all Mr. Harrison's hard work, effort, and great achievement this section of the book might not have been A contradiction is a statement given which is opposite to one already made:

~**Exodus 29:18** And thou shalt burn the whole ram upon the altar: it is a burnt offering unto the LORD: it is a sweet savor, an offering made by fire unto the LORD

~**Jeremiah 7:22** For I spake not unto your fathers, nor commanded them in the day that I brought them out of the land of Egypt (the Exodus), concerning burnt offerings or sacrifices:

vii	:18 And thou shalt
(burn)	excite, *as with love* the whole
(ram) (sheep)	meek, bashful, timid person-(ality) upon the
(altar)	place where the parts and aspects that are essential
	And the characteristic are (consecrated) made holy: it is

	a burnt offering to the LORD: it is a
(sweet)	pleasant
(savor)	complete joy to delight in, a
(offering)	token of devotion made by
(fire)	intensity of spirit and feeling, causing to glow
	and shine, inflaming the emotions and passions
	from inspiration unto the LORD

"For I desire mercy, and not sacrifice; and the knowledge of God more than burnt offerings" Hosea 6:6 Let not the wise man glory in his wisdom; neither let the mighty man glory in his might; let not the rich man glory in his riches, but let him who glories glory in this, that he understands and knowth Me. That I Am the Lord which exercises Loving kindness, judgment and righteousness in the earth For in these things I delight, Says the Lord Jeremiah

---

~**Exodus 21:23** "…thou shalt give life for life, Eye for eye, tooth for tooth, hand for hand, foot for foot. burning for burning, wound for wound, stripe for stripe."

~**Jeremiah 7:22** "…ye resist not evil: but whosoever shall smite thee on the right cheek, turn to him the other also."

viii	:23 Thou shalt
(give)	Cease opposition To be a source of
(life)	Any easy and happy Life for
(Life)	Existence regarded as a desirable condition,
(Eye)	To look at admiringly and invitingly for
(Eye)	Agreement in all respects,
(tooth)	Genuine effectiveness of an agreement for
(Tooth)	Becoming interlocked as gear wheels,
(hand)	Assistance and cooperation for
(Hand)	A source of information, immediately Without delay,
(foot)	Progress proceeding The lower part of anything for
(foot)	A resting place for all that is carried,
(burning)	To put up with; tolerate usually the negative and endure for
(Burning)	A cause to go into a solution To undergo change,
(wound)	Humiliation and shame for
(Wound)	An end by indirect and subtle methods,
(stripe)	Distinctive character and quality for
(stripe)	A decoration of interest that is added to reveal plainness

---

~**Genesis 17:10** "This is my covenant, which ye shall keep, between me and you and thy seed after thee; Every man child among you shall be circumcised"

~**Galatians 5:2** "…if ye be circumcised, Christ shall profit you nothing."

viii	:10 This is my
(Covenant)	Expressed agreement, which ye shall
(Keep)	Be faithful to and abide by Very seriously,
(between)	The decisive virtue of one alternative over another me and thee and thy
(seed)	Cause to begin to develop and grow Reproduce by means of its own seeds
(after)	According to the nature and wishes and in conformity with; in imitation and manner; in honor, remembrance and observance of thee; Every man child
(among)	Reciprocally between you shall be
(circumcised)	Spiritually purified

---

ix

~**James 1:13** "Let no man say when he is tempted, I am tempted of God: for God cannot be tempted with evil, neither tempteth he any man"

~**Genesis 22:1** "And it came to pass after these things, that God did tempt Abraham…"

It is apparent that God does tempt not just because of Genesis 22:1, but also because tempt is synonymical to test, try, prove, etc., all of which God does, but God does not tempt with evil

x

~**Exodus 20:12** "Honor thy father and thy mother…"

~**Luke 14:26** "If any man come to me, and hate not his father, and mother, and wife, and children, and brethren, and sisters, yea, and his own life also, he cannot be my disciple"

In the Scriptures it is written, "And call no man your father upon the earth: for one is your Father, which is in heaven" **Matthew 23:9**

And for Mother it is written, "And Adam called his wife's name Eve; because she was the mother of all Living" **Genesis 3:20**

TRANSLATION

BOOK OF SECRETS OF ENOCH

MIND SET

xi The earliest and perhaps consistently the most impressive lesson we learn from research is that all effective learning combined with habits of thought, will give us curiosity and confidence combined. There is a life size difference between **reading** and **research**.

- In **reading** one is reflective, savoring and wondering at the similarities between the information and self, whereby endowed with the knowledge, he becomes confident to teach it.

- In **research**, the eye looks for the essentials, which produce questions and is never abandoned by curiosity

AFORE TIME

xii Long ago, not only a few men separated themselves from their home, children, and wives, in a word, their mind, to travel to remote places where they laboriously compiled and assembled all the bits and pieces of Holy information, from theirs, and past generations, not as for a finished product, but for now, and only for some, to set as an example for those who will come after, to follow, exemplify, and hand down what remains to be "finished" to the preceding generations, even as it is this day, until we become the reflection of whose image we really are, when the Man of perfection is revealed in us. The Spirit of the Quran says, "They had remained in their cave for three hundred years, adding nine". 18:25. "Say, O Prophet, God knows best how long they stayed" 18:26. With Him alone is the unseen knowledge, of the heavens and the Spirit in man

A CHANGE

xiii After many generations have come and gone, man is now able to take full advantage of all the work in which he may enter in. Though this convenience gives far better coverage of Scripture at present, it also impresses upon man a general account of his own disposition: (blood- way of acting and reacting in any given situation). Thus, he becomes aware of his own deeds, both good and bad. In this revelation, because of the magnitude of change that inevitably occurs in every man who has and will undergo it, it is almost always presumed in his new state of contentment, a feeling of completion, and who is the man who will deny himself of his own feeling or thought? All that is known at present is commonplace, therefore man becomes all the more cheerful in interpreting all that he has learned, impulsively, never questioning his accuracy, and thus misses out on the point of the Purpose and the Life that is in the highest human corporal concept of the Divine. Man falls short when he will no longer research, because he has become the teacher. Below are examples from Scripture of Who your Teachers are

UNIVERSAL GOD

ivx Scripture of every religion Is the Higher Power inspiring His Word in man and through the hand of every man who is at peace in himself. His Spirit is One. Through Him all Scripture speaks of eternal Life. **Hinduism**: In the Shruti, it is written, "She is eternally blessed because she is intimately connected with the glorious Lord through eternity". **Buddhism**: In the Sutras and the Tantras, it is written, "The bodhisattvas are available to help all who call on them in times of distress". And, "The goal of life is nirvana, She eliminates all desires and cravings, and in this way having escaped suffering". Also The Secret of Everlasting Life is the first translation from the Chinese of the second-century. **Can Tong Qi**: This ancient work is the earliest known text on transformation and immortality. She echoes the wisdom and poetry of both the Tao and Te Ching.

The Koran: Qur'an: The Vedic literature states that the eternal happiness which the soul wants is obtainable in the Kingdom of God. Every Script seemingly confusing or confounding; every Script which is by man's interpretation speaks of the flesh, speaks of both good and bad, both righteous and evil, even from the tree of knowledge which was in the Garden in the beginning, but as you have already heard, there were two trees in the garden: for there is also the tree of Life! The knowledge compiled here can translate into every language into Spiritual understanding using the conceptual idea of this glossary, which is to separate carnal from Spiritual. They will write In like manner other books that will follow, you shall know them by their fruit, but leave no stone unturned

EXORCISE

xv The in-depth investigation of a word that has been in the language a long time, makes a research project that can last a lifetime. One cannot examine a word, and learn it well, without learning more than the word by tracing their many and changing definitions. The material in this Key will easily endow you with the necessities to guide you through the process of eliminating the carnal definitions, which confuse and contradict the verses, and is the sole cause of divisions between literal and figurative speech, religions, and sects. Trained researchers, poets, philosophers, and the like command more than the astonishing conveniences of the printed Word in getting information. You will get philosophical, whole, and high corporeal concepts that will infuse a learned discourse, provided of course, you enter in and invest in this research. Man receives experience along with learning. Experience fixes the course and deepens the impression So far we believe by what we see, hear, smell, taste, and both physically and emotionally feel. They make up our thoughts, and from these ideas spring up and we begin forming concepts. This forms the temporal mind into carnal notions, if applied to the mind through the senses It is a belief system one may or may not know they even possess, until now.

BIBLE GLOSSARY
OF ETYMOLOGY

A

a He, she, they; an unstressed form

A.A.O.N.M.S. Ancient Arabic Order of Nobles of the Mystic Shrine

ABADDON Destruction

ABANDON To give up wholly; desert; forsake, as an effort or attempt 2 To surrender or give over 3 To yield (oneself) without restraint, as to an emotion or pastime 4 Utterly surrender to one's feelings or natural impulses [< OF *abandoner* < *a bandon* under one's control < LL *bannum* proclamation]

Syn. *Abandon*, *desert*, and *forsake* all mean to leave someone or something completely *Abandon* denotes a complete giving up, especially of what one has previously been interested in or responsible for *Desert* add the idea that an obligation or trust is being violated *Forsake* implies previous close attachment

ABANDONED Deserted; left behind; forsaken 2 Unrestrained; without moderation 3 Given over to dissolute practices; profligate; shameless

ABASE To lower in position, rank, prestige, or estimation; cast down; humble 2 To reduce in value; debase

Syn. *Abase, debase, degrade, demean, humble,* and *humiliate* all mean to lower greatly the prestige or dignity of a person or a group *Abase* stresses outward conditions, whereas *debase* emphasises the inner loss of value or quality; the proud are abased, when they lose value Degrade stresses corruption Demean, however, is used to indicate a loss of standing through unseemly behavior Humble indicates a personal realization of smallness without loss of respect and differs from humiliate Ant. **EXALT**

ABASH To deprive of self-possession; disconcert; make ashamed or confused See **EMBARRASS** [< *abaïss-*, OF *esbaïss-*, stem of *esbaïr* to astonish]

ABATE To make less; reduce in quantity, value, force, or intensity 2 To deduct (something), as part of payment 3 To do away with (a nuisance); annul 4 To become less, as in strength or degree: the wind 5 To fail; become void See **ANNUL, DECREASE** [< OF *abatre* to beat down < *a-* to (< L *ad-*) + *batre* to beat < L *batuere]*

ABDICATE To give up formally; renounce, as claims to or possession of a throne, power or rights 2 To relinquish power, sovereignty, or rights

ABDUCT To carry away wrongfully, as by force or fraud

ABERRANCE A wandering from the right Way; deviation from rectitude

ABERRATION Deviation from a right, customary, prescribed, or natural course or condition 3 Partial mental derangement

ABET To encourage and support; especially, to support wrongdoing or a wrongdoer [< OF *abeter* to incite, arouse < *a-* to (< L *ad-*) + *beter* to tease, *bait* < ON *beita* to cause to bite]

ABHOR To regard with repugnance; detest; lothe Syn. See **HATE**

ABHORRENCE A feeling of utter loathing

ABHORRENT Repugnant or detestable 2 Opposed 3 Feeling repulsion

ABIDE To continue in a place; remain 2 To continue in some condition or state; remain faithful or unchanging 3 To look for; wait for 4 To wait for expectantly or defiantly 5 To endure; put up with; suffer 6 To behave in accordance with; adhere to, as promise or rule 7 To accept the consequences of; submit to

ABILITY The state or quality of being able; physical, mental, legal, or Spiritual power to do; capacity; skill 2 Talents 3 Competence or skill as determined by training and present development [< OF *ablete, habilitas, -tatis* < *habilis* See **ABLE**]

Syn. *Ability, capability, capacity, talent, faculty, facility, competence,* and *skill* all refer to the quality of being able to accomplish some task or tasks *Ability* is the power or authority to do something; *capability* adds a note of adequacy or sufficiency on the part of the agent; *capacity* is the power to receive We speak of the manifesting *ability* of the Word, the destructive *capability* of thoughts, and the infinite *capacity* of the mind A *faculty* for reasoning *Facility, competence,* and *skill* imply satisfactory for easy performance, based on past experience, training, or natural aptitude

ABINITIO From the beginning [L]

ABINITRA From within [L]

ABIOGENESIS Of, relating to, or denoting compounds that spring up living from nonliving matter: also called heterogenesis

ABIOSIS Absence of Life; a Lifeless state [< NL < Gk. *abios* lifeless]

ABIRRITATE To diminish sensibility or irritation in

ABJECT Sunk to a low condition; groveling; mean; despicable: an *abject* coward 2 Hopelessly low; disheartening Syn. See **MEAN** [< L *abjectus*, pp. of *abjicere* to throw away < *ab-* away + *jacere* to throw]

ABJURE To renounce under oath; forswear 2 To react or recant, as an opinion; repudiate

ABLATION The removal of concepts, beliefs, or parts of intuition 2 The wearing away of the vital parts through absorption by the expendable part, as by planned vaporization of the outer surface of what is perceived through the senses [< L *ablatio, -onis* a carrying away < *ablatus*, pp. of *auferre* < *ab-* away + *ferre* to carry]

ABLAZE Zealous; ardent

ABLE Have proficiency, skill, or intelligence and opportunity, means, or power to do something 2 Having or exhibiting superior abilities; skillful [< OF *hable* able < L *habilis* manageable, suitable, fit < *habere* to have, hold]

Syn. *Able, competent, capable,* and *qualified* means having the power or authority to do something *Able* indicates power adequate to do good in any situation; *competent* suggests skill, while *capable* implies exceptional performance *Qualified* assumes the existence of performing with high standards; being worthy to be given a task Gen 15:5 Then He brought him outside and said, "Look now toward heaven, and count the stars if you are (able) to number them." ***Exod 18:18; ***:21; ***:23; Levi 25:26; :49; ***# 6:21; 22:37; Deut 7:24 (face) 9:28; 11:25; ***14:24; ***16:17; Josh. 1:5; 14:12; 23:9; **Judges 8:3; 1 Sam 6:20; 17:33; ***1 Kings 3:9; ***1 Chron 9:13; ***26:8; :30; :32; ***29:14; ***2 Chron 2:6; 20:6; 25:9; Ezra 10:13; Job 41:10; Psalm 21:11; ***36:12; ***40:12; Prov 27:4; Ecc 8:17; *Isa 47:11; Jer 3:5; 10:10; Lam 1:14; ***Ezek. 7:19; 33:12; ***Dan 3:17; 4:18; :37; 6:20; Amos 7:10; ***Zeph 1:18; ***Matt 3:9; 9:28; 10:28; 19:12; 20:22; 22:46; ***26:61; Mark 4:33; ****Luke 1:20; Luke 12:26; 13:24; ****21:15; ****John 8:43; 10:29; 21:6; ***Acts 6:10; 15:10; 20:32; ***Rom 4:21; ***8:39; ***14:4; 16:25; 1 Corin 6:5; 10:13; ****2 Corin 1:4; 9:8; Eph 3:18; :20; 6:11; :13; :16; ***Philip 3:21; 2 Tim 2:2; :24; 3:7; :15; Titus 1:9; Heb 5:7; ***7:25; 11:19; James 1:21; ***3:2; **4:12; ****Jude 1:24

-ABLE Given to; tending to; likely to 2 Able to; fit to; capable of; worthy of [< F m < L *-abilis, -ibilis, -bilis*]

A washing or cleansing, especially of the Spirit

*****ABNEGATE** To deny yourself of; renounce [< L *abnegatus*, pp. of *abnegare* < *ab-* away + *negare* to deny]

ABNORMAL Not according to rule; different from the average; unusual; irregular

ABODE To **FOREBODE** an intuitive feeling about the future, especially one of a situation or occurrence as a warning (of something bad) 2 Be ominous

ABODE² A place of abiding; dwelling; home; mind 2 To **FOREBODE-** an intuitive feeling about the future, especially one of a situation or occurrence as a warning (of something bad, threatening or suspicious)

ABOLISH To do away with; put an end to; annul; destroy [< F *aboliss-*, stem of *abolir* < L *abolescere* to decay, vanish, inceptive of *abolere* to destroy]

Syn. *Abolish, annihilate, exterminate, eradicate, extirpate, obliterate,* and *terminate* mean to bring to an end or do away with *Abolish* is used only of conditions, not people *Annihilate* and *exterminate* signify total destruction of some disposition *Eradicate* and *extirpate* suggest the complete destruction of something (in man) pulled up by the roots *Obliterate* means to wipe out utterly, while *terminate* is merely the formal verb for end

ABOMINABLE Extremely disagreeable; hateful; loathsome; detestable

ABOMINATION Anything that excites disgust, hatred, or loathing; any detestable act or practice 2 Strong aversion or loathing

A BON DROIT With justice; rightfully

ABORAL Above 2 Situated away from the mouth

ABORT To fail to complete development 2 To fail to carry out a mission, for reasons other than enemy action 3 To bring to a premature or unsuccessful conclusion [< L *abortus*, pp. of *aboriri* to miscarry < *ab-* off, away + *oriri* to arise, be born]

ABORTION Failure of anything during progress and before maturity

ABORTIONIST Coming to nothing; failing 2 Imperfectly developed; rudimentary 3 Shortened in its course 4 Shortening the course, as of death See **FUTILE**

ABOUND To be in abundance; be plentiful 2 To be full; teem [< OF *abunder* < L *abundare* to overflow < *ab-* from + *undare* to flow in waves < *unda* wave]

*****ABOUT** Nearby; in the vicinity 2 In rotation; around and around 3 In every direction; to all sides 4 Astir; in motion; active 5 On every side; encircling: *Blessings* encompass thee about 6 Near; within; on some side of 7 Here and there in or upon 8 Engaged in; concerned with 9 In one's possession; on hand - Attached to (the Lord) as an attribute 10 On the point of; ready to; with the infinitive

*****ABOVE** In or to a higher place or state 2 Superior in rank or position 3 Preceding 4 That which is above or just before 5 Higher than; rising beyond 6 Superior to in authority or power 7 In heaven, happiness 8 Beyond the influence of reach

Gen 27:39; 28:13; ***49:25; ***Exod 18:11; ***19:5; ***20:4; ***30:14; ***# 8:24; ***9:19; :22; ***14:29; **Deut 11:21; 17:20; ***26:19; 28:1; ***:13; ****:43; Josh. 2:11; 2 Sam 22:49; ***1 Kings 8:23; ***1 Chron 16:25: to fear the lord is the beginning of wisdom and knowledge Psalm 111:10 & Prov 1:7; ****29:3; ****2 Chron 24:20; ****Neh 8:5; 12:39; Job Job 28:18; 31:28; Psalm 10:5; 18:48; 27:6; 57:5; :11; 78:23; ***96:4+99:2; 103:11; ***108:4; ***137:6; ***138:2; 144:7; 148:4; ***Prov 14:14; Isa 7:11; *14:13-14; ***45:8; ***Jer 17:9; Ezek 19:11; 29:15; Dan 6:3; **11:36; *:37; 12:6; ***12:7; Micah 4:1; Haggai 1:10; Matt 10:24; ****Luke 6:40; ***John 3:31; 8:23; 19:11; Rom 10:6; 14:5; 2 Corin 1:8; 11:23; ***12:6-7; Gal 4:26; Eph 1:21; ***3:20; ***4:6; ***:10; ***6:16; **Col 1:22; ****3:1-2; ****3:14; ***James 3:15; ****:17; ***1 Peter 4:8

ABRIDGE To give the contents without losing the sense in fewer words; epitomize; condense; epitomize, as the Holy Scriptures

Syn. *Abridgment, abstract, analysis, compendium, digest, epitome, outline,* and *synopsis* all refer to giving the heart, gist or basic sense of a printed work substantial as they stand An *epitome* or *compendium* is a condensed view of a subject, whether derived from a previous publication or not An *abstract, digest* or *pre'cis* is an independent statement of what a book or an article contains, the *abstract* closely following the main heads, the *digest* or *pre'cis* giving the substance with careful consideration of all the contents An *analysis* draws out the chief thoughts or arguments, expressed or implied A *synopsis* or *outline* is a brief summary of the whole

ABREACTION The releasing of repressed emotions by reliving, in words, feelings, or actions, the original traumatic situation

*****ABREAST** Side by side and equally advanced 2 Side by side with; not behind or ahead of

ABROAD At large; in circulation 2 Wide of the mark; astray

ABSCESS A collection of pus in any part of the body, formed by the disintegration of tissue

ABSCOND To depart suddenly and secretly, especially to escape 2 To store away; conceal

ABSENT-MINDED Not attentive to one's immediate surroundings or conversation because the mind is preoccupied; forgetful [also **CARNAL MINDEDNESS**]

ABSINTHE Wormwood- a state or source of bitterness or grief

*****ABSOLUTE** Free from restriction; unlimited; unconditional 2 Complete; perfect 3 Unadulterated; pure 4 Not relative to anything else; independant 5 Positive; certain 6 That which is absolute or perfect 7 The ultimate basis of all thought, reasoning, or being See **ABSOLVE**

*****ABSOLVE** To set free from blame, guilt, penalties, responsibility or consequences of an offence 2 To pardon or acquit, as from guilt or complicity 3 To grant release, as from **CAPTIVATION**

-ABSONANT Discordant; unreasonable

*****ABSORB** To engross completely; occupy wholly 2 To take in and incorporate; swallow up 3 To receive the force or action of; intercept

*****ABSTAIN** To keep oneself back; refrain voluntarily See **REFRAIN** [< OF *abstenir* < L *abstinere* < *ab-* from + *tenere* to hold]

*****ABSTRACT** Considered apart from matter or from specific examples; not concrete 2 Theoretical; idea, as opposed to practical 3 Considered or expressed without reference to a particular example 4 Generalized or universal, as opposed to concrete, specific, or representational; tending away from the realistic or literal 5 A part from concrete relation or embodiment 6 To take away; remove secretly 7 To withdraw or disengage (the attention, interests, etc.) 8 To consider apart from particular instances; from a general notion [< L *abstractus*, pp. of *abstrahere* < *ab-* away + *trahere* to draw]

-ABSTRACTED Lost in thought; absent-minded 2 Separated from all else; apart

Syn. *Abstracted, absorbed, preoccupied, absent-minded, inattentive,* and *oblivious* **all mean partly or fully unaware of one's surroundings or actions** *Abstracted, absorbed,* **and** *preoccupied* **refer to the cause of this unawareness;** *absent-minded, absent,* **and** *inattentive,* **to its effect The man** *absorbed* **in one thing will appear** *absent* **in others The** *absent-minded* **man is** *oblivious* **of ordinary** matters, **because his thoughts are elsewhere One who is** *preoccupied* **is intensely busy in thought One may be** *absent-minded* **simply through inattention, with fitful and aimless wandering of thought** *Inattentive* **refers to an obvious lack of concern for that which properly demande one's attention Ant. Attentive**

**Deut 9:4; 2 Sam 10:3; 2 Chron 13:8; 32:1; Esth. 4:13; Job 35:2; 41:32; Psalm 40:17; Prov 23:7; Isa 10:7; Jer 29:11; Zech 8:17; Matt 3:9; 5:17; 6:7; 9:4; 10:34; 17:25; 18:12; 21:28; 22:17; :42; 26:53; :66; Mark 14:64; ***Luke 7:7; 10:36; 13:4; :16; ***17:9; ***John 5:39;

:45; *16:2; Acts 13:25; ***17:29; 26:2; 28:22; Rom 2:3; 12:3; **1 Corinth 4:6; :9; *8:2 And if anyone thinks that he knows anything, he knows nothing yet as he ought to know; **10:12; 12:23; ***13:5; 14:37; **2 Corin 3:5; 10:2; **11:16; **12:6; :19; Gal 6:3; Eph 3:20; Phili

1:7; 3:15; James 1:26; 4:5; 1 Peter 4:12; 2 Peter 1:13

ABSTRACTION The process of separating qualities or attributes from the Individual to which they belong 2 Product of this process; a concept 3 A visionary or impractical theory 4 The act of withdrawing; separating 5 Absence of mind; preoccupation

-ABSTRUSE Incomprehensible; mysterious, enigmatic; hard to understand 2 Hidden; concealed See **COMPLEX, MYSTERIOUS**

-ABSURD Opposed to manifest reason of Truth; irrational; ridiculous [< F *absurde* L *absurdus* out of tune, incongruous, senseless < *ab-* completely + *sur-dus* deaf, dull]

Syn. *Absurd, ridiculous,* and *preposterous* refer to something beyond normal belief That is *absurd* which is contrary to reason or good sense *Absurd* implies obvious error, while *ridiculous* carries the added implication that the error is laughable *Preposterous* refers to what is overwhelmingly absurd

-ABULIA Loss or impairment of will power

-ABUSE To use improperly or injuriously; misuse 2 To hurt by treating wrongly; injure 3 To speak in coarse or bad terms of or to; revile; malign 4 To deceive 5 Ill-treatment 6 Vicious conduct, practice, or action 7 Abusive language; slander 8 Deception 9 Insulting; bitter 10 Used wrongly; misapplied

+ABY To redeem; pay the penalty for 2 To suffer; endure, as a fate [OE *abycgan* to buy, pay for]

-ABYSMAL Unfathomable; immeasurable; extreme: an abysmal ignorance

ABYSS Any profound depth or void: an abyss of shame

-ACARPOUS Not bearing fruit; steril

*ACCEDE To give one's consent or adherence; agree; assent 2 To come into or enter upon; dignity Syn. See **ASSENT** [< L *accedere* < *ad-* to + *cedere* to yield, go]

*ACCEPT To receive with favor, willingness, or consent 2 To give an affirmative answer to 3 To receive as satisfactory or sufficient; admit 4 To take with good grace; submit to 5 To believe in 6 To acknowledge as valid or received 7 To accept an offer, position, etc. See **ASSENT, RECEIVE** [< L *acceptare*, freq. *accipere* to take < *ad-* to + *capere* to take]

*ACCENTUATE To strengthen or heighten the effect of; emphasize

*ACCEPT To receive with favor, willingness, or concent 2 To receive as satisfactory or sufficient; admit 3 To take with good grace; submit to 4 To believe in 5 To acknowledge as valid or received

*ACCEPTABLE Worthy or capable of acceptance; pleasing; welcome

*ACCEPTANT Willing to accept; **receptive**

ACCEPTATION The accepted meaning of a word or expression

*ACCESS The act or opportunity of coming to or near; admittance 2 A way of approach or entrance; passage; path 3 The state or quality of being approachable; accessibility 4 Approach to God through all of His Words 5 An addition; increase Syn. See **ENTRANCE** [< L *accessus* an approach, pp. of *accedre*] See **ACCEDE**

*ACCESSION The act of coming to or attaining a dignity or right 2 An increase by something added; also, the thing added 3 Assent; agreement 4 Admittance; entrance

+ACCOMMODATE To do a favor for; oblige; help 2 To provide for; give lodging to 3 To be suitable for; contain comfortably 4 To adapt or modify; adjust or conform, as to new conditions 5 To reconcile or settle, as conflicting opinions 6 To be or become adjusted, as the mind to Spiritual things which are invisible

+ACCOMMODATING Disposed to make adjustments; pliable, to the will or wish of others

+ACCOMPANY To go with; attend; escort 2 To be or occur with; co-exist with 3 To supplement

-ACCOMPLICE An associate in wrongdoing; partner in crime, whether as **principle** or accessory

+ACCOMPLISH To bring to pass; perform; effect 2 To bring to completion; finish 3 To make complete -To fill up

ACCOMPLISHMENT An acquirement or attainment that tends to perfect or equip in character, manners, or person See **ATTAINMENT**

*ACCORD To render as due; greant; concede 2 To bring into agreement; make harmonize or correspond, as opinions 3 To reconcile, as former enemies 4 Harmony, as of sentiment; agreement 5 A settlement of any differences; reconciliation; especially, an agreement between churches See **HARMONY** [< OF *acorder* < LL *accordare* to be of one mind, agree < L *ad-* to + heart]

*ACCORDANCE Agreement; conformity 2 The act of according; corresponding See **THEREFORE**

ACCOST To speak to first; address; greet 2 To approach for sexual purposes; solicit 3 Salutation; greeting [< **F** *accoster* < **LL** *accostare* **to be side to side** < **L ad-** to + *costa* **rib**]

*ACCOUNT To provide a reckoning 2 To give a rational explanation; refer to some cause or natural 3 To be responsible; answer 4 To cause death, capture, or incapacitation 5 A statement of causes 6 A record of reckoning 7 Worth; importance 8 Judgment; estimation 8 Profit; advantage

*ACCRESCENT Continue to grow after flowering 2 Growing continuously; expanding with age

ACKNOWLEDGE To accept or admit the existence or Truth of a fault or mistake; confirm 2 To recognize the fact, importance, and impact of a fault or mistake 3 To be agreeable when

*ACQUAINT To make familiar or conversant 2 To cause to know; inform 3 Personal knowledge of a Person or thing

-ACRIMONIOUS Full of bitterness of speech, temper, or actions; sarcastic; caustic; sharp

*ACT To behave as suitable to 2 To behave or conduct oneself 3 To carry out a purpose or function in a particular way; preform 4 To produce an effect

*ACTINIUM The property of radiant energy that affects chemical change

*ACT OF GOD The inevitable events occurring by reason of the operations of nature unmixed with human agency or human negligence

*ACTUATE To incite or influence to action: actuated by motives of kindness

*ACUMEN Quickness of insite or discernment; keenness of intellect 2 A sharply tapering point [< L, point, sharpness (of the mind) < *acuere* to sharpen]

ADAGE A saying that has obtained credit or force by long use; a proverb

-ADAMANT Exceeding hardness; impenetrability 2 Immovable; unyielding 3 Admirably purposeful, determined, and unwavering

*ADD To join or unite so as to increase the importance or scope 2 Unite in total 3 To say or write further 4 To make sense

ADDICTED Given over to a

*ADMONISH To caution or warn against danger; reprimand or rebuke error; warn 2 Exhort; cautionary; a gentle reproof Job 5:17; **22:4; 37:13; 40:2; Psalm 39:11; 81:8; 94:10; Prov 3:11-12; 5:12; 7:22; 9:7-8; 10:17; 12:1; 13:18; 15:5; :10; :12; 16:22; 22:15; 23:13; 29:17; :19; Ecc 4:13; 12:12; Jer 2:19; :30; 5:3; 7:28; 10:24; 30:11; 42:19; 46:28; Amos 4:6; ****Hab 1:12; ***2:1; Zeph 3:2; Zech 3:6; Rom 15:14; Col 3:16; 2 Thes 3:15; 2 Tim 2:25; *** 3:16; Titus 2:4; Heb 12:9

*ADORN To make more beautiful or attractive; increase the loveliness of; enhance 2 To wreathe, or decorate Job 40:10; Psa 93:5; Isa 61:10; Jer 4:30; 31:4; Ezek 16:11; :13; :16; 23:40; Mat 23:29; Luke 21:5; 1 Tim 2:9; Titus 2:10; 1 Peter 3:3; :5; Rev 17:4; 18:16; 21:2; :19

-ADULTERY Any unchaste or lewd thought or act; **IDOLATRY~** One who is to an excessive degree loved or admired; object of infatuation 2 A misleading or false idea; devoted blindly Prov 6:32; Jerem 3:8-:9 (stones and trees); 23:14; Ezek 23:37; Hosea 3:1 (raisin cake); John 8:4; Rom 2:22; 2 Peter 2:14; Rev 2:22

AFFLICT Distress with suffering continually; greatly troubled 2 To throw down; overthrow; to strike or dash against, cast down; calamity
Gen 41:52; Exod 1:12; 4:31; 22:22; :23; Lev 16:29; :31; 23:27; :29; :32; # 11:11; 30:13; Deut 7:15; 16:3; 26:7; 2 Sam 16:12; 1 Kings 8:35; 11:39; 22:27; 2 Kings 14:26; 17:20; 2 Chron 20:9; 21:14; 33:12; Job 5:6; 6:14; 30:11; 34:28; 36:15; :21; Psalm 22:24; 25:18; 34:19; 44:2; 55:19; 66:11; 88:7 (waves); :15; 89:22; 107:10; :17; :41; 119:50

AFRAID Filled with fear or apprehension 2 Worried that something undesirable will occur or be done

AFTER According to the nature and wishes and in conformity with; in imitation and manner; in honor, remembrance and observance of
Gen 15:14; 17:7-:8; 18:5; :12; :19; 22:1; 32:20; 45:15; 48:6; Exod 5:1; 11:1; :8; 23:2; Lev 17:7; 19:31; 25:29; 26:18; :27; :33; # 25:8; :13; 32:22; Deut 1:8; 4:37; :40; 9:4; 10:15; 11:28; 12:30; 13:4; 17:7; 24:4; 24:21; 28:14; 29:22; *31:29; **Josh 2:16; 5:4; 5:12; 6:13; 8:34; **9:16; 10:14; 24:20; Jude 2:10; 19:5; Ruth 1:16; 1 Sam 8:3; **12:21

AGAIN Once more; anew 2 Once or twice repeated 3 To the same place or over the same course; back, as in previous condition 4 In reply; in return

AGAINST In contact with or pressing upon; in opposition 2 In hostility or resistance 3 In contrast or comparison with 4 Directly opposite

ALIKE Showing resemblance or similitude; similar 2 Equally; in the same manner, form or degree; in common

ALIVE In a functioning state of consciousness 2 In operation; in full vigor; active 3 In lively action; enthusiastic 4 Open or susceptible; sensitive: *alive* to the needs of others 5 Abounding in understanding 6 The ability to reason 7 The ability to express 8 The ability to consider 9 Effective communication by any means 10 The soul 11 The Spirit

ALMIGHTY Able to do all things; omnipotent 2 Great; extreme 3 Exceedingly

ALMOND A small tree

ALONE At peace; solitary 2 Excluding all thoughts 3 Without interruption; unique
Lev 13:46; # 23:9; Deut 1:12; 8:3; 29:14; 32:12; **2 Sam 16:11; 2 Kings 4:27; *1 Chron 29:1; Job 7:16; 10:20; 15:19; 34:29; **Psalm 4:8; 62:5; Prov 9:12; *Ecc 4:8; Isa 5:8; 14:31; 44:24; Lam 3:28; Hosea 4:17

ALPHA The beginning or first of anything 2 Designating in order of importance or discovery

ALTAR The **COMMUNION~** table -To honor; worship 2 Sympathetic intercourse 3 Fellowship 4 The place where the aspect or characteristic that is essential is consecrated-made holy -Difference in a particular size, style and course of tone or the like is the making of change and modifications
Exod 20:24; :25; :26; 21:14; *Lev 6:13; 9:7; 16:12; 16:33; 26:30; # 3:26; 16:38; Josh 9:27; 22:16; **22:19; :28; :29; Judges 6:24; 1 Sam 2:33; 2 Sam. 24:25; 1 Kings 8:31; 9:25; 13:2; 18:30; **2 Kings 23:9; 1 Chron 16:40; Isa 19:19; 56:7; 60:7; 65:3; Lamen 2:7; Ezekiel 40:46-47; Hosea 10:1; Joel 2:17; 1 Corin 9:13; Heb 13:10; Rev 16:7

AMATIVE Inclined toward and capable of Love [< L *amatus*, pp. of *amare* to Love]
Josh. 24:23; 1 Kings 8:58; Psalm 40:1; **45:10; 119:36; Prov 2:2; 4:20; 22:17; Isa 55:3; Jer 17:23; 25:4; 35:15

AMEND To change or make fit for the better; improvement; self edifying 2 To free from offences; correct; reform 3 To change or alter 4 To conduct better -To correct, adjust, adapt or qualify is to conform

Jer 7:3; :5; 26:13; 35:15 correct **Job 5:17; 22:4; 37:13; 40:2; ***Psalm 94:10; ***Prov 3:11-12; 5:12; 9:7-8; ***10:17; ***12:1; 13:18; 15:5; :10; 15:12; ***16:22; 22:15; 23:13: :19; Jer 2:19; 2:30; 5:3; 7:28; 10:24; 30:11; 46:28; Hab 1:12; 2:1; Zep 3:2; 2 Tim 2:25; ***3:16; ***Heb 12:9

AMIABLE Pleasing in disposition; kindly 2 Free from irritation; friendly 3 Lovable

AMICABLE Showing or promoting good will

Syn. Amicable, peaceable, neighborly, and friendly refer to the manifestation of good will toward others Amicable suggests formal politeness, but also stronger sentiment than peaceable, which refers merely to a disposition to avoid dispute The neighborly wants to live on good terms with his associates; friendly is the same, with an added note of greater warmth and personal regard

AMONG By the joint or concerted action of 2 Reciprocally between

AMOUNT The entire significance or effect 2 To be equivalent in effect or importance

ANCIENT Having existed from remote time

1 Sam. 24:13; 2 Kings 19:25; **Psalm 119:100; Pro 23:10; Ecc 1:10; Isa 19:11; 23:7; 44:7; 45:21; Jer 18:15; Ezek 36:2; Dan 7:22; **2 Peter 2:5

ANTIQUITY~ The people collectively of ancient times: the ancients 2 Belonging to or originating from times past] Ezek 26:20 3 **VENERATE~** Syn. Adore, revere, venerate, worship, mean to regard with absolute respect salted with soundness of character

Job 26:13; **40:10; Psalm 93:5; Isa 61:10; Jer 4:30; Ezek 16:16; 23:40; Matt 23:29; *1 Tim 2:9; **Titus 2:10; 1 Peter 3:3; :5; Rev 17:4; 21:2

*SAGE [1] Characterized by or proceeding from calm, far seeing wisdom and prudence

2 Chron 2:12; Job *11:6; 12:16; ***Prov 1:4; ***8:5; :12; Eph 1:8 2 Profound; learned, etc. 3 Greve; serious 2 Chron 2:12; Job 11:6; Prov 1:4; 8:5; :12; Eph 1:8 syn. **WISE SAGE** [2] Sagebrush Compare ***WORMWOOD**
Deut 29:18; Prov 5:4; Jer 9:15; Rev 8:11

ANGEL A Spiritual, immortal being attending upon Deity, a guardian, heavenly Spirit or ministering messenger -One of the nine orders of Spiritual beings: seraphim, cherubim, thrones, dominations or dominions, virtues, powers, principalities, archangels, and angels -An unenlightened immortal spirit; trouble maker -A person of real angelic qualities as of character; **PATIENCE**- An order of angels, also ones of contention and strife 2 A message from Truth and Love

11 ORDERS of ANGELS

KINGDOM	The Spiritual dominion of God
DOMINION	Sovereign or supreme; **AUTHORITY**; the **POWER** of ruling or governing: **domination**
ANGEL	1 of 9 orders of spiritual beings
CHERUBIM	The 2nd of the 9 orders of angels
DOMINATION	The 4th 0f 9 orders of angels, also
THRONES	The 3rd of the 9 orders of angels
PATIENCE	which is a virtue

VIRTUES	The 5th of the 9 orders of angels
POWER	The 6th of 9 orders of angels (See **POWER**)
PRINCIPALITIES	The 7th of the 9 orders of angels (See **PRINCIPALITY**)
ARCHANGELS	The 8th of the 9 orders of angels
SERAPHIM	The highest of the 9 orders of angels
SAINT	An angel **ALSO,**
ANGEL FALLS	The world's highest uninterrupted waterfall

1 Kings 19:7; Luke 8:15; 21:19; Rom 15:4-5; 2 Corin 6:4; Col 1:11; 1 Thes 1:3; 2 Thes 1:4; 3:5; 1 Tim 6:11; Titus 2:2; Heb 6:12; **James 1:3-4; 5:10; Revelation 1:9; 2:2-3; :19; 13:10; 14:12

ANGER A sudden and strong feeling of displeasure and antagonism directed against the cause of an assumed offence 2 Affliction; displeasure 3 Inflammation -To enrage or make angry; 4 To inflame; make unbearable -To burden; weigh down -Turn to the right or left; go out of the Way Ant. forbearance, gentleness, patience, peaceableness, self-control
Gen 49:7; # 11:1; 32:13; Deut 6:15; 7:4 31:17; :29; 32:16; 1 Kings 14:9; Neh 9:17; Job 18:4; Psalm **37:8; 38:3; *Prov 15:1; *:18; *16:32; *19:11; 20:2; *21:14; 22:8; 27:4; *Ecc 5:17; 7:9; Isa 1:4; 7:4; 13:3; 30:30; **Jer 2:35; 7:18-20; 8:19; 10:24; **23:20; 25:7; 30:24; 51:45; Lam 1:12; 2:21-:22; Ezek **16:26; 20:21; 35:11; Joel 2:13; Amos 1:11; Jonah 3:9; **Micah 5:15; Zep 2:3; Zec 10:3; Mark 3:5; Eph 4:31

ANIMAL A beastial man 2 Any creature, including man, but not a bird, fish or insect 3 Characteristic of, derived from or assuming the characteristics of an animal Neh 2:12; Ecc 3:18; :21; Dan 8:4; Rom 1:23 **DERIVED~** To draw or receive, as from a **SOURCE-** 2 Kings 2:21 or principle First in rank, character or importance 2 One who takes the role of a leader or authority in some action 3a One liable primarily for another who has become surety for 3b The utmost most importance of any given property to which other parts or things accompany but are not a major part of 3c The capital or body of an estate 4 One who is at the head of another; Col 2:8; Heb 5:12; 6:1 **PRINCIPALITY~** A reigning prince's territory Eph 1:21; Col 2:10 2 The 7th of 9 orders of angels; one in **AUTHORITY~** One who has special knowledge [< L To increase **POWER~**] A force or effect of great telling Rom 13:1-7; Prov 29:2; Dan 11:6; Matt 7:29; Luke 4:6; 20:20; 22:25; John 7:17; 11:51; 12:49; 16:13; 1 Corin 9:18; 11:10; 15:24; 2 Corin 10:7-:8; :12; 13:1 2 A large quantity or great in number 3 The 6 of 9 orders of angels Syn., Compare **ABILITY~** Faculty is the natural ability, talent is a natural suitability 2 The faculty and talent for jurisdiction, sway, impact, **DOMINION~** The power of ruling or governing 2 Chron 13:5; Neh 9:37; Job 25:2; Psalm 19:13; **119:133; 1 Peter 4:11; 5:11; Jude 1:25 **DOMINATION~** The 4th 0f 9 orders of angels (**cont. ANIMAL**)~ *4 Pertaining to the mental nature of man; carnal, sensual [< L, a living being < breath, soul, life] Syn. *Animal, brute and beast* are all applied to organic, **SENTIENT~** Beings possessing powers of sense or sense perception; having sensation or feeling 2 The **MIND~** The **AGGREGATE~** To bring together, as into a mass, sum, or body Rom 8:2-8 ([< L lit., to bring to the flock]) *Processes originating in or in associate with the **BRAIN~** Intellectual capacity; Mind; intellect *2 The principal center of energy, activity, or strength of anything lacking firmness or character; morally or intellectually powerless or effective; irresolute 3 The faculty of the will and emotions
1 Chron 28:9; Psalm 94:11; Isaiah 55:8; Isa 65:2; Jer 6:19; **23:20; Ezek 38:10; Matt 15:19; Luke 5:22; 1 Corin 3:20

ANNO MUNDI *Latin* In the year of the world: used in chronology, with the supposed date of creation set at 4004 B.C. Abbr. A.M. Gen 1:1

ANNOTATE To provide (a text, etc.) with explanatory or critical notes [< L *annotatus*, pp. of *annotare* < *ad-* to + *notare* to note, mark < *nota* mark]

ANTI One opposed to some policy, group, etc. [< Gk. < *anti* against]

ANXIOUS Experiencing fear; thoughts respecting some certain issue; matter at hand or far off; worrying; distressing 2 intent; eagerly desirous -To choke or distress
1 Sam 9:20; Job 20:2; Jer 17:8; Luke 2:48; 12:26; :29; Philip 4:6

APPEAR To come into view; to seem likely 2 To be clear to the mind and obvious 3 To come before the public; published
Gen 1:9; 17:1; 26:24; 29:17; 39:6; Exod 4:1; 6:3; 16:10; ****23:15; ****34:20; :23 (Gen 1:27 So God created man in His own image; in the image of God He created him; male and female); Levi 9:6; :23; ****13:14; 16:2; # 9:15; 16:42; 20:6; *** Deut 16:16; ****31:11; ****1 Sam 1:22; ***3:21***; 16:7; 25:3; *2 Kings 2:11; Neh 4:21; Job 4:16; ***Psalm 42:2; Psalm 90:16; Jer 31:3; Lam 4:7-8; Ezek 21:24; Dan 1:13; :15; 8:15; Mala 3:2; Matt 1:20; 6:16; :18; 13:26; 17:3; 23:27=28; 24:30; 27:53; Mark 9:4; Mark 16:9; :12; ***:14; Luke 1:11; 9:8; ***:29; ***:31; 19:11; 22:43; 24:34; :36; John 7:24; **Acts 2:3; 7:30; 9:17; 16:9; ***26:16; Rom 7:13; 2 Corin 5:10; :12; ***7:12; **10:7; 13:7; ***Philip 2:8; ***Col 2:23; ***3:4; ***1 Tim 6:14; 2 Tim 4:1; :8; ***Titus 2:11; 3:4; Hebs 9:26; ***:28; James 4:14; ***1 Peter 4:18; 5:4; ****1 John 2:28; Rev 4:3; 12:1

APPETITE A strong liking or inclination

APPRENTICE One who is bound by a legal agreement to serve another for a fixed period of time in order to learn a trade or business 2 Any learner or beginner 3 To bind or take on as an apprentice [< OF *aprentis* < *aprendre* to teach, learn < L *apprehendere* to **COMPREHEND** See **APPREHEND**]

ARBORVITAE From the pine family: also called *white cedar, tree of life* 2 The branching appearance of the white matter shown in a section of the cerebellum Also **arbor vitae** [<L *arbor vitae* tree of life]
Isaiah 41:19; 44:14; 60:13; Lam 4:9; Ezek 24:23; **33:10

ARC The part of a circle that represents the apparent path of a heavenly body 1 Thes 4:16; Jude 1:9

ARCH Preeminent of its kind; most eminent Job 16:13

ARDOR Passion; intensity and eagerness of affection 2 Great vehemence; strenuously toiling; energetic 3 Involving great hardship; difficult labor

ARISE To come into being; originate; issue 2 To result; proceed

AROUND On all sides; in various directions 2 In opposite direction 3 From place to place; here and there 4 Nearby; in the vicinity 5 In or to a particular place 6 To be experienced and up to date 7 To overcome or cope with (someone or something) 8 To give attention to or accomplish 9 To be experienced in the ways of the world 10 Surrounding; enveloping 11 Somewhere near or within

ARRAY An impressive display or range of a particular type of things 2 An orderly or impressive arrangement [< AF arai, OF arei, (noun), < a- to (< L ad-) + rei order < Gmc.]

ARROW Sharp words; to make a target of (someone) 2 Deadly words; to take away (someone's) joy; happiness; content; etc. 3 To cause emotional pain by calling (someone) names 3 Bad, very

ASHAMED Abashed by consciousness of fault or impropriety 2 Deterred by fear of shame; reluctant 3 Humiliated; mortified
2 Kings 8:11; Ezra 9:6; Job 19:3; Psalm 6:10; 69:6; 74:21; **119:6; :46; **:78; :116; **127:5; Isa 1:29; **30:5; 49:23; Jer 2:26; 6:15; 8:9; Rom 1:16; 6:21; Phil 1:20; 2 Thes 3:14; 2 Tim 1:8; Titus 2:8; 1 John 2:28

ASHES Become bitterly disappointing or worthless mortal remains

Lev 4:12; # 4:13; 19:9; :17; 2 Kings 23:6; Isa 44:20; Jer 25:34; Ezek 27:30; Jonah 3:6

MORTAL Subject to death

Job 4:17; Job 10:5; Psalm 26:4; Isa 13:12; Ezek 30:24; Rom 6:12; 8:11; 1 Corin. 15:53-54; 2 Corinth. 4:11; 5:4; Heb 7:8; Rev 13:3

ASIA Lively 2 The rising sun

ASK To need or require Matt 3:10

ASPIRE To have an earnest desire or ambition as for something high and Good 2 To rise or reach upward [< L To + breath]

ASS A beast of burden, also a person 2 A stupid person; fool

ASTRINGE To bind or draw together [to bind fast] -**MENT** Expressing the means or result of an action

ATONE To make explanation, as for sin 2 To agree 3 To expiate 4 To reconcile [< adverbial phrase at one in accord, short for to set at one]

Exo 30:15-:16; Lev 6:7; 10:17; 16:16; :33; **17:11; # 25:13; Prov 16:6; Ezek 16:63; 45:20 **PROPITIATE~ To cause to be favorably disposed; appease; conciliate Rom 3:25; Heb 2:17; 1 John 2:2; 4:10 Syn. *Propitiate* is any action which makes such a power more lenient toward the offender; *appeasement* nullifies by making concession to demands, and often suggests weakness, cowardice or bad judgment Gen 32:20; Prov 6:35; 16:14; Matt 28:14 *Atonement* originally meant reconciliation, but now denotes an offering or sacrifice sufficient to win judgment for an offence The word suggests some degree of equality between the injury suffered and the reparation made for it *Expiation* is a more legalistic word, and refers to the enduring of the full penalty for a wrong

ATONEMENT Satisfaction, reparation, expiation made for wrong, injury or amends 2 The redemptive work of Christ 3 The reconciliation between **God** and man affected by Christ 4 The exemplification of man's unity with **God** whereby man reflects divine Truth, Life and Love 5 To await; delay 6 To apply oneself to 7 To take care of; to consider [< toward + to stretch] Exod 29:33; :36-37; 30:10; Levi 1:4; 5:16; :18; 6:7; 16:6; 16:16; :33-34; 17:11; 19:22; ** 23:27-28; # 16:46-47; 25:13; 31:50; 35:33; Deut 32:43; 2 Sam 21:3; 2 Chron 30:18; Psalm 65:3; 79:9; **Prov 16:6; **Isa 22:14; Jer 18:23; ****Ezek 16:63; 43:26

ATTAIN To gain or arrive at by exertion of the mind; achieved, as a desired purpose or state [< L to reach < to + to touch]; unparalleled to some standard of Truth, accuracy and excellence Gen 47:9; 2 Sam 23:19; Psalm 139:6; **Prov 1:5; Ecc 1:16; Luke 20:35; Acts 26:7; Rom 9:30-:31; Phil 3:11-:12; :16; Col 2:2 -To

REVISE is to examine and change in any way, though a change for the better is implied **Genesis 35:2; 1 Sam 21:13; 2 King 25:29; Job 10:17; ***14:14; :20; 17:12; 23:13; ***Psalm 15:4; ***55:19; ***102:26; *106:20; ***Prov 24:21; **Ecc 8:1; Isaiah 24:5; **Jer 2:11; 13:23; 34:11; 48:11; Lam 4:1; Dan 2:21; 4:16; 5:9; :10; *7:25; Hosea 4:7; Micah 2:4; **Hab 1:11; Mal 3:6; ***Acts 6:14; **Rom 1:23; ***1 Corin 15:51-52; *Gal 3:15; *4:20; *Heb 1:12; ***7:12

ATTEND To wait on or go with as an attendant; escort 2 To visit or minister to 3 To give heed to; to listen to 4 To await; to expect 5 To be present # 8:26; 18:3-:5; :7; 1 Chron 23:32; **Pro 27:23; Jer 23:2; Luke 4:20

ATTIRE A beautified covering for the personality 2 To dress; aray; adorn

AUXILIARY Giving or furnishing aid 2 One who or that which aids or helps; assistant; associate 3 A verb that helps to express the tense, mood, voice, or aspect of another verb 4 A word that functions as a subordinate element in a sentence and is fully meaningful only in association with the main words [L *auxiliarius* < *auxilium* help < *augere* to increase]

Syn. Makeshift, substitute Secondary, subordinate, subservient, subsidiary dispensable, nonessential, superfluous, unessential Ant. All-important, essential, imperative, indispensable, integral, necessary, required, requisite, vital, chief, main, principal

AVAILABLE Capable of being used; at hand; useable 2 Valid 3 Effectual

AWAKE -To stir up; excite [< to watch] An arousing of attention or interest; revival
1 Kings 18:27; *Job 8:6; 14:12; Psalm 17:15; 73:20; 102:7; **119:148; **127:1; **Prov 6:22; Song of Sol 2:7; 4:16; Isa 29:8; Jer 51:57; Dan 12:2; Hab 2:19; Luke 9:32; Rom 13:11; 1 Corin 15:34; Eph 5:14

AWAY Out of existence; at or to an end 2 On and on continuously 3 From one's keeping, attention, or possession 4 At once; without hesitation

B

BACKSLIDE To return to wrong or sinful ways

BAPTIZE Purification by Spirit; **submergence into Spirit** Matt 3:11; Mark 1:8; 16:16; Luke 12:50; John 4:1-:2; **Acts 2:41; 8:12; 18:8; 1 Corin 1:16; **1 Corin 12:13; Gal 3:27 [< LL < Gk. **IMMERSION**]~ The disappearance of a heavenly body by passing behind or entering into the shadow of another;

IMMERSE~ To involve deeply; growing entirely under Scripture

BABEL Confusion of many voices or languages; tumult [from (Tower of) Babel] 2 Any impractical scheme or structure; a visionary project
Exod 23:27; Deut 28:20; :28; 1 Sam 14:20; Neh 4:8; Psalm 35:4; :26; 40:14; 60:3; Isa 24:10; 34:11; 41:29; 45:16; ***61:7; Jer 20:11; Zech 12:4; 1 Corin. 14:33; ****James 3:16

BABBLE To utter inarticulate or meaningless sounds 2 To make a murmuring or rippling sound 3 To talk wisely or foolishly 4 To utter unintelligibly 5 To blurt out thoughtlessly 6 Inarticulate or confused speech 7 To prattle as an infant
2 Kings 9:11; Ecc 10:11; Isa 44:25; Acts 17:18

BACK The farther or other side; the reverse 2 The part behind or opposite to the part used 3 Physical strength 4 In, to, or toward a former place 5 In, to, or toward a former condition 6 In withdraw or repudiation 7 To fail to keep (an engagement, promise, etc.) 8 To desert or betray

BACKSLIDE To return to wrong or sinful ways

BALD Without natural covering or growth, as a mountain
Lev 21:5; Isa 3:24; 22:12; Jer 16:6; 48:37; Ezek 7:18; 27:31; 29:18; Amos 8:10; Micah 1:16

BAND A range of frequencies or wavelengths between two stated **LIMPET** One that clings tenaciously to someone or something 2 To untie or tie with a band; encircle 3 A company of peron's associated for a common purpose 4 That which binds, ties, or unites; a bond Akin to **BIND**

BARE Not clothed or covered 2 Without addition; basic and simple Syn. plainly, essentially, fundamentally, straightforwardly, purely 3 To uncover and expose it to view 4 Very; really 5 Give

BE To have existence, Truth, and actual Light 2 To take place; happen 3 To stay or continue 4 To belong -To express purpose, duty, possibility, futurity, etc. -Respectively - Near, by

BEAM A gleam or ray; suggestion: a beam of Truth 2 The widest part of anything 3 In the right direction; just, right; correct

BEAR To support 2 To carry; convey 3 To show visibly 4 To conduct or guide 5 To spread; disseminate 6 To hold in the mind; maintain; entertain 7 Suffer or endure; undergo 8 Accept; acknowledge; assume as responsibility or expense 9 To produce; give birth to 10 To conduct or comport 11 To manage or carry (part or all of someone) 12 To move by pressing against; drive 13 To render; give; to be able to withstand; allow 14 To have or stand in (comparison or relation) 15 To possess as a right or power 16 To rest heavily; lean; press 17 To endure patiently; suffer 18 To produce fruit or young 19 To carry burdens 20 To move or lie in a certain direction; be pointed or aimed 21 To be relevant; have preference Syn. **CARRY, ENDURE** 22 To force down; overpower or overcome (temptation; fear; anger) with good 23 To exert oneself; to make a great effort; to support; confirm; justify; to keep strength and spirits when under strain; to carry, wear, suffer

Gen 49:15; **Lev 5:1; :17; 19:17-:18; 24:15; # 4:47; 11:14; :17; 18:32; Deut 1:12; 29:18; Job 16:8; 21:3; Psalm 28:9; 55:12; **Pro 9:12; *17:12; 30:21; **Isa 46:4; 52:11; Jer 10:19; 12:2; 17:21; 44:22; Ezek 16:52; 23:35; 32:24; 34:29; Hosea 9:16; Micah 6:16; 7:9; **Zech 6:13; Matt 3:8; Luke 11:48

BEAR A gruff, ill mannered or clumsy person Dan 7:5; Hosea 13:8

BEARD To defy courageously

BEAST A cruel, rude or filthy person 2 Disagreeable or unpleasant; nasty Very

Gen 7:14; *9:5; Exo 11:7; **23:11; Lev 26:6; **Job 18:3; Titus 1:12; 2 Peter 2:12; Jude 1:10; **Rev 13:18

BEAT To hunt over; search 2 To surpass; be superior to 3 To subdue or defeat; master 4 To win a victory or contest 5 Fatigued; worn out

BEAU A sweetheart or lover of a girl or woman A man very careful of his appearance and social etiquette; a dandy

BECOME To come to be; grow to be 2 To be appropriate to; benefit 3 To be suitable to; show to advantage [OE *becuman* to happen, come about]

Gen 2:24; 3:22; 24:60; 27:40; 32:10; *34:15-:16; 48:19; **Exod 15:2; Lev 19:29; ***25:35; :39; 27:29; ***Deut 15:9; **31:29; Josh. 6:18; **7:12; 1 Sam 2:5; 16:23; ***2 Sam 14:14; *2 Kings 7:13; 22:19; **Job 4:2; Psalm 14:3; 53:3; **119:56; Prov 10:9; **19:25; 29:12; Isa 1:22; 19:13; 29:11; 32:15; 63:19; Jer 2:5; 3:1; ***5:13; *:27; *7:11; *10:21; *13:11; **22:5; 50:37; Lam 1:6; Ezek 12:20; 17:8; 22:18; 23:30; 24:11; ***Hosea 12:8; Matt 13:22

BED Conjugal union; also, matrimonial rights and duties 2 To place firmly; embed 3 To cohabit with

BEFORE Under the consideration or perception of knowing

Gen 6:11; 18:22; 19:27; 23:12; 24:15; 30:30; 31:2; :5; :37; 33:3; :14; 42:6; 43:26; **45:5; 50:18; Exod 1:19; 6:30; 14:19; 19:7; 20:20; *22:26; 23:15; ***:20; :27; **:30; 27:21; 28:35; 30:6; ***33:19; 34:10; ***:23-:24; ***Lev 10:3; 18:30; ***19:14; ***:32; 23:40; -26:8; # ***15:15; :28; ***16:9; **27:17; Deut 4:8; ***:10; 6:25; ***8:20; ***9:4-:5; :25; **12:7; :18; :30; *16:16; **17:12; 18:13; **24:13; **26:13; **28:66; 29:15; **30:15; **:19; 31:21; ***Josh. 8:35; **22:29; Judges. 21:2; **Ruth 2:11; 1 Sam 2:11; :17-:18; ***:35; ***3:1; :3

BEGET To cause to be

Gen 48:6; Lev 25:45; # 11:12; Deut 4:25; 28:41; Prov 17:21; Ecc 6:3; Ezek 18:10; :14

BEGGAR To reduce to want

1 Sam 2:8; Luke 16:20; :22; Gal 4:9

BEGINNING Initial circumstances and earliest stage 2 Source or first cause

Gen 49:3; Exod 12:2; # 10:10; Deut 11:12; 21:17; Ruth 3:10; 2 Kings 17:25; Neh 4:7; Job 8:7; Psalm 111:10; Prov 1:7; 8:23; 9:10; 17:14; 20:21; Ecc 3:11; 7:8; Isa 1:26; 18:2; :7; 40:21; 41:26; 46:10; 48:3; 48:5; :7; :16; 64:4; ***Lam 2:19; Dan 9:23; Micah 1:13; Matt 19:4; :8; 24:8; :21; Mark 13:8; Luke 1:2; 24:27; ***:47; John 1:1-:2; 6:64; 8:9; :25; :44; 15:27; 16:4; Acts 8:35; 11:15; Eph 3:9; Col 1:18; 2 Thes 2:13; Heb 1:10; 7:3; 2 Peter 2:20; *1 John 1:1; 2:7; :24; 3:8; :11; 2 John 1:5-:6; Rev 3:14; 21:6

YAWN~ Stretching wide open deep space; **CHASM~** Divergence of opinions in relations marked an interruption in the **CONTINUITY~** Immediate connection and relation with the Whole, suggesting a more prolonged or elaborate, active and ingenious circumstance of entering in upon the broadest term applied freely to non-human activities -To furnished all that which is necessary for our existence and continuance

BEHALF The interest, part or difference -Formerly, *on behalf of* meant in support of or favor of, and *in behalf of* meant in the place or interest of, but in modern usage this distinction tends to disappear [OE *be halfe* by the side (of)]
Lev 22:20; :25; 2 Sam 3:12; *2 Kings 4:13; 2 Chron 16:9; **Isa 8:19; **Ezek 22:30; Rom 16:19; 1 Corin 4:6; 1:11; 5:12; ***:20; 7:4; 8:24; Phil 1:29

BEHIND Slow, as to watch 2 In reserve; to be made known 3 On the farther side of; beyond 4 In a condition left by (one) 5 Not so well advanced as; inferior to 6 Hidden by; not revealed about 7 Backing up; supporting 8 Following

BEHOLD To look at or upon; observe Syn. See **SEE~** Look! See! [OE to hold]
Gen 3:22; **6:13; 32:20; 45:12; ***Exod 16:4; 19:9; 23:20; 34:10; # 18:21; 23:9; ***:20; 24:17; ***25:12; ***Josh. 23:14; 1 Sam 3:11; ***15:22; 1 Kings 3:12; 2 Kings 6:17; 22:16; Job 1:12; 2:6; 5:17; :27; 8:19; 13:1; 19:27; **20:9; ***28:28; ***33:29; 35:5; 36:22; Psalm 27:4; 40:7; 51:6; 113:6

BEING [1] The supreme being **God** Gen 24:27; # 11:6; Deut 32:31

BEING [2] Essential nature; **SUBSTANCE~** The essential part of anything said or written 2 The essential nature that underlines phenomena; that in which qualities or attributes inhere 3 That which is eternal Job 5:5; ***Psalm 139:16: Micah 4:13: Luke 8:3; ***Colos 2:17; ***Heb 11:1 [< OF <L *substantia* < *substare* to be present < *sub-* under + *stare* to stand (**cont. BEING**)~ A thing **LIVING~** To remain operative; endure; last 2 To have one's home; dwell; reside 3 To lead or regulate one's life, as in accordance with rules, principles, etc. 4 To enjoy a varied or satisfying life; be joyously or enthusiastically alive 5 To escape destruction; stay afloat or in flight despite danger, as a vessel 6 To exemplify or put into practice in one's life; to be forbearing in regard to the conduct, characteristics, etc., of others; to live or behave so as to expiate or expunge the memory of an error, crime, inflicting pain on others, putting oneself before others, esteeming oneself above another, showing partiality, selfishness, concealing what should be known, table-bearing, cheating, being without justice, speaking without benefit, being ungrateful, unmerciful, falsifying, misleading, denying, self-projecting, etc. 7 To live or reside as a domestic servant 8 To fulfill a bargain; obligation, all in all that proceeds out of thy mouth!! 9 To put up with; to endure

BELIEF Acceptance of the Truth or actuality of anything without certain proof; mental conviction 2 A tent or a body of tents; Doctrine; creed 3 That which is believed; something held to be true or actual 3 Hypothesis, opinion, theory

BELIEVE To accept as True or real 2 To credit (a person) with veracity 3 To think; assume; with a clause as object 4 To accept the Truth, existence, worth, etc., of something 5 To have confidence; place one's trust in 6 To have faith from hearing the Scriptures 7 To think [ME *beleven* < *be-* completely + *leven* < OE *gelefan* to believe]
Gen 15:6; Exod 4:5; :31; 14:31; 19:9; # 14:11; 20:12; Deut 1:32; 9:23; 1 Kings 10:7; 2 Kings 17:14; ***2 Chron 20:20; ***Job 15:22; ***Psalm 27:13; 78:22; :32; Psalm 106:12; ***:24; 116:10; 119:66; Prov 14:15; **26:25; ***Isa 7:9; 28:16; 43:10; 53:1; Jer 12:6; Lam. 4:12; ***Dan 6:23; ***Jonah 3:5; ***Hab 1:5; ***Matt 8:13; 9:28; **18:6; 21:25; **:32; **27:42; ****Mark 1:15; ****5:36; ****9:23-24; ***16:11; :13-14; :17; Luke 1:20; ***:45; Luke 8:12-13; :50; 22:67; 24:11; :25; :41; John 1:7; :12; ****3:12; ****:15-16; :36; 4:41; ****:48; ****:5:24

BELLY The source of appetite 2 The womb

BETROTH [ME *bitreuthien* < *bi-* to + *treuthe* Truth} **AFFIANCE-** To pledge, especially of faith 2 With confidence [< OF *a fiancer* < *a fiance* trust, confidence < *a fier* **to trust** < Med. L *affidare* < L *ad-* to + *fidus* faithful]

BETWEEN The decisive virtue of one alternative over another 2 In the space that seperates [fusion]

BIRD A person, especially one who is peculiar or remarkable Job 12:7: Psalm 102:7; Prov 7:23; 27:8; Eccl 9:12; 10:20; Isa 31:5; 46:11: Jer 9:10; Ezek 39:17: 1 Corin 15:39; Rev 18:2

2 Deliberately; without passion 3 Cruelly; without mercy

BIRTH Beginning; origin 2 **PARTURITION-** Archaic **CONFINEMENT-** Archaic **LYING-IN-** Of an earnest request for aid, support, sympathy, mercy, etc.; entreaty; petition; plea 2 A request or reference to some person or authority for a decision, corroboration, judgment, etc. 3 Evoking attracting the interest, desire, curiosity, sympathy, or the like 4 To make a serious, urgent, or heartfelt request, apply to the higher court See **BEAR**

BITTER Unpleasant to accept; distasteful 2 Painful to the body or mind; harsh; severe 3 Feeling or showing intense animosity 4 Stinging; sharp words; a consequence that is especially humiliating or hateful

Exo 1:14; Deut 29:18; Judg 5:23; 21:2; 2 Sam 2:26; Ezra 10:1; Job 3:20; Psalm 64:3; **Pro 14:10; 27:7; Ecc 7:26; Isa 5:20; 22:4; 33:7; 38:15; 38:17; Jer 2:19; 4:18; ***6:26; ***13:17; ***22:10; Lam 1:2; 3:5; :15; Ezek 21:6; 27:30; Mic 2:4; Zep 1:14; Matt 26:75; Acts 8:23; Eph 4:31; Heb 12:15

BLACK Reflecting no Light 2 Destitute of Light; in total darkness 3 Gloomy; dismal; forbidding 4 Soiled; stained Indicating disgrace or censure 5 Angry; threatening 6 Evil; wicked; malignant 7 Confirmed; unchangeable, as in political views

BLASPHEMY Impious or profane speaking of God, or of a sacred person or things 2 The act of claiming the attributes of God 3 Any irreverent act or utterance See **PROFANITY**

BLEED To feel grief, sympathy, or anguish

BLEMISH A moral fault (stain) 2 A moral (taint) 3 Without pervading or spreading through 4 Being perceived in every part with emotions; ideas, etc. 5 To imbue with an offensive, noxious, or deteriorating quality or principle 6 Defect, as an error or lack of something needed for completion; (tarnish). Having a dim luster Dan 1:4; Mala 1:14; **Eph 5:27; 1 Peter 1:19; 2 Peter 2:13

BLESS To honor and exalt; glorify 2 To invoke **God**'s favor upon 3 To bestow happiness or prosperity upon; make happy 4 To endow, as with a gift 5 To guard; protect [To consecrate (with **BLOOD**)~ Disposition of the mind; way of acting and reacting in any given situation < blood]

Gen 5:2; 12:3; 14:20; 22:18; ***26:3; ***26:29; 27:12; ***28:3; :4; 30:30; ***33:11; 48:15; 49:25; :26; Exo 12:32; 23:25; 32:29; #'s 6:24; :27; 22:6; :12; 23:11; :20; :25; 24:1; Deut 8:10; 10:8; 11:26; :27; 12:7; :15; 14:24; :29; ***15:4; ***:6; ***:10; ***:14; ***:18; **16:10; :15; ***:17; 23:5; :20; 24:13; ***:19; 28:1; ***:2; :6; ***:12; ***29:19; 30:1; ***:16; ***:19; ***Josh. 8:33; ***Judg 5:2; ***:9; *Ruth 2:4; 3:10; 1 Sam 2:20; 23:21; 25:33; 2 Sam 7:29; 1 Kings 8:54; ***1 Chron 4:10; 17:27; 2 Chron 30:27; ***31:10; Nehem 8:6; 11:2; Job 1:21; 29:11; 31:20; Psalm 1:1; 2:12; 5:12; 10:3; ; 16:7; 29:11; 33:12; 34:1; :8; 37:22; 40:4; ***41:1; :2; 45:2; 66:20; 67:6; :7; 84:4; :5; 89:15; 94:12; 96:2; 100:4; 103:20; 106:3; 107:38; ***109:28; 112:1; 115:13; 118:26; ***119:2; ***133:1; ***:3; 145:2; Pr 5:18; 8:34;***20:7; ***22:9; ***28:20; 31:28; ***30:18; Isa 65:16; ***Ezek 28:25; ***Dan 3:28; 12:12; Joel 2:14; ***Zech 11:5; Mala 2:2; 3:10; 5:7; :10; :11; :44; Luke 1:45; 6:22; :28; 11:28; 12:37; 14:14; ***24:51; ***John 13:17; Acts 13:42; ***20:35; ***Rom 15:29; 1 Corinth. 4:12; 2 Corin 11:31; Hebrews 7:7; ***James 1:12; :25; 1 Peter 3:8; :14; 4:14; Rev 1:3

BLIND Lacking in perception or judgment 2 Acting or done without intelligent control; random 3 Unreasoning; heedless 4 Hidden; concealed 5 Insensible 6 Drunk 7 Difficult to understand; unintelligible; also illegible 8 Not producing buds or fruit 9 Something intended to deceive; subterfuge; decoy 10 To dazzle 11 To deprive of discernment or judgment 12 To darken; obscure 13 To outshine; eclipse

2 Sam 5:8 Exo 4:11; 23:8; Levi 19:14; Isa 29:9; :18; 35:5; 42:19; 56:10; Luke 4:18; ***14:13; John 9:2; :32; :41; 12:40; Rom 2:19; 11:7; :25; 2 Corin 4:4; Eph 4:18; 1 John 2:11; Rev 3:17

BLOCK A obstacle or hindrance 2 The act of blocking or obstructing, or the state or condition of being obstructed 3 The involuntary prevention of thought or action in an existing objective situation, traceable neither to physical sources nor to forgetfulness 4 To stop the progress of or prevent passage through; obstruct 5 To obscure from view

BLOOD Disposition of mind; temperament; mood 2 Everything that one can obtain 3 The vital **PRINCIPLE~** An accepted rule of conduct 2 An axiom or doctrine 3 Guiding sense of the requirements and obligations of right conduct 4 A composition or organization, method of operation 5 An originating or actuating agency or force 6 A constituent element, material, etc., serving to pose or make up a thing

Gen 15:4; Exod 4:26; 12:13; 23:18; 24:6; :8

BOAST Characterized by or addicted to boasting; to shape roughly with a broad chisel 2 To talk in a bragging or **VAIN~** manner Unproductive; worthless; fruitless; useless 2 Having no real basis or worth; frivolous; empty; unreal 3 Ostentatious; showy; to no purpose, and without effect

Judg 7:2; 1 Kings 20:11; Psalm 10:3; 12:3; 44:8; 52:1; 75:4; 94:4; 97:7; Prov 20:14; 27:1; Isaiah 16:6; 28:15; 45:25; 61:6; Jer 4:2; 9:23-24; 13:20; 48:30; 51:41; Ezek 35:13; Dan 7:11; Hos 12:8; Amos 4:5; Obad 1:12; * Zeph 3:11; Acts 8:9; Rom 1:30; 2:17; :23; 3:27; 5:2

BOAT In the same situation

BODY [1] The principal part of anything 2 A collection of persons as a whole 3 A distinct mass or portion of **MATTER~** That which is material and physical, occupies space and is perceived by the senses, as distinguished from that which is mental, Spiritual, etc. 2 A subject, event or situation that is or maybe an object of discussion, concern, feeling, etc. 3 Importance, consequence or moment 4 The ideas, content or meaning 5 An indefinite amount, quantity or amount 6 Pus

BODY [2] Matter as opposed to Spirit *carcass* usually refers to animal *bodies*, and **is used of humans only** contemptuously **or** harmoniously

BOIL SEETHE- To be filled with intense but unexpressed anger; be angry; furious; enraged; to be incensed; beside oneself; boil, simmer, rage, rant, rave, storm, fume, smolder 2 To give vent to one's rage or passion 5 To be stirred up or inflamed

BOOK A main division of a literary composition or treatise 2 Something regarded as a source of instruction 3 To arrange for beforehand

BORN Anything brought forth or into being 2 Natural: They are born into your belief of death

BOSOM The breast as the seat of thought and emotion 2 Inner circle; midst 3 Close; intimate; to have or cherish in the bosom; embrace; to hide in the bosom; conceal

BOW To submit; yield 2 To cause to yield; subdue

BOWL Drink (See **DRINK**) or convivial drinking 2 To express joy, delight, exaltation, etc., in an **IRREPRESSIBLE-** manner Not able to be controlled or restrained 3 To move smoothly or swiftly 4 To cause to be confused or helpless 5 The willingness to take bold risks Syn.

Boldness, daring, fearlessness, intrepidity, bravery, courage, heroism, pluck, grit; Spirit, mettle Guts, gutsiness, spunk, moxie

BRASS People in authority or of high rank 2 A person's hardness or effrontery

BREAD The necessities of life; **SUBSTANCE~** Means of support; livelihood 2 Inherent quality 3 Real being 4 A basis; a logical substance; hypostasis

BREADTH Freedom from narrowness; liberal 2 The impression of largeness and comprehensiveness

BREAK To crack without separating 2 To burst or cause to discharge 3 To destroy the order, continuity, or completeness of 4 To diminish the force or effect of ; moderate 5 To interrupt the course of 6 To reduce to discipline; tame 7 To disable by; render useless 8 To reduce in spirit, as by toil 9 To surpass; excel 10 To make well known; tell 11 To cause to discontinue a habit 12 To invalidate 13 To give way; become unusable or inoperative 14 To dissolve and disperse 15 To come into being or evidence 16 To become overwhelmed with grief 17 To fall off abruptly 18 To change from one quality to another 19 To suffer mental collapse 20 To yield, especially to strong feelings or grief 21 To cause to yield 22 To analyze or be analyzed 23 To decompose 24 To sever (relations); discontinue 25 To put an end to; stop 26 To become separate; detached 27 To disperse; scatter 28 To disseminate; dissolve 29 A breach of continuity; sudden interruption; change 30 A chance or opportunity 31 A rupture in friendship; falling out; quarrel 32 An unfortunate or ill-willed remark or action; blunder Akin to **BREACH**

BREAST The breast as the seat of afflictions or emotions

BREATH An articulate utterance; whisper

The process of speaking begins in the breath. The power of articulation separates man from all other breathing, creeping, crawling things which crawl upon the earth, birds of the air, fish of the sea, beasts of the field, and trees. If you noticed, when God spoke to each and everyone of you, when He hovered over you, did He articulate any word to you in all that was shown you? Or did you see Something for which you put words to at that moment? But then, in the next, it mysteriously faded, it vanished, just as it appeared, didn't it disappear? And without a trace Did or do you remember It?

BREATHE To utter, especially softly; whisper 2 To express; manifest 3 To utter with the breath only, without vibration of the vocal cords

BREATHING Words spoken; utterance Aspiration; longing

BRING To convey or cause (a person) to come with oneself to or toward a place 2 To cause to come about 3 To introduce into the mind; cause to appear 4a To cause to adopt or admit, as a persuasion, course of action, etc. 4b To set forth as evidence 5 To accomplish; to cause to happen 6 To revive; restore to consciousness 7 To give birth or produce fully 8 To give rise to 9 To reveal; cause to be evident, as the Truth 10 To cause to have reference, application, or influence 11 To rear; educate 12 To suggest or call attention to **-ING** Appropriate; suitable 2 Pleasing; attractive - A coming to be

BROIL A turmoil; noisy quarrel; brawl 2 To become impatient; burn with anger

BROKEN Violated; transgressed 2 Interrupted; disturbed 3 Incomplete; fragmentary 4 Rough; uneven 5 Veering abruptly 6 In disorder; routed; scattered 7 Humbled; crushed 8 Weakened or infirm; exhausted 9 Bankrupt; ruined 10 Trained in procedure; disciplined; adapted

BROOK To put up with; to tolerate; usually with the negative **BROTHER** Pertaining to or characteristic of a brother; a relationship; a state of mind

BRUISE To hurt or offend slightly, as the feelings
Gen 3:15; Levi 22:24; Job 5:18; Isa 1:6; 30:26; 42:3; 53:5; :10; Matt 12:20

BUCKLER A means of defence 2 To shield, defend, protect [< OF boucler having a boss See **BUCKLE**]

BUD Any immature person or thing 2 To begin to grow or develop

BUILD To make by assembling separate parts 2 To increase in intensity, excitement, etc.; to incorporate or add permanently 3 To renew or strengthen; also to increase [house]

BULL[1] One likened to a bull, as in manner 2 A speculator who buys so as to profit from a rise in prices he anticipates or hopes to cause 3 Empty talk; nonsense 4 To speculate for a rise in price of or in 5 To go or push ahead 6 Marked by rising prices

BULL[2] A funny blunder in speech [?< boule lie]

BURDEN Something that weighs heavily, as responsibility or anxiety 2 To load or overload; oppress, as with care 3 Something often repeated or dwelt upon; the prevailing ideas

BURN To be eager excited 2 To excite or enflame, as with love 3 To exhaust one's strength by overwork or dissipation 4 To put up with and tolerate; usually the negative and **ENDURE**! -Shine! -Sparkle, be inflamed with passion and desire -To burn, as with Love 5 Undergo change; lose one's original nature 6 Cause to go into a solution

BURNT Of strong emotion and passion undergoing **FISSION**- the act of **CLEAVING**- splitting and dividing along the natural line of division, as that of bone and marrow 2 Penetrate and advance through the water adhering closely; stuck; clung remaining faithful to the principles in spite of prosecution (**FISSION**) by exposing the one part to more Light by masking the other parts

BURST To give sudden expression to passion, grief, etc., also, to be filled with violent emotion 2 To fill or cause to swell to the point of breaking open

BUY To acquire the ownership 2 To obtain by some exchange or sacrifice 3 To get rid of the interference or opposition of a person or group, or obtain exemption 4 To win over interest by inducement

C

CALIB A dog 2 Faithful

CALLED Summon -To draw out 2 To arouse 3 To designate or characterize in any way 4 To bring to action or consideration 5 To make a brief visit 6 To invoke from heaven into action 7 To remember; recollect 8 To bring up for action or discussion 9 An inward urge to some specific work 10 To solemnly **INVOKE**- call on (a deity or Spirit) in prayer, as a witness, or for inspiration; supplicate, entreat, solicit, beg, implore; beseech

·**CANCER** Any dangerous and spreading evil; the presence of evil

***CAPTIVE** One enthralled by beauty, passion, etc. 2 Enslaved or rendered helpless by strong emotion, desire, etc.

***CAPTIVATE** To enthrall by excellence or beauty; fascinate; charm 2 To capture; subdue

CARCASS The human body, living or dead 2 Something from which the life or essence is gone from

CARNAL Related to bodily appetites; sensual 2 Sexual: to have carnal knowledge 3 Not Spiritual or intellectual; worldly 4 To perceive through the senses 5 Perception through the sense of taste, smell, sight, sound, and of both physical and emotional sense of feeling [< LL *carnalis* **fleshly** < L *caro, carnis* **flesh**]

Gen. 19:5; Lev. 18:20; 19:20; #'s 5:13; Judg. 19:22; Rom. 7:14; 8:6; :7; 1 Corin. 3:1; :3; :4; 2 Corin. 10:4; Colo. 3:1

CARNIFY To form into flesh or flesh like consistency [< L *carnificare* < *caro, carnis* flesh + *facere* to make]

CARRY To bear from one place to another; convey 2 To bear the weight, burden, or responsibility of 3 To give support to; corroborate; confirm 4 To bear as a mark or attribute; imply; involve 5 To be pregnant with 6 To conduct or comport (oneself) 7 To take by force or effort; capture; win 8 To gain the support or interest of 9 To gain victory or acceptance for; also, to achieve success in 10 To extend; continue 11 To have or keep 12 To bear; yield; sustain 13 To keep and follow 14 To keep up; keep going; continue [Doublet of **CHARGE**]

CAST To give birth to, especially prematurely; drop 2 To arrange by some system or into divisions 3 To revolve something in the mind; deliberate 4 To conjecture; forecast 5 To direct upward 6 An impression of anything 7 Something shaped or formed 8 Kind; sort; type 9 A stroke of fortune

CATTLE Human beings; a contemptuous term ***Gen 47:17; ***Exod 20:10; Levi 22:19; :21; # 31:9; :28; :30; :33; :38; :44; **35:3; Deut 5:14; Josh 8:2; 2 Kings 3:17; 1 Chron 5:9; 7:21; 2 Chron 35:8; :12; Nehem 9:37; 10:36; ***Job 36:33; Psalm 50:10; ***Psalm 104:14; 107:38; Isa 1:11; 30:23; ***Jer 9:10; Joel 1:18; Rev 18:13 -To fall in or down, as when undermined 2 To yield utterly; give in as to argument, hardship, or strain Syn **HOLE**

CAUSE Reason or motive for some human action 2 Good or sufficient reason 3 Any subject of discussion or debate 4 The ideal or goal, or set of these to which a person or group is dedicated 5a The general welfare of people seen as the subject of concern either to themselves or to others 5b The end or purpose for which a thing is done or produced 5c Any of the things necessary for the movement or the coming into being of a thing 6 To unite with joint effort; work together for the same end (reason, sake, make, create, produce) **BLOOD**- Disposition of mind and **PURPOSE**- The reason for which it exists and happens; an intended or desired result; end; aim; goal 7 Determination; resoluteness 8 The subject and point under consideration 9 Practical result, effect or advantage with intention and deliberately of the universe especially when considered as the creation of a superhuman agency or agencies 10 A point or matter of ethics or conscience

CENTER A place or point at which activity is concentrated or toward which people seem to converge: *center* of interest 2 A point from which effects, influences, etc., proceed; source

3 To place in or at the center; fix at the center 4 To direct toward one place; concentrate 5 To shape 6 To be centered or concentrated Syn. *Center, middle,* and *midst* all refer to an inner position away from the boundaries of a thing Strictly, the *center* is a point, while the *middle* is an area that may be only approximately central *Midst* commonly implies a group or multitude of surrounding objects

CHAIN Anything that confines or restrains 2 Any connected series; a succession 3 To bind

CHANGE To make different; alter; transmute 2 To exchange; interchange 3 To give or obtain the equivalent of, as coverings 4 To become different; vary 5 To enter upon a different phase

CHARACTER The combination of qualities or traits that distinguishes an individual or group; personality 2 Moral force; integrity 3 Reputation; also good reputation 4 A detailed description of a person's qualities or abilities 5 To represent; portray; indicating or constituting the distinctive quality, character or disposition 6 To represent; portray
Psalm 15:1; Rom 5:4; Philip 2:22; Job 1:6; Col 3:12

CHARGE [1] To place a load upon 2 To place in or on what is intended or able to receive 3 To diffuse something throughout; saturate 4 To fill as with electricity; make vibrant 5 To command

ENJOIN- To order authoritatively and empathetically; direct or command (a person or group) to a course of action, conduct etc. 2 To impose (a condition, course of action etc.) on a person or group -In the sense of direct or command **enjoin** is followed by *to* plus an infinitive

CHARGE [2] To instruct; exhort or warn solemnly or authoritatively 2 To entrust with a duty, responsibility, etc.; burden, as with care 3 Care and custody; superintendence 4 A person entrusted to One's care -A responsibility or duty 5 An address of instruction or admonition 6 An order or injunction 7 Having responsibility Doublet of **CARRY**

CHARITY Inclination to think well of others; tolerance; leniency 2 An act or feeling of benevolence or goodwill; Spiritual benevolence; brotherly love Syn. Benevolent; indulgent, kind, lenient, merciful 3 Philanthropic

CHASTE Pure in character or conduct; not indecent 2 Pure in artistic or literary style; simple

CHASTEN To discipline by punishment or affliction; chastise 2 To moderate; soften; temper 3 To correct; **CASTIGATE~** To rebuke or chastise severely; criticize

Syn. *Chasten, correct, discipline, chastise* and *castigate* suggest various degrees of punishment inflicted to cause a person to change his conduct *Chasten, correct* and *discipline* imply success in the effort, with *chasten* serving as a general term to cover mild or severe punishment, whether mild or severe punishment, whether physical or moral *Correct* suggests mild punishment or sometimes mere verbal reproof *Discipline*, like *correct*, looks to future conduct, and stresses training rather than punishment *Chastise*, and *castigate* refer to corporal punishment as retribution for past misconduct rather than as a corrective measure; of the two, *castigate* is harsher and more severe Compare **REPROVE, SCOLD**

CHILD A specific quality considered as a result or product of a specified condition

We know conception comes through the act of intercourse, all about the process of childbirth, and the miraculous result thereof This is a perception from the carnal mind We have all been led into the carnal perception of thinking, the result belief that we die, as it is written we were "born into sin", a consciousness that is fit for the senses, but not the eternal soul or the Eternal Spirit Everything that can be seen, heard, smelled, tasted, and both physically and mentally felt is matter and matter is the result of the carnal process of thought, currently called the state of our consciousness Our conscious state is determined by what we are conscious of All that is processed through the carnal mind is perceived by the senses, therefore all that matters is as temporary as the senses, all of which has an end because of the way it is known

There is in itself another much different definition that describes the **CONCEPT**ion of "childbearing" This is the Spiritual form of **SEXUAL INTERCOURSE**: This conception comes forth as a product of conversation, study, observation, etc., the means by which we take on characteristics prematurely, but not apparently, you see we are ourselves becoming like each other Though there are two different types of spirit children entities, both are conceived in like manner, conversation, study, observation, etc. Synonyms of sexual intercourse: **LIE, KNOWLEDGE, KNOW, CONVERSATION, INCEST, SEDUCE, MAKE** and **RAPE** It is written in the Holy Scriptures, "Outside, the sword will take their children, and inside, there will be terror; the young man and the young woman will be killed, the infant and the gray-haired" These are not as you or I, being a breathing soul, nevertheless, these are alive and at work in and around man by choice Some new lies and many old ones In this we are commanded, as it is written, "Therefore put away from among yourselves that wicked person" 1 Corinthians 5:13 Eat from the tree of Life; "That He might seek a Godly seed!" Malachi 2:15 You see, when we start becoming Christ like, it is because we are interacting with God's Word So this is how we become the children of God, so let every child of God become fully developed by His Word For this cause, He said, "Go and multiply" Genesis 1:28

CHRIST, JESUS

JESUS The highest human corporeal concept of the divine (idea)

CHRIST~ manifestation of **God**!

CHURCH A distinct body of Christians having a common faith and discipline 2 Whatever rests upon and proceeds from divine Principle 3 To call to account before the congregation; subject to discipline [OE *circe*, ult. < Gk. *kyriakon* (*dōma*) the Lord's (body) < *kyrios* Lord]

CIRCUMCISE In the Bible, to purify from sin; cleanse Spiritually

CIRCUMCISION Spiritual purification (The Catechism of the Catholic Church teaches that amputations and mutilations performed on innocent people without strictly therapeutic reasons are against the moral law. Pope Pius XII taught that circumcision is morally permissible if it prevents a disease that cannot be countered any other way (google))

CITY A situation characterized by a specified attribute

CLEAN Free from foreign undesirable matters, encumbrances or restrictions 2 Completely without something; having none of 3 Clever; dexterous 4 Well proportioned; trim; shapely 5 Neat in habits 6 Having few alterations; legible 7 To force out; drive away 8 To empty of contents or occupants

Gen 8:20; Lev. 10:10; 11:32; :47; # 31:23; Josh 22:17; 2 Kings 5:10-:14; 2 Chron. 30:19; Job 9:30; 17:9; 22:30; Psalm 24:4; 51:2; Prov. 20:9; 30:12; Isaiah 1:6; 1:16; 4:4; 66:20; Jere. 2:22; 4:11; 33:8; Ezekiel 16:4; 22:26; 24:13; 36:25; 36:33; 37:23; 43:26; **44:23; Zech. 3:1-:5; Matt 8:2; 10:8; 12:44; **23:25-:26; Mark 7:19; Luke 4:27; 11:25; ****11:41; *****John 15:3; Acts 10:15; 11:9; *****Roman 14:20; *****Eph 5:26; 2 Tim 2:21; *****Heb 6:2; consciousness 9:14; ****:22; 10:22

CLOTHE Endow with a particular quality

CLOUD A state or cause of gloom, suspicion, trouble, or worry 2 A frowning or depressed look 3 (Of such an emotion such as worry, sorrow, or anger) show in (someone's face) 4 Something that darkens, obscures, or threatens 5 Overshadowed by reproach 6 To render gloomy or troubled 6 To cover with calamity or disgrace; sully, as a reputation

CLUSTER A collection of people of the same kind growing or fastened together 2 A number of persons close together; group 3 To grow or form into a cluster or clusters

COAST To proceed easily without special application of effort or concern

COCKATRICE A fabulous serpent, said to be hatched from a cock's egg, deadly to those who felt its breath or met its glance Compare **BASILISK** In the Bible, an unidentified species of deadly serpent [< OF *cocatris* (infl. by *coq* cock) < Med. L *calcatrix*, lit., hunter, tracer [< L *calcare* to tread, trace), trans. of Gk. *ichneumon*, See **ICHNEUMON**]

COGNATE Allied derivation from the same source; belonging to the same stock or root 2 Allied in characteristics; having the same nature or quality; related; similar

COLD Not influenced by emotion; objective 2 Lacking in affection; displaying no affection 3 Chilling to the Spirit; depressing 4 Lacking freshness 5 Distant from the objective sought 6 Loss of courage; timidity 7 To discourage by being unenthusiastic or indifferent 8 Thoroughly; with certainty 9 Intentionally ignored

COME To exist as an effect or result 2 Turn out or proved to give and do what is requested 3 To return, revive; attain and attract 4 To regain former status by presenting and offering service 5 To be brought into use to be eligible to receive, acquire, and inherit entrance into and join those who acquitted themselves and became the descendants of those emerging from trial, making progress and developing to be made public; to be published and declared openly 6 Taking possession to change sides, and be successful 7 To survive, giving and doing what is required -To recover, revive, and amount to and result in being an equal 8 To purpose and produce a cause to emerge into

COMFORT A state of mental ease, especially one free from pain, want or other afflictions 2 Relief from sorrow, distress etc.; solace 3 One who or that which gives or brings ease or consolation 4 Help or support; aid and *comfort* 5 To cheer in time of grief or trouble 6 To aid; help -To strengthen

COMMAND To enjoin with authority 2 To direct authoritatively 3 To exact as being right and proper 4 The act of bidding 5 An invitation by a Sovereign -To thoroughly charge [Related to **COMMEND**]

COMMANDMENT The ability to use or control something Syn. knowledge, mastery, grasp, grip, comprehension, understanding; ability, fluency in

COMMENCE To start; begin; originate

COMMENCE Social or intellectual intercourse 2 Sexual intercourse

To express a favorable opinion of; praise 2 To accredit 3 To present with confidence; entrust 4 To present the regards of 5 To bestow in commend -To order, charge thoroughly [Related to **COMMAND**]

COMMIT To place in trust or charge; entrust 2 To consign for future reference or for preservation 3 To devote (oneself) unreservedly; pledge; bind Compare **TRUST** [< L *committere* to join, entrust < *com-* together + *mittere* to send]

COMPANION One who accompanies another or others 2 A person employed to live with and assist 3 A member of the lowest grade of knighthood 4 To be a companion to; accompany; associate with [< Du. *kampanje* storeroom < Med. L *campagna* provisions < L *com-* with + *panis* bread]

COMPASSION Pity for the suffering or distress of another, with a desire to help or spare [< L together + to feel, suffer]

COMPLEMENT That which fills up or completes a thing; that which must be added to make up a whole 2 One of two parts that mutually complete each other; supply a lack in

COMPLEMENTARY Serving as a compliment; complimenting 2 mutually providing each other's needs

COMPLEXION General aspect or appearance; quality; character 2 The cast of one's mind or thought; temperament

COMPOUND A combination of two or more elements, ingredients, or parts 2 A definite substance resulting from the combination of specific elements or radicals in fixed proportions: distinguished from mixture 3 To complicate or intensify, as by the introduction of a new element 4 To settle for less than the sum due, as a debt; compromise 5 To agree or come to terms, especially by way of compromise 6 Composed of or produced by the union of two or more elements, ingredients, or parts; composite 7 Made up of many distinct individuals functioning as a whole [< L *componere*]

COMPREHENSION The mental grasping of ideas, facts, etc., or the power of so doing; understanding 2 The complete conception of a term or idea, involving all the elements of its meaning and its correlations See **KNOWLEDGE**

CONCEIVE To form in the mind; developmentally 2 To understand; grasp 3 To express in a particular way 4 To believe or suppose; think 5 To become pregnant 6 To form a concept or notion of; imagine

CONCEPTION A beginning; commencement 2 The act or faculty of forming concepts; apprehension 3 That which is conceived mentally -Concept; idea See **JESUS**

CONCLUSION A judgment or opinion obtained by reasoning; inference; deduction 2 A final decision; resolve 3 A final arranging; settlement -To engage (someone) in a contest to determine superiority

CONCLUSIVE Putting an end to question or doubt; decisive

CONCORD Unity of interest; agreement; accord 2 Peace; friendly relations -**Agreement of words**

CONDESCEND To come down voluntarily to equal terms with inferiors; be affable 2 To lower oneself to do (something)

CONDESCENDING Showing conscious courtesy towards inferiors; especially, making a display of such courtesy; patronizing

CONFIDENCE A feeling of trust in a person or thing; reliance; faith 2 A relationship of trustful intimacy 3 Self-assurance; fearlessness 4 Excessive self-assurance; presumption 5 A feeling of certainty; expectation 6 Something told in trust; secrecy

To assure the validity of 2 To add firmness to; strengthen 3 To render valid and binding by formal approval or acceptance; ratify; sanction 4 To accept into the church by confirmation Syn. *Confirm, corroborate, prove, verify, establish,* and *substantiate* mean to show or discover a thing to be True, valid, or genuine We *confirm* that which is uncertain by removing all elements of doubt and making it firm or stable; usually the word suggests that the Truth of a statement has been settled beyond a doubt *Corroborate* is to support by additional testimony or evidence Correct reasoning from premise to conclusions *proves* a proposition or theory; examination of data or evidence *verifies* a statement by showing it to be True To *establish* is to *prove* or *verify* beyond doubt or question, while *substantiate* is to show to be real or valid

CONFOUND To confuse, amaze, or bewilder with something else; fail to distinguish 2 To confuse or mingle (elements, things, or ideas) indistinguishably 3 To damn: used as a mild oath (**MILD OATH** To express surprise or anger) 4 To put to shame; abash 5 To overthrow or defeat; ruin 6 To waste

CONGRUENT Agreeing or conforming 2 Exactly coinciding when superimposed

CONNOTATION The suggestive or associative significance of an expression, additional to the explicit literal meaning; implication 2 The total of the qualities constituting the signification of a term; intention

CONSCIENCE The faculty by which distinctions are made between moral right and wrong, especially in regard to one's own conduct; moral discrimination 2 Conformity in conduct to the prescribed moral standard 3 In Truth, in reason, and honesty 4 Inner thoughts 5 Certainly; assuredly [< OF < L *conscientia* < *conscire* to know inwardly < *com-* together + *scire* to know]

CONSENT To agree together; accord 2 A voluntary yielding to what is purposed or desired by another; acquiescence; compliance 3 Agreement in opinion or sentiment; harmony; concord

CONSEQUENT Following as a natural result, or as a logical conclusion 2 Characterized by correctness of reasoning; logical 3 An outcome; result 4 The conclusion of an argument, as of deductive reasoning as distinct from induction

CONSIDER To think about or deliberate upon; examine mentally; weigh 2 To look upon or regard (as) 3 To hold as an opinion; belief 4 To make allowance for; keep in mind 5 To take into account; have regard for 6 To observe closely

Syn.

CONSIST To be made up or constituted with 2 To have as source of basis; exist; inhere 3 To be compatible; harmonize 4 To stand together; subsist [< L *consistere* to stand still, be, exist < *com-* together + *sistere* To stand]

CONSISTENT Not contradictory or self-contradictory; compatible; harmonious 2 Conforming to a single set of principles, or to previous action or belief 3 Not to loose or fluid; solid

CONTAGION The communication of disease by contact, direct or indirect 2 A medium of transmission of disease 3 The impure or corrupting influence; harmful contact 4 The communication of mental states, ideas, etc. as by association -The *contagion* of graft See **CONTACT**

CONTAIN To hold or enclose 2 To include or comprise 3 To be capable of containing; be able to hold 4 To keep within bounds; restrain, as oneself or one's feelings 5 To be exactly divisible by 6 To be equivalent to [< OF *contenir* < L *continere* to hold, hang together < *com-* together + *tenere* to hold]

CONTENT Not inclined to complain or to desire something else; satisfied 2 Submissive to circumstances; resigned; accepting 3 Freedom from worry or unsatisfied desires; ease of mind; satisfaction 4 An affirmative vote in the House of Lords -To fulfill the hopes or expectations of
Job 36:11; Prov 13:25; ****19:23; Song of Songs 8:10; Luke 3:14; Phil 4:11; :12; 1 Tim 6:6; :8; Heb 13:5

CONTRADICTION Assertion of the opposite of a statement; denial 2 A statement that denies the validity of another 3 Obvious inconsistency, as between two statements; discrepancy

1 Corin 12:25; Heb 7:7; 12:3; 1 Tim 6:20; 4 Macc 7:20; # 20:13; :24; 2 Sam 22:44; Psalm 17:44; 30:21; 79:7; Jude 1:11

CONTRAST To place in opposition so as to set off differences or discrepancies 2 To set (one another) off by opposition 3 A dissimilarity revealed by contrasting 4 One who or that which shows unlikeness to another 5 The difference between Light and dark [< OF *contraster* to oppose < LL *contrastare* < L *contra* against + *stare* to stand]

CONVERSATION [1] Intimate association or social intercourse 2 Sexual intercourse See **CRIMINAL**
Psalm 37:14; 50:23; Amos 3:3; 2 Corin 1:12; Gal 1:13; Eph 2:3; 4:22; Phil 1:27; 3:20; 1 Tim 4:12; Heb 13:5; :7; James 13:3; 1 Peter 1:15; :18; 2:12; 3:1-:2; :16; 2 Peter 2:7; 3:11

CONVERSATION [2] Mode of life; conduct -Any interchange of ideas in which two or more persons participate

CONVOKE To call together; summon to meet [< L *convocare* < *com-* together + *vocare* to call, summon] 2 Kings 8:11

CORINTHIAN Given to luxury and dissipation 2 A man about town 3 A gentleman sportsman -A dissolute man

CORN Anything regarded as trite or overly sentimental

CORPOREAL Of a material nature

CORRECT To make free from error or mistake; to set right 2 To remedy or counteract(an error, malfunction, etc.); rectify 3 To indicate the error of; mark for amendment 4 To punish or rebuke so as to improve 5 To adjust, as to a standard 6 Free from fault or mistake; True or exact; accurate 7 [to make strait]

CORRECTION That which is offered or used for improvement 2 Rectification; revision 3 Tending or intentending to set right

COUNSEL Mutual exchange of advice, opinions, etc., consultation 2 Advice given as the result of consultation 3 A deliberate purpose; plan 4 A secret intent or opinion 5 A counsel of perfection 7 Good judgement; prudence 8 To advise in favor of; recommend

COUNTENANCE Innocent appearance of the facial features or expression 2 An encouraging look or expression, also, approval; support 3 Self control; composure 4 A look of approval; encouragement -**Fallen countenance**- Disconcerted; embarrassed; ashamed; abashed [< OF *contenance* < L *continentia* behavior < *continere*] See **CONTAIN**

COURAGE That quality of mind or Spirit enabling one to meet danger or opposition with fearlessness, calmness and firmness; bravery 2 Heart; Spirit 2 To overcome fear

*COURTIER One who seeks favor by flattery and complaisance [< AF *corteour*, OF *cortoyeur* (assumed forms)]

COVENANT An expressed agreement entered into by two or more parties; pledge

COVER To invest, as with a covering: covered with understanding 2 To provide protection, as from evil 3 To be sufficient to pay 4 To protect or guarantee against the risk or loss of life or property: *God's Word will cover you* 5 To pardon, as by putting out of one's memory 5 To clothe

COVET To desire eagerly; long for; especially, to desire something belonging to another

COW ¹ To overawe; intimidate; daunt; tyrannize

COW ² To cut short; lap off

CREATE To cause to come into existence; originate 2 To be the cause of; occasion 3 To produce a characteristic, personality, disposition, etc., from nothing by one's own thought and imagination 4 To be the first to portray, as a character or part [< L *creatus*, pp. of *creare* to produce, create]

CREATION Anything created; especially, an original product of human intelligence or imagination

CREATURE That which has been created 2 One who is dependant on, influenced by, or subordinate to something or someone

CREDULIYT Readiness to believe on slight evidence; gullibility

CREED A formal or authoritative statement of religious belief or doctrine; a confession of faith 2 Any organized system or statement of beliefs, principles, etc. [< OE *creda* < L *credo* I believe]

CREEP To act servilely; cringe A repugnant person

CROWN The highest part 2 Something that imparts splendor, honor, or finish 3 The most perfect or complete state or type 4 To endow with honor or dignity 5 To surmount; be the topmost part of 6 To enthrone 7 To finish or make complete; consummate

CRUSH To put down, subdue; conquer 2 To burden or oppress 3 To become broken or misshapen by pressure 4 An infatuation or the object of it -To break; crush; crack

CRY To call out or appeal loudly 2 To beg for; implore

CUCUMBER widely cultivated but very rare in the wild

CULMINATE To reach the highest point or degree; come to a final result or effect [< LL *culminatus*, pp. of *culminare* to mature [< L *culmen* top, highest point]

CULTIVATE To care for so as to promote growth and abundance 2 Raise from seed 3 To improve or develop by study, exercise or training; refine 4 To give one's attention to in order to acquire 5 To promote the development or advancement of [< L till < to care for, cherish]

CUNNING Skill in deception; craftiness; guile 2 Knowledge combined with manual skill; dexterity 3 Crafty or shrewd; artful; guileful 4 Executed with skill; ingenious 5 Innocently amusing; cute 5 Knowing; adept 6 Syn. **ASTUTE** [OE < *cunnung* knowledge < *cunnan* to know, be able Akin to **CAN**]

CUP One's lot in life 2 Sam 12:3

CUT To cause mental pain to; hurt the feelings 2 To pretend not to know 3 To absent oneself from 4 To shorten or deeply edit by removing parts 5 To reduce or lesson 6 To dissolve or break down 7 To perform; to present 8 To veer sharply in one's course 9 To flashback (which see) 10 To be suited for 11 To intercept 12 To effect

D

DAGGER To scowl at 2 Depression of spirits 3 A discouragement; check 4 To discourage; dull (energy, ardor etc.)

DANCE To move the body and feet rhythmically 2 To move about lightly or excitedly; leap about

DAN Sir; mister: a title of honor : *Dan* Cupid

DANIEL In the Bible, a young Hebrew prophet, captive in Babylon

DANGER Exposure to evil, injury or loss; peril; risk 2 Power; control; ability to injure [< OF, power of a lord, power to harm [< L *dominium* lordship < *dominus* lord]

DAMNATION The act of damning, or being damned ((self inflicted)) 2 A cause for eternal punishment; a mortal sin 3 Ruin by adverse criticism; tending to convict or condemn; detestable; outrageous; to cause injury; hurt or damage; to **INCULPATE~** To charge with a fault; blame 2 To involve in an accusation; incriminate [< in + fault]

DARE ¹ To have the courage or boldness to undertake; venture on 2 To challenge someone to attempt something as proof of courage 3 To oppose and challenge; defy; a taunt -The third person singular present indicative appears in two forms: *dare*, with the infinitive without *to*, or the infinitive understood

DARE ² To daunt; scare; bedazzle 2 To be in fear [OE to lurk]

DARK Cheerless or disheartening; dismal; threatening 2 Sullen in appearance; frowning; dour 3 Unenlightened in mind or spirit; lack of clarity; ignorant; blindness 4 Evil or sinister; wicked; atrocious 5 Not understandable; mysterious; obscure 6 Not known; concealed; secret; to obscure; confuse 7 Ignorance, wickedness; evil; lack of clarity; obscurity; concealment; secrecy absence of Light and lack of knowledge

DARK AGES So called because the period was considered to be characterized by ignorance and reaction

DARKNESS Ignorance, wickedness; evil; lack of clarity; obscurity; concealment; secrecy; absence of Light and lack of knowledge 2 Cheerless, disheartening, dismal things of concealed evil, sinister, wicked, atrocious, ignorant, unenlightened mind of the spirit

DARLING Beloved; very dear

DASH To frustrate; confound 2 To daunt; discourage 3 To put to shame; abash 4 A small addition of some other ingredient 5 Vigor of style

DATELESS Without end or limit 2 Of permanent interest

DAWN An awakening; new beginning or unfolding 2 To begin to be understood 3 To begin to expand or develop

DAY A point in time marked by the beginning of a new development an interval of time memorable for extraordinary events, important influences, and unusual circumstances 2 A conflict or its result 3 A time considered as propitious or opportune 4 A day of contest or the contest itself 5 A period of success, influence, accomplishment; etc.

DAZZLE To bewilder or charm, as with brilliant display; as from thought or through the senses 2 To excite admiration 3 The art of dazzling; the condition of being dazzled

DEAD Not responsive; insensible 2 No longer in force; ineffective 4 Not productively employed 5 Without spiritual life or vitality 6 Exhausted; worn out 7 Barren 8 Lacking activity, excitement or interest 9 Without luster 10 without resonance; muffled 11 Without resilience 12 Tasteless; flat 13 Complete; absolute 14 Having full or unrelieved force 15 Having no outlet or opening certain 16 Incapable of being moved emotionally 17 Utterly tired; exhausted, infertile; barren; without resonance; without resilience without vitality, spirit, enthusiasm, or the like 18 Not fruitful; unproductive 19 The period of greatest darkness, coldness 20 Not having a potential difference from that of the earth

DEADLY Excessive; deliberation 2 *Informal* Very

DEAF Unwilling to listen; determined not to hear

DEAR[1] Beloved; precious 2 Highly esteemed 3 Intense; earnest 4 Noble; glorious

DEAR[2] Severe; dire; difficult [OE wild]

DEATH Unreal and untrue 2 Absence of Spiritual Life 3 Mortal 4 A matter of time

DEBASE To lower in character, quality or worth; degrade 2 To lower in esteem See **ABASE, POLLUTE**

DEBAUCH To corrupt in morals; seduce; deprave 2 To cause to forsake allegiance 3 Dissipate [< F *debaucher* to lure from work < OF *desbaucher*]

DEBT The condition of owing something 2 A sin; trespass

DEBTOR One under obligation to another for any reason or thing

DECAY To fail slowly in any form of excellence 2 Gradual decline in mental power 3 All matter decays

DECEIT Concealment or misrepresentation of the Truth 2 An instance of deception or a device that deceives; a trick 3 To mislead into falsehood; lead into error; delude 4 To while away (life) -The quality of being deceptive; falseness

DECENT Characterized by propriety of conduct, speech or dress; respectable 2 Free of coarseness and indelicacy; modest; chaste 3 Adequate; passable; satisfactory 4 Generous; kind -Comely [< L To be fitting; proper]

DECIDE To determine; settle as a controversy; arbitrate 2 To determine the issue or conclusion of 3 Free from uncertainty; definite; unquestionable 4 Exhibiting determination; resolute; emphatic

DECIPHER To determine the meaning of (something obscure etc.) 2 Define; portray; depict

DECISIVE Ending uncertainty or dispute; conclusive 2 Characterized by decision and firmness; prompt; determined 3 Unquestionable; unmistakable

DECLARE To make known or clear; especially, to announce formally; proclaim 2 To say empathetically; assert; avow 3 Reveal; prove

DECREE A formal and authoritative order or decision; a law or ordinance 2 The foreordained and eternal purpose of God See **DISCERN**

DEDICATE To set apart for sacred use 2 To inscribe to someone as a mark of affection or esteem 3 To commit (oneself) to a certain course of action or thought 4 To open or unveil to the public, especially with a formal ceremony -Dedicated; devoted

DEDUCT To derive as a conclusion by reasoning; infer; conclude 2 To trace, as derivation or origin

DEED Anything done; an act 2 A notable achievement; feat; exploit 3 Actions in general, as opposed to words -in deed In fact; in Truth; actually

DEEP The most profound and intense part 2 Difficult to understand; obscure 3 Grave; serious 4 Heartfelt; sincere 5 Absorbing; engrossing 6 Sound and heavy; profound 7 Having penetrating intellectual powers 8 Profoundly cunning and artful 9 Mysteriously involved 10 In difficult, serious circumstances; in trouble 11 In a vast extent, as of space, time, ect. 12 The part of greatest intensity; in a way that is impossible to disentangle or separate 13 Sagacious, wise, profound, shrewd

DEEP-LAID Made with extreme care and cleverness, usually in secret

DEFACE To mar the surface or appearance of; disfigure 2 To obliterate wholly or partially, as an inscription; efface 3 Lack of something necessary for perfection or completeness 2 A blemish; failing; fault Syn. See **BLEMISH** -To desert; yield to the opinions or decisions of another [< MF *deferer* < L *deferre* < *de-* down + *ferre* to bear, carry]

DEFENCE The act of defending against danger or attack; protection 2 A plea or argument in justification or support of something 3

DEFILE To make foul or dirty; pollute 2 To tarnish or sully the brightness of; corrupt the purity of 3 To sully or profane (a name, a reputation, etc.) 4 To violate the chastity of [to trample]

DEFINE To state precisely the meaning of (a characteristic or a word etc.) 2 To describe the nature or properties of; explain 3 To determine the boundary or extent of 4 To bring out the outline of; show clearly 5 To fix with precision; specify, as the limits of power [< OF *definer* < L *definire* < *de-* down +*finire* to finish < *finis* end]

DEFINITION The act of stating what a word, phrase, set of terms, etc., mean or signifies 2 A statement of the meaning of a word, phrase, etc. 3 The determining of the outline or limits of anything 4 The state of being clearly outlined or determined **Syn.** see **EXPLANATION**

DEFLATE To take the conceit, confidence, or self-esteem *out*

To turn aside; swerve or cause to swerve from a course

DEGENERATE To revert to a lower type; decline; deteriorate 2 Having become worse, inferior, or debase; degraded 3 A morally degraded person

DEIFIC Making or tending to make divine 2 Divine

DEIL (del) The devil 2 Mischievous fellow

DEIPOTENT Having divine power

DEJECT To depress in spirit; dishearten 2 To throw down

DELIGHT Great pleasure; gratification; joy 2 The quality of delighting; charm 3 To take great pleasure; rejoice 4 To give great enjoyment 5 To please or gratify highly

DELILAH A voluptuous but treacherous woman

DELIVER To give forth; send forth; emit; discharge 2 Free from restraint, evil, danger, etc.; set free rescue 3 Liberate Syn. Free, release, let out, let go, discharge, set/let loose, deliver, save, rescue, extricate; unshackle, unfetter, unchain, unmanacle, unbind, unyoke; give rights to; ransom; manumit; disenthrall

DEMON An evil spirit 2 A very wicked or cruel person 3 A person of great zeal 4 A supernatural being of secondary rank (orig. spirit, god) **EBLIS~** In Muslim, the devil

DENOMINATION The act of naming or calling by name 2 A specific class of units in a system of measures, weights and money See **RELIGION** Syn. Sect, cult, movement, body, branch, persuasion, order, school; church

DENY To declare to be untrue; contradict 2 To refuse to believe; declare to be false or invalid, as doctrine 3 To refuse to give; withhold 4 To refuse to acknowledge; disown; repudiate 5 To refuse access to 6 To refuse to accept; decline -To refuse oneself of something desired; practice self-denial [< OF *denier* < L *denegare* < *de-* completely + *negare* to say no, refuse]

DESERT A place so lacking that it is uninhabitable by any living thing 2 Any region or mind that is uncultivated and desolate because it lacks the necessities to sustain life 3 Of or like a desert; uninhabited; barren 4 The state of deserving reward or punishment

DESPISE To regard as contemptible or worthless; disdain; scorn

DESTROY To ruin utterly; consume; dissolve 2 To tear down; demolish; raze 3 To put an end to; do away with 4 To kill 5 To make ineffective or useless

DEVIL Any subordinate evil spirit 2 Evil; a lie; error; opposes Truth 3 A belief in death, sickness and matter 4 A wicked, malicious or ill-natured person 5 A wretched fellow -Between equally bad alternatives; in a dilemma -Exclamation of anger, disgust, etc. -Trouble to be expected as a consequence -To acknowledge the ability or success of a bad or disliked person; antagonist etc. -To annoy or harass -To slander

DEVOUR Destroy completely Syn. Destroy, consume, engulf, envelop, demolish, lay waste, wipe out, annihilate, devastate; raze, gut, ravage, ruin, wreck 2 Be totally absorbed by a powerful feeling Sytn. Afflict, torture, plague, bedevil, trouble, harrow, rack; consume, swallow up, engulf, swamp, overcome, overwhelm

DEW Anything gentle, pure, or refreshing

DIE To become indifferent or insensible 2 To desire exceedingly

DIFFRACT To separate into parts

DIG To discover or bring out by careful effort or study 2 To understand or like 3 To entrench (oneself) 4 To begin to work intensively 5 To study hard and steadily; plod 6 A sarcastic remark; gibe; slur

DIGEST Mental perception and assimilation 2 To arrange in systematic form, usually by condensing; summarize and classify 3 To tolerate patiently; endure

DILIGENT Showing perseverance and application in whatever is undertaken; industrious 2 Pursued with painstaking effort **BUSY**

DIMENSION Any measurable extent, as length, breath, or thickness 2 Extent or magnitude 3 A factor used to characterize a term, counting all the exponents

DIRECT To order or instruct with authority; command 2 To lead as a conductor 3 To tell (someone) the way 4 To cause to move or face in a desired direction; aim 5 To indicate the destination of (your soul) 6 To guide the production or translation of 7 Having or being the straitest course; strait, shortest; nearest 8 Free from intervening agencies or conditions; immediate 9 Strait forward, as in meaning, statement, or intention; clear, candid, plain 10 Complete; absolute 11 Continuous as opposed to alternating 12 Having the same direction as the primary 13 Designating motion on the celestial sphere from the west towards the east, in the direction of the sun's movement among the stars 14 In a direct line or manner; directly 15 Positive [< L *directus* pp. Of *dirigere* to arrange, direct < *dis-* apart + *regere* to guide, conduct]

DIS To fill with consternation or apprehension; petrify with uneasiness; appall 2 To make downhearted or greatly troubled; dishearten and depress

DISCERN To recognize as separate or different; discriminate mentally 3 The mental power of discernment; keenness of judgment; insight See **SENSE**

DISCIPLINE Training of the mental, moral and physical 2 The state or condition of orderly conduct etc., resulting from such training 3 Systematic training in obedience to rules and authority 4 The state of order and control that results from subjection to rule and authority 5 Punishment or disciplinary action for the sake of training or correction, chastisement 6 Knowledge or training gained from misfortune, troubles etc. 7 A system of rules, or method of practice, as of a church 8 A branch of knowledge or instruction 9 To train to obedience or subjection 10 To drill; educate 11 To punish See **DISCIPLE**

DISGUST To offend the sensibilities, moral values, or good taste of; sicken

DISK The figure of a heavenly body as it appears to the naked eye **2** cause to think, and feel

DISPENSATION The act of dispensing; a dealing out; distribution 2 A specific plan, order or system of dispensing or administering 3 A special exemption from something, as from a law, rule or obligation, especially an exemption by ecclesiastical authority from a vow or similar obligation; also the document containing such an exemption 4a The arrangement or ordering of events, as by a divine Providence 4b A religious or moral system viewed as divinely established 4c the period which such a system is operative

DISPOSITION One's usual frame of mind, or one's usual way of reacting 2 Acquired tendency or inclination, especially when habitual, as a kind *disposition* 2 Blood 3 A particular ordering, arrangement or distribution 4 Management, adjustment or settlement 5 A getting rid of something, as by throwing away 6 Liberty to deal with or dispose of in any way; dispensation

DISSEMINATE to scatter as if sowing; diffuse far and wide: to disseminate knowledge

DISSOLVE To ruin utterly; consume; dissolve 2 To put an end to; do away with 3 To kill 4 To make ineffective or useless

DITAT-Deus God enriches: motto of Arizona

DIVIDE To separate into sections 4 To separate into groups; classify 5 To split into opposed sides; cause dissent in; disunite 6 To cause to be apart; cut off 7 To subject to the process of division 8 To split up through disagreement; be at variance 9 To share

DIVINE Supreme being addressed, appropriated, heavenly, extremely good Spiritual aspects of man, devoted in like character in attributes and qualities to that of Christ, to discover and declare (obscure things now) by divination and prophecy, by perception of epiphanies, intuition and insight, by the constant exercise and practice of the Word through hearing, reading, and a constant reciting of the Lord's prayer

DIVINE RIGHT of KINGS Divine authority considered as God given

DIVINITY The state or quality of being divine; especially, the state or quality of being God or a god 2 A Godlike character or attribute; especially, supreme excellence

DIVISION To cause to think, and feel 2 The state of being at variance, as in opinion, agreement, discord 3 The distribution of something separated into parts 4 Disagreement between two or more groups Syn. Disunity, discord, disagreement, dissension, disaffection, conflict, alienation, isolation, estrangement, disunion 5 Any subsidiary category between major levels of classification 6 The state of being at variance in sentiment or interest

DIVORCE Any radical or complete separation 2 To separate; cut off; disunite [< MF < L *divortium* < *divertere* to divert]

DOCTRINE That which is presented for acceptance or belief; teachings, as of a Spiritually inspired text 2 A particular principle or tent that is taught, or a body of such principles or tents

DONKEY The ass 2 A stupid or stubborn person

DONE Completed; finished; ended; agreed

DOOR Any means of entrance, exit, or approach; access [Fusion of OE *dor* gate]

DOUBT To hold the validity or reliability of as uncertain; hesitate to believe or accept 2 To be apprehensive or suspicious of 3 To be unconvinced; mistrustful 4 Lack of certainty about the Truth or facts of something 5 Fear; dread

DOVE A symbol of the Holy Ghost 2 A symbol of peace 3 A gentle, innocent, tender person

DOWN To or at a place perceived as lower (often expressing casualness or lack of hurry) 2 So as to lie or be fixed flush or flat -To or at a lower level of intensity, volume, or activity 3 In or into a weaker or worse position, mood, or condition 4 Out of action or unavailable for use (especially temporarily) 5 Not in play, typically because forward progress has been stopped 6 throughout 7 Directed or moving toward a lower place or position 8 Denoting a flavor of quark having a charge of – 1/3 protons and neutrons are thought to be composed of combinations of up and down quarks 9 Unhappy; depressed; sad, melancholy, miserable, wretched, sorrowful, gloomy, dejected, downhearted, despondent, dispirited, low 10 Supporting or going along with someone 11 To knock or bring to the ground 12 To consume 13 A feeling or period of unhappiness or depression

DRAGNET A systematic search for someone or something

DREAM Having an unreal, beautiful, charming experience, so perfect and wonderful that it can hardly be accepted as real 2 To imagine or envision 3 To consider as possible to be able to imagine [< ME *dreme* < OE *dream* **joy**; infl. By ON *draumr* a dream]

49

NOTE:

DRINK To receive or absorb eagerly through the senses or the mind

DRIP A disagreeable, insipid, or inept individual

DROUGHT Long continued lack of what is needed to sustain Life 2 Scarcity; dearth

DRUNK Overwhelmed by some powerful stimulus or influence

DRY Plain; unadorned, devoid of interest and life; dull; boring 2 Devoid of emotion; cold and stiff 3 Quietly shrewd, and impersonal 4 To become unproductive
Genesis 1:8

DUNG Anything foul 2 Exhausted; finished [[to bang; smash]

DUST Earthly matter reduced to particles so fine as to be easily born in the air 2 Confusion; turmoil; stir 3 A low or despised condition 4 Something worthless 5 To be defeated

DUTY That which one is morally bound to do; obligation 2 The controlling or impelling force of such obligations or responsibilities 3 Action or conduct required by one's position
Syn.
Duty, *obligation*, and *responsibility* denote an action that one is bound to perform In origin, *duty* is that which is owed or due; *obligation*, that by which one is bound; *responsibility*, that for which one must answer *Duty* arises from external circumstances; *responsibility*; form one's own undertaking The *duty* of man is to Love The *obligation* of God is to His Word The *responsibility* of the soul is to his Spirit

DWELL To linger as on a subject 2 To continue in a state or place See **LIVE** [OE to go astray; to delay]

E

EAGLE To have a keen sense of sight or insight **CHARACTERISTICS of**: a. Fearless- Never surrenders to its prey, regardless of strength or size b. Attentive c. Tenacious d. High flyers e. Nurture their young The eagle conveys the powers and messages of the Spirit; it is man's connection to the divine because it flies higher than any other bird When the eagle appears it bestows freedom and courage to behold the future The eagle is symbolic of the importance of honesty and Truthful principles -An eagle flies from 75- 100 mph -The constellation Aquila (Aquila & Priscilla)

EAR Attentive consideration; heed -To **be eagerly attentive** -To be submerged in work, problems etc. -To **pay attention**

EARTH The unrefined, coarse mortal body; also, **those who inhabit it** 2 Worldly or temporal affairs, as contrasted with Spiritual ones [Danish for **Jordan**] 3 The world, as distinguished from, and as opposed to heaven and hell **EARTHLY** Of or relating to the earth and its material qualities; worldly; secular 2 Possible; imaginable; **of no use**

EARTHY Unrefined; coarse 2 Natural or robust; lusty 3 Worldly

EASE Freedom from mental agitation 2 Freedom from great effort or difficulty 3 Freedom from a studied pretense; display 4 Artificiality of manner or behavior; affectedness or embarrassment; naturalness; poise 5 To relieve the mental pain or oppression of; comfort 6

To make less painful or oppressive; alleviate 7 To lessen the pressure, weight, tension etc., of 8 To make easier; facilitate 9 To move lower or put into place slowly and carefully 10 To lessen in severity, tension, speed etc. [< L close at hand, within easy reach]

EAT To gain knowledge; learn; study; find out; research; look into 2 To absorb; pay full attention 3 To make (forget) from lack of practice; deteriorate; fade 4 To retract what one has said

ECCE HOMO ¹ Behold the Man: in the **VULGATE~** *Common; popular; generally accepted 2 *Everyday speech 3 *Any commonly accepted text; the common people

ECCE HOMO ² A representation of Christ crowned with thorns **EDGE** Advantage; superiority 2 Keenly sensitive; tense; irritable 3 Eager 4 The point or state immediately before something unpleasant or momentous occurs 5 An intense, sharp, or striking quality 6 A quality or factor that gives superiority over close rivals or competitors 7 To move gradually, carefully, or furtively in a particular direction, as in conversation 8 To defeat by a small margin 9 To give an intense or sharp quality to

EDIFY Intellectual or moral enlightenment and improvement -To enlighten and benefit, especially Spiritually [< OF *edifier* < L *edificare* < *aedes* building + *facere* to make] -To enlighten and uplift; instructive, as by good example

EFFETE Having lost strength or virility; lacking vigor 2 Incapable of further production; * barren [< L worn out + a breeding]

EFFICACY Power to produce desired or intended result

EFFICIENCY The quality of being **EFFICIENT~** Productive results with a minimum of wasted effort

EFFRONTERY Shameless or impudent boldness; barefaced audacity 2 An act or instance of this See **IMPUDENCE** [< L *effrons* shameless, barefaced < *ex-* out + *frons, frontis* forehead, face]

EFFULGE To shine forth; radiate

EGO The thinking, feeling and acting self that is conscious of itself and aware of its distinction from the selves of others and from the objects of its thought and other operations 2 The conscious aspect of the psyche that develops through contact with the external world and protects the organism by resolving conflicts between the id and the superego so as to conform best with reality 3 Self centeredness; conceit; egotism

EGYPTIAN The ancient Hamitic language of Egypt, in its final stage called Coptic 2 A **GYPSY~** A member of a wandering dark-haired, dark-skinned, Caucasian people believed to have migrated to Europe from India in the 15ᵗʰ century and known throughout the world as fortune tellers, musicians etc. [Earlier *gypcyan*, **APHETIC VAR~** The gradual developmental loss of short or unaccented vowel variations from the beginning of a word, as in *mend* from *amend*, of *Egypcyan* Egyptian]

ELDER Superior in rank

ELECT To set aside by divine will for salvation: used in the passive voice

ELECTRICITY The science that deals with the phenomena, laws, theory, and application of electric energy 2 The property of many substances, as amber or fur, **to attract or repel each other when subjected to friction**

ELEMENT A part or **ASPECT** of something **ABSTRACT** especially one that is essential or characteristic 2 **ATMOSPHERIC**- Any surrounding thoroughly penetrating or permeating element or influence of **POWER**- With the ability to act; capability 2 Strength or force actually put forth 3 Any agent that exercises power as in control or dominion 4 Of a great and telling force or affect 5 A mental faculty or forces 6 The 6th of 9 orders of angels (**ELEMENT** cont.) 3 A principle, factual item, etc., essential to the solution of some problem 4 An infinitely small portion of a magnitude; a generator 5 A subdivision of an organization or formation BWE

ELDER Superior in rank, office, etc. 2 An influential senior member of a family, community, etc. 3 A predecessor, governing, or counseling member Syn. Forerunner, precursor, antecedent

EMBRACE To influence or attempt to influence, corruptly [back formation < **EMBRACER**]

EMPTY Without value, substance or significance; unsubstantial 2 Destitute or devoid

ENCOURAGE To inspire with courage, hope resolution; hearten 2 To help or foster; be favorable toward See **COURAGE**

END The purpose of an action; aim 2 An inevitable or natural consequence 3 Ultimate state 4 To bring to a finish; conclude See **PURPOSE**

ENDURE To bear up under 2 To put up with; tolerate 3 To continue to be; last 4 To suffer without yielding; hold out

ENEMY One who harbors hatred or malicious intent toward another; also one who opposes or works actively against a person, cause etc.; adversary; foe 2 Hostile power; also a member of a hostile force 3 Unfriendly [not + friend] An *enemy* is one who manifests ill will; and may be applied to a friendly *opponent* or to the most implacable

2 Chronicles 20:27 Then they returned, every man of Judah and Jerusalem, and Jehoshaphat in the forefront of them, to go again to Jerusalem with joy; for the Lord had made them to rejoice over their enemies

ENMITY Deep-seated unfriendliness accompanied by readiness to quarrel or fight; hostility; antagonism

ENRAPTURE

ENTER To become a member 2 To cause to be admitted 3 To take an interest in and contribute actively

ENTICE To lead on or attract by arousing hope of pleasure, profit, etc.; allure [< OF *enticier* to set afire < L *in*- in + *titio* firebrand]

ENTITY Something existing in the mind; an actual or conceivable being 2 Existence as opposed to non existence; being 3 Essence; substance [< L *entitas*, *-tatis* < *ens*, ppr. of *esse* to be] See also **CITY** Isaiah 2:6, 3:12

ENTRAILS The internal parts of anything [< L *inter* between, in the midst of]

ENTREAT To beseech with great intensity; implore; beg 2 To make an earnest request of or for; petition

EPHESUS Was an ancient Greek city on the western shore of Asia Minor It became a major trading center and played an important role in early Christianity (= **worldly**) 2 One of seven gatherings of bishops from around the known world under the presidency of the Pope to regulate matters of faith (= **works**) and morals (= **labor**) and discipline (= **patience**) = **Spiritual NICOLAITANS** One of certain corrupt persons in the early church at Ephesus, who is censured Ephesus is located approx. 40 miles from Smyrna

EPHOD A Jewish priestly **VESTIGE(ment)~** Visible trace, impression or sensible evidence or sign of something absent, lost or gone; trace **VESTURE~** Garments; clothing; **fig leaf** 2 All that covers land, except trees 3 A covering or envelope

EPHRAIM The plain of Jezreel 2 The kingdom of Israel

EPIPHANY A moment of sudden revelation or insight

EQUITY Fairness or impartiality; justness; reasonable 2 Something that is fair or equitable

ERR To make a mistake; be wrong 2 To go astray morally; sin 3 To wander; go astray [< L wonder]

ERROR Something done, said, or **believed incorrectly**; a mistake 2 The condition of deviating from what is correct or true in judgment, belief or action 3 An offence against morals; sin 4a The difference between the observed value of a magnitude and the true or mean value 4b Any deviation from the true or mean value not due to gross blunders of observation or measurement 5 **The contradiction of Truth; a belief without understanding** [< OF < L *errare* to wander]

Job 4:18; 19:4; ****Psalm 19:12; Ecc 5:6; *10:5; ***Isa 32:6; *Jer 10:15; *51:18; Dan 6:4; Rom 1:27; 1 Thes 2:3; 1 Tim 6:3; ***James 5:20; 2 Peter 2:18; 3:17; 1 John 3:24; 4:6; Jude 1:11 Did not believe- Deut 1:32; 9:23; 1 Kings 10:7; 2 Kings 17:14; 2 Chron 9:6; Psalm 78:22; :32; 106:24; Matt 21:25; :32; Mark 16:11; :13-14; Luke 1:20; Luke 24:11; :41; ***John 6:64; John 7:5; 9:18; ***11:40; 12:37; :47; ***20:30; Acts 9:26; ***19:2; :9; ***Rom 3:3; *4:17; **1 Corin 1:21; *2 Thes 2:12; *Heb 11:31; *Jude 1:5

ESCAPE To manage to avoid or remain untouched by some imminent or present evil 2 To come out gradually from 3 To fade away and disappear; vanish: All remembrance of sin had escaped from her mind 4 To grow wild, as a newly introduced plant 5 To get away from the notice, observation or recollection of; to slip by 6 To slip out from inadvertently or unintentionally 7 A means of escaping reality, boredom etc. 8 Gradual emergence 9 That provides a means of getting away from reality etc.; literature

ESSENCE ¹ That which makes something what it is; that in which the real nature of a thing consists; intrinsic or the fundamental nature 2 The distinctive quality(s) of something 3 That in which the attributes of something inhere; substance 4 An existent being especially, an immaterial being; Spirit 5 A perfume [< L to be]

ESPOUSAL Adoption or support, as of a cause 2 To make one's own; support, as a cause or doctrine

ESSENCE ² A member of ancient Jewish sect that existed from about the 2ⁿᵈ century B.C. to about the 2ⁿᵈ century A.D. and that stressed rigorous asceticism and a distinctive sort of mysticism [< L *Essent* < Gk. *Esse not*? < Hebrew *senu'm* the humble, pious ones]

ESSENTIAL Of, belonging to or constituting the intrinsic nature of something; fundamental and inherent; basic: the *essential* qualities of an intelligent being 2 That cannot be done without or disregarded; extremely important; vital; indispensable 3 **Fulfilled, realized or existent**

to the greatest possible extent; complete, total or absolute 4 Something **fundamental, indispensable or extremely important**

ESTEEM To have a high opinion of; look upon with appreciation or respect; value greatly 2 To think of (<u>**every person**</u>) as having the Spirit of the Living **God**; rate 3 High regard of respect; great appreciation 4 Judgment; opinion [< L to value]

ETIQUETTE The usage or rules conventionally established for behavior in polite society or in official or professional life [< F < OF *estiquette*; orig., label, hence order, manners Doublet of **TICKET**]

ETYMOLOGY A HISTORY OF A WORD AS SHOWN BY BREAKING IT DOWN INTO BASIC ELEMENTS OR BY TRACING IT BACK TO THE EARLIEST KNOWN FORM AND INDICATING ITS CHANGES IN FORM AND MEANING; ALSO A STATEMENT OF THIS 2 THE STUDY OF THE DERIVATION OF WORDS [< GK. <*ETYMON T*RUE MEANING + WORD, STUDY] Etymon~ The earliest known form of a word [< L <Gk. original meaning; orig. neut. sing. of *etymos* true, genuine]

EUDEMONISM Of, relating to or intending to produce happiness -A system of ethics in which actions are evaluated morally according to their ability to produce happiness

EVENING Period during which something gradually draws to a close; especially the declining years of life

EVIL Morally bad; wicked 2 Causing injury, damage or any other undesirable result 3 Marked by, full of or threatening misfortune or distress; unlucky or disastrous 4 Not high in public esteem; not well thought of -Those who are morally bad; wrongdoing -Those who are injurious or otherwise undesirable -Those who cause suffering, misfortune or disaster 5 Some particular thing as an act, condition or characteristic, that is evil

EVINCE To indicate clearly; demonstrate convincingly; make evident; prove 2 To give an outward sign of having; exhibit; display 3 **To overcome; also to convince** [< L *evincere*, See **EVICT**]

EVIDENCE That which serves to prove or disprove something; **that which is used for demonstrating the Truth** or falsity of something; support; proof 2 That which serves a ground for knowing something with certainty or for believing something with conviction; corroboration -In the condition of being readily seen or perceived; especially, conspicuously present 3 **To give a clear indication of; show unmistakably -Inward character is revealed by outward signs** -A *palpable* thing is **perceived by a sense other than sight, and so presumably more certain than that which is merely visible** -A similar depreciation of sight is suggested by a secondary sense of apparent

EXALT The state or feeling of great, often extreme, exhilaration and well being, rapture or ecstasy 2 To raise in character, honor etc. 3 To glorify or praise; pay honor to 4 To fill with delight, pride etc.; elate

EVANGEL Of, relating to, contained in or in harmony with the New Testament, especially the Gospels 2 Of, relating to or maintaining the doctrine that the Bible is the only rule of faith and that salvation is attained chiefly by faith in the redemptive work of Christ (See introduction)

EVER At any time; on any occasion 2 By any possible chance 3 In any possible or convincing way 4 At all times; invariably 5 Throughout the entire course of time; always; forever 6 To an extremely great extent or degree; extraordinarily; exceedingly 7 Extremely often; repeatedly

EVERYTHING Whatever exists; all things whatsoever 2 Whatever is relevant, needed or important 3 The essential Thing

EVIL Morally bad; wicked deeds 2 Causing injury, damage, or any other undesirable result; harmful or prejudicial 3 Marked by, full of, or threatening misfortune or distress; unlucky or disastrous 4 Not highly thought of in public esteem; not well thought of 5 That which is morally bad; wrongdoing; wickedness 6 That which causes suffering, misfortune, or disaster 7 Some particular thing, as an act, condition, or characteristic, that is evil Syn. Pernicious, hurtful, destructive, immorality, and illness

EXAMPLE Something deserving to be imitated or copied; model; exemplar 2 Designed to serve as a warning or deterrent to others by way of illustration; as a typical instance -To act in such a way as to arouse others to imitation; **now only in the passive**

EXAMINE To inspect or scrutinize with care; investigate critically; inquire into 2 To test by questions or exercises as to qualifications, fitness, etc., as a pupil 3 Questions formally in order to elicit facts etc. [< L tongue of a balance < out + root of *agere* to drive. Akin to **EXACT**]

EXERCISE To exert, as influence 2 To occupy the mind of 3 A putting into use, action or practice 4 A lesson, problem etc., designed to train some particular function or skill 5 An **act of worship or devotion** See **PRACTICE**

EXERCISED Harassed; agitated; excited -The exercise or practice of certain skills, powers etc. 2 A display of skill

EXERT To put forth or into action as will, strength, or influence; exercise vigorously; to put forth effort

EXHORT To urge by earnest appeal; advise or recommend strongly 2 Completely to urge

EXILE Separation by necessity or choice

EXIST To have actual being or reality; be 2 To be present; occur

EXISTENCE The state or fact of being or continuing to be 2 Anything that exists; an entity; actuality 3 All that exists

EXPERIENCE

EXPONENT One who or that which explains or expounds 2 One who or that which represents or symbolizes something [< L *exponens*, -entis, ppr. of *exponere* to explain]

EXPONIBLE Needing explanation, as a proposition in logic that must be restated to be intelligible

EXPRESSION An outward indication or manifestation of some feeling, condition, quality, etc. 2 A conventional sign or set of signs used to indicate something; symbolization 3 A particular way of looking, acting, etc., that is indicative of something; especially, a cast of the features 4 A particular way in which one expresses oneself 5 The quality of expressing oneself with understanding, insight, sensitivity, etc. 6 The ability to communicate through feeling, etc.: **a concept beyond expression**

EYE Attentive observation; watchful care 2 Capacity to discern with discrimination 3 A particular expression; **MEIN**- The outward manifestation of personality or attitude 4 Interest; desire 5 A manner of viewing; judgment; opinion 6 To get the attention of 7 To look at admiringly or invitingly 8 To look at amorously or covetously 9 To agree in all respects 10 With a view to 11 One's own interests 12 To look at carefully; scrutinize

F

FACE Awareness of the literal or most evident meaning of what is apparent, that is most important or designed to fulfill a purpose 2 To meet with courage and confront 3 To become or be made aware of, realizing 4 In each others immediate presence 5 The expression of the countenance 6 A grotesque or grimacing expression 7 Effrontery; audacity 8 The front or principle surface of anything

FACTION A group of people operating within, and often in opposition to, a larger group, to gain its own ends 2 **Internal dissention** [< L to do]

FAIL To turn out to be deficient or wanting, as in ability, quality or effect; prove disappointing 2 To miss doing or accomplishing something attempted, requested, expected etc. 3 To prove of no help to; **disappoint the expectations** of; forsake; desert; fault; defect; shortcoming; default; lacking; unsuccessful; inefficient [< L *fallere* **to deceive**]

FAIN Gladly; preferably 2 Willing or content to accept an alternative or substitute 3 Obliged or compelled 4 Glad; rejoiced

FAINT To lose consciousness; swoon 2 To fail in courage or hope 3 To grow weak 4 Lacking in distinctness, brightness, etc. 5 Without enthusiasm, purpose, or energy; feeble; weak - A temporary loss of consciousness [< OF, pp. Of faindre See **FEIGN**]

FAIR Free from blemish or imperfection 2 Showing no partiality; just; upright 3 According to rules, principles, etc.; legitimate 4 Properly open to attack: He is *fair* game 5 moderately satisfactory or acceptable; passably good or large 6 Likely or promising 7 Apparently good and plausible, but actually false 8 Gracious or courteous; pleasant 9 Open; unobstructed 10 Accurately trimmed; even; regular 11 In fair manner - Play fair 12 Squarely; directly - To seem probable or favorable 13 To become fair or clear 14 A fair woman; sweetheart

FAITH Confidence in or dependence on a statement, or thing as trustworthy; trust 2 Belief in God or a testimony about God as recorded in the Scriptures or other Spiritually inspired writings 3 Anything given adherence or creedence 4 Allegiance or fidelity Syn. See **TRUST BELIEF RELIGION**

FAITHFUL True or trustworthy in the performance of duty, the **fulfillment of promises** or obligations etc.; constant; loyal 2 **Worthy of belief or confidence**; Truthful 3 True in detail or **accurate in description** 4 **To betray one's own beliefs or principles** 5 With honorable intentions 6 Anything given adherence or credence

FAITHLESS Untrue to promise or obligation; unfaithful; disloyal 2 Not dependable or trustworthy; unreliable 3 Devoid of faith or trust 4 Deceitful; perfidious

FALL To drop from a higher to a lower place or position because of removal of support or loss of hold or attachment; to God 2 To be taken or captured 3 To yield to temptation; sin 4 To pass into some specified state or condition 5 To experience or show direction 6 To be classified or divided 7 **To conflict with** 8 To quarrel or argue with 9 To leave or withdraw 10 To attack; to assail 11 To be or prove deficient 12 To set about; to begin (time) 13 To begin eating 14 To begin fighting 15 A moral lapse 16 **A loss or diminution of esteem**

FALLOW Left unseeded after being plowed; uncultivated -To remain unused, **idle**, dormant etc. 2 Land left unseeded after plowing 3 The process of plowing or working land and leaving it unseeded for a time -To make, keep or become fallow ~Light, yellowish brown pale [< L to be pale]

FALSE Deceptive or misleading; false impression 2 **Given to untruth**; lying 3 **Wanting in fidelity**; disloyal; faithless 4 Supplementary; substitutive 5 Not correct in pitch; out of tune 6 Not properly so called [< L *fallere* to deceive]

FAMILY A group of persons forming a household 2 Any class or group of like things 3 Of, belonging to, or suitable for a family [< L *familia* family < *famulus* servant]

FAMINE A widespread scarcity of anything; dearth 2 Without or diminishing Word of God 3 Starvation

FAST Firm in place; not easily moved 2 Not liable to fade **ABSTINENCE**- The act or practice of **abstaining as from conversation and the company of others; pleasure** 2 Total self denial 3 To keep oneself back; refrain voluntarily from action; forbear 4 To be still (for three days); effective 3 Deep or **SOUND**

FAT Well filled or supplied with rich or desirable elements 2 Abundant; plentiful 3 Yielding abundantly; profitable 4 The richest or most desirable part of anything

FATHER Eternal Life; the divine Principle, commonly called **God** 2 To found, create, or make

FAULT Whatever impairs excellence; a blemish; **offence**; misdeed; negligence; flaw; err; mishap; blunder; default; lack See **OFFENCE~** Open to blame; in the wrong; culpable 2 At a loss; perplexed; astray 3 Off the scent -Immoderately; excessively -**To seek out and complain** about some imperfection, error, misdeed etc. 4 To find fault with -To crack, so as to produce a fault -**To deceive**

FAVOR An attitude of friendliness, liking or approbation 2 **The condition of being looked upon with liking or approval** 3 **Kind permission; gracious consent** 4 **Something that helps or furthers an undertaking**; aid 5 Some little *fides* faith Syn. Honesty, integrity 6 loyalty, faithfulness, **constancy, devotion**

FEAR To have a deep reverential awe of: **The fear of the LORD is the beginning of knowledge**

Note: A person can not have a deep reverential awe of anyone unless he knows him as well or almost as well as he knows himself

FEAST Something affording great pleasure to the intellect 2 A day or days of celebration 3 To entertain lavishly 4 To delight; gratify 5 To dwell delightedly

FECUNDATE To make prolific or fruitful 2 To impregnate -Made fruitful -Fertilized

FEEBLE Lacking intellectual or moral vigor 2 Lacking energy, direction or effectiveness; altogether inadequate; ineffective 3 Lacking point or substance 4 Scarcely able to be seen or heard; indistinct; faint; [< weak; lamentable; to weep] gift or remembrance given as a token of esteem, affection or hospitality 5 Attractiveness; charm 6 General appearance -Having approval or support -Of such a kind as to help one or promote one's interests, approval or support 7 To show special consideration to, often in an unfair way; show partiality to 8 To lean toward approving or supporting 9 To increase chances of success of; help along 10 To be careful of; treat gently; spare

FEED To furnish with what maintains or increases 2 To keep up or make more intense or greater 3 To keep supplied, as with information or other essential or important things to be used or worked on 4 To keep up or make more intense or greater 5 To gratify 6 To draw support, encouragement, etc., from *Informal* a **MEAL**

FEET Into a condition of stability; well-established 2 In or into a condition of restored health

FEIGN To make a false show of; put on a deceptive appearance; sham 2 To think up (a false story, a lying excuse, ect.) and give out as true; fabricate 3 To imitate so as to deceive; counterfeit 4 To portray or tell (something imagined) in a story, verse, ect.; also, to conjure up in the impagination 5 To make pretense of something [< OF *feindre* < L *fingere* to shape]

FELICITY Happiness, especially when very great; bliss 2 A cause or source of happiness or bliss 3 An agreeably pertinent effective manner or style 4 An instance of this manner or style, as a pleasantly appropriate remark or observation See **HAPPINESS** [< OF *felicite* < L *felicitas*, *-tatis* < *felix*, *-icis* happy

FELL [1] Cruel; vicious; inhuman 2 Lethal; deadly [OE *felen*]

FELL [2] **The skin of a human being** [OE hide] Genesis 1:27 Genesis 2:23 Isaiah 10:18 Jeremiah 31:22

FELL [3] A barren hill

FELLOW FEELING A statement closely paralleling or harmonizing with that of another; sympathetic understanding

FELLOWSHIP The state of being joined to or associated with another by reason of being one of the same kind, class or group 2 Close association with or adoption into a body of individuals having common interests, origins, ideas, experiences, beliefs etc.; comradeship; also, the body of individuals joined together through such interests, beliefs etc.; brotherhood

FERVENT Moved by or showing great warmth or intensity, as of emotion or enthusiasm; ardent [< L *fervere* to boil]

FICKLE Inconstant feeling or purpose; changeful; capricious

FIDUCIAL Fiduciary 2 Prompted by or based on trust or religious faith

FIDUCIARY Of, pertaining to or acting as a trustee 2 Held in trust

FIDUS ACHATES As he was called, was a close friend of Aeneas; his name became a byword for "intimate companion" *2 Any faithful, trustworthy friend

FIELD The whole extent or particular division of knowing, research, study etc.; also, a particular area of activity, experience, interest, etc. 2 A region of active operations or maneuvers; sphere of action 3 To remain firm against opposition -To give one's energies, interest, or attention to the entire range of something [< OE *folde* earth Cf. **PLANE**]

FIERY Eagar or fierce in Spirit; passionate; impetuous

FIG To dress; array 2 Condition; form: in good *fig* -According to this definition, the tree is a metaphor for the Jewish nation, i.e., it had the outward appearance of godly grandeur (the leaves), but it was not producing anything for God's glory (the lack of fruit). The fig-tree that had no fruit, when Jesus came when He saw there was no fruit (for He was *hungry*), He cursed the tree and it soon lost its leaves [Var. of obs. *Feague* whip < G *fegen* polish]

FIGURATIVE Based on, of the nature of or involving a figure of speech; not literal; metaphorical 2 Representing by means of a form or figure; emblematic -Departing from a literal use of words representing forms that are recognizably derived from life

FIGURE The visible form of anything; shape; outline; appearance 2 The appearance of impression that a person or his conduct makes 3 A representation or likeness 4 One who, or that which represents or symbolizes something 5 A figure of speech (which see) 6 To make an image, picture or other representation of; depict 7 To express by a figure of speech; symbolize 8 To solve; compute 9 To make out; understand

FIND Discover or perceive by chance or unexpectedly 2 Recognize or discover (something) to be present Syn. Be present, occur, exist, be met with, be existent, appear, show itself, manifest itself, be; obtain 3 A discovery of something valuable, typically something of Spiritual interest 4 Discover (information) after a deliberate search 5 Summon up (a quality, especially courage) with an effort 6 Become aware of; discover to be the case 7 Discover the fundamental Truths about one's own character and identity 8 Officially declare to be the case Syn. Judge, adjudge, adjudicate, deem, rule, hold, consider, count, rate, reckon, see as; declare, determine, pronounce 9 Reach the understanding or conscience of (someone) 10 A person who is discovered to be useful or interesting in some way

FINE Superior in quality; excellent; choice 2 Highly satisfactory; very good 3 Possessing superior ability or skill 4 Keen; sharp 5 Trained to the highest efficiency 6 Subtle; nice 7 Delicate of perception; discriminating 8 Elegant; polished; fastidious: *fine* manners 9 Cloudless; clear 10 Free from impurities; pure 11 Very well [< OF *fin* finished, perfected, ult. < L *finire* to complete < *finis* end]

FINE ² End; conclusion; death [< OF fin settlement < L finis end]

FIRE Light; brilliance and splendor of 2 The intensity of Spirit, feeling, and passion 3 Inflamed; burning; hence, eager; Ardent and zealous 4 To become excited; or enthusiastic 5 To commence 6 To get a reaction 7 To cure 8 To cause to glow or shine 9 To inflame the emotions or passion of Spiritual feeling; inspire -To start and proceed with energy and rapidity, especially in asking questions 10 Being subject to severe criticism 11 Failing to explode; braving any danger and enduring every trial

FIRMAMENT To make firm; support 2 A sphere or world viewed as a collection of people

FIRST Highest or foremost in character, rank etc.; leading; best; chief 2 The beginning 3 In preference to anything else; preferably Syn. Prime, primary; original, primordial; principle, preeminent, primordial

FIRSTFRUIT The first outcome, result or reward of anything

FIT[1] Adapted to an end, aim or design; suited 2 Proper or appropriate; becoming 3 Possessing the proper qualifications; competent 4 A state of preparation; ready See **APPROPRIATE~** To be suitable or proper for 2 To make or alter to the proper size purpose 3 To provide what is suitable or necessary; equip 4 To prepare or make ready or qualified 5 To put in place carefully or exactly See **ADAPT~** Condition or manner of fitting

FIT[2] A sudden overmastering emotion or feeling 2 Impulsive and irregular exertion or action [OE *fitt* struggle]

FIX To make firm or secure 2 To render permanent and unchangeable 3 To place firmly in the mind 4 To hold or direct (the attention, gaze etc.) steadily or piercingly 5 To settle or decide definitely 6 To determine or establish 7 To arrange or put in order; adjust 8 To repair 9 To prepare 10 To prearrange or influence the outcome, decision etc. 11 To become firm or stable 12 To get ready -To decide upon See **PREDICAMENT** [< Med. L *fixare* to fasten]

FLAME Intense passion or emotion; ardor 2 To light up 3 To become enraged or excited

FLANK To have one side directed toward (something specific)

FLAT Smooth and regular with few or no hollows or projections 2 Absolute and unqualified 3 Lacking interest spontaneity, or sparkle; lifeless; dull 4 Lacking tastiness or zestfulness 5 Monotonously devoid of variety in tone 6a Lower than the right, true pitch 6b Having flats in the key signature 7 Without interest -To fail to achieve desired effect 8 A shallow tray of earth for germinating seeds

FLATTER To praise excessively, especially without conviction or sincerity 2 To try to gain favor of by praising this way 3 To play upon the hopes or vanity of; beguile 4 To make pleased or gratified, as by compliments, also to please by pampering 5 To show as more attractive than is actually the case -To have the vain conviction, feeling or notion that you will succeed [< OF flatter to fawn, caress. Akin to **FLAT**]

FLAVOR A special, suitable quality pervading something 2 Odor ~Regard or estimation [< L *flare* to blow: added on analogy with *savor*]

FLESH The body of anything corporeal and incorporeal 2 The main or central part of something, especially a building or text 3 The representation of a soul's abstract qualities; attribution of a personality 4 The basic inherent disposition, personality, temperament, mentality, pleasurable, interesting and exciting mood of man 5 The soul of a male or female **without the skin** (because of the **FALL**[2])

FLESHLY Corporeal 2 Sensuous; carnal 3 Worldly

FLOCK A group of persons who are members of the same church or congregation; also the whole body of Christians 2 Any group of persons under the care of or supervision of someone 3 Like bands of people traveling or otherwise grouped together, coming or going into crowds

FLOUR To break up into **NONCOALESCING**- The absence of growing together or into one body 2 The opposite of uniting so as to form one mass, community, etc.

FLY To move swiftly or with a rush 2 To pass swiftly 3 Escape 4 To flee 5 To enter into suddenly 6 A light hackney coach while in great haste

FOLLOW To go or come after in the same direction 2 To succeed in order 3 To hold to the course of 4 To conform to 5 To use or take as a model; imitate 6 To watch or observe closely 7 To have an active interest in 8 To understand the course, sequence or meaning of, as an explanation 9 To come after as a consequence or result 10 To move or act in the cause of 11 To accompany; attend 12 To pay attention 13 To follow to the end 14 To comply with, as orders or instructions 15 To perform fully; complete 16 To bring to full completion 17 To increase the effectiveness of by further action

FOOD Anything that is used or consumed in a manner suggestive of food; **intellectual**

FOOL [1] A person lacking understanding, judgment or common sense 2 One who has been duped or imposed upon; victim; butt 3 An imbecile; idiot 4 To act, speak etc., in a playful or teasing manner 5 Make a fool of; impose upon; deceive 6 To waste time on trifles 7 Loiter about idly -To spend or waste foolishly; squander 8 To meddle with 9 To play or toy aimlessly with -Stupid or silly

FOOL [2] Crushed stewed fruit

FOOT In progress; proceeding 2 The lower part of anything 3 A resting place for all that is carried

FORBEARANCE Refraining or abstaining from an action 2 **Patient**; **self-control** 3 A refraining from enforcing a right -Disposed to **FORBEAR~** To cease or desist from (some action) 2 **To put up with**; **endure** 3 To be patient or **act patiently** See **FOREBEAR~ An ancestor**. See **PATIENT**

FOREHEAD The front part of anything

FOREVER Throughout eternity; to the end of time; everlastingly; always 2 Incessantly; constantly

FORGET To lose interest in or regard for; overlook purposely; disregard or slight 2 To leave unmentioned; fail to think of 3 To lose self control and act in an unbecoming manner 4 To be lost in thought 5 To neglect (to do something) unintentionally

FORGIVE To grant pardon for or remission of (something); cease to demand the penalty for 2 To grant freedom from penalty to (someone) 3 To cease to blame or feel resentment against 4 To remit, as a debt 5 To show forgiveness; grant pardon; absolve 6 A disposition to forgive

FORM Proper arrangement or order in the manner in which something is done 2 Constructed, devised, developed and acquiring in the mind; as habit and liking to give specific exemplified character to that which makes up an element 3 **Shaped by discipline and training**; to mold 4 **To begin to exist** 5 **With fitness of mind for performance and intrinsic nature as distinguished from the matter that embodies its essence**

FORGIVE To grant pardon for or remission of (something); cease to demand the penalty for 2 To grant freedom from penalty to (someone) 3 To remit, as a debt 4 To show forgiveness; grant pardon

FORSAKE To renounce or relinquish 2 To abandon; desert Syn. See **ABANDON** [OE *forsacan* to repudiate, deny < *for-* away + *sacan* to renounce]

FORTE That which one does with excellence; strong point

FORTIFY To give moral strength to; invigorate; encourage 2 To strengthen the structure of; reinforce 3 To confirm; corroborate

FORTITUDE Strength of mind in the face of pain, adversity, or peril; patient and persistent courage

FOUND To give origin to; set up; establish and lay the foundation on the basis; (of a)

PREMISE- A proposition that serves as a ground for reasoning, and conclusions: "If the premise is True, then the conclusion must be True" 2 A assertion or proposition which forms the basis for a work

FOUNDATION The act of giving existence to (someone) or setting up and establishing (someone) 2 The state of being founded or established **3 A base on which something rests**

FOUNTAIN The Origin or Source of anything Jere. 2:13; 17:13; Rev. 7:17

FRINGE One of the alternate light and dark bands produced by the interference of Light as in a **DIFFRACTION** See **DIFFRACT**

FRANK Open, honest, and direct in speech or writing, especially when dealing with unpalatable matters 2 Open, sincere, or undisguised in manner or appearance 3 Unmistakable; obvious

Syn. Open, undisguised, unconcealed, naked, unmistakable, clear, obvious, transparent, patient, manifest, evident, perceptible; blatant, barefaced, flagrant

FRANKINCENSE In the general sense inflame or excite someone with a strong feeling [< OF *incenser* < L *incendere* set fire to < from *in-* in + the base of *candere* 'to glow < OF franc **pure** + *encens* **INCENSE**]- **Anger; enrage**

FRANKPLEDGE In old English law, a system that required all men of a community to combine in groups of ten to stand for sureties for one another's good behavior 2 A member of one of the groups in this system; also, any group (*tithing*) in this system [< AF *franc-plege*, lit., a freeman's pledge; erroneous trans. [< Of < OE *frith-borg* a pledge **to keep the peace**]

FRESH Newly obtained, received, etc. 2 Recent; latest 3 Additional 4 Not spoiled 5 Retaining original vividness; not faded or worn, as (some) instance of occurring to the mind 6 Pure and clear 7 Not fatigued; energetic 8 Inexperienced; untrained 9 Moderately rapid and strong 10 Having a renewed supply of Syn. Untried, unskilled, naive 11 Saucy; impudent; disrespectful

FRIEND One who is personally well known by oneself and for whom one has **warm regard or affection** 2 A patron or supporter -To be on (or enter into) friendly terms (with)

FRIEND AT COURT An influential person well disposed toward another and able to promote another's interest

FRIENDLY Well disposed; not antagonistic 2 Helpful; favorable

FRIENDLY SOCIETY A benefit society (which see) 2 **Mutual liking and esteem -Friendly feelings or inclination**

FRUIT The outcome, consequence, or result of some action, effort, situation, etc. [To enjoy]

FURNACE A grueling test or trial

FUNDAMENTAL Pertaining to or constituting a foundation; basic; primary; essential 2 Of or pertaining to a root 3 Anything that serves as a basis of a system, as Truth, law, principle, etc.; an essential

FUTILE Being of no avail; unproductive; worthless; fruitless; useless 2 Having no real basis or worth; empty; unreal, no purpose; without effect 3 Frivolous; trivial [< F < L *futilis* pouring out easily, useless]

FUTILITY Complete lack of effectiveness or point; uselessness 2 Unimportance; triviality

G

GAD To roam about restlessly, aimlessly, frivolously or capriciously; ramble 2 Vagabond

GAMBLE To take a risk to obtain a desired result 2 To lose or squander by wagering or taking risks 3 Any risky or uncertain venture

GARDEN Any fertile, highly cultivated territory remarkable for the beauty of its vegetation

GARMENT To decorate; adorn; **DRESS** To prepare for use 2 To clean for translating 3 To till or prune 4 To put in proper alignment 5 To come into proper alignment See **DIRECT**

GATE Anything that gives access 2 A particular way of doing something or behaving 3 A course or path

GATHER Through induction or observation; infer 2 Come aware of it through deduction and observation 3 To summon up or muster, as one's energies, for an effort

GAUNT [< OF gent elegant, infl. in meaning by ON]

GAVE Transfer freely without asking anything in return; to be the source performance and to do the action indicated 2 To devout free gifts, making donations; furnish a view or passage; conduct creditably, as in difficult situations; exchange on equal terms 3 To hand over the bride to the Bridegroom 4 Making known the secret

GEM One who or that which is treasured or greatly admired for perfect or nearly perfect qualities

GENERATION Of such a group regarded as having similar opinions, behaviors, etc., and a bringing of them into being; by production and origination

GENEROUS Marked by or **showing great liberality; munificent; unselfish** 2 Having **gracious** qualities; manifesting **generosity** in **forgiving insults or injuries; not given to resentment or envy; great of soul; high minded; unselfish** 3 **Abundant and overflowing; large; bountiful** 4 **Stimulating or strong as wine** 5 **Fertile or fruitful** 6 Being of noble ancestry -**A person who gives freely etc., of great worth; emphasizes the warm feeling of sympathy, tenderness, regard, etc., that prompts the giving; stresses the amount (not in $) of the gift and points to the absence of stinginess or meanness -**The *bountiful* **person gives both lavishly and continuously; one who displays princely liberality 7 Considerate, unselfish, charitable 8 Ample, plentiful**

*****GENIAL Kindly pleasant or cordial in disposition or manner 2 Imparting warmth, comfort, Life or growth; supporting Life or growth -Exhibiting or relating to genius**
[< L *genialis* of one's tutelary deity < *genius*, See *****GENIUS**]

GENIUS Extraordinary intelligence that of most intellectually superior individuals: also, one who posses such intelligence 2 An aptitude for doing or achieving a particular thing: especially, an outstanding gift for some specialized activity 3 The essential Spirit or distinguishing characteristic of a particular individual 4 A supernatural being appointed to guide a person throughout life: a guardian Spirit 5 A person who exerts a strong, formative influence over another for good [< L tutelary Spirit < *gen-* stem of *gignere* to beget] Syn. *Genius, talent, gift, aptitude,* and *faculty* refer to superior mental ability *Genius,* the strongest word, is conceived as a mental power far beyond explanation in terms of heritage or education and manifests itself by exceptional originality *Talent* is a natural readiness in learning and doing in a particular field; it is conceived of as an inborn resource that may or may not be developed *Gift* is akin to *genius* on a lower plane; it is also an innate quality or ability that manifests itself without cultivation *Aptitude* is special ability to learn and become proficient, while a *faculty* is a particular mental skill or knack, inborn or acquired [< L *genialis* of one's tutelary deity < *genius*, See **GENIUS**]

GENTEEL Well-refined; elegant; polite Doublet of GENTLE~ Mild and amiable in nature or disposition; kindly; patient 2 Not harsh, rough, or loud; soft; moderate; mild 3 Not steep or abrupt; gradual 4 Easily managed; docile; tame 5 To make easy to control; tame 6 The Spirit or principles of knighthood 7 The ideal qualities of knighthood, as courtesy, valor, charity; to appease the anger of; pacify 8 To elevate in social rank

GENUINE Being actually of the origin, authorship, or **character claimed**; authentic; real 2 **Not spurious, adulterated or counterfeit**; **properly so named** 3 Not affected or hypocritical -**Frank; sincere** 4 Being of the original or true stock

GIFT A natural endowment; aptitude 2 The right or power of giving See **GENIUS**

GILT A young sow

GIRD¹ To encircle; surround 2 To prepare (oneself) for action 3 To clothe, equip or endow, as with some quality or attribute [OE *gyrdan*]

GIRD² To attack with sarcasm; gibe 2 To taunt

GIVE To transfer freely (what is one's own) to the permanent possession of another without asking anything in return 2 To make available; furnish; proffer 3 The quality of being resilient 4 To grant or concede, as permission 5 To impart; administer 6 To part with relinquish or yield 7 To devote, as oneself, to a cause 8 To furnish a view or passage; open -To conduct (oneself) creditably, as in a difficult situation 9 To hand over (the bride) to the Bridegroom in the marriage ceremony 10 To make known, as a secret; reveal 11 To yield to something, as demands 12 To cease opposition; acknowledge oneself vanquished 13 To become completely used up or exhausted -To cause to understand; (or know) 14 To devote wholly 15 To cease objecting 16 To be a source of [Fusion]

GLAD Having a feeling of joy, pleasure or content; gratified 2 Showing joy; brightly cheerful 3 Giving reason to rejoice; bringing joy -To gladden -Shining

GLADIATE Sword-shaped [< L *gladius* sword + ate (used to form the names of salts)]

GLADIOLUS See **THORAX**~ enclosed by the ribs, and containing the lungs, heart etc.

GLASS To reflect the image or character in

GLEAN To collect (facts) by patient effort

GLOOM Darkness or depression of the mind or spirits 2 To look sullen, displeased or dejected 3 To be or become dark or threatening 4 To make dark, sad or sullen [ME *glom*(be)en to look sad]

GLORY The state of being invested with glory 2 A glorified state 3 Distinguished honor or praise; exalted reputation 4 Something bringing praise or renown; an object of special distinction 5 Worshipful praise; adoration: To give *glory* to **God** 6 Magnificence; splendor 7 The bliss of heaven 8 The state of exaltation, extreme well being, prosperity etc. 9 A nimbus halo

GLORIOUS Full of or deserving glory; renowned; illustrious 2 Bringing glory or honor 3 Resplendent; beautiful 4 Very pleasant; delightful

GLOSS An explanatory note; especially, a marginal or **INTERLINEAR~** Situated or written between the lines 2 An artful or deceptive explanation designed to cover up a fault, defect etc.; **ANNOTATE~** To provide (a text, etc.) with explanatory or critical notes 2 To excuse or change by false explanations, over the Truth [< L *glossa* a difficult word (in a text) < Gk. *glossa* foreign word orig., tongue]

GLOSSARY A lexicon of the technical, obscure or foreign words of a work or field

GLOTTOCHRONOLOGY Total or partial removal of the tongue -The probable dates when the various members of a language family separated from one another, from their parent language etc. 2 The study of the time during which a separation process in language took place

GOAD A signal or permission to move ahead or proceed

god Any person or thing made the chief object of one's love interest or aspiration

GOD The divine, creative Principle; Life, Truth and Love; Mind; Spirit 2 This Being regarded as the source or embodiment of some specific attribute, principle, virtue, etc. 3 The self-existent and eternal creator, sustainer and ruler of the universe

GOD FEARING Having reverence for **God** 2 Pious; devout 3 Having reverence for the whole creation; principles and virtues; all Truth; Life; and Love 4 Having reverence for the mind, who is the Spirit with you, while you remain in this consciousness

GODLY Filled with reverence and love for **God**; pious 2 Belonging to or emanating from **God**

GOD SEND Something received or acquired unexpectedly most welcome that happens by a stroke of good luck [< **GOD** + ME *sande* message]

GOLD A characteristic considered to be precious, beautiful, or of the most superior quality

GOLDEN AGE An early period of civilization marked by perfect innocence, peace and happiness 2 A period of prosperity or excellence

GONE Moved away; left 2 Beyond hope; ruined; lost 3 Departed 4 Ended; past 5 Marked by faintness or weakness 6 Consumed; spent 7 Causing, feeling, or expressing intense satisfaction; ecstatic 8 Exhausted; wearied 9 Greatly involved

GOOD Morally excellent; virtuous 2 Honorable; worthy 3 Generous; loving; kind 4 Well behaved; tractable 5 Proper; desirable 6 Favorable; approving 7 Pleasant; agreeable 8 Having beneficial effects; **SALUTARY~** Calculated to bring about a sound condition by correcting evil or promoting good; wholesome 9 Reliable; safe 10 Suitable; qualified 11 Skillful; expert 12 Genuine; valid 13 Excellent in quality, degree or kind 14 **ORTHODOX~** Correct or sound in doctrine; conforming 15 Of sufficient quality or extent; ample 16 Unspoiled; fresh 17 Being in sound condition 18 Satisfactory or appropriate for specific action, purpose etc. -Altogether; completely; very 19 Capable of lasting, surviving or remaining valid or in operation for (an indicated period of time) 20 Able or willing to pray, give or produce (something indicated) 21 Entitling one to or acceptable for 22 Used to show approval 23 That which is desirable, serviceable, fitting etc. 24 Benefit; advantage; profit 25 That which is morally or ethically desirable -For the last time; permanently; forever 26 To be successful 27 To compensate for; replace; repay 28 To fulfill (a promise, agreement etc.) 29 To prove; substantiate -To credit, profit or advantage Syn. Upright 30 Dutiful, obedient 31 Advantageous, profitable 32 Secure 33 Able, competent 34 Adequate 35 Wholesome

GOOD BOOK The Bible, also Good Book

GOOD CHEER A mood or Spirit of joy, optimism, courage, etc.

GOOD NATURED Having a pleasant disposition; not easily provoked

GOODNESS The state or quality of being good; especially 2a Excellence of character, morals etc.; virtue 2b Generous and kindly feelings ; benevolence 3 The best or most nourishing part of anything; essence; strength 4 **God**: used alone or with other words **in various empathetic or exclamatory utterances**

GOODS The necessary qualifications or abilities for a specific purpose, act, etc. 2 To produce what is specified, promised or expected

GOOD SAMARITAN A human, compassionate person, helpful to those in trouble

GOOD USAGE Standard use; said of diction, phraseology and idioms acceptable to cultivated speakers and writers of the Spiritual language

GOOD WILL A desire for the well being of others; benevolence 2 Cheerful, ready consent or willingness

GOODWILL AMBASSADOR Any person traveling in a foreign country to promote friendly relations and understanding

*GOSPEL** Any sentiment or information accepted as unquestionably true 2 A doctrine, principle or course of action considered to be of major importance [OE *godspell* good news]

GRACE Beauty or harmony of motion, form manner or proportion 2 Any attractive or excellent quality or endowment 3 Favor or service freely rendered; goodwill 4 The act of showing or granting such favor 5 Clemency; mercy 6 The perception of what is appropriate and right 7a The unmerited but freely given Love and favor of **God** toward man 7b The divine influence operating in man to regenerate, sanctify and strengthen him 7c The state or condition of being pleasing and acceptable to God in man 7d Any divinely inspired Spiritual virtue or excellence -To be regarded with favor -In a cheerfully willing manner 8 To add grace and beauty to; adorn 9 To dignify; honor: "For by grace you are saved [< OF < L *gratia* favor]

*GRACEFUL** Characterized by grace, elegance or beauty of form, movement, language etc. Syn. *Graceful* and *beautiful* are compared as they mean possessed of pleasing qualities Syn. In their narrowest sense, *graceful* refers to movement, *beautiful* to appearance When used more broadly, *graceful* may refer to a person who displays any admirable qualities, one of which may be inner beauty; *beautiful* can and no doubt should only be perceived by the mind's eye

GRACIOUS Characterized by or showing kindness, affability, politeness etc. 2 Condescendingly polite or indulgent, as to inferiors 3 Full of compassion; merciful 4 Loosely; elegant; refined 5 Happy; fortunate; prosperous -An exclamation of mild surprise

*****GRAFT** To attach or incorporate, as by grafting new ideas on outworn concepts

GRAIN Natural disposition or temperament **-against the grain:** Contrary to one's natural temperament or inclinations [Fusion of OF *grain* seed and *graine* seed, grain, both < L *granum* seed]

GRAPEVINE A secret or unofficial means of relaying information, usually from person to person

GRANT To confer or bestow, as a privilege 2 To accede to; yield to as a request 3 To admit as true, as for the sake of argument; concede [< L *credere* to believe] Syn. We *grant* out of generosity, often in response to supplication

GRANTED To assume to be true; believe unquestioningly 2 To accept as one's due; be complacently neglectful

GRAY MATTER The reddish gray nervous tissue of the brain and spinal cord, composed largely of nerve cell bodies: distinguished from *white matter* 2 Brains; intelligence

GRAVE[1] Of great importance or concern; weighty 2 Filled with or indicative of danger; critical 3 Solemn and dignified; sober; sedate [< F < L *gravis* heavy]

GRAVE[2] Any place or state regarded as an end, extinction, or final loss

GRAVE[3] To impress firmly; fix indelibly, as on the memory

GRAVEL To confound; baffle 2 To irritate; annoy 3 To run aground

GREAT More than ordinary; considerable; extreme 2 Being more important than others of the same kind 3 Of unusual importance or consequences; momentous; significant 4 Marked by or possessing loftiness or nobility of thought, action, etc. 5 Unusual in ability or achievement; highly gifted 6 Impressive; remarkable 7 Characterized by or manifesting constant and absorbed interest; enthusiastic 8 Much favored; popular 9 Proficient; skillful 10 Excellent; first rate 11 Pregnant: often followed by *with* 12 To be well informed or enthusiastic about; excel in 13 Those who are eminent, powerful, etc. 14 An outstanding or distinguished person -Very well; splendidly

GREE[1] To bring or come to agreement

GREE[2] Satisfaction; to set right, as a wrong, by compensation or by punishment of the wrongdoer; make reparation for 2 To make reparation to; compensate 3 To remedy; correct 4 Satisfaction for a wrong done; amends 5 A restoration; reformation; correction [< L dresser] See **DRESS**~ Pertaining to or having the properties of medicine; healing; curative; alleviating 6 Goodwill; favor [< OF *gre* ult. < L *gratus* pleasing]

GREE[3] Superiority; victory 2 The prize of victory

GREED Excessively eager for acquisition or gain; covetous 2 Selfish and grasping desire for possession, especially of wealth; avarice

GREEN Not fully developed; immature; unripe 2 Not cured or ready for use; unseasoned 3 Lacking training or skill; inexperienced 4 Easily duped; credulous; gullible 5 Untreated or unprocessed; fresh; raw

GREET To express friendly recognition or courteous respect to, as upon meeting; address a salutation to; welcome 2 To meet or receive in a specific manner 3 To present itself to; be evident or perceptible to

GROUND The fundamental cause, reason or motive for an action, belief, etc.. 2 A foundation or basis as for a decision, argument, or relationship; footing See **REASON** To base on or as on a foundation; establish; found 4 To train (someone) in basic principles or elements; teach fundamentals to

GROW To undergo the process of developing characteristics

GUARD To keep vigilant watch over or care for so as to keep from harm; protect 2 To keep vigilant watch over so as to prevent insubordination, etc. 3 To serve as a **SENTRY~** Any watcher, as a soldier placed on guard to see that only authorized persons pass his post and to warn of danger 4 To maintain cautious control over; keep in check 5 To escort 6 To take precautions; be alert 7 One who has supervisory control over a point of entry, exit, etc., and keeps protective watch over something of value; watchful care -Watchful, as against attack, danger or untoward circumstances; cautious 8 That which provides protection; defense; safeguard

Ant. Unprepared for attack or adverse circumstances; not vigilant or alert [< Gme. Akin to **WARD**]

GUIDE To lead or direct, as to a destination; show the way to 2 To lead or direct the affairs, standards, opinions, etc., of 3 One who or that which is taken as a model for or example 4 A Book that explains, outlines, or gives practical instructions

H

HABIT An act or practice so frequently repeated as to become relatively fixed in character and almost automatic in performance 2 A tendency or disposition to act consistently in a certain manner or to repeat frequently a certain action 3 Mental or moral disposition or attitude 4 A characteristic action, aspect or mode of growth 5 To dwell in 6 To accustom 7 To dwell [< OF < L *habitus* condition < *habere* to have]

HAGIOGRAPHA The writing or study of the lives of the saints

HAIR Any exceedingly minute space, measure, degree, etc. -To show or reveal no sign of embarrassment, fear, anger, etc. 2 With the utmost exactness or perfection, in minute detail

HAIRY Dangerous; menacing 2 Superb; excellent

HALAKHAH The legal elements of Talmudic literature, consisting of those decrees, ordinances, usages and customs that seek to interpret, but are not included in, the Scriptures: distinguished from *Haggadah* [< Hebrew *halakhah* a rule to go by < *halakh* to walk, go]

HALF Either of two equal or approximately equal parts into which a thing is or may be divided; also a quantity equal to such a part -One's wife or husband 2 Being either of two equal, or nearly equal, parts of a thing, amount, value etc. 3 Not complete; imperfect; partial 4 To a considerable extent; very nearly 5 To any extent; at all

HALLOW To make holy; consecrate 2 To look upon as holy; reverence

HALO A splendor or glory investing a person or thing held in affection, reverence, etc. [< L <Gk. circular threshing floor]

HALO Of or relating to salt

HAMMER To force, impress etc., by empathetic repetition 2 To have the sound or feeling of rapid pounding 3 To work at persistently

HAMSTRING To destroy the efficiency of; frustrate

HAND Assistance; cooperation 2 Possession or control; supervisory care 3 A pledge or promise 4 A source of knowledge, information, etc. 5 Considered as producing something 6 Nearby; readily available 7 About to occur 8 By the action of; directly from innocence -Freedom from guilt -Without thought for the future, or the possibility of saving or planning 9 So as to satisfy all the needs or wishes -Each holding the hand of another; in close association 10 In one's possession; available for use 11 Finished and done; Immediately; without delay 12 To be engaged in an excessive amount of work -To continue an activity or interest so as not to lose skill or knowledge 13 To bless, consecrate, ordain, etc. -To disclose one's involvement or intentions -To engage in; undertake -The controlling advantage 14 To give, offer, or transmit 15 To assist or lead -To give deserved praise or recognition to -To give to the next in succession -To distribute or offer among individuals

HANDLE To have control over; manage; direct 2 To treat of or discuss 3 To act of behave toward 4 To trade or deal in, as matters of the heart 5 To respond to manipulation or control ^ That which serves as an opportunity or advantage in achieving a desired end

HAPPEN To occur by chance rather than design 2 To befall 3 To become

HAPPINESS The state or quality of being pleased or content *Happiness* is a general term, often indicating little more than freedom from sadness, sorrow etc. *Gladness* is joyful, overflowing *happiness*, but falls short of *bliss*, which is ecstatic, perfected *happiness Blessedness* is *happiness* so profound as to be attributed to divine favor 2 The expanse of space surrounding a place resembling a state of supreme beauty and happiness 3 Heaven

HAPPY Produced or uttered with skill and aptness **FELICITOUS~** Particularly well chosen; most appropriate; apt 2 Marked by an agreeably pertinent or effective manner or style, as a pleasantly appropriate remark or observation 3 Happiness, especially when very great; bliss

HARDSHIP A difficult, painful condition, as from **PRIVATION~** The state of lacking something necessary or desirable; especially the common comforts of life 2 Deprivation See **PRIVATE**

HAREM [< Arabic harim (something) forbidden, sacred]

HARKEN To listen; harken: usually in the imperative 2 To heed; pay very close attention

HARLOTRY The trade or behavior of an unchaste woman [< OF harlot fellow, rogue] -One who is innocently mischievous or playful 2 A variation from a standard

HARM Injury; damage hurt 2 Offence against morality; wrong; evil

HARMFUL Having power to injure or do harm

HARMONIOUS Manifesting agreement and accord in views, attitudes etc.; free from dissension 2 Pleasing to the ear; euphonious

HARMONIST One who collates parallel passages in different writings, as the Gospels, in order to emphasize similarity of ideas, languages etc.

HARMONIZE To make or become harmonious, suitable or agreeable 2 To show the harmony or agreement of, as the Gospels

HARMONY A state of order, agreement or aesthetically pleasing relationships among the elements of a whole Syn. *Harmony, concord, accord, consonance* and *congruity* characterize unity among persons or things. *Harmony* and *concord* among persons is more than the absence of dissension; these words imply some mutual regard, goodwill and cooperation

HARP To utter; express 2 To talk or write about persistently and vexatiously

HARSH Grating, rough, or unpleasant to any of the senses 2 Unpleasing to the mind or artistic sense; ungraceful; crude 3 Manifesting severity and rigor; cruel; unfeeling [rancid]

HARVEST The product of any effort, action or event

HASTE Undue or reckless hurry; precipitancy 2 The urge or necessity to act quickly; urgency; expedite

HATE To be unwilling

HATRED Intense dislike or aversion; animosity; enmity

HAVE To be connected with by some bond of relationship resembling possession; be possessed of 2 To be characterized by; be possessed of, quality, etc. 3 To hold in the mind or among the feelings; find in oneself; entertain; cherish 4 To receive, take, or acquire 5 To achieve control, or mastery of 6 To suffer from; be stricken with 7 To take part in; engage in 8 To undergo; experience 9 To plan and execute; arrange and carry out; hold 10 To give birth to; bring forth 11 To manifest or exercise; act or behave with 12 To cause to or cause to be 13 To allow or permit; tolerate; brook 14 To assert or announce; maintain; declare 15 To know 16 Prevail over

HAWK ¹ A person who preys on others

HAWK ² [Back formation]

HEAD Mind; intellect 2 Self-control; self-possession; sanit 3 Progress in the face of opposition; headway 4 Mind 5 **CULMINATION~** To reach the highest point or degree; come to a final result or effect **(head cont.)** 6 Pertaining to or at the highest or culminating point of development, eminence etc. -To give someone freedom of action or unrestrained authority -Position; rank of a leader 7 The source -The superior part of

HEAD LONG Head first 2 Without deliberation; recklessly; rashly 3 With unbraided speed or force 4 Advancing impetuously 5 Steep

HEAL To restore to health; soundness; make healthy again; cure 2 To bring about the remedy or cure of, as Spiritual refining 3 To remedy, repair, or mend (quarrel, breach etc.) 4 To cleanse of sin, grief, worry, etc.; purify: to heal the Spirit 5 To become well or sound 6 To perform a cure or cures

HEALER One who undertakes to heal through prayer and faith

HEALTH Soundness of any living organism; vigor of body or mind; tone; good [OE *<hal* whole]

HEALTHY Sound; well 2 **Salutary** 3 Indicative or characteristic of sound condition skepticism

HEAR To listen to officially or judicially 2 To respond to; acced to 3 To be informed or made aware; perceive or understand the meaning of See **LISTEN**

HEART The seat of emotion, especially Love and affection, as distinguished from the head; the center of intellect and reason 2 Tenderness; affection; Love 3 The capacity for kindness and sympathy 4 Firmness of will; courage 5 One's inmost thoughts and feelings 6 Enthusiasm; energy 7 The state of mind; mood 8 A person, especially a dear or courageous one 9 The central or inner part of anything 10 The vital or essential part; essence 11 The capacity to produce in abundance; fertility -In one's deepest thoughts or feelings; essentially; basically; with all and complete sincerity; with deep feelings; entirely; wholly -The most deepest and most intimate part of one's being -To cause deep disappointment and sorrow to 12 To endure great remorse or grief 13 To have a great longing -To be sympathetic and generous -To change one's opinions, attitudes, feelings, etc. -To be callous or cruel enough -To become discouraged 14 To consider seriously 15 With great willingness

HEAT A single effort or trial, especially a course in a trial 2 Great intensity of feeling, especially of anger or irritation; excitement; passion 3 The highest point of intensity; greatest excitement or fury

HEAVEN God, the Supreme Being; the celestial powers 2 Full of the peace befitting happiness 3 Having general expressions of approval

HEBREW [< Hebrew *'ibhri*, lit., one from beyond (Jordan)]

HEDGE To set barriers and restrictions to, so as to hinder freedom of movement or action

HEED To pay attention to; take more than casual notice of; listen to 2 Careful attention or consideration

HEEL A habitually dishonorable person; contemptible chiseler; crumb 2 Shabby; slovenly; run down -To act or agree reluctantly

HEIR One who or that which takes over or displays the qualities of some forerunner

HELL Any condition of great mental or physical suffering; agony; also anything causing such suffering 2 Mortal belief; error; death; suffering and destruction 3 Very much, very fast, very bad, very loud, etc. 4 Not at all; never 5 To be damaging or harmful to 6 To be unpleasant or difficult for 7 To be very strict or harsh with -To be roundly scolded or punished, as for a misdeed -To upbraid or punish (someone) severely -To create a disturbance; make an uproar -An exclamation used as an imprecation or an expression of anger or impatience

HERB Any seed-bearing plant that does not have a woody stem and dies down to the ground after flowering

HERD A large crowd of people, a contemptuous term -The common people; the masses 2 To bring or group together and to care for and drive as a Shepherd (sheep/cattle)

HEREAFTER In the state of life after death -A future state or existence

"Distressed and hungry, they will roam through the land; when they are famished, they will become enraged and, looking upward, will curse their king and their God" "Then they will look toward the earth and see only distress and darkness and fearful gloom, and they will be thrust into utter darkness" Isaiah 8:21-:22

HERITAGE That which is inherited, as characteristics, conditions, etc. 2 A body of knowledge handed down from past times

HERMENEUTICS The science or art of interpretation, especially of the Scriptures

HIEROPHANT One who explains or interprets any esoteric cult or doctrine [sacred + to show]

HIGH Superior, loftly, or exalted in quality, character, rank, kind, etc. 2 Most important; principal, main 3 Having serious consequences; grave 4 Elated; joyful 5 Advanced to the fullest extent or degree 6 Arrogant; haughty 7 Strict or extreme in opinion; doctrine 8 Complex; advanced

HIM His Imperial Majesty

HIT To arrive at, achieve, or discover, either by intention or inadvertently 2 To accord with; suit 2 To begin to journey on 3 To arrive in or reach (a state of mind) 4 To make use of or indulge in to excess 5 To request or obtain from 6 To come or Light; happen: followed by on or upon 7 To depict, characterize, or satirize cleverly and accurately 8 A popular or obvious success 9 A fortunate chance or circumstance 10 An apt or telling remark, witticism, piece of sarcasm, etc. [OE *hittan* < ON *hitta* to come upon]

HOLD To keep in a specified state 2 To keep under control; restrain; check or influence 3 To keep in reserve; designate for disposition 4 To have the use, benefit, or responsibilities of 5 To regard or consider in a specified manner 6 To bind by contract or sense of duty 7 To adjudge; decide 8 To prolong or sustain 9 To have title to 10 To maintain in the mind; harbor 11 To conduct or engage in 12 To maintain a grip or grasp 13 To withstand strain or pressure; remain firm or unbroken 14 To remain or continue in a specified state 15 To remain relevant or True 16 To adhere resolutely, as to a principle, belief, or purpose; cling 17 To forbear 18 To keep apart or aside; retain, as for an undisclosed purpose 19 A fortification; stronghold

HOLE A defect; fault

HOLY Having a divine nature or origin 2 Having great Spiritual or moral worth; saintly 3 Designated or set apart for studying Scripture or observance; consecrated 4 Characterized by Spiritual exaltation, reverence, etc.; Spiritually pure 5 Evoking or meriting reverence or awe Syn. *Holy, sacred, blessed and hallowed* are applied to things regarded with great reverence in religious worship *Holy* is the strongest word, being applied only to things which have the most immediate connection with God *Sacred* is applied to that which is inviolate on any account, and thus has less force than *holy* Blessed means especially favored by God *Hallowed* refers to that which has been made *sacred* by long continued worship

HONEST Not given to lying, cheating, stealing, etc.; acting honorably and justly; trustworthy 2 Not characterized by falsehood or intent to mislead; meriting belief; Truthful 3 Giving or having full worth or value; genuine; fair 4 Performed or earned in a reliable and **CONSCIENTIOUS**- wishing to do what is right, especially to do one's work or duty in a well and thorough manner; relating to a person's conscience 5 Characterized by openness and sincerity; frank 6 Chaste; virtuous -Uprightness of character, conduct, etc.; integrity 7 The state or quality of being honest -(A garden plant of the mustard family) Syn. Diligent, industrious, punctilious, painstaking, sedulous, assiduous, dedicated, careful, meticulous, attentive, hard-working, studious, rigorous, particular; strict

HONEY An excellent example of something **COMB-** Search carefully and systematically

HONEYCOMB To penetrate or pervade so as to undermine or weaken with discontent; infiltrate and undermine High regard, respect, or esteem 2 Glory; fame; credit 3 An outward token, sign, act, etc., that manifests high regard or esteem 4 A strong sense of what is right; keen moral judgement 5 A reputation for high standards of conduct 6 A cause or source of esteem or pride 7 High rank or position; dignity 8 Chastity in women; also, reputation for chastity 9 Pledging one's word on the Truth on something stated or on the keeping of a promise 10 To show esteem for; pay homage to 11 To bring respect or credit to 12 To treat with courtesy

HONOR High regard, respect, or esteem 2 Glory; fame; credit 3 An outward token, sign, act, etc., that manifests high regard or esteem 4 Strong sense of what is right; keen moral judgement 5 A reputation for high standards of conduct 6 A cause or source of esteem 7 Dignity 8 A privilege or pleasure 9 Chasity in women; also, a reputation for chasity 10 Pledging one's Word on the Truth of something or on the keeping of a promise 11 To show esteem for; pay homage to 12 To bring respect or credit to 13 To regard with honor or respect 14 To treat with courtesy 15 To worship or venerate 16 To confer an honor upon; dignify

HOOK Something that catches or ensnares; trap 2 To trick; dupe 3 To pilfer; steal

HORIZON The bounds or limits of one's observation, knowledge or experience 2 The great circle of the celestial sphere whose plane, parallel to the sensible horizon, cuts the center of the earth midway between the (**celestial** or **rational horizon**)- [Arabic opposite] of the zenith, or the highest point of the celestial sphere vertically above the observer **ZENITH-** The time at which something is most powerful or successful [Arabic the way over one's head] **NADIR-** The lowest point in the fortunes of a person or organization

HORN In the Bible, a symbol of glory and power 2 The imaginary projections from the forehead of a **CUCKOLD~** The husband of an unfaithful wife 3 One of two or more alternatives of a dilemma 4 To check one's anger, zeal etc.; restrain oneself 5 To retract or withdraw, as a previous statement -One who announces a True foretelling -A True prophet

HORSE A CONTRIVANCE~ The issue being devising or adapted to, especially to a particular purpose, also the ability to do this 2 An ingenious plan; stratagem; trick; plot 3 A man; friendly, joking, or **OPPROBRIOUS~** Contemptuously abusive; imputing disgrace 2 Shameful; disgraceful term 3 In schools, a translation or other similar aid used **ILLICIT**ly~ Not permitted; unlawful; [L *illicitus* <in- not + *licitus*] by students working out lessons -From the most direct and reliable source 6 To support a cause already lost -To act haughtily or scornfully -To restrain one's impetuosity or impatience 7 To subject to horse play or ridicule -**A horse of another (or different) color - A completely different matter!**

HOST [1] A man who extends hospitality to others, usually to guests in his own home

HOST [2] A large number of men; a multitude

HOST [3] The Eucharistic bread or wafer [< OF *hoiste* < L *hostia* sacrificial victim]

HOT Constantly in use or action 2 Marked by or showing strong or violent emotion; excited; passionate 3 Marked by intense activity; raging 4 Exciting; lively 5 Strongly disposed toward; eager; enthusiastic 6 Controversial 7 So new as not to have lost it's freshness, currency, excitement, etc. 8 Excellent, skillful, lucky, etc. 9 Dangerous or uncomfortable 10 To make the situation extremely uncomfortable for

HOUSE The body as a dwelling place for the Spirit, soul, etc. 2 An **ADVISORY**- Having or consisting in the power to make recommendations but not to take action enforcing them or **LEGISLATIVE**- Having the power to make laws (**HOUSE** cont.) Group, especially in **ACADEMIC**- Not of practical relevance; of only theoretical interest (**HOUSE** cont.) **or** ecclesiastical matters See **RELIGIOUS** 2 To get rid of undesirable conditions, entities, or persons: to clean house

HOVERING Remaining in an uncertain and irresolute state

HOW In what way 2 To what degree, extent or amount 3 In what state or condition 4 For what reason or purpose 5 To what effect; with what meaning 6 By what name or designation -A manner, method or means of doing -Why

HUB The center part of a wheel into which the axle is inserted 2 Any center of great activity or interest

HUMAN Compound of many individuals functioning as a whole

HUMANE Having or characterized by kindness, sympathy, tenderness etc.; compassionate; benevolent 2 Tending to refine or civilize; learning

HUMANISM A system or attitude in thought, religion etc., in which human ideas and the perfection of human personality are made central, so that cultural and practical interests rather than theology and metaphysics are at the focus of attention 2 An emphasis on human interests rather than on religion or the world of nature

HUMANITARIAN One who seeks to promote the welfare of mankind by eliminating pain and suffering; philanthropist

HUMANITARIANISM In ethics: The doctrine that man's chief duty is to work for the welfare of the human race

HUMANIZE To make humane; make gentle, kindly, etc. 2 To become human or humane

HUMANLY In a human manner 2 Within human power or ability 3 In accordance with man's experience or knowledge

HUMAN EST ERRARE To err is human

HUMBLE Free from pride or vanity; modest; meek; unassuming 2 Lowly in station, rank, condition, etc.; unpretentious; modest 3 Servile; fawning 4 Respectful 5 To reduce the pride of; make meek 6 To lower in rank or dignity [< F <L *humilis* low < *humus* ground] **ABASE**

HUNGER Any strong desire or craving Deut 8:3; 28:48; **32:24; ***1 Sam 2:5; Neh 9:15; **Psalm 34:10; ***Prov 19:15; Isaiah 49:10; ****Lam 2:19; 4:9; Ezekiel 34:29; ***Micah 6:14; ***Matt 5:6; Luke 6:25; 15:17; ***John 6:35; 1 Corin 4:11; 2 Corin 11:27; Rev 6:8

HUNGRY Not fertile; poor or barren 2 Eagerly desirous; craving 1 Samuel 2:5; Job 5:5; **22:7; **24:10; Psalm 50:12; 107:5; *:9; ***146:7; *Prov 16:26; **25:21; 27:7 (HONEYCOMB); ***Isa 8:21; 9:20; 29:8; 32:6; 44:12; ****58:7; ****58:10; ***65:13; ***Ezek 18:7; Matt 15:32; 25:35; :37; 25:42; :44; Luke 1:53; *** 4:2; Acts 10:10; Rom 12:20; 1 Corin 11:21; **:34; Philip 4:12

HURT To cause distress, fear, false hope to; injure 2 Damage, injure. or impair in some way; do harm to 3 To grieve or distress; cause mental suffering to 4 To cause discomfort, suffering, or damage 5 To give out a feeling of pain 6 Any injury, wound, ache etc. 7 Impairment 8 Any injury to the feelings; affront Gen 31:7; # 16:15; ***1 Sam 25:15; :34; ***Psalm 15:4; 35:4; :26; 38:12; 41:7; 70:2; 71:13; :24; Prov 20:30; ***Ecc 5:13; ***8:9; 10:9; ****Isa 11:9; 27:3; 65:25; Jer 6:14; 8:21; **10:19; ***25:7; Dan 3:25; 6:22; Mark 16:18; Luke 4:35; 10:19; ***Rev 2:11; 9:10

HUSBAND FUSION- The process or result of joining two or more things together to form a single entity 2 A combination or mixture of two or more elements **BETROTH-** [< OE < *betreuthe* < *be-* + Truth (expressing **TRANSITIVITY-**)] Being or relating to a relation with the property that if the relation holds between a first element and a second and between the second element and a third, it holds between the first and third elements equality, it is a transitive relation

HUSBAND MAN One who tills the soil

HUSBANDRY The occupation or business of farming -Careful management; economy; thrift 2 Management of household affairs

HYLO Matter; of or pertaining to matter 2 Wood; of or pertaining to wood

HYPOCRITE The pretense of having feelings or characteristics one does not possess; especially the deceitful assumption of praiseworthy qualities; insincere [< OF *hypocrisie* < L *hypocrisies* < Gk. *hypokrisis* pretense] Syn. Denotes a false show of qualities not actually possessed *Hypocrisy* is the most extreme word; it denotes the feeling of admirable qualities, as goodness sincerity, honesty etc., by those who actually have the opposite qualities of badness, insincerity, dishonesty etc. *Pretense* is even milder, and may be worthy: to make a *pretense* of not hearing a slur *Sanctimonious*, originally meant worthy, holiness or nobility of nature, has become the *hypocritical* pretense of *piety*; this condition of getting worse is even stronger in *sanctimoniousness Pharisaism* is the hypocritical observance of the letter of the law, especially a moral law, while actually disregarding its spirit *Cant*, in the sense here compared, refers to the pious utterances of the *sanctimonious* person, or simply to *sanctimonious* character itself

I

ICE To dispel reserve or formality, especially at a social gathering -To have no influence; to be of no account 2 Certain to be achieved or won

~ICE Condition, quality, or act

IDEA That which is conceived in the mind as a result of conscious thinking 2 That which is established in the mind as a result of passive perception; an impression or notion 3 A conviction; opinion; belief 4 An intention; aim; plan 5 Vague knowledge; inclination; inkling 6 A fleeting thought; passing fancy; whim 7 Significance; meaning; purpose 8a The platonic concept of an archetype or fundamental example of which an existing thing is but an imperfect representation 8b That which is immediately perceived by the mind or the senses 8c The concept of absolute Truth or reason 9 The concept of anything in its highest or most desirable state

IDEAL That which exists only as a concept in the mind 2 Capable of existing as a mental concept only, by virtue of unattainable perfection; utopian; imaginary

IDEALISM The envisioning of things as they should be or wished to be rather than as they are 2 Any of several theories that there is no reality, no world of objects or thing in itself apart from a reacting mind or conscious, that only the mental is knowledgeable, and therefore that reality is essentially Spiritual or mental

IDEALIST An impractical dreamer; romantic

IDEALITY Existence in the mind only; also that which exists in the mind only

IDEALIZE To consider or represent things in their ideal form

IDEATE To form an idea of; frame in the mind; conceive 2 To form mental concepts; think -The object corresponding to an idea: so distinguished by those who view the object as distinct from the perception or **COGNITION~** The act or facility of knowing or perceiving 2 A conception or perception 3 Knowledge [< L *cognitio, ~onis* knowledge < *cognoscere* to know < *co~* together + *(g)noscere* to know]

IDEOLOGY The ideas or manner of thinking characteristic of an individual or group; especially, the ideas or objectives that influence a whole group, or national culture, shaping especially their political and social procedure 2 The science that treats of the origin, evolution and expression of human ideas 3 Fanciful or visionary

IDIOM A expression peculiar to a language, not readily understandable from its grammatical construction or from the meaning of its component parts

IDOL One who is loved or admired to an excessive degree; object of infatuation 2 A false or misleading idea; a fallacy -Excessive or undiscerning admiration or veneration

IGNORANT UnenLightened 2 Lacking awareness; unaware 3 Lacking information or experience; uninformed; inexperienced 4 Resulting from or indicating lack of knowledge

IGNORE To refuse to notice or recognize; disregarded intentionally

IHS A monogram of the name Jesus, derived from the Greek **IH(ZOT)Z = Jesus**

ILL Destructive in effect; harmful 2 Hostile or malevolent in attitude or intent; unfriendly; spiteful; bitter 3 Portending danger or disaster; unfavorable 4 Morally bad; evil; unsavory 5 Improper; incorrect 6 Not proficient; unskilled 7 Evil; wrong: Do good in return for *ill* 8 Injury; harm 9 A cause of unhappiness, misfortune, injustice etc. 10 Disaster; trouble 11 Malady 12 With difficulty 13 Unsuitably; poorly -Uncomfortable; nervous; fidgety

ILLEGITIMATE Contrary to good usage; incorrect 2 Contrary to logic; illogical; unsound

ILLOGICAL Not logical; neglectful of the rules of logic or reason

ILLUMINATE To shed light upon; clarify 2 To enlighten, as the mind 3 Spiritual enLightenment -Serving to illuminate

ILLUSION Misconception 2 A general impression not consistent with fact 3 A sensory impression that results in misinterpretation of the True character of the actual thing

ILLUSTRATE To explain or make clear by means of examples, comparisons etc.; exemplify 2 To enLighten 3 To give distinction to [< L *illuminate]*

ILLUSTRIOUS Greatly distinguished 2 **CONFERRING~** To compare; collate 2 To hold a conference; consult together; take counsel [< *com* together + *ferre* to bring, carry] -Greatness or glory 3 Luminous [< L *illustris* < *in* in + *lustrum* Light]

IMAGE The process of forming mental images of the objects of perception or thought in the absence of the concrete external stimuli; the picturing process of the mind

IMMANENCE A permanent abiding within; an indwelling 2 The presence of **God** pervading all creation

IMMERSE To involve deeply; engross

IMMERSION The disappearance of a heavenly body by passing behind or entering into the shadow of another

IMMORAL Contrary to conscience 2 Sexual impurity or misconduct Syn. *Immoral, amoral, unmoral,* and *nonmoral* agree in meaning not moral The *immoral* person violates moral principles knowingly; consciously wicked, dissolute, evil, etc. The *amoral* person lacks the sense of right and wrong, and thus may violate morality without evil intent *Unmoral* and *nonmoral* mean not within the realm of morality; a baby is *unmoral*

IMMORTAL Pertaining to immortality or to beings or concepts that are immortal; divine

IMMORTALITY Unending existence; eternal Life 2 Eternal fame

IMMUNITY Resistance to harmful influences 2 Diplomatic immunity (which see)

IMPARADISE To place in paradise; make supremely happy

IMPERATIVE Urgently necessary; obligatory; unavoidable 2 Having the nature of or expressing a command; peremptory; authoritative 3 Designating the mood used to express commands, requests, exhortations etc. 4 The mood used to express command, exhortation etc.

IMPERCEPTIBLE That can barely be perceived as by reason of smallness, extreme delicacy, subtlety, gradualness etc. 2 Not discernible by the mind or senses

IMPERFECT Falling short of perfection; faulty; defective; *imperfect* knowledge 2 Wanting in completeness; not fully adequately formed or made; unfinished; deficient 3 Denoting a tense that indicated action, usually past action, as uncompleted, continuing, or synchronized with some other action 4 Lacking certain parts normally present 5 Without binding force; not legally enforceable, said of (a person's) thoughts

IMPERIALISM Imperial character, authority or Spirit

IMPERTINENCE Deliberate disrespectfulness; unwarranted boldness; insolence; rudeness 2 Lack of pertinence; irrelevancy 3 Unsuitability; inappropriateness; incongruity 4 An impertinent remark, unmannerly act etc. -Impudence

IMPERTURBABLE Incapable of being disturbed or agitated; unruffled; calm

IMPERTURBATION Freedom from agitation; calmness

IMPETRATE To obtain by entreaty 2 To beseech; supplicate -To obtain by request [<*in~* in + *patrare* to bring to pass]

IMPETUS The force that sets a body in motion; also the energy with which a body moves or is driven 2 Any motivating force; stimulus; incentive

IMPIOUS UNHOLY- Denoting an alliance with potentially harmful implications between two or more parties that are not natural allies Awful; dreadful (used for emphasis) **IRRELIGIOUS**- indifferent or hostile to religion **SINFUL**- Highly **REPREHENSIBLE**- deserving censure or condemnation **WICKED**- Intended to or capable of harming someone or something 2 Extremely unpleasant **IMMORAL**- Not conforming to accepted standards of morality **UNRIGHTEOUS**- Wicked **IRREVERENT**- Showing a lack of respect for people or things that are generally taken seriously **AGNOSTIC**- Having a doubtful or noncommittal attitude toward something **HEATHEN**- An unenlightened person; a person regarded as lacking culture or moral principles

IMPLANT To install in the mind: to *implant* new ideas; inculcate

IMPLEMENTATION A putting into effect, fulfillment or carrying through

IMPLORE To call upon in humble or urgent entreaty; beseech; 2 To beg for urgently 3 To make urgent supplications [< L *implorare* < *in-* thoroughly + *plorare* To cry out]

IMPORTUNATE Urgently or stubbornly persistent in demands; insistent 2 Of a demand or request; repeatedly made; pressing 3 Troublesome; vexatious

IMPORTUNE To harass with persistent demands or requests 2 To ask or beg for persistently or urgently 3 To annoy 4 To impel; urge See **OPPORTUNE**

IMPOSTER One who deceives; especially one who assumes the name or character of another

IMPOTENCE The condition or quality of being a: helplessness; ineffectiveness 2 Lack of self-control; powerless to act or accomplish anything; unrestrained

IMPOVERISH To exhaust the fertility of, as soil

IMPREGNABLE Incapable of being taken by force; proof against attack 2 Incapable of being overcome; firmly resistant; unyielding

IMPREGNABLE [2] Capable of being impregnated

IMPREGNANT To fill or imbue, as with ideas

IMPRESSION An effect, especially a profound effect, produced on the mind, the senses or feelings 2 A generalized effect or feeling 3 A vague remembrance or uncertain belief 4 A material change caused by any agency -To have a vague notion (that); think

IMPRINT To fix firmly in the heart, mind etc.

IMPROVE To raise to a higher or more desirable quality, value or condition; to make better 2 To increase the value or profit of, as land by cultivation 3 To use to good advantage; utilize 4 To become better than

IMPURE Containing elements not properly belonging; especially, of language, containing foreign idioms or grammatical or rhetorical errors

IMPUTE

IN AETERNUM Latin Forever; everlasting

IN BEING Inherent existence 2 Essential nature

INCARNATE Embodied in flesh, especially in human form 2 Personified; exemplified 3 To give bodily form to 4 To invest with or present in concrete shape or form 5 To represent in living form; typify

INCARNATION The assumption of bodily form, especially human form 2 The assumption by Jesus Christ of the human form and condition 3 The bodily form assumed by a deity or supernatural being 4 A person in which some idea, quality or other abstract idea is incarnated

INCENSE [1] To inflame with anger; enrage -To set on fire

INCENSE [2] Pleasing flattery; homage [< OF *encens* < L *incensus*, pp. of *incendere* to set on fire]

INCEST Sexual intercourse between persons forbidden to marry because of a Spiritual relationship

INCIPIENT Just beginning to appear

INCISIVE Sharp; keen; penetrating 2 Cutting; biting; sarcastic *incisive* wit

INCITE To spur to action; urge on; stir up [Thoroughly + to rouse, of *ciere* to set into motion]

INCLINE To cause to bend, lean 2 To impart a tendency or leaning to (a person); dispose; influence 3 To bow or nod as the head -To hear with favor; heed 4 Willing; to work hard

INCOGITANT Unthinking; thoughtless [<*in-* not + *cogitare*] See **COGITATE**

INCONGRUENT Inconsistent with what is suitable, reasonable or proper; not suited to the circumstances; out of place; inappropriate 2 Not corresponding or conforming; at odds: a plan *incongruent* with reason 3 Consisting of elements or qualities not properly belonging together; lacking harmony or consistency; incompatible; *not agreeing*

INCORPORATE having a bodily form; embodied

INCORPOREAL Not consisting of matter 2 Of or pertaining to non material things; Spiritual 3 Having no material existence, but regarded as existing by the law; intangible

INCREASE A growing or becoming greater, as in quality **AUGMENT~** To become greater in size **-ATION** That by which something is increased

INCUMBENT Resting upon one as a moral obligation, or as necessary under the circumstances; obligatory 2 Resting, leaning or weighing wholly or partly upon (someone)

INDEED In fact; in Truth; used to emphasize an affirmation, to mark a qualifying word or clause, to denote a concession, or interrogatively to elicit confirmation of a fact stated

INDIGNATION Anger aroused by injustice or baseness; righteous anger -To think unworthy

INDULGENCE Remission of temporal punishment due for a sin after it has been forgiven through sacramental absolution 2 In English history, the granting through royal proclamation (**Declaration of Indulgence**) of a larger measure of religious freedom to nonconformists, especially during the reign of Charles II and James II The Protestant Reformation began as an attempt to reform the Roman Catholic Church On October 31, 1517, Martin Luther supposedly nailed his 95 theses against the selling of indulgences at the door of All Saints', the Castle Church in Wittenberg, Pr

INELUCTABLE Not to be escaped from or avoided; inevitable [< L *ineluctabilitis* < *in-* not + *eluctabitis* resistible < *eluctari* to struggle out < *luctari* to struggle]

INEQUITY Lack of equity; in**justice** 2 An unfair act or course of action

INEXPUGNABLE Not to be taken by force; impregnable [< OF <L *in inexpugnabilis*, *in-* not + *ex-* intens, + *pugnare* to fight]

INFATUATE To inspire with a foolish and unreasoning love or passion 2 To make foolish 3 Possessed by folly

INFER To derive by reasoning; conclude or accept from evidence or premises; deduce 2 To involve or imply as a conclusion; give evidence of; said of facts, statements, etc. 3 Loosely, to imply; hint 4 To draw an inference [< L *inferre* to bring into < *in-* in + *ferre* to bring, carry]

INFIDELITY Adultery

INFINITE Boundless limits; without end and perfect

INFLICT To cause (another) to suffer or endure

INFLUENCE The power of persons or things to produce effects on others, especially by imperceptible or indirect means 2 One who or that which possesses the power to affect others 3 An ethereal fluid or occult force supposedly flowing from the stars to affect the destiny of men 4 To produce an effect upon the actions or thought of; persuade; mold 5 To have an effect upon; affect; modify [< OF < LL *influentia* < L *influens, -entis*, ppr. of *influere* < *in-* in + *fluere* to flow Doublet of **INFLUENZA**]

INFLUENZA [< Ital., (illness due to) the influence (of the stars) [< L *influentia* < L *influere* to flow in]

INFORM[1] To acquaint (someone) with facts, data, opinion etc.; make something known to; notify 2 To pervade or animate; give quality or character to 3 To shape or form (in the mind, character, etc.) [< OF *enformer* < L *informare* to give form to <*in-* in + *forma* form]

INFORM[2] Shapeless; unformed

INFORMATION Knowledge acquired or derived; facts; data 2 Specific knowledge 3 Communication theory,

INFUSE To instill or **INCULCATE~** To impress upon the mind by frequent repetition or forceful admonition [< L *inculcatus*, pp. of *inculcare* to tread on [< *in-* on + *calcare* to tread < *calx, calcis* **heel**], as principles or qualities 2 To inspire; imbue 3 To pour in 4 To steep, as to make an extract or infusion

INFUSIONISM The doctrine that the human soul is of divine origin and is infused into the body at conception or birth of a concept as an epiphany

INGENIOUS Showing ingenuity; cleverly conceived; skillful 2 Having inventive and adaptive ability 3 Displaying genius or great intellectual power [< MF *ingenieux* < L *ingeniosus* talented < *ingenium* natural quality, ability < *in-* in + *gignere* to beget]

INGRATIATE To bring (oneself) deliberately into the favor or confidence of others

INGREDIENT Anything that enters into the composition of a mixture 2 A component of anything [< L *ingrediens, -entis*, ppr. of *ingredi* to enter < *in-* in + *gradi* to walk]

INHERE To be a permanent or essential part; be inseparably associated, as rights, qualities etc.

INIQUITY Grievous violation of right or justice; wickedness 2 Wrongful act; unjust thing or deed; sin [< OF *iniquite* < L *iniquitas* < *iniquus* unequal < *in-* not + *aequus* equal]

INNER LIGHT The Divine presence in man, source of guidance and certainty: also, **INNER WORD**

INNOCENT Free from blame or guilt 2 Not tending to harm or injure; **INNOCUOUS~** Having no harmful qualities or effects; harmless 2 Not maliciously intended 3 Lacking in worldly knowledge 4 A simple or unsuspecting person lacking in guile Syn. Chaste, virtuous 2 Unoffending 5 Unsophisticated

INOCULATE To implant ideas, opinions, etc., in the mind

IN OMNIA PARATUS *Latin* Prepared for anything

INORDINATE Exceeding proper limits; immoderate; excessive 2 Unrestrained, as in conduct, feeling, etc.; intemperate 3 Lacking order or regularity; disorderly

INQUIRE To seek information by asking questions; ask 2 To make an investigation, search, or inquiry

I.N.R.I. Jesus of Nazareth, King of the Jews (L *Iesus Nazarenus, Rex Iudaeorum*

INROAD A serious encroachment; harmful trespass: with, on, or upon one's happiness

INSANE Not sane; mentally deranged or **unsound**

*INSECT An insignificant or contemptible person

INSECURE Liable to break, fail, collapse etc.; unsafe 2 Troubled by anxiety 3 A condition of anxiety; apprehensiveness; threatened

INSEMINATE To sow (seed); also to implant (ideas etc.) 2 To sow seed in

INSIDE The internal nature or workings that are concealed

INSIGHT Perception into the inner nature or real character of a thing; penetrating discernment and understanding 2a Discernment and evaluation of one's own mental processes, powers etc.; self-knowledge 2b The ability of one who is mentally ill to recognize the nature of his disorder

INSIPID Lacking spirit and vivacity; vapid; dull 2 Lacking flavor or savor; tasteless; flat; bland [< L *insipidus* < *in-* not + *sapidus* savory < *sapere* to savor, taste]

INSOMUCH To such a degree

INSPECT To look at or examine carefully; especially, to examine for faults or defects 2 To examine or review officially and with ceremony

INSPIRATION Divine influence exerted upon the mind or Spirit

INSPIRE To impart or suggest by divine intervention 2 To direct or guide, as by special divine influence: Let **God**'s will *inspire* you 3 To breathe in; inhale: opposed to expire 3 To breathe or blow upon or into

INSPIRIT To fill with renewed Spirit or life; animate; exhilarate; **ENLIVEN~** To make lively, cheerful or sprightly 2 To make active or vigorous; stimulate

INSTIGATE To spur on or goad to some drastic course or deed; incite 2 To bring about by inciting; foment; provoke [< L *instigatus*, pp. of *instigare* < *in-* against + the root *-stig-* to prick, goad]

INSTRUCTION Knowledge or factual matter imparted; also, an item of such knowledge taught, as a rule, precept, or lesson 2 Directions; orders **TO BUILD**

INSTRUMENTALISM The doctrine that reflective thought is an instrument to successful action, and that ideas are true or valid to the extent that they are useful in guiding action

INTEGRAL Being an indispensable part of a whole; essential; constituent 2 Formed of parts that together constitute a unity 3 Whole; entire; complete 4 An entire thing

INTEGRATE To bring together into a whole; fit together; unify 2 To make the use or occupancy of available to persons of all races 3 To make whole or complete by the addition of necessary parts 4 To become available to all persons of all races, as reformation of the Spirit etc. [< L *integratus*, pp. of *integrare* to make whole, renew]

INTEGRATION The interaction of different cellular and nervous processes in such a way as to secure maximum unity in the performance of bodily functions 2 The orderly balancing of the physical, emotional or mental components of the personality into a more or less stable pattern or behavior

INTELLECT The power of the mind to grasp ideas and relations, and to exercise dispassionate reason and rational judgment; reason; understanding 2 Mental power collectively **Syn.** *Intellect, mind, reason,* intelligence, *wits* and *brains* are compared as they denote the human power of thinking *Intellect,* reflecting an older psychological use that has been abandoned, refers specifically to the powers of knowing and thinking, as distinguished from those of feeling and willing, while *mind* is the sum of all these powers or faculties Reason is the ability to think, or at its simplest the ability to elaborate sense impressions into concepts; we speak of *reason* as distinguishing man from the lower animals *Intelligence* is chiefly used to mean the capacity to learn or to deal with new situations; this power can be tested and measured *Wits* and *brains* are popular words for *intelligence* as it is applied to specific situations; *wits* suggests inborn *intelligence,* and *brains,* the competence and resourcefulness that are achieved through effort

INTELLECTION Exercise of the intellect 2 A specific act of the intellect

INTELLECTUALISM Devotion to intellectual interests 2 The exercise of the intellect 3a The doctrine that pure reason is wholly or largely the source of knowledge 3b The doctrine that the ultimate principle of all reality intellect or reason

INTELLECTUALITY Intellectual force, ability or endowment 2 To think; reason

INTELLIGENCE The faculty of perceiving and comprehending meaning; mental quickness; active intellect; understanding 2 The ability to adapt to new situations, and to learn from experience 3 The inherent ability to seize the essential factors of a complex matter 4 An intelligent or rational being, especially one that is not embodied 5 The primal and eternal quality of infinite Mind, **God**

INTELLIGENT Having an active, discerning mind; mentally perceptive; acute 2 Endowed with intellect or understanding; reasoning 3 Cognizant [< L *intelligens, -entis,* ppr. of *intelligere* to understand, perceive < *inter-* between + *legere* to choose Syn. quick-witted, sharp-witted, knowing, alert Ant. stupid

INTENSION Increase in degree -Resolution; determination 2 Intensification 3 Depth; force 4 All the implications in a concept or term; **CONNOTE~** To suggest or imply along with the literal meaning 2 To involve as a condition; consequence, etc. [< Med. L *connotare* [< L *com-* together + *notare* to mark] (**cont. INTENSION~** Distinguished **EXTENSION~** That property of matter by virtue of which it occupies space 2 The class of things to which a term or concept is correctly applicable: distinguished from intension See **EXTEND~** To cause to last until or for a specified time; continue 2 To increase or broaden the range, scope, meaning etc., of 3 To hold out or put forth, as the hand 4 To give or offer to give 5 To access; appraise

INTENTION Purpose, either ultimate or immediate

*****INTERCOURSE** Mutual exchange; commerce; communication 2 The interchange of ideas

INTERDISCIPLINARY Pertaining to or involving two or more branches of knowledge

INTEREST A feeling of curiosity or attentiveness 2 The power to arouse curiosity or attention 3 That which is of advantage; profit; benefit 4 Involvement or concern in something 5 Something added in making a return; something more than is due; equity 6 Legal right, claim or share, as in an estate 7 To excite or hold the curiosity or attention of -To cause to be concerned in; involve 8 To relate to; concern; effect 9 Not impartial; biased [< OF < L *interest* it is of concern or advantage; 3ʳᵈ person sing. of *interesse* to lie between, be important < *inter-* between + *ease* to be]

INTERNAL Pertaining to the inner self or the mind; subjective -An essential quality or attribute

INTERNALITY Devotion to or concern with matters of the mind, Spirit etc.; subjectivity

INTERPRET To give the meaning of; explain or make clear; especially, to restate in clear language; construe 2 To judge (a person) in a personal or particular way 3 To restate orally in one language what is said in another

INTERPRETATION Elucidation; explanation 2 The meaning assigned to actions, intentions, etc. 3 One's concept of a work expressed in a representation

INTERVENE To interfere or take a decisive role, especially with a view to correction, solution or settlement 2 To occur so as to modify an action, expectation etc.

INTIMACY The state of being intimate; confidentiale friendship; close association 2 An instance of this

INTIMATE Characterized by a pronounced closeness of friendship, relationship, or association 2 Deeply personal; private 3 Resulting from close study or familiarity with 4 Pertaining to the inmost nature or being; essential; intrinsic See Friend

INTIMATE ² To make known without direct statement; hint; imply

INTO To and toward the inside of from the outside 2 Passing through the outer boundary or limit of the form, state and condition of

IN TOTO In the whole; altogether; entirely

INTOXICATE To elate or excite to a degree of frenzy 2 Unduly elated or excited

INTREPID Unshaken by fear; dauntless; bold [< L *intrepidus* < *in-* not + *trepidus* agitated]

INTROSPECTION The observation and analysis of one's own mental processes and emotional states; self examination

INVISIBLE The Supreme being; God "For the invisible things of him from the creation of the world are clearly seen, being understood by the things that are made, even his eternal power and Godhead; so that they are without excuse

INVOCATION The act of invoking or appealing to a deity, or other agent for help, inspiration; witness

INWARD In or into the mind or thoughts 2 Pertaining to the mind or Spirit 3 Inherent; intrinsic 4 Within the mind or heart -Peaceful in purpose; conciliatory 2 The -ology concerned with Christian unity

IRIS The rainbow

IRON That which is firm, harsh, unyielding, or indestructible; great power or strength 2 To be engaged in many enterprises 3 To act at the right moment; take advantage of an opportunity 4 Inexorable; unyielding; indefatigable 5 Inferior; debase 6 To smooth over; remove, as difficulties

IRRADIATE To make clear or understandable; enlighten, as with intellectual or Spiritual insight 2 To make radiant; suffuse, as with emotion 3 To be radiant; shine 4 Made bright; illuminated [< L *irradiatus*, pp. of *irradiare* < *in-* thoroughly + *radiare* to shine < *radius* ray]

IRRADIATION Enlightenment, as of the mind or Spirit 2 Treatment with any for of radiant energy, as for therapeutic or preservative purposes

IRRATIONAL Not possessed of or incapable of exercising the power of reason 2 Contrary to reason; absurd; senseless

IRRATIONALITY The state of mind or quality of being irrational 2 That which is irrational; absurd or senseless thought or behavior

IRRESOLUTE Not resolved 2 Lacking firmness of purpose; wavering; hesitating 3 Faint hearted

ISLAM submission (to the will of God) from root of ʿaslama- he resigned, he surrendered, he submitted caus., conj., salima- he was safe, and related to salam "peace [< Arabic *islam* submission < *salama* to be **RESIGNED~** characterized by resignation; submissive]

Quran 3:85 "Whoever seeks other than Spiritual as a religion, it will not be accepted from him, and in the Hereafter he will be among the losers" 3:144. "Muhammad is no more than a messenger Messengers have passed on before him If he dies or gets killed, will you turn on your heels? He who turns on his heels will not harm God in any way And God will reward the appreciative"

IT To represent the implied idea, condition, action, and situation

-IVE Tending to; having the nature of

J

JACKAL One who does menial work to serve another purpose

JAW A talk 2 Impudent talk 3 To talk; jabber 4 To scold or abuse

JAY A stupid, gullible person; **GREENHORN~** An inexperienced person; beginner 2 One easily imposed upon or duped [< GREEN immature + HORN]

JEALOUS Fearful or suspicious of being displaced by a rival in affection or favors 2 Vindictive toward another because of supposed or actual **RIVALS~** One who strives to equal or excel another, or is in pursuit of the same object as another; a competitor See **ENEMY (jealous cont.)** 3 Vigilant in guarding; closely watchful 4 Demanding exclusive worship and love 5 **ZEALOUS~** Enthusiastic devotion; ador, especially for a cause [< OF *zele* < L *zelus* < Gk. *zelos* < *zeein* to boil] See **ENVIOUS** Doublet of **ZEALOUS**

JEHOVAH In the Old Testament, **God**; the Lord: the common transliteration of the Tetragrammaton See YAHWEH [< Hebrew *JHVH* Yahweh, either Creator or Eternal < *hayah* to be, with the substitution of vowels from *adhonay* my Lord]

JEJUNE Lacking in substance or nourishment; barren 2 Lacking interest; insipid; dry 3 Loosely, lacking sophistication; naive [< L *jejunus* hungry]

JEREMIAD A lament or tale of woe; complaint [< F *jeremiade* < *Jeremie* **JEREMIAH**]~ God loose (from the womb)

JERUSALEM [< Hebrew *Yerushalayim* Possession, or City of Peace (**Shalom**)] The new Jerusalem **JERU-** The peaceful place **SALEM-** Meaning. Peaceful, complete. Salem (Arabic: سالم, properly transliterated as Sālim; it can also be a transliteration of the Hebrew: שָׁלֵם

Shalem; the Arabic name is also transliterated as Salim) is an Arabic-origin given name and surname, also a Sephardic Jewish surname

JESUS [1] The highest human corporeal concept of the divine (idea)

JESUS [2] The son of Sirach, lived about the third or fourth century B.C.; author of *Ecclesiasticus*

JEWEL A person or thing of rare excellence or value

JIHAD A religious war of Muslims against enemies of their faith 2 Any crusade for or against a belief or faith

JEZREEL A bold, vicious woman, evil actions Also **ESDRAELON~** (Plain of) Jezreel; insipid; dry Loosely, lacking sophistication; naive [< L *jejunus* hungry]

JOB An affair; circumstances 2 Attending strictly to the matter at hand

JOB'S COMFORTER One who discourages and disheartens under the guise of offering sympathy and consolation

JOKE One who or that which excites mirth; laughing- stock; butt 2 A matter of **little importance**; trifle

JOCKER Any hidden or unknown factor causing difficulty 2 An ineffectual person

JONAH [< Hebrew *Yonah*, lit., **DOVE**]

JOVIAL Possessing or expressive of good-natured mirth or gaiety; convivial; jolly [< F < LL *Jovialis* born under the influence of Jupiter]

JOY A strong feeling of happiness arising from the expectation of some good, or from its realization; gladness; delight 2 A state of contentment or satisfaction 3 Anything that causes delight or gladness 4 An expression or manifestation of this feeling See **PLEASURE~** To be glad; rejoice

JUBILEE In Jewish history, an institution of the Levitical law (**Lev. XXV 8-17**) to be observed during every fiftieth year, at which time Hebrew slaves were to be freed, alienated lands returned, and the fields left uncultivated

JUDAH The southern part of ancient Palestine under Persian, Greek and Roman dominion; also **JUDAEA**

JUDGMENT The faculty of judging; ability to judge wisely; discernment; discrimination 2 The form of thought in which two terms are compared and their fitness to be joined under a given relation is confirmed or denied 3 Uprightness; rectitude Syn. See **SENSE~** That which commends itself to the understanding as being in accordance with reason and good judgment 2 The capacity to perceive or appreciate

JUDICIOUS Having, showing or exercising good judgment; prudent 2 Proceeding from or done with good judgment

JUICE The essence of anything 2 Vital force; strength

JURAMENTADO Moro Muslim of the Philippines who swore to die in the act of killing a Christian [< Sp., orig. pp. of *juramentar* to bind oneself by oath]

JURE DIVINO By divine law

JURE HUMANO By human law

JUS DIVINUM *Latin* Divine law

JUSSIVE Expressing mild command -A *jussive* mood, word or construction

JUST Fair, even handed, and impartial in acting or judging 2 Adhering to high moral standards; upright; honest 3 Morally right; equitable 4 Legally valid; legitimate 5 Rightly given; merited; deserved 6 Well founded; substantial 7 True; correct; accurate 8 Fitting; proper 9 Righteous in the sight of **God** 10 To the exact point; precisely 11 Simply; really; very

JUSTICE The abstract principle by which right and wrong are defined Syn. *Justice, equity, fairness,* and *impartiality* are compared as they mean conformity to principles of right judgment

JUSTIFY To show to be just, right or reasonable; vindicate 2 To adjust to the proper length by spacing 3 To cause to be free of grievous sin, and reconciled with **God** 4 To fit; be properly

SPACED~ That which is characterized by dimensions extending indefinitely in all directions from any given point, and within which all material bodies are located

JUVENESCENCE The state of being or becoming young

JUVENESCENT Becoming young; growing young again 2 Making young; rejuvenating

K

KAFFIR A member of a powerful group of South African Bantu tribes 2 *Xhos*, the language of these tribes 3 A non-Muslim: term used contemptuously by Arab Muslims Also *Kaffer* [< Arabic *kafir* unbeliever] -The transcendental philosophy of Immanuel Kent, a doctrine of a priori knowledge stating that man experiences the material world through sense perception, but its reality is determined by purely mental forms and categories

KARMA In Buddhism and Hinduism, the doctrine of responsibility for all one's acts in all incarnations, that explains and justifies good and evil fortune

KEEN [1] Able to cut or penetrate readily; very sharp 2 Having mental acuteness, penetration, refined perception etc. 3 Manifesting intense absorption or eagerness 4 Having a piercing, intense quality or impact 5 Eager; enthusiastic 6 Fine; excellent -See **ASTUTE**

KEEN [2] A wailing lamentation for the dead -To wail loudly over the dead

KEEP To hold or continue to hold in some specified state, condition, relation, place etc. 2 To continue or cause to continue; maintain 3 To be faithful to or abide by (a promise, vow, one's word etc.) 4 To do the required work of; manage; conduct 5 To defend from harm 6 To care for; be in charge of; tend 7 To observe, as by discerning 8 To be the support of 9 To write down and preserve in good order 10 To stay in or on 11 To maintain for use 12 To preserve in good condition 13 To persist in; continue 14 To remain 15 To remain good for a later time -To remain in the graces of 16 To maintain good condition 17 To cause to continue 18 Means of subsistence 19 Guard or custody; care 20 Very seriously; not for mere amusement 21 Permanently [OE *cepan* to observe] 22 Something that keeps without spoiling

KEN To know 2 To recognize as heir 3 To see 4 To have knowledge or understanding -Range of sight or knowledge; cognizance

KENNING The smallest recognizable portion; a trace; shade 2 recognition

KENOSIS The action of Christ in putting aside His divinity in the incarnation

KIDNEY Temperament, nature or type 2 Any of several doctrines regarding this [< Gk. *kenosis* an emptying < *kenoein* to empty < *kenos* empty]

KETTLE A trying or difficult situation

KEY Anything serving to disclose, open or solve something 2 Something that opens or prepares the way 3 Level of intensity of expression, a characteristic tone or style 4 A key fruit 5 To provide with a cross-reference or a system of cross-references 6 To provide with a solution 7 To cause excitement, expectancy etc. in -Of chief and decisive importance

KIBBUTZ A cooperative or collective farm in Israel [< Hebrew, gathering]

KILL To make a very strong emotional impression upon, as for amusement from embarrassment, etc. 2 To destroy the active qualities of; neutralize 3 To spoil the effect of; cancel by contrast

KILL-JOY One who spoils pleasure for others

KIN Similar in one or more ways; alike

KIND [1] Gentle and considerate in behavior; good hearted; benign 2 Proceeding from or manifesting good heartedness 3 Affectionate; loving 4 In accordance with nature; natural; appropriate; lawful Syn. sympathetic, kindly, gracious, compassionate, benevolent. Compare **CHARITABLE, HUMANE**

KIND [2] Nature in general; the ordained and proper course of things

KINDLE To excite or inflame, as the feelings or passions

KINDLESS Unnatural; degenerate

KINDLY Having or showing kindness; sympathetic 2 Having a favorable effect; beneficial 3 Proper to its kind; natural 4 In a kind manner or Spirit 5 Enthusiastically; heartily 6 To accept with liking or interest 7 To be naturally attracted to

KINDNESS The quality of being kind; goodwill; kindly disposition 2 A kind act or service; a favor 3 A kindly feeling See **BENEVOLENCE**

KINDRED Having like nature or character; similar; **COGNATE~** Allied by derivation from the same source; belonging to the same stock or root 2 Allied in characteristics; having the same nature or quality [< L *cognatus* < *co-* together + *(g)natus*, pp. of *(g)nasci* to be born] Jesus said to them, "How then does David in the Spirit call Him Lord? Matt 22:45

KING One who is **PREEMINENT~** Distinguished above all others; outstanding; **CONSPICUOUS~** Clearly visible; easily seen 2 Readily attracting attention [< L *conspicuus* < *conspicere* < *com-* together + *specere* to look at] **DOM-** Denoting a state or condition of being 2 Denoting a class of people or the attitudes associated with them, regarded collectively **dom-** Domain 2 Domestic 3 Dominion -dom- The totality of those having a certain state of mind or condition of disposition See **BLOOD**

KINGDOM Any place area of concern in the mindset of It as a sovereign domain; sphere -The spiritual dominion of **God**

KINGLET A young or insignificant king 2 Any of several small birds

KINGLY Pertaining to or worthy of a king; regal; kinglike *Kingly* is used chiefly of personal qualities: *kingly* forbearance *Princely*, in extended use, opulence or generosity

KITHE To make or become known

KNACK The ability to do something readily and well 2 Cleverness; **ADROIT~** Skillful or ready in the use of bodily or mental powers; dexterous; expert [< F < *d* to (< *Lad-*) + *droit* right < L *directus]* Syn. Clever, deft, handy

KNOCK To make a strong emotional impression upon, especially of great amusement

KNOW To distinguish between; discriminate: to know good from bad 2 To have sexual intercourse with

KNOWING Perceptive; astute; shrewd; also hinting at having sly or secret knowledge concerning something 2 Conscious; intentional

KNOWLEDGE The cumulative culture of the human race 2 Specific information 3 Sexual intercourse 4 Evidence obtained from the five corporeal senses, the opposite of Spiritual Truth [ME *knowlechen, knowlegen* to admit, recognize]

Syn. *Knowledge, information, learning, erudition* and *lore* are compared as they refer to a store of facts in the mind Knowing is more than this store

KNOWN Past participle of know Recognised as the Truth by all; understood; axiomatic

KOINE ¹ The modified Attic dialect of Greek used during the Hellenistic Age and in the Septuagint and the New Testament Its spoken form is the parent of modern Greek Also called *Hellenistic* Greek [< *koine (dialektos)* common (language)]

KOINE ² Any mixed dialect that becomes the lingua **FRANCA~** Of a region any language that is widely used as a means of communication among speakers of other languages

KOOKABURRA A large Australian bird allied to the kingfisher, noted for its harsh, laughing cry: also called laughing jackass

KOR A homer, the Hebrew measure

KORAN The sacred book of the Muslims, recording in Arabic the revelations of Allah (**GOD**) to Mohammed: also *Alcoran, Alkoran.* [< Arabic *Qur'an*, lit., recitation < *qar'd* to read]

KULTURKAMPF The political struggle from 1872 to 1887 between the German imperial government and the Roman Catholic Church over the state's attempts to control educational and ecclesiastical appointments [< G < **KULTUR** + *kampf* struggle]

KYRIE ELEISON In the Roman Catholic and Eastern Orthodox churches, an ancient liturgical petition for mercy beginning with the words Kyrie eleison ("Lord, have mercy")

KYTE The belly; stomach

L

LABOR Arduous mental exertion; toil 2 Heavy rolling and pitching of a vessel 3 To exert oneself for a cause or purpose 4 To progress with great effort or painful exertion 5 To be oppressed or hampered 6 To work out laboriously; over work; over elaborate 7 To till; plow cultivate [< L labor toil, distress]

LABORIOUS Requiring much labor; toilsome 2 Diligent; industrious

LACK Deficiency or complete absence of something needed or desired 2 To be without; have none or too little 3 To be wanting

LACONISM BREVITY~ Condensation of language; conciseness and **PITH~** concentrated force; vigor 2 The essential part; quietness; gist of utterance 3 A **TERSE~** Short and to the point; concise 2 Clean; polished; refined Syn. *Terse, concise, pithy, succinct, compendious* and *laconic* characterize speech that says much in relatively few words *Terse* emphasizes the finish and the convincing power of the result; *concise* suggests that all unnecessary words have been pruned away *Pithy* describes something both brief and forceful, while *succinct* suggests that which is highly compact because all extraneous detail has been removed

LADEN Burdened; oppressed, as with cares 2 Weighed down; loaded

LADY A woman showing the refinement, gentility, and tact 2 The woman a man loves; beloved 3 A wife or consort [OE *hlaefdige*, lit., bread-kneader < *hlaf* bread, loaf + *dige*, a stem akin to *dah* dough]

LADY The virgin Mary

LAIR Lare; learning

LAMARCKISM The theory of organic evolution holding that species have developed through the inheritance of characteristics acquired by the individual in response to environmental influences

LAMB Any gentle or innocent person, especially a child -Christ -To give birth

LAMBERT The CGS unit of brightness, equal to that of a perfectly diffusing surface emitting or reflecting light at the rate of one lumen per square centimeter

LAME Weak; ineffective: a lame effort

LAMENT To feel or express sorrow over; feel remorse or regret over 2 An expression of grief

LAMENTATIONS A lyrical poetic Book of the Old Testament, attributed to Jeremiah the prophet Abbr. Lam.

LAMP The eyes -To look at literally: A source of Spiritual or intellectual inspiration [< OF *lampe* < L *lamps* <Gk. < *lampein* to shine]

(LAMP)STAND (these characteristics should be found in the seven churches:) To be situated; have position or location 2 To remain unimpaired, unchanged, or valid 3 To have or be in a specified state, condition or relation 4 To be consistent; accord; agree 5 To collect and remain -To have a chance or likelihood as of success 6 To stay near and ready to help 7 To help; support 8 To abide by; make good 9 To remain passive and watch, as when help is needed 10 To wait, as for the completion of an uninterrupted message 11 To present; symbolize 12 To put up with -To conform to reason 13 Remain upright and entire rather than fall into ruin or be destroyed 14 Rest without disturbance 15 Remain on a specified course 16 Act in a specified capacity 17 Withstand (an experience or test) without being damaged

LAND A conceptual realm or domain 2 Any **HEREDITAMENT- Any item of property, either a CORPOREAL-** Bodily, fleshly, carnal, somatic, human, mortal, earthly, physical, material, tangible, concrete, this-worldly, orand **INCORPOREAL-** Intangible, impalpable, nonphysical; bodiless, disembodied, discarnate, immaterial; Spiritual, ethereal, insubstantial, transcendental; ghostly, spectral, supernatural 3 To bring to some point, condition, or state 4 To succeed in obtaining or achieving especially in the face of strong competition 5 Denoting a particular sphere of activity or group of people to -To obtain; win

LANGUAGE Translation of emotions or ideas between any living creature by any means 2 The words forming the means of communication among members of a single nation or group at a given period; tongue 3 The impulses, capacities, and powers that induce and make possible the creation and use of all forms of human communication by speech and hearing 4

One's characteristic manner of expression or use of speech [< OF *langage* < *langue* tongue < L *lingua* tongue, language. Akin to **TONGUE**]- The power of speech or articulation 2 Mere speech, as contrasted with fact or deed 3 utterance 4 A people or race regarded as having its own language; a Biblical use 5 A jet flame

LANGUOR A lack of energy or enthusiasm; spiritless 2 A mood of tenderness or sentimental dreaminess

LAODICEA An indifferent or lukewarm person

LAO TZU Founder of Taoism

LAP [1] Control, care, or custody -To give over the responsibility or control of something to someone else [OE *laeppa*. Akin to Du. L *labi* to slip]

LAP [2] To surround with love, comfort, etc.

LAP [3] To listen or take in with eagerness

LAPIDATE To hurl stones at 2 To stone to death [< L *lapidatus*, pp. of *lapidare* < *lapis -idis* stone]

LAPSE Imperceptible slipping downward or onward 2 A pronounced fall into ruin, decay or disuse 3 A slip or mistake, usually trivial 4 A failure or miscarriage through fault or negligence 5 A forfeiture brought about by the failure to perform some necessary act 6 Apostasy or backsliding 7 To fall into ruin or a state of neglect 8 To deviate from one's principles or beliefs; backslide 9 To become void, usually by failure to meet obligations

LARES In ancient Rome, tutelary deities, especially the spirits of departed ancestors presiding over the household: associated with the *penates*

LARGE Having considerable breadth of sympathy or comprehension 2 Free and open handed in giving 3 In general; not divided or classified

LARK [1] Any of numerous small singing birds, chiefly of the Old World, as the skylark

LARK [2] A hilarious time; frivolous adventure; prank 2 To jump (a fence) on horseback 3 To play pranks; frolic

LASCIVIOUS Having or manifesting wanton desires; lustful 2 Arousing sensual desires [< LL *lasciviosus* < L *lascivia* wantonness < *lascivus* sportive, lustful]

LASH Anything that wounds the feelings 2 To break into angry verbal abuse

LAST To remain in existence; continue to be; endure 2 To continue unimpaired or unaltered -To suffer no diminution 3 To be as much or more than needed; hold out -To follow a track, continue, accomplish -To attend to one's proper business

LASTING Continuing; durable; permanent -Endurance; continuance

LAST JUDGEMENT 1a The final trial and sentencing by **God** of all mankind 1b The time of this

LAST WORD The definitive and most authoritative utterance 2 The most fashionable and desirable thing

LATCH To comprehend

LATENT Not visible or apparent, but capable of developing or being expressed; dormant 2 Undeveloped [< L *latens*, -*entis*, pp. of *latere* to be hidden]

LATINATE Designating a style or diction in English heavily dependent upon words and sentence patterns derived from Latin

LATINISM An **IDIOM~** A group of words established by usage as having a meaning not deducible from those of the individual words in another language taken from or imitating Latin

LATITUDE Freedom from narrow restrictions or customary limitations; independence or breadth of scope in thought, conduct etc. 2 The angular distance of a heavenly body from the ecliptic (celestial latitude)

LATRIA In the Roman Catholic Church, the supreme worship that can properly be given to **God** only; distinguished from dulia and hyperdulia [< LL *latria* < Gk. *latreia* service, worship < *latreuein* to work for hire, worship < *latris* hired servant]

LAUD To praise highly; extol Syn. See **PRAISE~** An expression of approval or commendation 2 The glorifying and honoring of **God** especially, worship of **God** expressed in song 3 The ground or reason for praise 4 To express approval and commendation of; applaud; eulogize 5 To express adoration of; glorify, especially in song [< OF *preisier* < LL *pretiare* to prize < L *pretium* price] *Praise, laud, extol, eulogize, applaud, acclaim* and *celebrate* mean to commend highly *Praise* is the weakest word, and may refer to the mere speaking of compliments To *laud* is to *praise* highly, possibly to excess *Extol* stresses the intention to elevate or magnify a person or thing by praise; *eulogize* is to *extol* in a formal way, especially by public speech, *Applause*, and *acclaim* point to a public show of approval, as by clapping the hands or shouting *Celebrate* almost always implies the use of poetry, and refers to the singing of hymns or the writing of a poem in another's honor

LAUREL To be content with what one has already achieved or accomplished

LAUS DEO Praise be to **God**

LAVATION A washing

LAVER A means or agency of spiritual cleansing, as the water of baptism

LAW A rule of conduct, recognized by custom or decreed by formal enactment, considered by a community, nation or other authoritatively constituted group as binding upon its members 2 A system or body of such rules 3 An authoritative rule or command; governing force: His will is law 4 Divine will, command or precept, especially as expressed in the Scriptures; also a body or system of rules having such divine origin 5 A rule of conduct, moral principle etc., derived from a generally recognized concept of universal justice 6 In science and philosophy, a formal statement of the manner or order in which a set of natural phenomena occur under certain conditions {karma} 7 A rule or formula governing a function or operation 8 A start given to a weaker competitor Syn. A canon was originally a church law; it has since been extended to mean any principle which is regarded as established by common practice or by eminent authority 9 See **AXIOM~** A self-evident or universally recognized Truth 2 An established principle or rule -A self-evident proposition accepted as true without proof Abbr. *ax* [< L *axioma, -atos* < Gk. *axioma* a thing thought worthy, a self-evident thing < *axioein* to think worthy < *axios* worthy Syn. *Axiom, theorem, law* and *principle* are compared as they denote a proposition universal in form and widely accepted as true An *axiom* is self-evident;

a *theorem* is a proposition deduced from axioms, or, in general, any proposition susceptible of proof A scientific *law* is an assertion about cause and effect, or the regularity of phenomena, or the like, formulated by induction from data A *principle* is a generalization useful as a guide to understanding or study See **TRUISM~** An obvious self-evident Truth

LAY To construct, produce, or establish as a basis or support 2 To have sexual intercourse with

LAYMAN One without training or skill in a learned profession or specialized branch of knowledge 2 A man belonging to the laity, as opposed to the clergy

LAZY Unwilling to engage in energetic activity; insolent; slothful 2 Moving or acting slowly or heavily; sluggish 3 Conducted or characterized by idleness or languor -Loose [feeble]

LEAD To influence the actions of; motivate 2 To be the principal participant in 3 To experience or Live; also to cause to experience or go through 4 To direct or affect the course of 5 To be led; yield readily to being guided 6 To afford a way or passage; extend 7 To approach or arrive at gradually or cautiously 8 Position of primary importance, responsibility, etc. 9 Guidance; leadership; example

LEAF To begin anew, especially with the intention of improving one's ways

LEAGUE In close alliance; working or acting in cooperation [< OF *ligue* < Ital. *liga, lega* < *legare* to bind < L *ligare*]

LEAL Loyal; faithful

LEAN To rest or incline for support 2 To depend for support, comfort etc.; rely

LEARN To acquire knowledge of or skill in by study, practice etc. 2 To find out; become aware of 3 To commit to memory 4 To acquire by experience or example -Characterized by or devoted to practice 5 Modification of behavior, mental processes etc., as a result of

LEASING A lie; lying; falsehood

LEAVE To allow to remain behind or in a specific place, condition etc. 2 To have or cause as an aftermath; result in 3 To cause to be placed, given or made available in one's absence 4 To commit for action or decision etc.; entrust 5 To let; permit 6 To allow to remain solitary or unattended

LEAVEN Any component, addition, or pervasive influence that produces a significant change 2 To affect in character; temper 3 To cause **FERMENTATION~** To excite with emotion or passion; agitate [< F < L *fermentum* < *fervere* to boil]

LEECH One who clings or preys upon another for gain; a parasite [OE *lxce*, orig., physician]

LEFT Relating to a person or group favoring liberal, socialist, or radical views 2 Go away from Syn. Depart from, withdraw from, retire from, take oneself off from, exit from, take one's leave of, pull out of, quit, be gone from, decamp from, disappear from, abandon, vacate, absent oneself from, evacuate; say one's farewells/goodbyes, make off, clear out, make oneself scarce, check out; abscond from, run away from, flee (from) 3 Allow to remain 4 Remain to be used or dealt with 5 Bequeath Syn. Will, endow, hand down, transfer, convey, make over; demise, devise 6 Cause (someone or something) to be in a particular state 7 Let (someone) do or deal with something without offering help or assistance 8 Cause to remain as a trace or record Syn. Cause, produce, generate, give rise to, result in 9 Deposit or entrust to be kept, collected, or attended to 10 Entrust a decision, choice, or action to (someone else, especially someone considered better qualified)

LEFT HANDED Ironical, insincere or ambiguous in intent or effect 2 Clumsy; awkward 3 Morganatic

LEGAL [1] A division or section of a course or journey

LEGAL [2] Pertaining to the Doctrine of salvation by works rather than grace Abbr. *leg.* Doublet of **LOYAL**

LEGITIMATE Based on or resulting from orderly, rational deduction or inference; logical; reasonable 2 Authentic; valid 3 To show reason or authorization for; justify

LENGTH The limit of one's effort, ability, etc.

LENITIVE Having the power to allay pain or distress; soothing -That which soothes or mitigates; a palliative

LET Discharge, dismiss and excuse, as from work or obligation, allowing to escape punishment or penalty 2 To make known; reveal and reduce tension 3 To permit to pass, come, go, etc. 4 To cause 5 To grant 6a An exhortation or command 6b Willingness; acquiescence 7 To cause to flow -To leave unmolested; refrain from disturbing or tampering with -To insert into the substance, material or body of something 8 To allow to make it known; reveal

LEVEL Any of various devices used to find the conformity of a line or surface with the horizontal plane, as a Spirit level (which see) 2 Without equivocation or deception; fair and square -A calm and sensible mind -The best one can possibly do; one's utmost 3 To bring to a common state or condition; remove inequalities, as of rank or importance 4 To aim or direct (something) with force of emphasis 5 To bring person's into a common state or condition 6 To be straightforward or honest [< OF *livel, nivel* < L *libella,* dim. of *libra* a balance]

LEVIATHAN A gigantic unidentified water beast mentioned several times in the Bible 2 Any enormous creature or thing

LEWD Characterized by or inciting to lust or debauchery 2 Obscene; ribald; bawdy 3 Unprincipled; worthlessness [OE *lxwede* lay, ***unlearned**, fusion < L *latcus* lay and OE *lxwan* to betray]

LIBERAL Characterized by or inclining toward opinions or policies favoring progress or reform 2 Characterized by generosity or lavishness in giving

LIE To exist; be **INHERENT**- Existing in something as a permanent, essential, or characteristic attribute 2 To continue or extend -To be confined or engaged in the process of childbirth -To remain in concealment; conceal one's intentions 3 To have sexual intercourse with 4 That which creates or is intended to produce a false impression -A false statement made knowingly but with the intent of being polite or kind; a minor or trivial untruth 5 To put or promote (oneself or someone) into a specified situation by telling a lie

LIEGE Bound in vassalage or owing allegiance to a lord or sovereign 2 Pertaining to or characteristic of the relationship between vassal and lord [< OF < Med. L *ligius* free < *laeticus* free < *letus* freedman < OHG *ledig* free]

LIEGEMAN A loyal follower or subject

LIFE The divine principle, **God** 2 A Spiritual state regarded as continuation or perfection of animate existence 3 A living being; soul; Spirit; mind 4 The period of an individual's existence between birth and death or translation 5 The period during which something continues to be effective, useful, etc. 6 Manner of existence; characteristic activities 7 A source or support of existence; essential necessity 8 Energetic force; vitality; animation 9 A source of liveliness; animating Spirit 10 A Living Model; also a representation of such a Model 11 Existence regarded as a desirable condition -As though to save someone's Life; with urgent effort, speed, etc. -Under any circumstances -Any easy and happy Life; the sweet Life 12 To recall vividly to the mind or senses 13 To regain consciousness 14 To become animated 15 To seem to be real or alive

LIFT To hold up; support 2 To bring to a higher or more desirable degree or condition; cause to increase in quality, estimation, etc.; exalt 3 A feeling of exhilaration or well-being

LIGHT [1] Spiritual understanding or insight; enLightenment 2 The state of being unhidden and observable 3 Way of being regarded; aspect 4 Ability and understanding 5 A lively or intense expression on the face, especially the eyes 6 The Inner Light (which see) 8 To come into being 9 Full of Light; not dark; bright 10 To make known 11 Unhidden, and observable Spiritual understanding, (inner-Light) (which see)

LIGHT [2] Not burdensome or oppressive; easily borne 2 Not difficult; arduous; easily done 3 Not great in degree or concentration 4 Intended or enjoyed as entertainment; not lofty or heroic 5 Designating the less massive types of weapons or equipment, as with an enLightened exhortation

LIGHTEN To make less oppressive, troublesome etc.; diminish the severity of 2 To relieve, as of distress, uneasiness etc.; ease

LIGHTNESS Freedom from sorrow or care; blitheness 2 Lack of seriousness

LIGHTNING The discharge of **LIGHT** (Spiritual knowledge) itself

LIKE [1] To take pleasure in; enjoy 2 To feel warmly or affectionate toward; be fond of 3 To wish or desire; prefer 4 To feel disposed; choose 5 To be pleasing to 6 Preference; inclination

LIKE [2] Indicative of; likely to result in 2 As though having the need for; desirous of 3 Equal or nearly equal 4 One of equal value, standing 5 With great intensity, force, effort, etc. 6 With the characteristics or qualities of; in the manner of; typical of 7 Indicative of; likely to result in 8 With great intensity 9 Having the same or similar characteristics; belonging in the same category; related 10 Equal 11 Similar to what is portrayed or represented 12 One of equal value, standing, etc. 13 In the manner that

LIKENESS Characteristic or typical of 2 Having the same or similar characteristics; belonging in the same category; related 3 Having a close resemblance to; similar to 4 With the characteristics or qualities of; in the manner of 5 Similar to what is portrayed or represented 6 As (the one is), so (is the other) -One of equal value standing 7 As; in the manner that 8 To represent as similar; comparable See like-minded

LIKE-MINDED Having the similar opinions, purposes, tasks etc.

LILT A lively quality of speech, voice, song etc., with pronounced variation of pitch 2 A Light, buoyant motion or manner, as in walking -To speak, sing, move etc. in cheerful rhythmic manner [ME *lulte*. Cf. Du. *lul* pipe]

LIMB [1] A mischievous child; young rascal -In a risky, vulnerable or questionable position

LIMB [2] The edge of a **DISK**~ The figure of a heavenly body as it appears to the naked eye (cont. **LIMB** [2]) of the sun, moon or other heavenly body

LIMIT A definite quantity or value that a series is conceived or proved to approach but never reach 2 One who or that which tries one's patience, credulity etc., to the utmost

LIMITED Falling short of fullness or impressiveness

LIMP [1] To progress in an irregular, defective or labored manner

LIMP [2] Lacking force or vigor

LIMPID Characterized by clarity, lucidity or purity, as of style See **CLEAR**

LINE A demarcation or limit separating contrasts, kinds of behavior, etc. 2 General plan or concept, as of form, content etc. 3 A **GLIB**~ Characterized by facile insincere compliments and a manner of speech intended to ingratiate or persuade [OE *line* cord; infl. by F *ligue* < L *linea* linen thread < *linum* **FLAX**]

LINGUISTIC STOCK A family of languages, including a parent language together with all the languages and dialects derived from it

LION A representation of a lion, as a heraldic 2 One having qualities considered characteristic of a lion; especially a man of noble courage, great strength etc. 3 A prominent or notable person, especially one much sought after socially

LIP Brash and impudent talk; sass 2 Merely spoken; insincere; hypocritical

LISSOME Flexible; pliant; supple 2 Moving with ease and grace; agile; lithe

LIST Be pleasing or expedient to; suit 2 To desire; wish; choose

LISTEN Be attentive in order to hear 2 Give attention; give heed 3 To be influenced or persuaded

LITERAL Conforming or restricted to the exact, stated meaning; not figurative or inferred: The literal sense of the Scriptures 2 Following the exact words and order of an original; verbatim: a literal translation 3 Tending to recognize or accept stated meaning only: matter-of-fact; unimaginative 4 Free from figurative language, embellishments etc. as a literary style; factual; unadorned

LITTLE Having small force or effectiveness; weak 2 Not having great influence or power; of minor status 3 Not important or significant; inconsiderable; trivial 4 Narrow or limited in view point; petty; mean 5 Appealing, endearing, or amusing because of affectionate association, familiarity, etc. 6 To treat or regard as inconsequential

LIVABLE Worth living; capable of being endured; tolerable

LIVE [1] To remain valid or operative; endure; last 2 To use something as one's soul or customary nourishment; subsist 3 To be joyously alive 4 To escape destruction; stay afloat or inflight despite danger 5 To exemplify or put into practice in one's life -To be forbearing or unprejudiced in regard to the conduct, characteristics etc. of others -To live or behave so as to expiate the memory of (an error, crime etc.) -To reside as a domestic servant -To have fun -To survive or withstand (an experience) 6 To satisfy (an expectation) 7 To fulfill (a bargain, obligation etc.) 8 To reside with 9 To cohabit with 10 To put up with; endure -One may *sojourn* in a place for several years, but with the feeling that one may someday return to a permanent home elsewhere

LIVE [2] Pertaining to, characteristic of, or abounding in Life 2 Of present interest and importance; currently valid 3 Vivid or brilliant 4 ready or retained for use, not to be destroyed or disregarded

LIVER One who lives in a specified manner 2 A dweller

LO See! Observe!

LOATHE Strongly disinclined; reluctant; unwilling

LOCK('s) And interlocking, fastening, or jamming together of parts or elements 2 A wrestling grip or hold 3 To shut, fasten, or secure by means of constant study 4 To keep, confine, imprison, etc., in or as in a locked enclosure 5 To fit together securely; interlock; link

LOFT A large, open room where parts of a vessel are drawn at full scale or assembled [Late OE < ON air, sky, **upper room** Akin to **LIFT**]

LOFTY Elevated in character, quality, style etc.; noble 2 Exalted in rank or position 3 Showing contemptuous pride; arrogant; haughty

LOGIC The science concerned with the principles of valid reasoning and correct inference, either deductive or inductive See **FORMAL LOGIC, SYMBOLIC LOGIC** 2 Method of reasoning, inference, argument etc.; especially, correct or sound reasoning 3 Effective or convincing force, influence etc. 4 The basic principles of reasoning developed by and applicable to any field of knowledge 5 A system of or treatise on logic [< F *logique* < L *logica* < Gk. *logike* (*techne*) logical (art) < *logikos* of speaking or reasoning < **Logos Word, speech, thought**]

LOGICAL Relating to or of the nature of logic 2 Conforming to the laws of logic; consistent in point of reasoning 3 Capable of or characterized by clear reasoning

LOGICAL POSITIVISM A movement in philosophy that stresses sensory observation as the basis for assessing claims to knowledge about matters of fact, as well as the use of modern techniques of logical analysis in clarifying the meaning of statements

LOGOMACHY Strife over mere words; verbal contention -Abnormal talkativeness

logos Greek and Hellenistic philosophy, the cosmic reason giving order, purpose, and intelligibility to the world [Gk., Word]

LOGOS The creative Word of **God**, identified with the cosmic reason 2 In the Christian religion, **God**, the second person of the Trinity, incarnate as Jesus Christ

LOIN Regarded as the seat of strength and procreative power

LONGANIMITY Patient endurance of trials and sufferings

LONGHAIR Of or pertaining to intellectuals or their tastes 2 Of or pertaining to serious rather than popular music 3 A longhair person; intellectual

LONG SUFFERING Patiently enduring injuries, misfortune etc. for a long time

LOOM To appear or come into view indistinctly, as through a mist, especially so as to seem large or ominous 2 To appear to the mind as large or threatening; great difficulties

LORD God 2 Jesus Christ -The highest human corporeal concept of the divine manifestation of **God**

LORD of HOSTS Jehovah; **God**

LORD'S DAY ACT A federal regulatory statute intended to preserve Sunday as a day of rest

LORD SHIP The dominion, power or authority of a lord 2 Sovereignty in general

LOSS The harm, inconvenience, deprivation, etc. caused by losing something or someone -A state of confusion or perplexity

LOST No longer possessed, seen or known 2 Bewildered; perplexed 3 Helpless 4 Destroyed; ruined 5 No longer known or practiced -To be absorbed or engrossed in 6 To no longer belong to 7 To be impervious or insensible to: to be lost to all sense of justice 8 To be no longer available to -To have no effect upon

LOT One's portion in life as ascribed to chance, fate, destiny, custom 2 A specified type of (person)

LOUD MOUTHED Possessed of a loud voice; offensively clamorous or talkative

LOVABLE Worthy of love; amiable

LOVE A deep devotion or affection for another person or persons 2 One who is beloved 3 A term of endearment 4 A very great interest in, or enjoyment of someone, also the person so enjoyed 5 The benevolence and mercifulness of **God** toward mankind 6a The adoration or devout affection of man toward **God** 6b The kindness and charitableness man should show toward others 7 **God** -As a favor; without compensation -For any consideration; under any circumstances -For the sake of; in loving consideration of -To conceive a strong and devoted feeling for someone 8 To take pleasure or delight in; like very much Syn. *Love, affection, devotion,*

attachment and *fondness* denote a warm feeling of regard, usually between persons *Love* is the strongest term, describing the warmest, most intense regard of one person for another; it frequently includes and often implies a Spiritual quality: love of **God** *Affection* is a degree short of *Love*; it is always felt for persons, and suggests a strong liking or sympathy characterized by kindness *Devotion* is steadfast loyalty and service, which may be rendered to a cause or person *Attachment* is weaker than *devotion*, often denoting no more than the wish to play an active part in another's life *Fondness* refers to a strong liking or preference which is often demonstrative

LOVELY Possessing mental qualities that inspire admiration or Love 2 Beautiful 3 Delightful; pleasing 4 Affectionate

LOVER One in love with or making love to another person of the opposite sex: in the singular now used only of the man 2 One who enjoys or is strongly attracted to some diversion, object, persuit, etc.

LOW-CHURCH Of or belonging to a group in the Anglican Church that stresses evangelical doctrine and is, in general, opposed to extreme ritualism

LOWLY Humble or low in rank, origin, nature etc. 2 Full of humility; meek 3 In a low condition, manner, position etc. 4 Modestly; humbly; confident etc. Indicating loyalty See **FAITHFUL** Doublet of **LEGAL**

LOYAL Constant and faithful in any relation or obligation implying trust, confidence etc. 2 Indicating or professing loyalty

LUCID Easily understood; rational; clear 2 Mentally sound; sane 3 Shining bright Syn. See **CLEAR**

Lucifer A friction match

LUCIFER The planet Venus when it appears as the morning star [< L light-bearer < *lux*, *lucis* light + *ferre* to bear]

LUKEWARM Lacking ardor, enthusiasm or conviction; indifferent

LUMINOUS Easily understood; clear 2 Brilliantly intelligent or wise

LURE Anything that attracts or entices by the prospect of advantage, pleasure, etc.

LURK To exist unnoticed or unsuspected 2 To move secretly or furtively; slink 3 To lie hidden, as in ambush

LUST Sexual appetite 2 Excessive sexual appetite, especially that seeking immediate or ruthless satisfaction 3 Strong or overwhelming desire or need 4 Pleasure; inclination 5 To have passionate or inordinate desire, especially sexual desire

LUSTRATE To purify by an offering or ceremony [< L *lustratus*, pp. of *lustrare* to purify by propitiatory offerings < *lustrum* purification]

LUXURIANT Growing lushly and profusely, as fruit; prolific; rank 2 Abundant, exuberant, or ornate 3 Abundantly fertile, as the Spirit

LUXURY Anything, usually rare, that ministers to comfort or pleasure but is not a necessity to life

M

MACROCOSM The whole universe or great world, especially when regarded in contrast to man 2 A large system regarded as a unity [< Gk. *makros* long, great + *kosmos* world]

MAD Suffering from or manifesting severe mental disorder; insane; psychotic 2 Feeling or showing anger 3 Going beyond the bounds of reason, decorum or safety; wildly foolish; rash 4 Subject to an overpowering emotion 5 Turbulent and confused; extremely disorderly 6 Showing a passionate infatuation with or desire for 7 Flamboyant; daring produced by

MADE Produced by fabrication, invention, or skill; not occurring naturally 2 The time from the beginning to be sure of success 3 Admirable, and well situated See **MAKE**

MAGI The three wise men from the east who came to Bethlehem to pay homage to the infant Jesus 2 The priestly cast of the Medes and Persians

MAGNANIMOUS Manifesting generosity in forgiving insults or injuries; not given to resentment or envy; great of soul; high minded 2 Characterized by or arising from magnanimity

MAHOUND Mohammed

MAIDEN Of or pertaining to the first use, trial or experience 2 Untried; unused

MAKE To bring about the existence of by shaping or combining of materials; produce; build; construct; fashion 2 To bring about; cause 3 To bring to some state or condition; cause to be 4 To form or create in the mind, as a plan, conclusion, or judgment 5 To entertain mentally 6 To understand the meaning or significance To utter or express, as for the record 7 To represent as being or appearing 8 To put forward or proffer 9 To carry on; engage in 10 To earn or acquire 11 To act in such a way as to win or gain 12 To amount to; add up to 13 Draw up, enact, or frame, as laws, wills. Treaties, etc. 14 To affect or form as characteristics or personality 15 To estimate to be;recon 16 To prepare or arrange for use 17 To induce, or compel 18 To be the essential element or determinant of 19 To afford or provide 20 To become through development; have the essential qualities of 21 To cause the success of 22 To complete (a circuit) 23 To win a place or position 24 To have sexual intercourse with 25 To cause (someone) to assume a specified condition 26 To act or behave in a certain manner 27 To start or appear to start to do something 28 To be made 29 To get along with what is available, especially with an inferior substitute 30 To bring about the success 31 To see; discern 32 To comprehend; understand 33 To establish by evidence 34 To succeed 35 To be the parts of; constitute 36 To settle differences and become friendly again 37 To supply what is lacking in 38 Compensate; atone 39 Eager for amorous conquest

MAKER God, the Creator

MALE Adapted to fertilize, but not to produce fruit, as **STAMENS-** The pollen-bearing organ of a flower, standing inside the floral envelopes and consisting of the **FILAMENT-** The stalk or support of another [< L *stare* to stand] and the **ANTHER-** [< F anthere < L anthera, medicine obtained from flowers < Gk. anthera, Fem.]

MAMMON Riches regarded as an evil influence and ignoble goal 2 Worldliness; avarice, and worldly gain

MAN Akin to mind 2 Human being collectively 3 One having pronounced **VIRTUES~** The quality of moral righteousness or excellence **RECITUTED-** The practice of moral duties and the abstinence from immorality and vice; sexual purity; chastity especially in Spirit 2 Particular type of moral excellence, especially one of those considered to be of special importance in philosophical and religious doctrine 3 Compare cardinal virtues 4 Any admirable quality or trait, inherent or essential qualities, power, etc. 5 Efficacy; Potency; Valor; by or through the fact, quality, force, or authority of 6 To seem to do freely and from principal what is or must be done necessarily strength; bravery

Syn. **VIRTUE, GOODNESS, MORALITY, RECTITUDE** and **RIGHTEOUSNESS** are compared as they denote the disposition to be good, moral, honest, and upright We regard virtue, as acquired through self discipline I predicate of human beings only Goodness is an innate quality and so may be ascribed to God as well as you Morality involves conformity to an accepted code of right conduct being less elevated but more concrete than virtue Rectitude also implies conformity to a moral code, but stresses intention and disposition Hence a man's morale may arise from fear of punishment or of sensors, but his rectitude can only come from a Love of the right and a conscious desire to follow it The rectitude of an action is to be found more in its purpose than its consequences Righteousness is a very close synonym of rectitude but suggest a religious point of view **VIRTUOSITY** ~ virtuoso technical mastery of an art ~A servant; member of a team; you; you there; A ship or vessel The compound idea of infinite spirit to be independent **HOLY~** regarded with reverence because of the association with and derived from God Having divine nature and origin Sacred: Scripture Completely devoted to the service of compassion Having great spiritual and moral worth; saintly Designated and set apart to bring happiness to those who do not have it Consecrated characterized by kind exaltation reverence etc.; Spiritually pure: Love Invoking and meriting reverence and awe: mysterious A sacred and holy place ~syn. Holy, sacred, consecrated, blessed and hallowed are applied to things regarded with great reverence Holy is the strongest word being applied only to things that have the most immediate connection with Love Blast means especially favored by Love (not human love) Hallowed refers to that which has been made sacred by long-continued attention Akin to mind

~~God~~

Self existent, eternal Creator, Sustainer, and Ruler of Life and the universe This Being regarded as the source or embodiment of some specific attributes; principal; virtue etc.; the divine, creative Principle; Life, Truth, and Love; Mind and Spirit [< OE *monn, mann* Akin to L men's mind]

MANA A pervasive supernatural power that may inhere in persons or things

MANGER A trough or box for feeding **HORSE**s- A man; friendly, joking, **OPPROBRIOUS**-term The public disgrace arising from someone's shameful conduct 2 A trough or box for feeding cattle (See **CATTLE, HORSE**)

MANIA An extraordinary interest, enthusiasm, absorption, craving etc.

MANIFESTO A public and formal declaration or explanation of principles, intentions etc.

MANIPULATION To deal with (ideas, relations etc.) by means of the mind

MANKIND The whole human species

MANLY Having the qualities and virtues of a man, as courage, determination, strength etc. Syn. *Manly, manful* and *manish* characterize qualities proper or peculiar to men. *Manly* may be applied to almost any admired quality: *manly* fortitude, *manly* gentleness

MANNER A way of doing or a way in which something happens or is done; mode; fashion 2 One's bearing and behavior; style of speech and action 3 Social conduct; etiquette; especially, polite and civil social behavior 4 Distinguished 5 Character; nature; disposition

MAN ON HORSEBACK A military leader whose popularity is a threat to civil government

MANQUE Lacking fulfillment; in wish but not fact

MANTA Mildness; gentleness [< L *mansuetudo, -inis* < *mansuetus*, pp. of *mansuescere* to tame < *manus* hand + *suescere* to accustom]

MANTIC Of, pertaining to, or having powers of divination or prophecy

MANTLE Anything that envelops or conceals

MARK That which indicates the presence of a thing, quality, process, etc., characteristic; symptom, position, etc., assumed or imposed on a person; token 2 A visible indication of some quality, trait 3 Notice; attention; heed 4 To make known or clear; manifest; display 5 To take notice; pay attention; consider

MARKED Clearly evident; noticeable; prominent; distinguished

MARKETPLACE The imagined place where ideas, opinions, works, etc. are tested and traded

MARRIAGE Any close union

MARRIED Closely related or joined

MARROW The inner meaning or purpose 2 Inmost or central part 3 Chamber 4 The mind; most inner part 5 The essence of anything; pith 6 Vitality 7 To associate or marry

MARRY An exclamation of surprise, indignation, etc. [Alter. of MARY; with ref. to the Virgin Mary]

MARTIAL In astrology, under the evil influence of the planet Mars

MARTYR One who suffers or sacrifices everything for a principle, cause, etc. 2 To torture or prosecute [OE < LL < Gk. *martyr*, Aeolic form of *martyrs, martyros* witness]

MASORA A false show, disguise or pretense 2 To disguise one's true characters; assume a false appearance

MASTER One who has control, direction or authority over someone 2 One who has the ability to control or influence 3 Something considered as having the power to control or influence 4 Principal; main

MASTER BUILDER One who supervises building construction

MASTERY The state of dominion; control 2 Superior knowledge or skill 3 A companion; comrade 4 To join or match closely together 5 To consort; associate {< MLG < *gemate* < *ge-together* + *mat* meat, food. Prob. akin to **MEAT**]

MATERIAL Anything that may be used in creating, working up or developing 2 Of, related to, or affecting the body or sensual appetites 3 Concerned with or devoted to things primarily physical rather than Spiritual or intellectual 4 Pertaining to matter as opposed to form

MATERIALIST Undue regard for the material rather than the Spiritual or intellectual aspects of life

MATEY Friendly; chummy

MATHEMATICAL EXPECTATION The sum of each possible value or outcome of a given event multiplied by the probability of a particular outcome

MATTER That which is material and physical, occupies space, and is perceived by the senses, as distinguished from that which is mental, intellectual, Spiritual, etc. 2 That which makes up the substance of anything, especially of material things 3 A subject, event, or situation that is or may become an object of discussion, concern, feeling, etc. 4 Importance, consequence, or moment 5 The ideas, content, or meaning of a speech, book, etc., as distinguished from style or form 6 The opposite of God; illusion 7 To be of concern or importance; signify [< OF *matere* < L material *materia* stuff]

MATTER-OF-COURSE Following or accruing as a natural or logical result 2 Accepting or regarding things as a matter of course

MATTER-OF-FACT Something having actual and undeniable existence or reality

MATTOID A mentally unbalanced person

MATURE Completely developed or grown; fully ripe, as fruit 2 Highly developed or advanced in intellect, moral qualities; outlook etc. 3 Fully or thoroughly developed, perfected, detailed etc. 4 To perfect; complete

MAUNDY The religious ceremony of washing the feet of others in commemoration of the washing of the feet by Christ at the Last Supper See **MANDATE**

MAXIM A brief statement of a general Principle, Truth or rule of conduct See **MAXIMUM**

MAY Desire, prayer or wish 2 Contingency, especially in clauses of result, concession, purpose etc. 3 Obligation or duty 4 Ability; power See **CAN** and **MIGHT**

MAY The prime of life

ME The objective case of the pronoun

MEALY MOUTHED Unwilling to express facts or opinions plainly and frankly; insincere; euphemistic

MEAN To have in mind as a purpose or intent 2 To intend or design for some purpose, destination etc. 3 To intend to express or convey 4 To have disposition or intention; be disposed 5 Selfishly unwilling to oblige or accommodate; disagreeable; nasty 6 Ashamed; humiliated 7 Ill; out of sorts 8 Vicious; ill-tempered; dangerous 9 Difficult; troublesome

Mean, ignoble, base, sordid and *abject* describes persons or action regarded as being far below common worth or dignity *Mean* suggests a contemptible smallness of mind, or a petty, ungenerous nature; *ignoble* denotes a lack of noble or praiseworthy qualities and frequently implies a failure to meet ordinarily accepted standards of worth or excellence *Base* is a strong word, used to condemn that which is openly evil, selfish or dishonorable *Abject* is the least derogatory of these words; it denotes a low condition, degree or estate, often without further implication: the *abject* spirits of the condemned

MEANING That which is intended or meant; aim; purpose; end 2 That which is signified; sense; import 3 Interpretation or significance 4 Having purpose or intention 5 Significant; suggestive; expressive

MEAT The essence; gist or main idea of something 2 Anything one particularly enjoys or does with ease

MEATY Full of substance; significant

MEDIATE To settle or reconcile differences by intervening as a peacemaker 2 To bring about or effect by one's intervention 3 To serve as a medium for effecting (a result) or conveying (information) 4 To act between disputing parties in order to bring about a settlement, compromise etc.

MEDICINE Any object or rite supposed to produce supernatural effects

MEDIUM An intervening substance through or in which something may act or an effect be produced

MEEK Having a patient, gentle disposition; mild 2 Submissive; compliant 3 Compassionate; kind

MEET To come into the observation, perception or recognition of 2 To experience; undergo 3 To deal or cope with; handle 4 To comply or act in accordance with; conform to 5 To fulfill (an obligation, responsibility, need etc.) 6 To come together in union; join 7 To assemble 8 To agree; concur

MEETING Observation, perception, and recognition; face to face

MEGALOMANIA A mental disorder in which the subject thinks himself great or exalted 2 A tendency to magnify and exaggerate

MEGIDO An ancient city in NW Palestine at the western edge of the plane of Jezreel, probably Armageddon of the Bible

MEGRIM Depression of spirits; dullness 2 A whim 3 Migraine

MELANCHOLIA Mental disorder characterized by great depression of spirits and excessive brooding without apparent or sufficient cause

MELLOW Soft, sweet and full-flavored by reason of ripeness, as fruit 2 Well matured 3 Rich and soft in quality 4 Made gentle and sympathetic by maturity or experience 5 Soft and friable, as soil -To make or become mellow; ripen; soften

MELT To disappear or cause to disappear; dissipate 2 To blend by imperceptible degrees; merge 3 To make or become softened in feeling or attitude 4 A single operation of fusing

MEMENTO Either of two prayers in the Canon of the Mass beginning with the word *Memento*, the first being for the living and the second for the deceased [< L remember, imperative of *meminisse* to remember]

MEMORY The mental function or capacity of recalling a recognizing previously learned behavior or past experience 2 The period of time covered by the faculty of remembrance

MEND To make sound or serviceable again by repairing; repair 2 To correct the errors or faults in; reform; improve 3 To correct (some defect) 4 To become better

MENSE Defined conduct

MENS SANA IN CORPORE SANO A sound mind in a sound body

MENTAL Of or pertaining to the mind or intellect 2 Of or taking place in the mind, especially without the aid of written symbols

MENTAL DEFICIENCY A condition including all types of idiocy, imbecility and mormonism, characterized by subnormal intelligence to the extent that the individual is handicapped from participating fully in ordinary life

MENTAL HEALING The alleged curing of any disorder, ailment or disease by mental concentration and suggestion

MENTAL HYGIENE The scientific study and application of methods to preserve and promote mental health

MERCY Kind or compassionate treatment of an offender, advisory, prisoner etc., in one's power; compassion where severity is expected 2 A disposition to be kind, forgiving or helpful 3 The power to show mercy or compassion 4 A thing to be thankful for

MERIDIAN A great circle drawn from any point on the earth's surface and passing through both poles 2 An imaginary great circle of the celestial sphere passing through its poles and a zenith of an observer at any point 3 The highest or culminating point of anything; development; eminence

MERIT Worth or excellence; high quality; a reward 2 That which deserves esteem, praise or reward; a commendable act or quality 3 The quality or fact of being entitled to reward, praise etc.

MERRY Full of mirth and laughter; joyous; gay 2 Characterized by or conductive to mirth, cheerfulness and gay spirits; festive

METANEPHROS Complete transformation of character, purpose, circumstance etc.

METAPHOR A figure of speech in which one object is likened to another by speaking of it as if it were that other -A figurative expression in which two or more incongruous metaphors are used 2 A figure of speech in which a term that ordinarily designates an object or idea is used to designate a dissimilar object or idea in order to suggest comparison or analogy [< Gk. < *metapherein* < *meta-* beyond, over + *pherein* to carry]

METAPHRASE To translate word for word -A literal translation

METAPHYSICAL Of or pertaining to ultimate reality or basic knowledge 2 Beyond or above the physical or the laws of nature; transcendental

METAPSYCHIC Of or pertaining to the phenomena apparently resulting from mental action and having no physical basis or explanation

METEMPSYCHOSIS Transmigration of souls

METONYMY A figure of speech that consists in the naming of a thing by submitting one of its attributes or an associated term for the name itself

METAPHERICAL Lying beyond the bounds of experience; not derived from experience

METTLE Inherent quality, as of character or temperament 2 Dauntless spirit; courage -Aroused to one's best efforts; putting forth one's utmost

MICHAEL One of the archangels represented as a militant protector and defender of the faithful

MICROLOGY Undue attention to minute and unimportant matters

MIDRASH The traditional body of commentaries on the Old Testament, dating from the fourth to the twelfth century Compare **HAGGADAH, HALAKHAH**

The condition of being surrounded, as by entities, spirits, God, Love, knowledge, etc., engaged or involved 2 The central or interior part; middle See CENTER

MIEN Manner, bearing, expression or outward appearance Syn. **AIR**

MIGHT Power or capacity to dominate, be preeminent, etc., strength; force 2 Mental strength 3 With all one's ability; with utmost endeavor Syn. awfully, majorly, mega, plumb, right 4 Earnestness 5 Extremely

MILD Kind or amiable in behavior, disposition or manners; not rough or severe; gentle 2 Expressing or signifying kindness or gentleness, as words, behavior etc. 3 Gentle or moderate in action, effect or degree; temperate; clement 4 Not harmful, extremely painful or dangerous 5 Not intense 6 Kind or considerate

MILL A trying or grueling experience; ordeal

MILLSTONE A heavy or burdensome weight

MIND Way or state of knowing or feeling; mental disposition; temper 2 Intellectual power or capacity; correct or accurate understanding 3 The faculty of cognition and intellect, as opposed to the will and emotions 4 Sound mental condition; sanity 5 Attention! 6 Spirit or knowing regarded as the basic substance of the universe and sometimes distinguished from matter; physical being 7 The divine Principle; **God**: also, **Divine Mind** See INTELLECT

"One man

Esteemeth	Have a high opinion; looking upon with appreciation and respect; valuing greatly To think of (every person) as having the Spirit of the Living High regard Judgment; opinion [to value] one
Day	Point in time marked by the beginning of a new development an interval of time memorable for extraordinary events, important influences, and unusual circumstances A conflict and its result A time considered as propitious and opportune A day of contest or the contest itself A period of success, influence, accomplishment; etc.
Above	In and to a higher place and state; above Superior in rank and position Preceding That which is above and just before Higher than; rising beyond Superior to in authority and power In heaven, happiness Beyond the influence of reaching another: another
Esteemeth	Have a high opinion; looking upon with appreciation and respect; valuing greatly To think of (every person) as having the Spirit of the Living High regard Judgment; opinion [to value] every
Day	Point in time marked by the beginning of a new development an interval of time memorable for extraordinary events, important influences, and unusual circumstances A conflict and its result A time considered as propitious and opportune A day of contest or the contest itself A period of success, influence, accomplishment; etc.
Alike	Showing resemblance and similitude Equally; in the same manner, form and degree; in common. Let every
Man	One having pronounced The quality of moral righteousness and excellence The practice of moral duties and the abstinence from immorality and vice; sexual purity; chastity especially in Spirit Particular type of moral excellence especially, one of those considered to be of special importance in philosophical and religious doctrine Compare cardinal virtues Any admirable qualities and traits, inherent and essential qualities, power, etc. Efficacy; Potency; Valor; by and through the fact, quality, force, and authority of What is and must be done necessarily and seem to be done freely and from principal be fully persuaded in his own
Mind	Spirit within." — Romans 14:5

To understand this verse one must have the reflection of what defines a man For everyone who reflects what defines a man, than you are the reflection of whose image Created you For this is not for a carnal man to understand, but to gather what he can for that Man who is in him

MINDED Having or characterized by a (specific kind of) mind 2 Disposed of; having an inclination

MINE To obtain useful information from, as by purposeful effort, diligent search etc.

MINISTER One who acts as the servant of another person 2 To give attendance or aid; to be helpful or useful; contribute 3 To administer 4 To supply; furnish

MINOR ORDERS HOLY ORDERS

MIRABILE DICTU Wonderful to relate

MIRABILIA Miracles; wonders

MIRACLE An event that appears to be neither a part nor result of any known natural law or agency and is therefore often attributed to a supernatural or divine source 2 Any wonderful or amazing thing, fact or event; marvel 3 One who is of surprising merit or excellence

MIRROR Whatever reflects or depicts Truly 2 Something deserving imitation [< L *mirari* to wonder at, admire]

MIRTH Spirited gaiety, especially when accompanied by jesting or laughs; social merriment

MISERABLE Being in a state of poverty or wretched unhappiness 2 Causing extreme discomfort 3 Of inferior quality; worthless 4 Paltry or meager; skimpy 5 Deserving of pity 6 Disreputable; shameful

MISTRESS A woman who has mastered a branch of learning

MITZVAH A commandment or rule of conduct, as found in the Bible -The fulfillment of such commandment Any meritorious act

MNEMONIC Aiding or designed to aid the memory

MNEMONICS A system of principles and formulas designed to assist or improve the memory

MOCK To imitate; counterfeit 2 To defy; make futile or meaningless 3 To deceive or disappoint; delude 4 Merely imitating or resembling the reality; sham 5 A deceitful, impudent, or contemptible imitation 6 Something ludicrously futile, inadequate, or unstable

MOLD To influence, determine, or direct 2 To follow the contours of; cling to See **INFLUENCE**- To assume or come to fit a particular shape or pattern

MOLEST To disturb or annoy by unwarranted, excessive or malicious interference

MOLLIFY To make less angry, violent or agitated; sooth 2 To reduce the harshness, severity or intensity of; mitigate

MONEY The True exchange of deeds for opinion or judgement

MONOGENESIS The doctrine that the whole human race is of one **BLOOD**- (See **BLOOD**) or species

MORAL Of or related to conduct or character from the point of view of right and wrong; concerned with the goodness and badness of an action, character, disposition, etc. 2 Of good character or disposition; right and proper in behavior; righteous 3 Sexually virtuous; chaste 4 Teaching or attempting to teach standards of right and wrong; moralizing 5 Capable of distinguishing right and wrong: Man is a moral agent 6 Concerned with the establishment of principles of right and wrong, and their application; dealing with the study of ethics 7 Arising from a sense of duty and right conduct; based on principles of right and wrong: A moral obligation 8 Acting not by physical force or practical means but by appeal to character, conduct or disposition; moral support 9 Based on probability or on a general knowledge of human nature rather than on objective evidence or clear demonstration: Moral certainty 10 Conduct or behavior with regard to right and wrong, especially in sexual matters 11 A **MAXIM**

MORAL State of mind, with reference to confidence, courage, hope, zeal etc.

MORNING early part or stage of anything is the morning of the world

MORTAL Arising from or as from fear of death 2 Incurring spiritual death unless repented of and forgiven: distinguished from *venial* 3 Very great 4 Possible; conceivable

MOTHER The divine Principle; **God** 2 To bring forth; produce; create 3 To care for or protect

MOURN To feel or express grief or sorrow 2 To lament or sorrow for 3 To grieve over or bemoan 4 Bewail;deplore

MOUTH Entrance into or exit out from anything or anyone 2 Utter very clearly and distinctly 4 One source of communication

MUNIFICENT Extraordinarily generous or bountiful; liberal

MURDER Something exceedingly difficult, painful or hazardous

MUSE The Spirit or power regarded as inspiring

MYRRH Also, **SMYRNA** [OE *myrra* < L *murrha* < Gk. *mȳrra* < semitic. Cf. Arabic *murr*, Hebrew *mōr, mar* **BITTER**]

N

NAIL To secure or make certain through quick decisive action 2 Not to be moved by sentiment, pity etc.; unfeeling 3 To detect and expose, as a lie or liar 4 To focus or bring to bear on a subject, as the intellect

NAKED (paraphrased**)** Without defense or protection from knowledge; being vulnerable to Lucifer 2 Being without His Light of **God**'s sustenance; destitute 3 Therefore lacking conditions necessary for validation, as of contract; agreement; promise; terms and conditions; understanding; void of, characterized by, the state of being without astringents

NAME A word by which a Concept is known or referred to; especially, a name or title of a person 2 Semblance or form, as essence or actuality; opposed to and distinguished from, resemblance and outward form 3 The sacred and powerful **APPELLATION**- The action of giving a name to **God** 4 Distinction 5 To designate; assign for a particular job, duty 6 To achieve 7 To entitle 8 To identify 9 To specify; determine Syn. Designation, byname, nickname; moniker; denomination

NARROW Exhibiting or characterized by small means or resources 2 Minute or detailed; careful; painstaking

NASCENT Beginning to exist or develop; newly conceived **NASCENT STATE** ~ The uncombined condition of an atom in its most active state at the moment of its liberation from a compound

NATION Lit., a body of persons [< F < L *natio, -onis* birth, race < *nasci* to be born] See **PEOPLE**

NATURAL Belonging to or existing in one's nature; not acquired; innate 2 Being so because of one's inherent ability, disposition etc. 3 Conforming to nature or its usual or expected course; not exceptional; normal 4 Free from distortion; lifelike 5 Untouched by man or by the influences of civilization; untutored 6 Free from affectation or awkwardness; not forced; easy 7 reasonable or expected 8 Physical or actual, as distinguished from spiritual etc. 9 Determined by innate moral conviction 10 Founded upon reason rather than faith 11 Born out of wedlock 12 One who is naturally gifted, especially well suited to some purpose

NATURE The fundamental qualities or characteristics that together define the identity of (someone); essential character 2 The overall pattern or system of natural objects, existences, forces, events etc.; also the principle or power that appears to guide it 3 The entire material universe and its phenomena 4 The basic character or disposition of a person; heart 5 A force, drive or tendency that influences or determines the behavior or condition of a person; instinct 6 A particular character or temperament; also the person possessing it 7 Powers essential to life 8 The ingenerate state of man, as distinguished from a state of grace -By birth or disposition; innately

NAZARENE A Christian -The Nazarene Jesus 2 Anyone who takes the oath -A man or woman who shall separate themselves to vow a vow of a Nazarite, to separate themselves unto the Lord # 6:2; :13; :18- :21; Judg 13:5; :7; 16:17; Lament 4:7; Amos 2:11- :12

NEAR Closely touching one's interests or affections 2 In close relation; intimate Compare **NIGH**- Convenient; direct

NEAT [1] Characterized by or in a state of orderliness, tidiness or cleanliness 2 Free from sloppiness, vagueness or embellishment; precise 3 Ingeniously done or said; clever; smart 4 Undiluted 5 Wonderful; splendid

NEAT [2] Bovine collectively

NECESSARY Absolutely needed to accomplish a certain result; essential; indispensable 2 Being of such a nature that it must exist or occur; inevitable 3 That cannot be logically denied 4 That which is indispensable; an essential requisite Syn.

Necessary, *essential*, *indispensable*, *requisite* and *needful* refer to a person whose presence is urgently desired or required in a system, series, group, arrangement etc. A *necessary* thing may supply a wide range of wants, from mere convenience to logical completeness *Essential* refers to that which is required for the continued existence of a thing; *indispensable* may denote that which is only an adjunct, but which cannot be spared **Love is essential to be alive**

NECESSITY Urgent or desperate need, as because of poverty or accident; also a time of such need

NECK To make Love to (God) in such a manner

NEED To be obliged or compelled; have to 2 Intensive or compulsive desire or longing 3 A condition of want, danger or helplessness 4 Poverty, hardship, indigence

NEGATION Expressing, containing or characterized by negation, denial, or refusal 2 Marked by the absence of or opposition to positive or affirmative qualities

NEGATIVE Expressing, containing or characterized by negation, denial or refusal 2 Marked by the absence of or opposition to positive or affirmative qualities 3 Having the lights and darks reversed 4 By or with an expression of refusal; no: to answer 5 On the negative or opposing side 6 To prove to be false; disapprove 7 To make ineffective; counteract

NEIGHBOR One who lives near another 2 One who is near another 3 Friend; mister 4 A fellow human being [OE *nehgebur* < *neah* near + *gebur* dweller < *ge* together + *bur* dwelling]

NEO-HEBRAIC The form of the Hebrew language used in **HEBRAIC** literature after the Bible -Pertaining to post Biblical Hebrew

NEOLOGISM A new word or phrase 2 The use of new words or of new meanings for old words 3 A new doctrine, especially in theology

NERVOUS SYSTEM As with animals, so also is man with the additional function of directing and conditioning consciousness

NERVE Courage or boldness; daring 2 Arrogant assurance; brashness; effrontery 3 The source of sensitivity, patience, emotional steadiness, etc. 4 Unsteadiness of mind and muscle; nervousness 5 Muscle; sinew [< L *nervus* sinew Akin to Gk. *neuron* sinew] See **SINEW**

NERVE CENTER The focus of command and communication; headquarters

NESCIENCE Lack or absence of knowledge; ignorance; Agnosticism [< L *nesciens*, ppr. of *nescire* to be ignorant of < *ne-* not + < *scire* to know]

NEST A place containing or fostering something bad, vulgar, or dangerous; haunt; den; also, those occupying such a place

NET Anything that traps or entangles; a snare 2 Free from anything extraneous; fundamental; basic

NIGHT A condition of ignorance, gloom, painful confusion of the soul 2 Darkness; the dark 3 Mental or moral darkness; sorrow; grief 4 Anything unknown 5 The state of not knowing; obscures; hidden; mysterious -Unrevealed, unlearned, and Unknown information

NIMBLE Characterized by a quick and ready intellect -Quick at grasping and receptive

NIMBUS A luminous emanation or atmosphere believed to envelop a deity or holy person

NIRVANA The state of absolute felicity, characterized by freedom from passion, desire, suffering etc., and attained through the annihilation of the self or through the liberation of the individual from all passions and desires 2 Loosely, a similar state achieved through the merging of the self into **BRAHMA~ God** comprising the trinity; especially the personification of the first of the trinity as supreme Creator 2 The supreme soul of the universe, **(God)** self-existent, and eternal, from which all things emanate and to which all return; the absolute **PRIMORDIAL** essence~ First in order or time; original; **ELEMENTAL~** Chemically uncombined; not compounded 2 Of, belonging to or suggestive of the powerful forces at work in nature or in man 3 Relating to or concerned with first principles; **RUDIMENTARY~** A first principal, step, stage or condition 2 That which is as yet undeveloped or only partially developed 3 Being or remaining in an imperfectly or incompletely developed state; functionless; **VESTIGE~** A visible trace, impression or a sensible evidence or sign, of something absent, lost or gone; trace 2 A part or organ, small or degenerate

NISUS The exercise of power in acting or attempting to act (well pleasing in the eyes of others indiscriminately); an effort, endeavor or exertion

NO A negative reply; a denial

NOBEL Alfred Bernhard, 1833-96, Swedish industrialist, inventor of dynamite; founded by his will the Nobel Prize, awarded annually in the fields of physics, chemistry, medicine, literature and furtherance of world peace.

NOBLE Having or indicative of excellence or dignity; eminent; illustrious; worthy: a noble effort 2 Characterized by or displaying superior moral qualities; magnanimous; lofty 3 Magnificent and imposing in appearance; grand; stately 4 Of or pertaining to the nobility; aristocratic 5 Chemically inert [< MF < L *nobilis* noble, well-known. Akin to L *noscere* to know]

NOBLESSE OBLIGE Those of high birth, wealth or social position must behave generously or nobly toward others; literally, nobility obligates

NOETIC Of, pertaining to or originating in intellectual or rational activity

NOLI ME-TANGERE A warning caution against touching or meddling

NOMISM Strict adherence to religious or moral law in human conduct

NORMAL Conforming to or consisting of a pattern, process or standard regarded as usual or typical; regular; natural 2a Well adjusted to the outside world; without marked or persistent mental aberrations 2b An average skill, ability, intelligence etc. 3a Not exposed to infection or modified by experimental treatment 3b Occurring naturally

NOTABLE Worthy of remembering; memorable; distinguished 2 Capable of being noted or perceived 3 Industrious or efficient

NOTE A sign, suggestion or element by which a quality, condition, fact etc., may be recognized or known; a distinctive mark 2 A record of impressions, observations, reflections etc. 3 A written comment amending, criticizing or explaining a passage in a book, manuscript etc., as in the margin of a page 4 Distinction; importance; reputation 5 Notice; observation; attention 6 Manner of speaking; attitude 7 To become aware of; observe 8 To pay attention to; heed carefully

NOTED Well known by reputation 2 Taken note of 3 Committed to memory

NOTICE The act of noticing or observing; attention; cognizance 2 Respectful treatment; civility [< OF < L *notitia* fame, renown < *notus* known]

NOUMENON An object of intuition that can be perceived by the intellect only and not by the senses 2 The necessarily postulated ground or cause for phenomena, transcending sense perception and theoretically unknowable 3 An object in itself, independent of our perception of it

NOW In such circumstances; things being the way they are

NUCLEUS A central point or part around which other things are gathered; inner or essential element; core 2 A center of growth or development; basis; **KERNEL~** The central part of anything **(cont. NUCLEUS)~** A complex **SPHERICAL BODY~** Pertaining to the heavenly bodies; celestial **(cont. NUCLEUS)~** surrounded by a thin **MEMBRANE~** A thin, pliable, sheet like layer of tissue serving to cover or line an organ or part, separate adjoining cavities, or connect adjoining structures [< L *membrana*, lit., **LIMB ~** (The edge of a heavenly body) coating] **(cont. NUCLEUS)~** and embedded in the **PROTOPLASM~** The physicochemical basis of living matter **(cont. NUCLEUS)~** of most cells containing chromatin and essential to the process of heredity and to other vital activities, as growth, **ASSIMILATION~** The process by which all new experiences, when received into the consciousness, is modified so as to be incorporated with the results of previous conscious processes, **REPRODUCTION~** The process by which an animal or plant gives rise to another of its kind **(cont. NUCLEUS)~** Any of certain masses of gray matter composed of nerve cells and found in the brain and spinal cord 2 The brightest portion in the head of a comet or in the center of a **NEBULA~** Any interstellar mass of cloudlike appearance and vast extent, often luminous, and composed of gaseous matter in various degrees of density -A **GALAXY~** Any very large system of stars, nebulae, or other celestial bodies 2 Any brilliant group, as of persons

NUMINOUS Evoking awe or reverence, as the presence of something holy or divine -The numinous The part of religious experience that is characterized by feelings of fascination and awe

NURSE A person who cares for the sick, injured or **INFIRM~** Lacking resolution, stability or firmness of purpose **(cont. NURSE)** 2 One who or that which fosters, nourishes, protects or promotes 3 To look after the wants of; to minister to 4 To take steps to cure 5 To use or operate carefully so as to preserve from injury, damage or strain 6 To preserve or prolong deliberately

NURTURE The aggregate of environmental conditions and influences acting on an organism subsequent to its conception 2 To bring up or train; educate

O

O An exclamation used in direct address, especially in earnest or solemn appeal, as in prayer or invocation: O Lord, my countrymen!

OATH The careless or profane use of the name of **God** or other sacred person

OBDT Obedient

OBEDIENCE Submission; compliance 2 Spiritual jurisdiction or control; also, an area or group of persons under such jurisdiction

OBEDIENT Complying with or conforming to a command, restraint etc.; dutiful 2 Deferring habitually to laws, superiors etc., docile; compliant

OBEISANCE Courtesy, reverence or homage; also an act or gesture expressing this

OBEY To comply with or carry out the command, request etc., of; be obedient to 2 To comply with or execute (a command, request etc.) 3 To be guided, controlled or actuated by; act in accordance with [< OF *obeir* < L *obedire, var,* of *oboedire* to give ear, obey < *ob-* towards + *audire* to hear]

OBJECT Anything that is or may be apprehended by the senses; especially, a tangible or visible thing 2 The purpose or end of an action; goal; aim 3 One who or that which is the focus or center of thought

OBJECTIVE Free from or independent of personal feelings, opinions, prejudice etc.; detached; unbiased 2 Pertaining to what is external or independent of the mind; real 3 Treating, stressing or dealing with external phenomena, as distinct from inner or imaginary feelings and thoughts Syn. **PURPOSE**

***OBJECTIVITY** Material reality

OBLATE Consecrated or devoted to a religious life See ***OFFER**

OBLATION Any grateful or solemn offering

OBLATION The duty, promise, contract etc., by which one is bound 2 The constraining or binding power of a law, promise, conscience, word, etc. 3 What one owes in return for a service, favor etc.; also the favor or service itself 4 The condition of being indebted for a kindness, benefit etc. Syn **DUTY**

OBLIGATORY Imperative

OBLIGE To place (one) under obligation, as for a service, favor etc.; give (one) cause for gratitude 2 To compel, bind or constrain, as by command, promise etc. 3 To do a favor or service for

OBLIGING Disposed to do favors; accommodating; kind

OBLIQUITY Mental or moral deviation

OBLIVION The state or fact of being completely forgotten 2 The state of fact of completely forgotten; forgetfulness 3 Heedlessness; disregard [< OF < L *oblivio, -onionis* < *oblivisci* to forget]

OBLIVIOUS Not conscious or aware; unmindful 2 Forgetful or given to forgetfulness See **ABSTRACTED**

OBLOQUY Abusive and defamatory language, especially when directed at one by a large group of people; vilification 2 The state or condition resulting from such abuse; disgrace [< LL *oboloquium* contradiction < *obloqui* < *ob-* against + *loqui* to speak]

OBSCURE Not clear or plain to the mind; hard to understand; obtuse 2 Not clear or distinct to the senses; difficult to discern; indistinct; faint 3 Not readily discovered; hidden; remote 4 without distinction or fame; inconspicuous; humble 5 To render obscure, vague, indefinite etc.

OBSECRATE To supplicate [< L *obsecratus*, pp. Of *obsecrare* to beseech < *ob-* on account of + *sacrare* to make sacred < *sacer* sacred]

OBSEQUIOUS Excessively obedient or submissive; sycophantic; servile 2 Dutiful; obedient [< L *obsequiosus* compliant < *obsequium* compliance < *obsequi* to comply with < *ob-* towards + *sequi* to follow]

OBSERVANT Attentive, careful or quick in observing; heedful; alert 2 Strict or careful in obeying

OBSERVE To see or notice; perceive 2 To watch attentively 3 To make careful observation 4 To follow or comply with; abide by 5 To celebrate or solemnize in the proper or customary manner 6 To make a remark or comment 7 To take notice 8 To look at or attend without taking part Syn. **CELEBRATE, SEE** [< L *observare* to watch < *ob-* towards, against + *servare* to keep, protect]

OBSESS To occupy the mind to an excessive degree; preoccupy; harass; haunt [< L *obsessus*, pp. of *obsidere* to occupy, besiege < *ob-* before + *sedere* to sit]

OBSESSION That which obsesses, preoccupies or vexes, as a persistent idea or feeling 2a An unwanted or compulsive idea or emotion persistently coming to awareness 2b The compulsive state itself 3 The act of obsessing or the state of being obsessed

OBSOLETE Syn. *Obsolete, obsolescent, archaic* and *rare* are applied to words that are now seldom or never used An *obsolete* word is no longer used either in speech or writing, usually because it has been supplanted by a different word; *oscitate*, meaning to yawn, is now *obsolete*. An *obsolescent* word, tho still in use, is becoming *obsolete*; *mercaptan*, a former chemical term, is such a word. *Archaic* words were current at some time in the past, and appear in the works of Shakespeare, the Bible etc., but unlike *obsolete* words they are still used for effect because they have an unmistakable flavor of their period or milieu, or are used by persons whose vocabularies were formed in a distinctively earlier era. *Rare* words may be *archaic* or current, but are little used; *trow* is an *archaic* word, and *obsecrate* is an example of a *rare* word

OBSTINATE Unreasonably fixed in one's purpose or opinion; unyielding; inflexible; stubborn 2 Difficult to overcome, control or cure [< L *obstinatus* stubborn < *obstinare* to persist < *obstare* See **OBSTACLE**] Syn. *Obstinate, stubborn, dogged, pertinacious, headstrong, obdurate, pig-headed* and *mulish* mean unyielding in opinion or action One may be *obstinate* in a particular instance, but is *stubborn* by disposition *Dogged* also refers to character or disposition, but it alone of all these words is not necessarily deprecatory, and frequently refers to a commendable perseverance: a dogged determination to find out the meaning of the Word *Pertinacious* refers to perseverance in action that annoys others, while *headstrong* implies persistence in behavior that is foolish, reckless or arrogant *Obdurate* describes a person who is hard and unfeeling, and unmoved by compassion, pity etc. *Pig-headed* usually suggests a stupid obstinacy, *mulish*, an irrational stubbornness See **INFLEXIBLE**

obt. Obedient

OBTAIN To gain possession of, especially by effort; acquire; get 2 To arrive at; reach 3 To be prevalent or in effect 4 To succeed; prevail [< to hold]

OBTEST To invoke as a witness 2 To beseech; implore

OBVERSE Turned toward or facing One 2 **INVERSE~** Reversed or opposite in order, effect etc. 2 Inverted 3 Having an opposite direction of change in variables 4 That which is in direct contrast or opposition; the reverse; opposite 5a The performance or result of an inversion 5b A reciprocal (**cont. OBVERSE**) 3 Constituting a counterpart 4 The front or principle side of anything

OBVERT To present the principle or other side of

OBVIATE To prevent or counter (an objection, difficulty etc.) by effective measures; dispose of; provide for [< L *obviatus*, pp. of *obviare* to meet, withstand < *obvius* See **OBVIOUS**]

OCCASION An important or extraordinary event 2 A favorable condition; opportunity 3 The immediate grounds for some action or state; reason 4 A need or requirement; exigency 5 Personal needs or wants 6 To cause or bring about, especially in an accidental or incidental manner

Od God; a euphemism used in oaths Also Odd. [Alter. of **God**]

-ODE [1] Way; path

-ODE [2] Like; resembling; having the nature of [< Gk. *-odes* < *eiods* **form**]

OFFEND To be disagreeable

Syn. *Offend, insult, affront, exasperate* and *outrage* mean to deal with so as to arouse hostility, anger, resentment etc. To offend is to cause displeasure, whether intentionally or not; to *insult* is to treat with deliberate contempt, in order to humiliate or mortify One *affronts* another by belittling him to his face, by discourtesy, or by insolence To *exasperate* is to annoy or irritate exceedingly The strongest of these words is *outrage*, which implies the arousal of extreme resentment and indignation in the offended person
Job 34:31; Prov 18:19; ***Isa 29:21;

OFFENSE Syn. *Offense, crime, sin, error, fault* and *wrong* denote a violation of what is regarded as right or proper *Offense* is the broadest of these words, embracing any transgression of law, morals or good manners More specifically, a *crime* is a violation of common or statute law, such as envy or anger An *error* is primarily a mistake as to fact or Truth; the word stresses a person's ignorance, rather than his deliberation A *fault* is a trifling or petty offense with regard to the harm or injustice it does
***2 Chron 19:10; ***Ecc 10:4; Hosea 5:15; Haba 1:11; Matt 16:23; 18:7; Luke 17:1; ***Acts 24:16; Rom 4:25; 5:15; ***:17; 14:20; 16:17; 1 Corin 10:32; ***2 Corin 6:3; ***Philip 1:10; 1 Peter 2:8

OFFER To present or suggest for acceptance or rejection; consideration; a purpose, idea or ideal kept before the mind as an end of effort or action 3 To present yourself with solemnity or in worship 4 To show readiness to do or attempt; purpose 5 To present; appear 6 Token of devotion; plan; design; aiming at a particular thing to be effective or attained with a practical result; settled resolution; with determination in constancy; in proposition 7 Having the intention of doing and accomplishing, with determination and a clear exercising will
Gen 22:2; **Exod 18:12; **22:29; **23:18; **29:36; :38-:39; :41; 30:9; **34:25; Levi 1:3; ***2:12-:14; 3:1; **:3; :7; 6:22; 7:12-:16; :18; **:25; :33; 10:1; **10:15; 12:7; 14:12; :19; :30; 16:6; :9; :24; **17:4-:5; **:7-:8; 19:5-:6; ****21:6 (the bread of their God); ****21:8 (the bread of your God); 21:17; :21; ;22:4; :18-:25; :27; ****23:8; :12; *:27; *:36; ****Deut 12:13-:14; *****20:10-:11; ****23:18; **27:7; **28:68; 32:38; ****33:19; Josh 22:23; **:27-:29; *****Judge 5:2; *****:9; 6:26; ***11:31; ***1 Sam 2:29; ***2 Kings 17:36; ***1 Chron 29:1; :14; ***:17; ***Ezra 1:4; Nehem 4:2; 10:37; :39; ****11:2; **Job 6:22; 42:8; *****Psalm 4:5; ***27:6; *******Psalm 40:6 (my ears You have opened); 50:14; *******50:23; ****51:16; :19; ****96:8; ****Psalm 119:108; Prov 7:14; Isa 1:11; 43:23; 56:7; 57:6-:8; 66:3; :20; **Jerem 6:20; 7:21-**:22; 14:12; 33:18; Ezek 16:21; 20:31; :40; ****36:38 (flocks of men); 43:19; 44:11; Dan 9:27; Hosea 4:13; ***:14 (the people who do not understand ...); *******6:6; ******8:13; *9:4; **14:2; Joel 1:13; 2:14; Micah 6:6; Zeph 3:10; Haggai 2:14; Malachi 1:7-:8; :10; :13; 2:12-:13; 3:3; ***3:8; **Matt 5:24; Mark 12:33; *Acts 7:42; *8:18; 1 Corin 8:1; Philip 2:17; Heb 5:1; :7; 10:5-:6; :11; :14; ***:18; ****13:15; James 2:21; ****1 Peter 2:5; Rev 8:3

OFFICE The duty, charge or trust of a person 2 Any act done or intended to be done for another; a service; favor Gen 41:13; 1 Chron 6:32; 9:22; :26; :31; Psalm 109:8; Isa 22:19; Jer 52:25; **Acts 1:20;

OFFICIATE To act or serve as a minister [< Med. L *officiatus*, pp. of *officiare* to perform **your** duty]

OFFSCOURING A social outcast Lam 3:45; 1 Corin 4:13

OIL To bribe or flatter

OIL To bribe or flatter

OLIVE BRANCH Anything offered as an emblem of peace

OMEGA Is translated as the end; the last

OMNIA VINCIT AMOR *Latin* **Love conquers all things**

OMNIFARIOUS Producing all kinds

OMNIPOTENCE Unlimited and universal power, especially as a divine attribute 2 **God** 3 Unlimited power or authority

OMNISCIENCE Infinite knowledge

ONENESS Singleness; unity; sameness 2 Agreement; concord 3 The quality of being unique
OPEN Affording approach, view, passage or access because of the absence or removal of barriers, restrictions, etc. 2 To become receptive or enlightened; to begin to be 3 Officially declared to be undefended, and so immune under international law from bombardment 4 Frank and communicative; not given to deception or concealment 5 Accessible to new ideas; unprejudiced 6 Receptive 7 With no restrictions on those allowed to attend or participate 8 Not containing any of its limit points 9 Improvd or made possible access to or through 10 Made available or more widely known 11 Become more communicative or confiding 12 To begin or be formally established
OPEN MINDED Free from prejudices conclusions; amenable to reason; receptive 2 Free from captivation
OPINION A conclusion or judgment held with confidence, but falling short of positive knowledge 2 A judgment or estimate of the excellence or value of a person 3 A common or prevailing sentiment
OPPORTUNIST One who uses every opportunity to contribute to the achievement of some end, and who is relatively uninfluenced by moral principles or sediment
ORACLE A person of unquestioned wisdom or knowledge, or something regarded as infallible authority 2 A wise saying 3 A divine command or communication; also the Holy of Holies in the Temple [< OF < L *oraculum* < *orare* to speak, pray,? < *os, oris* mouth]
ORDAIN To order or decree; enact; establish 2 To predestine; destine: said of **God**, fate etc. 3 To invest with ministerial or priestly functions [< OF *ordener* < L *ordinare* to set in order < *ordo, -inis* order, arrangement]
ORDEAL A severe test of character or endurance; a trying course of experience
ORDER A condition in which there is a methodical, proper and harmonious arrangement of successive things 2 A social condition of peace and harmony 3 A class or body of persons united by some common bond or purpose 4 Any 1 of the 9 grades or choirs of angels 5 Suitable care; preparation 6 In accordance with rule or proper procedure 7 Neat; tidy -For the purpose of -Quickly; without delay 8 To decide or will 9 To ordain 10 The arrangement or disposition of people or things in relation to each other according to a particular sequence, pattern, or method 11 Used to describe the quality, nature, or intention of something
ORDERLY Having regard for arrangement, method or system 2 Peaceful 3 Characterized by neatness and order
ORDINATION The state of being ordained, regulated or settled 2 Natural or proper order
ORGAN An instrument or agency of communication 2 An agency for or a means of getting something done
ORGANIC Inherent in or pertaining to the fundamental structure of something; constitutional
ORGANIZATION A number of individuals systematically united for some end or work
ORGANIZE To bring together or form as a whole or combination, as for a common objective 2 To arrange systematically; order

ORGANON A system of rules and principles considered as an instrument of knowledge or thought

ORIENT The eastern sky; also, dawn; sunrise 2 To adjust according to recognized facts or Truths 3 Resembling sunrise; bright 4 Ascending; rising

ORIENTAL Very bright, clear and pure

ORIENTATION Awareness of one's own temporal, spatial and personal relationships 2 The particular disposition of the constituent atoms in a compound, especially as determined by electrical forces

ORISON A devotional prayer

ORMUZD The supreme deity of the Zoroastrian religion, the Creator of the world, source of Light and embodiment of the principles of good, essentially opposed to Ahriman, the spirit of darkness and evil: also called Ahura Mazda Also **Or'mazd** (mazd) [< Persian Ormazd, ult. < *Avestan Ahuro-Mazdao*, lit., wise lord]

ORNAMENTS A person regarded as a source of honor or credit

ORTHODOX Adhering to traditional practice or belief; conventional 2 Holding the commonly accepted or established faith, especially in representing a number of different Christian creeds; conventional [< LL *orthodoxus* < Gk. *orthodoxos* < *orthos* right + *doxa* **opinion** < *dokeein* **to think**]

OSCULANT Intermediate in character between two groups of organisms 2 Adhering closely; embracing

OSCULATE To bring or come into close contact or union 2 To touch so as to have three or more points in common 3 To have (characteristics) in common

OSMOSIS Any gradual process of assimilation, as of facts, ideas or habits, that seems to occur without conscious or deliberate effort

OSTENSIBLE Offered as real or genuine

OSTENSIVE Manifest 2 Set forth as a principle that manifestly includes the proposition to be proved

O TEMPORAL! O MORES! O the times! O the morals! [L]

OTHERWORLDLY Of, characteristic of an ideal or Spiritual world, as of heaven 2 Concerned with matters of the Spirit or intellect, especially to the neglect of material things

OUGHT To have a moral duty; be obliged 2 To be advisable, expedient or proper

OUT Away from specified and usual places 2 From among others 3 So as to remove, deplete, or exhaust 4 To a result or conclusion; to the end 5 Into being or activity, or out of a state manifest to the senses 6 Aloud and boldly; without constraint 7 So as to be extended or projecting 8 Into the care or control of another 9 From a state of tension, irritation, or dispute to a state of ease or composure 10 Into consciousness 11 By far; incomparably 12 Past or beyond the point of danger or trouble 13 Beyond the limits, scope, or usual position 14 Influenced, inspired, or caused by 15 Not in office or a position of power 16 A way of dodging responsibility or involvement; a means of escape 17 To be revealed 18 To a greater extent; surpassing; more; better; beyond

OUT-CLASS To surpass decisively in skill, quality or power

OUTWIT To trick or baffle by superior ingenuity or cunning 2 To surpass in intelligence

OVERCOME To get the better of in any conflict or struggle; defeat; conquer 2 To prevail over or surmount, as difficulties, obstacles etc. 3 To prevail over or surmount, as difficulties, obstacles, etc. 4 To render (someone) helpless, as by emotion, sickness, etc. 5 To gain mastery; win [OE *ofercuman*]

OVERHAUL To examine carefully for needed repairs; also to take apart for this purpose 2 To make all needed repairs in; renovate 3 A thorough inspection 4 Examination and complete repair

OVERHEAR To hear (something said or someone speaking) without the knowledge or intention of the speaker

OVERJOY To delight or please greatly

OVERSEE To survey; watch 2 To examine; **PERUSE~** To read carefully or attentively 2 To examine; scrutinize

OVERSET To overcome a disorder mentally or physically; disconcert 2 A turning over; upset 3 Excessive of composed type

OVERSHADOW To render unimportant or insignificant by comparison

OVERSOUL The spiritual being or element of the universe that unites and influences all human souls

OVERTURE An act or proposal intended to initiate a relationship

OVINE Of or pertaining to sheep; sheep like

OWE To have or possess by virtue some condition or cause 2 To cherish (a certain feeling) toward another 3 To be indebted; to be obliged to pay or repay 4 To be obligated to render or offer 5 To be in debt

OWN Belonging to oneself; peculiar; particular; individual; as an intensive or **to indicate the exclusion of others** 2 Being of the nearest degree 3 To receive one's reward; come into one's rightful position 4 To admit or acknowledge 5 To confess forthrightly and fully -To possess, have; later, to owe 6 To receive one's reward; come into one's rightful position 7 To keep up with one's work, or remain undefeated Syn. See **CONFESS; HAVE**

OX A man who is persistent, but stubborn, cautious, but hesitant, moody, and quick-tempered

OXIDATION The process or state of undergoing combination with oxygen 2 The process by which atoms lose or are deprived of valence electrons, or begin sharing them with a more electronegative element

OXIDATION NUMBER The number of electrons an atom has lost or is sharing with a more electronegative element, if electrons shared by atoms of the same element are divided equally between them

OXIDATION REDUCTION Oxidation or reduction considered in regard to their reciprocal relationship

P

PACE With the permission (of): used to express courteous disagreement [< L, ablative of *pax, pacis* peace, pardon]

PACIFIST One who opposes military ideals, war or military preparedness, and proposes that all international disputes be settled by arbitration

PACIFY To bring peace to; end war or strife in (an area) 2 To allay the anger or agitation of; appease; calm; quiet; soothe [< L *pacificare* < *pax, pacis* peace + *facere* to make]

PAIN The unpleasant sensation or feeling resulting from or accompanying some derangement, overstrain or obstruction of the physical powers 2 Any distressing or afflicting emotion 3 Care, trouble, effort or exertion expended on anything 4 To cause pain to; hurt; grieve; disquiet [< OF *peine* pain, penalty < L *poena* < Gk. *poine* fine, penalty]

PAIR PRODUCTION The instantaneous conversion of a **PHOTON~** A quantum of radiant energy moving with the velocity of light and an energy proportional to its frequency (cont. **PAIR PRODUCTION**) into an **(ELECTR)ON~** An atomic particle carrying a unit charge of negative electricity [< Gk. *elektron* amber], and a **POSITRON** by its passage through a strong electrical field

PAL A friend or chum [< Romany *pal* brother, mate, ult. < Skt. *bharate*, Akin to **BROTHER**]

PALATAL Produced with the blade of the tongue near the hard palate

PALATINE A VASSAL~ A dependent, retainer or servant of any kind; a slave or bondman -Having the character of or pertaining to a vassal; tributary 2 Servile -The state of being a vassal; also, the duties and obligations of a vassal 3 Servitude in general (cont.

PALATINE~ Exercising royal privileges over his territory

PALE Feeble and unimpressive Syn. Feeble, weak, insipid, bland, poor, inadequate; uninspired, unimaginative, spiritless, lifeless; pathetic 2 To seem less impressive or important

PALI The sacred language of the early Buddhist writings, still surviving in the religious literature of Burma and Thailand [< Skt. *pali* line, canon; *pali* (bhasa) *canonieal* (language)]

PALINGENESIS A new or second birth, as into a higher life or form of being 2 The theory or belief that souls are continually reborn

PALLADIAN Characterized by wisdom or learning

PALM The reward or symbol of victory or preeminence 2 Triumph

PALSY To cause to tremble or become helpless as from fear or rage

PALATAL Produced with the blade of the tongue near the hard plate

PALTER To speak or act insincerely; equivocate; lie 2 To be fickle or capricious; trifle 3 To haggle or quibble

PALTRY Having little or no worth or value; trifling; trivial 2 Compatible; petty

PAMPER To treat very indulgently; gratify the whims or wishes of; coddle 2 To feed with rich food; glut

PAN All; every; the whole 2 Comprising, including or applying to all

PANSOPHY Comprehensive or universal knowledge [< **PAN~** + Gk. *sophia* wisdom]

PANTOLOGY A system of comprehending all departments of human knowledge

*PARABLE A short narrative making a moral point by comparison with natural or homely things [< OF *parabole* < LL *parabola* allegory, speech < Gk. *parabole* a placing side by side, a comparison < *para* beside + *ballein* to throw Doublet of **PALAVER, PARABOL, PAROLE**]

PARACLETE One called to the aid of another; an advocate -The Holy Spirit as a helper or comforter [< Of *paraclet* < LL *paracletus* < LGk. *parakletos* comforter, advocate < *parakalein* to call to one's aid < *para~* to + *kalein* to call]

PARALLELISM The doctrine that the relation between mind and matter is one of **CONCOMITANT~** Existing or occurring together; attendant -An attendant circumstance, state or thing [< L *concomitans, -antis*, ppr. of *concomitari* < *com-* with + *comitari* to accompany]

PARALLELISM Essential likeness; similarity 2 The doctrine that the relation between mind and matter is one of concomitant or parallel variation, and not one of cause and effect

PARALOGISM False or illogical reasoning See **FALLACY** [< Gk. *paralogismos* < *paralogizesthai* to reason falsely, ult. < *para* beside + *logos* word, reason]

PARALIZE To render powerless, ineffective, or inactive [< F *paralyser*, back formation < *paralysie* palsy]

PARAMOUNT Superior to all others; of chief importance 2 Having the highest authority or rank Syn. See **DOMINANT** A supreme lord; highest ruler [< L *ad montem* to **the hill**]

PARAPHRASE A restatement of the meaning of a passage, work etc., as for clarity

PARLEY A conference, as with an enemy; a discussion of terms -To hold a conference, especially with an enemy See **PARABLE**

PARTURIENT Bringing forth or about to bring forth young 2 Producing or about to produce an idea, discovery etc. [< L *parturiens, -entis*, ppr. of *parturire* to be in labor, desiderative of *parere* to bring forth]

PASS To succeed in meeting the requirements of (a test, trial etc.) 2 To go beyond or surpass; exceed; transcend: It passes all comprehensions 3 To cause or allow (a specified period of time) to elapse; spend 4 To cause or allow to move, go past, proceed, advance etc. 5 To approve or sanction; ratify; enact 6 To be approved or sanctioned by 7 To cause or allow to get through (a test, trial etc.) 8 To convey or transfer from one to another; circulate; transmit: to pass the Word 9 To permit to go unnoticed or unmentioned 10 To pledge or promise 11 To obtain a way; secure a passage 12 To lead or extend; run 13 To come to an end; draw to a close 14 To go about or circulate; be current 15 To change or move from one condition; place, etc., to another; to be altered or transferred 16 To be mutually exchanged 17 To take place; happen; occur 18 To be allowed or permitted without challenge, pressure etc. 19 To undergo a test etc., successfully; fulfill the requirements 20 To be approved, sanctioned 21 To come to an end; disappear 22 To give out or circulate as genuine; palm off 23 A permit, order or license giving the bearer authority to enter, move about, depart etc., without the usual restrictions 24 A state of affairs; situation -To cause to be fulfilled, accomplished or realized

PASSABLE Capable of being passed, crossed etc. -Fairly good or acceptable; tolerable

-PASSION Any intense, extreme or overpowering emotion or feeling 2 Ardent affection or love 3 Overwhelming anger or rage 4 An outburst of strong feeling, especially of violence or anger 5 Formerly in philosophy and psychology, the state or condition of being acted upon

[< OF *passiun* < L] *passio, -onis* suffering < *passus* pp. of *pati* to suffer] Rom 1:26; 7:5; 1 Corin 7:9; Gala 5:24; Col 3:5; 1 Thess 4:;

-**PASSIVE** Submitting or yielding without resistance or opposition; submissive 2 The passive voice

-**PASSIVE RESISTANCE** A method of demonstrating opposition to some authority or law by nonviolent acts as voluntary fasting etc.

PASTOR A shepherd [< AF *pastour*, OF *pastur* < L *pastor, -oris* shepherd, lit., feeder < *pascere* to feed] Eph 4:11

PASTORAL Of or pertaining to shepherds, rustic or rural life 2 Having the characteristics usually associated with rural life, as innocence, simplicity, charm etc. 3 Pertaining to a clergyman or to his duties 4 A letter from a pastor to his flock or from a bishop to a clergy or people of his **DIOCESE~** [< L *dioecesis* district < Gk. *dioikesis*, orig., management of a house < *dia-* completely + *oikein* to dwell, manage] 1a A book or treatise on the function of a pastor 1b The pastoral epistles (which see)

-**PATER** Short for **PATERNOSTER**; from the rapid repetition of the prayer

PATH A course of life or action Gen 49:17; # 22:24; 2 Sam 22:37; Job 6:18; 8:13; 13:27; 19:8; 24:13; 28:7; 30:13; 38:20; Psalm 1:1; 16:11; 17:5; 18:36; 25:10; 65:11; 78:50; **85:13; 119:105; 139:3; Prov 1:15; 2:8; :15; :18; :19; ***3:6; :17; 4:11; :18; ***:26; 5:6; 8:2; ***12:28; Isa 2:3; 40:14; 42:16; 59:7; Jer 6:16; ***Hebrews 12:13;

PATHETIC FALLACY The ascribing of human emotions and characteristics to nature or things of nature

*PATHFINDER** One skilled in leading or finding or finding a way, especially in unknown regions

PATHO- Suffering; disease: *pathogenesis* [< Gk. *pathos* suffering]

PATHOS A quality that evokes or arouses pity or sadness Syn. Poignancy, tragedy, sadness, pitifulness, piteousness, pitiableness

PATHOLOGY The branch of medical science that treats of the origin, nature, causes, and development of disease 2 The sum of the conditions, processes, and effects in the course of a disease

-**PATHY** Suffering; affection: *sympathy* 2 Disease, or the treatment of disease [< Gk. -patheia < -pathos suffering]

*PATIENT** Possessing or demonstrating quiet, uncomplaining endurance under distress or annoyance; long suffering 2 Tolerant, tender and forbearing 3 Capable of tranquility awaiting results or outcomes 4 Capable of bearing 5 Preserving; diligent 6 Anything passively affected by external actions or impressions [to suffer] Psalm 37:7; 40:1; Ecc 7:8; Acts 26:3; Rom 2:7; 12:12; 1 Thess 5:14; 2 Tim 2:24; Heb 6:15; James 5:7; :8; 1 Peter 2:20

*PATRON** One who protects, fosters, countenances or supports some person; a protector; benefactor 2 A patron saint (which see)

*PATTERN** An original or model proposed for or worthy of imitation 2 A complex of integrated parts functioning as a whole 3 A representative, example, sample or instance Ezek 43:10; Phil 3:17; 1 Tim 1:16; 2 Tim 1:13; Titus 2:7

*PAX** Peace [< L, peace]

*PAX VOBIS CUM** *Latin* **Peace be with you**

*PAY To render or give, as attention 2 To be worthwhile 3 To afford full return; be fully effective 4 Reward; also retribution 5 A person considered with respect to his ability to pay or his promptness in paying -To appease Exo 22:16; :17; Deut 23:21; 2 Sam 15:7; 2 Kings 18:14; Job 22:27; 41:11; Psalm 22:25; ***Psalm 76:11; Prov 5:1; 7:24; ***19:17; ***29:12; ***Ecc 5:4; *:5; *Isa 23:18; **Ezek 16:31; ***Micah 3:11; ****Mark 12:14; ****Acts 21:24; Rom 13:6; **James 2:3

*PEACE A state of mental or physical quiet or tranquility; calm; repose 2 The absence or cessation of war 3 Public order and tranquility; freedom from riot or violence 4 A state of reconciliation after strife or enmity 5 Freedom from mental agitation or anxiety 6 In a state or condition of order AND harmony -To become quiet or silent ...Gen 26:29; ...28:21; ***Exod 14:14; ***18:23; ***20:24; ....Lev 10:3; 17:5; 19:5; 26:6; # 6:26; ***25:12; 30:4; Deut 2:26; ....20:10; ***23:6; 27:7; 29:19; Josh. 9:15; ....Judg 6:23; :24; 11:31; 18:6; ....19:20; ....1 Sam 10:27; 16:4; 20:42; 25:35; 2 Sam 17:3; 20:19; *1 Kings 2:6; 4:24; 5:12; 20:18; ****22:17; ****2 Kings 18:31; 20:19; 22:20; 1 Chron 4:40; ***12:17; 22:9; 2 Chron 15:5; ****18:16; ****30:22; ***31:2; 34:28; Est 9:30; ***10:3; ***Job 5:24; **11:3; 13:13; 22:21; 25:2; Psalm 4:8; 7:4; 28:3; 29:11; ****34:14; ***37:11; ***37:37; 39:2; 55:18; 72:3; :7; 83:1; 85:8; :10; ****119:165; ***120:6; ****120:7; 122:6; :; :7; ***:8; Prov 3:2; ****:17; ***11:12; ***12:20; ****16:7; 17:28; Isa 9:6; :7; ***26:3; :12; 27:5; ****32:17; :18; ****33:7; 39:8; ***42:14; 45:7; 48:18; ****52:7; 54:1; ***:10; ....:13; 55:12; 57:2; ***:11; ********:19; 62:6 Isaiah 62:6 I have set watchmen on your walls, O Jerusalem; They shall never hold their peace day or night. You who make mention of the Lord, do not keep silent; 66:12; Jerem. 29:11; 33:6; Ezek 38:11; ****Dan 4:1; ***6:2; 10:19; ***11:21; ***:24; Micah 5:5; ***Nahum 1:15; Zechariah ********6:13; ********8:16; ****:19; Mal 2:5; :6; Matt 5:9; 10:13; Mark 5:34; 9:50; Luke 1:79; ....2:29; ....7:50; ....8:48; 10:5; :6; ****19:42; 24:36; ****John 14:27; **; 16:33; Acts 9:31; 10:36; Rom 5:1; 8:6; 12:18; 14:19; 15:13; 2 Corin 13:11; ****Gal 5:22; Eph 2:14; *****6:15; Philip 4:7; 4:9; Titus 3:2; Heb 12:14; ***James 2:16; 3:17; :18; 1 Peter 5:14; 2 Peter 1:2; *Rev 6:4

GRAY Characteristic of **VENERABLE**- Exciting reverential feelings because of sacred or historic associations

-It means to *regard* with profound respect mingled with other feelings We *venerate* that which we judge objectively to be of great worth, as a holy person *revere* implies respect, which have been added personal affection and awe; *revere* is chiefly applied to persons but should be applied only to God who is in every person and not the person himself: to *revere* God In strict usage, we *worship* or *adore* that which we consider Divine; *worship* refers to participation in all God says, and *adar*, to the sense of personal gratitude for Divine favor which the worshiper feels In extended use, we *worship* God by the giving of thanks for all things, and adore the invisible attributes of Him who excites our ardent admiration

PEACE CORPS A U.S. Government organization, established in 1961, that trains and sends volunteers to live in and aid underdeveloped countries by teaching farming, building etc.

PEACE OFFERING An offering made for the sake of peace or reconciliation 2 Formerly, a Levitical sacrificial offering

PEACH Any particularly inner beautiful, pleasing or excellent person

PEAK [1] The maximum development, strength, value etc., of something 2 To assume the form of a peak or peaks

PEAK [2] To become sickly, weak or dispirited

PECCAVI Latin A confession of guilt; literally, I have sinned

PECULIAR Having a character exclusively its own; unlike anything else or anything of the same class or kind; specific 2 Singular; odd; strange 3 Select or special; separate 4 Belonging particularly or exclusively to one 5 A member of the sect known as the **PECULIAR PEOPLE** See **CHARACTERISTIC**

PECULIAR PEOPLE A denomination of Christians who hold that sinless perfection is immediately obtainable by those willing to seek and accept it

PEER An equal, as in natural gifts or in social rank 2 An equal before the law 3 A companion; mate

PEERLESS Of unequal excellence

PEG A reason or excuse for an action

PEOPLE Human beings as distinguished from animals 2 Animals collectively

PERCEIVE To become aware of (something) through the senses, see, feel, hear, taste, smell Or 2 To come to understand; apprehend with the mind [< OF *perceveir* < L *percipere* to seize, perceive < per- thoroughly + *capere* to take]

PERDITION Lesson; diminution [< OF *perdiciun* < L *perditio, -onis* < *perditus*, ppr. of *perdere* to destroy, lose < *per-* throw, away + *dare* to give]

PERFECT Having all the elements or qualities requisite or necessary to its nature or kind; complete 2 Thoroughly and completely skilled or informed 3 Accurately or closely reproducing or corresponding to a type or original; exact 4 Thorough; total; utter 5 **Completely effective** 6 Assured; positive 7 To bring to perfection; complete; finish

PERFECTION The embodiment of something that is perfect: As a hostess

PERFIDY The act of violating faith, trust or allegiance; treachery

PERFORM To carry out in action; execute; do 2 To act in accord with the requirements or obligations of; fulfill; discharge, as a duty or command 3 To act (a part) or give a performance of 4 To carry through to completeness an action, undertaking etc. [to accomplish entirely]

PERFUNCTORY Done or performed mechanically and merely for the sake of getting through

PERICOPE A selection from a book, especially a passage of Scripture read as part of a religious service

PERK To recover one's spirits or vigor 2 To make one trim and smart in appearance

PERPETUITY Something that has perpetual existence or worth

PERPLEX To cause to hesitate or become confused, as from doubt, difficulties encountered etc.; puzzled 2 To make complicated, intricate or confusing

PERSEVERANCE The continuance in grace and certain salvation of those chosen by **God**

PERSIST To continue firmly in some course, state etc., especially despite opposition or difficulties

PERSON One's characteristic appearance or physical condition One considered somewhat inferior in status; a mere nobody

PERSONA The personality assumed by an individual for purposes of concealment, defense, deception or adaption to his environment

PERSONAL EQUATION The tendency to error in observation, reasoning etc., resulting from individual characteristics

PERSONALITY Distinctive qualities or characteristics of (Love, goodness, someone who is good, etc.) 2 An entity, especially one of outstanding or distinctive qualities 3 personal existence 4 A condition in which two or more relatively distinct sets of experiences and behavior patterns reveal themselves alternately in the same individually

PERSONALLY In person; not through an agent

PERSPICACIOUS Keenly discerning or understanding 2 Sharp-sighted

PERSPICACITY Keenness in mental penetration or discernment

PERUSE To read carefully or attentively 2 To read 3 **To examine; scrutinize**

PERVASIVE Thoroughly penetrating or permeating

PERVERT To turn to an improper use or purpose; misapply 2 To distort the meaning or intent of; misconstrue 3 To turn from approved opinions or conduct; lead astray 4 To deprave; debase; corrupt [< F *pervertir* < L *pervertere* to turn around < *per-* away + *vertere* to turn]

PERVIOUS Capable of being penetrated; permeable 2 Open to reason, suggestion etc. [< L *pervius* having a way through < *per* through + *via* way]

PESTILENCE A noxious or malign doctrine, influence etc.

PESTILENT Having a malign influence or effect 2 Making trouble; causing irritation; vexation

PETITION A formal request, supplication or prayer

PHARISAIC Observing the form, but neglecting the spirit; self-righteous; censoriousness or hypocrisy

PHARISEE A formal, sanctimonious, hypocritical person

PHILANTHROPY Disposition or effort to promote the happiness of mankind 2 Love or benevolence toward mankind in general

PHILISTINE An ignorant, narrow-minded person, devoid of culture and indifferent to art -Blind conventionalism

PHILOSOPHER One who is calm and patient under all circumstances

PHILOSOPHICAL Pertaining to or founded on the principles of philosophy 2 Proper to or characteristic of a philosopher 3 Self-restrained and serene; rational; thoughtful 4 Pertaining to or use in the study of natural philosophy or physics

PHILOSOPHY The inquiry into the most comprehensive principles of reality in general, or some limited sector of it such as human knowledge or human values 2 The love of wisdom, and the search for it 3 Practical wisdom; fortitude as in enduring reverses and suffering 4 Reasoned science; a scientific system 5 The sciences as formerly studied in the universities

PHOSPHOR The morning star, especially Venus, as the harbinger of the day

PHOTOBIOTIC Living in the Light 2 Requiring Light for Life or development

PHYLACTERY One of two small leather cases containing a strip or strips of parchment inscribed with Scriptural passages, and having thongs for binding on the forehead or around the left arm during morning prayer, except Sabbath and holy days

PHYSICAL Of or relating to the human body, as distinguished from the mind or spirit; carnal 2 Of the nature of or pertaining to matter or material things

PHYSICAL SCIENCE Any of the sciences that treat the structure, properties, and energy relations of matter apart from the phenomena of life, as physics, astronomy, chemistry, geology etc.

PHYSICIAN Any healer

PIERCE To pass into or through; penetrate 2 To force a way into or through 3 To affect sharply or deeply, as with emotion, pain, etc. 4 To penetrate to the source or meaning; solve; understand 5 To enter

PIT An abyss so deep that one cannot return from it, as the grave or hell 2 Great distress or trouble 3 To match as antagonists; set in opposition

PITH Concentrated force; vigor; substance 2 The essential part; quintessence; gist

PLACE Particular point, part, passage; right and proper position 2 In its natural or original position,

PLAGUE Anything troublesome or harassing, producing mental distress; affliction 2 Any great evil or calamity 3 Nuisance; bother 4 To harass or torment -Pestilence

PLANK To put down emphatically

PLANT An apparently trivial passage early that later becomes important in shaping the outcome of the action 2 To found; establish 3 To introduce into the mind; implant, as ideas or principles

PLATONIC Purely spiritual, or devoid of sensual feeling

PLEASE To be agreeable to; gratify 2 To be the wish or will of 3 **To be so kind as to; to be willing to** 4 To give satisfaction 5 To have the will or preference; wish

PLEASURE An agreeable sensation or emotion; gratification; enjoyment 2 Something that gives a feeling of enjoyment, delight, or satisfaction 3 Amusement or diversion 4 Sensual gratification One's preference or choice

PHYSIOGNOMY The face or features considered as revealing character or disposition 2 The outward look of a thing 3 The practice of discerning character in the features in the face or form of the body

PIERCE To affect sharply or deeply, as with emotion, pain etc. 2 To penetrate to the source or meaning; solve; understand

PIETY Reverence or devoutness toward **God** 2 Honor and obedience due to parents, superiors etc.; dutifulness

PIG A person regarded as like a pig, especially one who is filthy, gluttonous or coarse

PILGRIM One who journeys to some sacred place from religious motives

PILGRIMAGE Any long arduous journey

PILGRIM'S PROGRESS A religious allegory in two parts (1678 and 1684) by John Bunyan

PILLAR One who strongly supports a work or a cause

PILOT To guide or conduct, as through difficult circumstances 2 Serving as a trial situation

PIN To seize and hold firmly; make unable to move, as with the mind 2 endure (something) without complaint or resistance; tolerate 3 To force (someone) to make up his mind, follow a definite course of action, etc.

PINE[1] Any of a genius (*Pinus*) of cone- bearing trees having needle-shaped evergreen leaves growing in clusters, and including many important timber trees 2 Loosely, any tree of the pine family (Pinaceae), including the cedar, fir, etc.

PINE ² To grow thin or weak with longing, grief, etc. 2 To have great desire or longing 3 To grieve for [OE *pin* torment, ult. < L *poena* punishment]

PINEAL Pertaining to the **PINEAL BODY~** A small, reddish gray, vascular, conical body of rudimentary glandular structure found behind the third ventricle of the brain and having no known function: sometimes called *epiphysis* [< F *pineal* < L *pinea* pine cone < *pinus* pine tree]

PIONEER To prepare the way [< L *pes, pedis* foot]

PIOUS Actuated by reverence for a Supreme Being; religious; godly 2 Marked by reverential Spirit [< L pius dutiful, respectful]

PIP An admirable person

PIPAL (pepl) The sacred fig tree

PIT An abyss so deep that one cannot return from it, as the grave or hell 2 Great distress or trouble

PIQUANT Lively and charming; interesting; stinging; sharp

PLANT An apparently trivial passage early in a story that later becomes important in shaping an outcome of the action 2 A trick; dodge; swindle 3 To set or place firmly; put into position 4 To found; establish 5 To introduce into the mind; implant, as an idea or principle 6 To place or station for purpose of deception, observation, etc.

PLAY To engage in diversion; amuse oneself 2 To act or behave in a specified manner 3 To act in a way that shouldn't be taken seriously 4 To deal carelessly; behave insincerely 5 To act 6 To pretend to be 7 To assume the character of 8 To attempt to gain something 9 To attempt to seduce

PLEAD To make earnest entreaty; implore; beg 2 To discuss or maintain (a belief) by reasoning Syn. sue, petition Compare **ENTREAT**

PLEASANCE A secluded garden

PLEASANT Agreeable in manner 2 Merry; gay [< OF *plaisant*, ppr. *paisir* to please L *placere*]

PLEASE To be agreeable to; gratify 2 To be the wish or will of 3 To be so kind as to; to be willing to 4 To have the will or preference Syn. cheer, gladden, delight, rejoice, exhilarate Ant. displease, offend, anger

PLEIAN Anyone who is coarse or vulgar [< L plebeius < plebs the common people]

PLEDGE To bind (oneself) to a statement 2 To offer (one's word, Life, etc.) as a guaranty or forfeit 3 To make a promise; statement; agreement to perform or fulfill some act, duty, etc. 4 A statement suggestive of doing or not doing (something) Syn. Syn. security

PLEIAD One of any cluster of brilliant people, usually seven

PLENARY Full in all respects or recisites; entire; absolute; complete 2 Fully or completely attended, as a conversation

PLENTIFUL Existing in great quantity; abundant 2 Yielding or containing plenty; affording ample supply

PLOW To move or cut through 2 To advance laboriously 3 To undertake vigorously to accomplish, finish or solve

PLUCK Confidence and Spirit in the face of difficulty or danger; courage

POLLUTE To make unclean or impure; dirty; corrupt; profane 2 To defile

Syn. *Pollute, contaminate, taint, infect, defile,* and *debase* refer to the process of making (someone) dirty, impure, or worthless *Pollute* suggests the end of this process, and *contaminate,* it's beginning A *polluted* conversation is completely unfit for hearing, understanding, or believing because of impure, foregin, inaccuracies in it, while a *contaminated* conversation is only partially or temporarily unsafe for the same reason A similar distinction exists between *taint,* and *infect,* both of which suggests the presence of decay- or disease-causing emotions That which is *tainted* is already decayed or corrupt, but that which is infected in in the early stages of decay or disease and may be corrected and cured *Defile* often suggests the malicious or thoughtless dirtying or profanation of that which should be pure and clean, or held in reverence: to *defile* the mind *Debase* suggests a loss of dignity, value, honor, etc. by a person formerly held in high esteem

POLLYANNA One who finds good in everything

POOR Lacking in abundance or good qualities; scanty; meager: a *poor* crop 2 Lacking in fertility; sterile: *poor* soil 3 Inferior in workmanship or quality 4 Deficient in vigor; feeble; frail: *poor* spirit 5 Lacking in nobility of character; contemptible; mean 6 Lacking proper ability; unsatisfactory 7 Deserving of pity; wretched; unhappy

POSITRON An antiparticle corresponding to an electron [< **POSI(TIVE) + (ELEC) TRON**] **PAIR PRODUCTION** by its passage through a strong electric field

POSSIBLE Capable of happening or proving true; not contrary to fact, natural laws or experiences

POT To secure, capture, or win

POTENCY Mental or moral power 2 Authority 3 Strength and effectiveness 4 Capable of influencing greatly; very convincing 5 One having great power or sway

POTTER To **PUTTER** To act work or proceed in a dawdling or ineffectual manner 2 To waste or spend

POVERTY The condition or quality of being poor or without sufficient substance, said of knowledge 2 Absence or scarcity of necessary qualities, characteristics, or understanding

POWER Ability to act 2 The right, ability, or capacity to exercise control; legal authority, capacity, or competency 3 Great or telling effect 4 A mental faculty 5 Any form of energy available for doing work; especially, Spiritual energy 6 Magnifying capacity

PRAISE An expression of approval or commendation 2 The worship of **God** expressed in song 3 The ground or reason for praise

PRATE To talk idly and at length; chatter 2 To idle emptily

PRAY To make earnest request or entreaty; beg 2 To ask (someone) earnestly; entreat 3 To ask for by prayers or entreaty 4 To cause to move by prayer: pray a soul out of purgatory [< OF *preier* < LL *precare* < L *precari* < *prex, precis* request, prayer]

PRAYER Spiritual communion with **God**, and awareness of His presence, as in praise, thanksgiving, confession etc. 2 A religious service in which praying plays the most prominent part 3 Any earnest request [< OF *preiere,* ult. < L *precarius* obtained by prayer < *precari* See **PRAY**]

PREACH To advocate or recommend urgently: to *preach* patience 2 To proclaim or expound upon: to *preach* one must possess his soul by patience -To minister; administer See **MINISTER** [< OF *prechier* < L *praedicare* to proclaim < *prae-* before + *dicare* to make known]

PRECEPT A rule prescribing a particular kind of conduct or action 2 A proverbial standard or guide to morals; a maxim 3 A direction, as for technical matters

PRECIOUS Greatly esteemed, as for moral or Spiritual qualities: the *precious* ideal of Truth 2 Beloved; cherished 3 Affectedly delicate or sensitive 4 Surpassing 5 Extremely; very [< OF *precio*s < L *pretiosus* < *pretium* price]

PRECISE Sharply or clearly determined or defined; strictly accurate 2 Exact or distinct in sound, statement etc. 3 Scrupulously observant of rule

PREGNANT Having considerable weight or significance; full of meaning 2 Teeming with ideas 3 Bearing issue or results; fruitful; prolific

PRESENT To put forward for consideration or action; submit, as a petition 2 To exhibit to view or notice 3 To suggest to the mind 4 Ready at hand 5 Not delayed 6 For the time being 7 To nominate to a **BENEFICE**- A permanent Church **APPOINTMENT**- To make a priest or minister; confer holy orders on

PRESERVE To keep in safety; protect from danger or harm; guard 2 To keep intact or unimpaired; maintain 3 To keep from decomposition or change

PREVAIL To gain mastery; be victorious; triumph 2 To be efficacious; succeed 3 To use persuasion or influence successfully 4 To be or become a predominant; be prevalent feature or quality 5 To have general or widespread use or acceptance; be in force [< OF *prevaloir* or L *praevalere* < *prae-* before + *valere* to be strong]

PRIEST A man in like character to that of Jesus Christ

PRIMORDIAL First in order or time; original; elemental -An elementary principle

PRINCE The son of the Sovereign 2 One of a high order of nobility 3 A chief or leader, or One of the highest ranks of any class [< OF < L *princeps* first, principal < *primus* first + stem of *capere* to take]

PRINCIPALITY The territory of a reigning prince, or one that gives to a prince a title of courtesy 2 The seventh of nine orders of angels

PRINCIPLE A general Truth or law, basic to other Truths 2 A law or rule of personal conduct 3 Moral standards collectively 4 That which is inherent in anything, determining its nature; essence 4 A source or cause from which a thing proceeds 6 An established mode of action or operation in natural phenomena 7 An essential constituent of a compound or substance that gives it character to it (God or the devils) [< L *principium* beginning]

PRISON A place of confinement

PRIVY Participating with another or others in the knowledge of a secret transaction

PROCLAIM To announce or make known publicly or officially Declare officially or publicly to be 2 To make plain; manifest [< L *proclamare* < *pro* before + *clamare* to call]

PROCURE To obtain by some effort or means; acquire 2 To bring about -To attend to

PRODUCE To bring forth or bear; yield as young or natural product 2 To bring forth by mental effort

PROFANE Manifesting undue familiarity toward the Deity or sacred things: blasphemous -Not religious or concerned with religious things; secular 2 Not initiated into the inner mysteries 3 Common

PROFIT Any advantage or gain; benefit; return 2 To derive, gain, or benefit

PROMISE The assurance given by one person to another that the former will or will not perform a specified act 2 Reasonable ground for hope or expectation, especially of future excellence or satisfaction [< L *promissum*, pp. of *promittere* to send forward < *pro-* forth + *mittere* to send]

PROMOTE To contribute to the progress, development or growth of; further; encourage 2 To work in behalf of; advocate actively

PROPHECY A prediction made under divine influence and direction 2 Any prediction 3 Discourse delivered by a prophet under divine inspiration 4 A Book of prophecies

PROPHESY To utter or foretell with or as with divine inspiration 2 To predict 3 To point out beforehand 4 To speak by Divine influence, or as a medium between God and man 5 To explain properly or teach accurately the Sacred Scriptures

PROPAGATE To spread from person to person, as a doctrine or belief 2 The action of widely spreading and promoting an idea, theory, etc

PROPERTY Any of the qualities or characteristics that together make up the nature or basic structure of a thing; a constituent part or element 2 A quality or feature that belongs distinctively to a particular class; peculiarity 3 That which is not a part of the essence of a thing but is necessarily connected with the essence 6 See **CHARACTERISTIC 7 ATTRIBUTE**

PROPITIATE To cause to be favorably disposed; appease; conciliate Syn. *Propitiation* is any action which makes such a power more lenient toward the offender *Appeasement* mollifies by making concession to demands, and often suggests weakness, cowardice or bad judgment *Atonement* denotes an offering or sacrifice sufficient to win forgiveness for an offence The word suggests some degree of equality between the injury suffered and the reparation made for it *Expiation* is a more legalistic word, and refers to the enduring of the full penalty for a wrong

PROPITIOUS Attended by favorable circumstances 2 Kindly disposed; gracious *Propitious* and *auspicious* may both be applied to circumstances that appear to favor a project or bode well for the future

*PROPORTION Relative magnitude, number or degree, as existing between parts, a part and a whole 2 To form with a harmonious relation of parts which is not a part of the essence of a thing but is necessarily connected with the essence See **CHARACTERISTIC ATTRIBUTE**

PROPRIETY PROPERTY

PROSAIC Lacking those qualities that impart animation or interest; unimaginative; commonplace; dull 2 Pertaining to or like prose

PROSE Speech or writing without metrical structure: distinguished from *verse* 2 Commonplace or tedious discourse 3 Tedious; tiresome 4 To write or speak in prose [< OF < L *prosa (oratio)* straightforward (discourse) < *prorsus* < *provertere* < *pro-* forward + *vertere* to turn]

PROSER A dull tedious writer or talker; a bore

PROSPEROUS Successful; flourishing 2 Favoring or tending to success; auspicious 3 Promising; favorable [Prosper akin to *sperare* to hope]

PROSY Like prose; prosaic 2 Dull; tedious; common place

To show to be True or genuine, as by evidence 2 To determine the quality or genuineness of; test 3 To establish the authenticity or validity of 4 To verify the accuracy of 5 To learn by experience; undergo 6 To be shown to be by the results or outcome; turn out to be See **CONFIRM**

PROVERB A **PITHY**- concise and forcefully expressive saying, in a clever and amusing way, having a witty or ingenious ending, especially one condensing the wisdom of experience; **ADAGE**- A statement expressing a general Truth; **APHORISM**- A concise statement of a scientific principle, typically by an ancient classical author; **MAXIM**- A statement expressing a general Truth or rule of conduct **ENIGMATIC**- Difficult to interpret or understand; mysterious saying 2 A typical example; deliberately obscure

PROVERBS An Old Testament book of moral sayings

PRUDENT Careful to avoid errors and follow the most profitable course 2 **Exercising sound judgment** 3 Characterized by practical wisdom or discretion; not extravagant

PSALTRIES The reading of the Psalms from the joy of one's heart

*PSYCHE The mind; intellect 2 The aggregate of the mental components of an individual, including both conscious and unconscious states, and often regarded as an entity functioning apart from or independently of the body

PUBLIC Well known; open to all; without concealment 2 For the use of the people at large or those that may be grouped together for any given purpose 3 participated by the people as

PULL To put into effect; carry out 2 To make or obtain by impression from type 3 Any steady continuous effort 4 A means of influencing those in power 5 Attraction; appeal [OE *pullian* to pluck]

*PURE Free from mixture or contact with that which weakens, impairs or pollutes 2 Free from adulteration; clear 3 Genuine 4 Free from moral defilement; innocent; chaste; unsullied; also free from coarseness; refined 5 Free from imported elements, as language 6 Free of harsh qualities; correct in form or style; finished 7 Considered apart from its attributes or from concrete experience; abstract 8 Concerned with fundamental research, as distinguished from practical application 9 Breeding true with respect to one or more characters; homozygous 10 Nothing but; sheer *Pure* suggests the absence of any element felt to be alien or nonessential

PURIFY To rid of extraneous or noxious matter 2 To free from foreign or debasing elements

PURIST One who believes in or practices exact or meticulous usage, as of language, style, etc.

PURPLE Imperial; regal

PURPOSE An idea or ideal kept before the mind as an end of effort or action; plan; design; aim 2 A particular thing to be effected or attained 3 Practical advantage or result 4 Settled resolution, determination; consistency -To have the intention of doing or accomplishing (something); aim

PURSE A valuable resource or means

PUT To bring into a specified state, condition or relation 2 To ascribe or attribute 3 To bring forward for debate, answer, consideration etc. 4 To express in words 5 To write down; record 6 To humble or deflate 7 To grow 8 To exert 9 To enter 10 To give a representation of 11 To accomplish successfully 12 To bring to successful completion 13 To cause to undergo 14 To provide -**To endure; tolerate**

Q

QUADRAGESIMA The forty fast days before Easter; Lent

QUAKE See **SHAKE** 2 For **EARTHQUAKE** see **EARTH** and **SHAKE**

QUALIFY To make fit or capable, as for a privilege 2 To attribute a quality to; describe; characteristics 3 To make less strong or extreme; soften; moderate 4 To change the strength or flavor of 5 To modify 6 To be or become qualified or fit; meet the requirements, as for entering a race [< MF qualifier < Med. L *qualificare* to define limit < L *qualis* of such a kind + *facere* to make]

QUALITY That which makes something such as it is; a distinguishing element or characteristic 2 The basic or essential character, nature etc., of (someone) 3 Excellence 4 The degree of excellence; relative goodness 5 A moral or personality trait or characteristic Syn. See **ATTRIBUTE**

QUANTITATIVE ANALYSIS The process of finding the amount or percentage of each element or ingredient present in a material compound

QUANTUM THEORY The theory that energy is not a smoothly flowing continuum but is manifested by the emission of radiating bodies of discrete particles or *quanta*

QUARREL [1] An unfriendly, angry or violent dispute 2 A falling out or contention; breach of amity 3 To break off a mutual friendship; fall out; disagree 4 To find fault; cavil [to complain]

QUARREL [2] A dart or arrow

QUEER Being out of the usual course of events; singular; odd 2 Of questionable character; open to suspicion 3 Counterfeit

QUICK Responding readily or eagerly to impressions or instruction 2 Alert; sensitive; perceptive 3 Easily aroused or excited; hasty 4 Characterized by readiness of action 5 Refreshing; bracing 6 The feelings 7 Having Life; Living 8 The Living flesh

R

RABBLE [1] A disorderly crowd or mob 2 The common people; hoi polloi: a contemptuous term -Of, suited to, or characteristic of a rabble; disorderly

RABBLE [2] To speak or utter in an incoherent or disconnected manner; gabble

RABBLE-ROUSER One who tries to incite mobs by arousing prejudices and passions; a demagogue

RACE Any class of beings having characteristics uniting them or differentiating them from others

RAIMENT Personalities; characteristics

RAISE To cause; occasion, as a smile or laugh 2 To cause to move upward or to a higher level; ellevate 3 To make greater in value 4 To advance or elevate in rank, estimation, etc. 5 To increase the strength, intensity, or degree of 6 To breed; grow 7 To cause; occasion 8 To stir to action or emotion; arouse 9 To weaken, animate, or reanimate 10 To gather together; obtain or collect 11 To bring up for consideration 12 To put an end to 13 To make great disturbance; stir up confusion [These things are made with leaven See **RAISED**]

RAISED Elevated in low relief 2 Made with leaven

RALLY To bring together and restore to effective discipline

RAM A male sheep- meek, bashful, timid 2 To charm; stuff 3 The unimaginative; meek, bashful and timid personality of people who are easily influenced, led; and who are regarded as protected followers of God

RANGE The extent to which any power can be made effective 2 To occur; be found 3 To extend or proceed 4 To exhibit variation within specified limits Doublet of **RANK**

RANK Utter; complete: used **PEJORATIVELY~** The condition of becoming worse; deterioration 2 A degeneration or lowering in the meaning of a word 3 Producing a luxuriant growth; fertile 4 Inequitable; excessive 5 Lustful

RANSOM To secure the release of (a person) for a required price, as from captivity Doublet of **REDEMPTION**

RAPE The act of forcing a woman to have SEXUAL INTERCOURSE; especially the forcible and unlawful carnal knowledge of a woman against her will

RAPPORT Harmony and sympathy of relation; agreement; accord [< F < *rapporter* to bring back]

RAPPROCHEMENT A state of harmony or reconciliation; restoration of cordial relations, as between nations

RAPTURE The act of breaking apart, or the state of being broken apart 2 Breach of friendship or concord between individuals 3 To affect with or suffer a rapture

RAREFY To make rare, thin, less solid or less dense; expand by dispersion of the particles 2 To refine or purify 3 To become rare 4 To become more pure

RATHER With preference for one of two things or courses; more willingly 2 With more reason, justice, wisdom etc. 3 More precisely, strictly or accurately 4 In a greater or lesser degree; to a certain extent 5 On the contrary 6 Yes indeed! [OE *hrathor* sooner, compare, of *hrathe* soon, quickly]

RATIFY To give sanction to, especially official or authoritative sanction; make valid by approving; confirm [< OF *ratifier* < Med. L *ratificare* < L *ratus* fixed, calculated + *facere* to make]

RATIOCINATIVE Of or pertaining to the act or process of reasoning 2 Given to or characterized by ratiocination

RATIONAL Possessing the faculty of reasoning 2 Having full possession of one's mental faculties; sane 3 Conformable to reason; judicious; sensible 4 Pertaining to reason; attained by reasoning 5 Pertaining to rationalism Syn. *Rationable* and *reasonable* refer to the power of reasoning We call man a *rational* being because he possess this power When we call a particular man *rational*, we may mean that he is not insane, or that he is being guided by his intellect rather than by his emotions A *rational* proposition is one that is derived logically from facts, data or circumstances *Rational* indicated only that human reasoning is at work; *reasonable* goes further and says that it is working well A *reasonable* man bases his views or actions on good reasons; a reasonable proposition is not only logical, but also displays good judgment, sagacity, practicality etc. Ant. Irrational, insane, unreasonable, absurd

RATIONALISM The formation of opinions by relying upon reason alone, independently of authority or of revelation

RATIONALIZE To explain or base (one's behavior) on grounds ostensibly rational, but not in accord with unconscious motives 2 To explain or treat from a rationalistic point of view 3 To make rational or reasonable 4 To remove the radicals containing variables from (an expression or equation); also, to alter the radicals so as to change (the expression) into more workable form -To think in a rational or rationalistic manner

RAVISH To fill with strong emotion, especially delight; enrapture 2 To commit rape upon 3 To carry off by force; with ulterior motives, as with the mind

RAY A line of propagation of any form of radiant energy 2 To issue forth, as reasons 3 To send forth, as an example 4 To irradiate

RAZOR See **SCRAPE**

REACTION The reciprocal action of substances subjected to chemical change, or some distinctive result of such action

REACTION FORMATION The development of character traits, attitudes, and forms of behavior in direct opposition to unconscious trends

REACTIVITY The relative tendency of an element to enter into chemical reaction

READ To apprehend the meaning of by perceiving the meaning of the printed or written characters 2 To understand the significance, intent etc. 3 To apprehend the meaning of something written 4 To make a study of; also, to obtain knowledge of 5 To discover the true nature of (a person, character etc.) by observation or scrutiny 6 To interpret (something read) in a specified manner 7 To take as the meaning of something read 8 To have as its wording: the passage reads "principle", not "principal" 9 To bring into a specified condition by reading -To perceive or infer what is not expressed or obvious, as a hidden or true meaning, implication, or motive

READER A textbook containing matter for exercising in reading: as the Holy Scriptures

READILY In a ready manner; promptly; easily 2 Willingly; without reluctance

READINESS The quality or state of being ready 2 The quality of being quick or prompt; facility; aptitude 3 A disposition for prompt compliance; willingness

READY Prepared for use or action 2 Prepared in mind; willing 3 Likely or liable 4 Quick to act, follow, occur or appear; prompt 5 Immediately available or at hand; convenient; handy 6 Quick to perceive or understand; alert; facile 7 Here; present -prepared

READY MADE Not made to order; prepared or kept on hand for general demand: said especially of clothing 2 Prepared beforehand; not impromptu 3 Lacking in originality; borrowed; trite

READY WITTED Quick to apprehend or learn; alert

REAGENT Any substance used to ascertain the nature or composition of another by means of their reciprocal chemical action

REALITY PRINCIPLE The adjustment of the ego to meet the requirements of the external world Compare **PLEASURE PRINCIPLE**

REALM A kingdom or domain 2 The scope or range of any power or influence

REASON The faculty of thinking logically; power of drawing conclusions or making inferences 2 Good judgment; common sense 3 A normal state of mind; sanity 4 One of the premises of an argument, especially the minor premise -By reason of -Because of -In reason -In accordance with reason or good sense -It stands to reason -It is logical or reasonable -With reason -Justifiably; properly 5 To think logically; obtain inferences or conclusions from known facts 6 To talk or argue logically 7 To think out carefully and logically; analyze 8 To influence by means of reason; persuade; dissuade

Syn. *Reason, purpose, motive, ground* and *argument* are compared as they denote the basis of a human action A *reason* seeks to explain or justify an action by citing facts, circumstances, inducement and the like, together with the working of the mind upon them *Reason* may include *purpose* and *motive* as internal or subjective elements and also *grounds* and *argument* that are external or objective The *purpose* of an action is the effect that it is intended to produce; its *motive* is the inner impulse that sets it in motion and guides it *Grounds* are the facts, data etc., that the mind weighs in reaching a decision; and *argument* is the logical demonstration of how these facts and data determine the decision

9 See **CAUSE** 10 See **INTELLECT**

REASONED Founded upon or characterized by reason; premeditated or studied

REBORN Born again; having undergone emotional or mental regeneration

REBUKE To reprove sharply; reprimand 2 To check or restrain (oneself) by command 3 A strong authoritative expression of disapproval [< AF *rebuker,* OF *rebuchier* < *re-* back + *buchier* to beat]

REBUT To refute by contrary evidence or proof, as in formal argument; disprove

RECEIVE To gain knowledge or information of 2 To take from another by hearing or listening 3 To bear; support 4 To experience; meet with 5 To undergo; suffer 6 To contain; hold 7 To allow entrance to; admit into one's presence; greet 8 To perceive mentally; understand 9 To accept as true, proven, authoritative

RECIPROCATE To give, feel, do etc., in return; requite, as an emotion 2 To make a return in kind 3 To correspond; be equivalent

RECIPROCITY Reciprocal obligation, action or relation 2 A trade relation between two countries by which each makes concessions favoring the importance of the products of the other

RECK To have a care or thought (for); heed; mind 2 To be of concern or interest (to)

RECON To look upon as being; regard 2 To make computation; count up; to recon for -To pay for; receive the penalty of -To reckon with 3 To settle accounts with 4 To take into consideration; bear in mind; consider

RECLAIM To bring (a person) into a condition to support cultivation or Life, as by draining or irrigating 2 To obtain a (soul/Spirit) from used or waste products 3 To cause to return from wrong or sinful ways of life; reform 4 To tame, as a hawk -The act of reclaiming or the state of being reclaimed [< OF *reclamer* to call back < L *reclamare* < *re-* back + *clamare* to cry out]

RECOLLECTION A state or condition of inner tranquility or prayerfulness

RECOMMEND To commend with favorable representations; praise as desirable, worthy etc. 2 To make attractive or acceptable 3 To advise; urge 4 To give in charge

RECOMPENSE To give compensation to, pay or repay; reward; requite 2 To give compensation for; make up for as a loss 3 An equivalent for anything given or done; payment

RECOMPOSE To restore the composure of; tranquilize -To compose or form anew; rearrange; reconstitute; recombine

RECONDITE Remote from ordinary or easy perception; abstruse; secret 2 Hidden; not readily observed [< L *reconditus*, pp. of *recondere* to hide < *re-* back + *condere* to store < *con* together + *dare* to put]

RECTITUDE Uprightness in principles and conduct 2 Correctness as of judgment 3 Straightness

red Communistic 2 An ultra radical in political views **RED** A member of the Communist party of any country 2 Any person who supports or approves of the aims of the Communist party 3 An ultra radical; antichrist

REDD To put in order; make ready 2 To empty 3 To adjust Also spelled red [OE *raedan* to arrange; infl. by OE *hreddan* to free from]

REDEEM To regain possession of by paying a price; especially, to recover, as your Spirit (in you) 2 To pay off; receive back and satisfy, as a commandment 3 To set free; rescue, as (your) mind 4 To rescue from consciousness of matter (though present) and the penalties therein 5 To fulfill, as your oath and promise (upon conception) 6 To make amends for; compensate for

REDEEMABLE Capable of being redeemed 2 Tha is to be redeemed, as the consciousness which has been overcome by matter, the same shall be set free and released from matter

REDRESS To set right, as a wrong, by compensation or by punishment of the wrongdoer; make reparation for 2 To make reparation to; compensate 3 To remedy; correct 4 To adjust, as balances 5 Sanctification for wrong done; reparation; amends 6 A restoration; reformation; correction [< F *redresser* to straighten < *re-* again (< L) + *dresser*. See **DRESS**]

REFERENT The object, concept, etc., to which reference is made in a statement or its symbolic equivalent

REFINE To make fine or pure; free from impurities or extraneous matter 2 To become fine or pure 3 To make fine distinctions; used subtly in thought

REFINEMENT Fineness of thought, language etc.; freedom from coarseness or vulgarity 2 The act, effect or process of refining; purification 3 A nice distinction; subtlety Syn.

Refinement, *cultivation* and *breeding* denote a quality we attribute to persons regarded as superior in intellect, sensitivity or manners Refinement is perhaps the strongest word, implying not only the elimination of vulgarity and grossness but also the development of delicate perception and understanding Cultivation is the self-discipline, study and exercise that brings learning Breeding suggests the training that manifests itself in good manners, tact and consideration for others

REFLECT To cause as a result of one's actions, character, etc., cast 2 To manifest as a result of influence, imitation, etc. 3 To send back rays, as of Light 4 To shine back 5 To think carefully; ponder

REFORM To make better by removing abuses, altering etc.; restore to a better condition 2 To improve morally; persuade or educate to a better life 3 To put an end to; stop 4 To give up sin or error; become better 5 An act or result of reformation; change for the better, especially in administration; correction of evils or abuses 6 Improvement in one's personal life, especially by abandonment of bad habits

REFRACT Of (information) make (a statement, belief, or understanding) change directions when it enters at an angle

REFRAIN [1] To keep oneself back; abstain from action; forbear [< OF *refrener* < L *refrenare* to curb < *re-* back + *frenum* bridle] Syn. *Refrain*, *abstain*, and *forbear* mean to check oneself from performing an action *Refrain* may indicate mere nonperformance, or may imply a positive subjection of an impulse or inclination: to *refrain* from making an angry retort *Abstain* indicates a considered policy, usually of self-denial *Forbear* suggests patience, kindness or leniency

REFRAIN [2] One who flees to a refuge 2 One who flees from invasion, persecution or political danger

REFUSE To turn back (the wing of a line of troops) so that it stands at an angle with the main body **1 Sam 16:7

REFUTE To prove the incorrectness or falsity of (a statement) 2 To prove (a person) to be in error; confute Syn.

Refute, *disprove*, *rebut* and *confute* mean to show to be incorrect or fallacious *Refute* emphasizes the fact of opposing a statement or argument; *disprove* emphasizes the result of such opposition To *rebut* is to *refute* in formal debate, while *confute* is to *disprove*, overthrow or put to confusion; *confute* may include the use of ridicule, as well as of logical argument

REGARD To look at or observe closely or attentively 2 To look on or think of in a certain or specified manner; consider 3 To take into account 4 To have relation or pertinence to 5 To care for 6 To pay attention 7 To gaze or look Syn. See **ADMIRE, CONSIDER**- Careful attention or notice; heed; consideration 2 Esteem; respect 3 Reference; relation 4 A look or aspect 5 Good wishes; affection Syn. See difference [< OF *regarder* to look at < *re-* again + *garder* to guard, heed < Gmc. Akin to **REWARD**]

REGENERATE To cause complete moral and Spiritual reformation or regeneration in 2 To produce or form anew; re-create; reproduce 3 To make use of 4 Having new life; restored 5 Spiritually renewed

REGENERATION The imparting of Spiritual Life by divine grace 2 The reproduction of a lost part or organ

REINS The region near temperament, nature or type 2 The loins, considered as the seat of the affections and passions

REJECT To refuse to accept, recognize, believe, etc. 2 To refuse to grant; deny, as a petition 3 To refuse (a person) recognition, acceptance, etc. 4 To expel, as from the mouth; vomit 5 To cast away as worthless; discard 6 One who or that which has been rejected

RELATION Conditions or connections in general that bring an individual in touch with his fellows

RELATIVITY The quality or condition of being relative; relativeness 2 Existence only as an object of, or in relation 3 A thinking mind 4 Condition of dependence or of close relation 5 The principle of interdependence of matter, energy, space and time -The special theory of relativity states that the velocity of light is the maximum velocity possible in the universe, that it is constant and independent of the motion of its source, that motion itself is a meaningless concept except as between two bodies moving relatively to each other, and that energy and mass are interconvertible in accordance with the equation energy = mass X the square of the speed of light or $E=mc^2$ -The general theory of relativity extends these principles to the law of gravitation and the motion of the heavenly bodies

RELATIVITY OF KNOWLEDGE The theory that knowledge of what things really are is impossible, since knowledge itself is dependent upon the subjective nature of the mind

RELEASE To set free; liberate 2 To deliver from worry, pain, obligation etc. 3 To free from something that holds, binds etc. 4 A deliverance or final relief, as from anything grievous or oppressive 5 A discharge from responsibility or penalty, as debt

RELEGATE To send off or consign, as to an obscure position or place 2 To assign, as to a particular class or sphere 3 To banish; exile

RELENT To soften in temper; become more gentle or compassionate 2 To cause to relent

RELIABLE That may be relied upon; worthy of confidence; trustworthy 2 Exhibiting a reasonable consistency in results obtained distinguished from valid Syn.
Reliable, *dependable*, and *trustworthy* characterize that in which we have great confidence A *reliable* person acts rightly, competently or consistently; a *reliable* thing is adequate, serviceable or true: we may say that a reference dictionary is *reliable* if the information it presents is accurate, or that a man is a *reliable* judge of personal issues if his opinions are sound *Dependable* is akin to *reliable*, but a little more subjective; we go to a *dependable* person confident of receiving loyalty, support or aid *Trustworthy* is stronger than either of the foregoing words, implying that our confidence is complete and profound: a *trustworthy* servant

RELIEF Charitable aid given in the form of money or food to the needy

RELIEVE To free wholly or partly from pain, embarrassment etc. 2 To lessen or alleviate, as pain or anxiety 3 To give aid or assistance to 4 To free from obligation, injustice etc. 5

To release from duty, as a sentinel, by providing or serving as a substitute 6 To make less monotonous, harsh or unpleasant; vary 7 To bring into relief or prominence; display by contrast [< OF *relever* to raise again < L *relevare* to lift up < *re-* again + *levare* to lift, rise < *levis* light]

RELIGION The beliefs, attitudes, emotions, behavior, ect., constituting man's relationship with the powers and principles of the universe, especially with a deity or deities; also, any particular system of such beliefs, attitudes, etc. [< OF < L *religio, oins < religare < re-* back + *ligare* **to bind**]

To bring back or recall again to the mind or memory To keep in mind carefully

REMOVE

RENOUNCE To give up, especially by formal statement 2 To disown; repudiate

RENT A violent separation; schism

REPARATION The act of making amends; atonement 2 That which is done by way of amends or satisfaction 3 The act of repairing or the state of being repaired

REPENT To feel remorse or regret, as for something one has done or failed to do; be contrite 2 To change one's mind concerning past action because of disappointment, failure, etc. 3 To feel such sorrow for one's sins as to reform 4 To feel remorse or regret for (an action, sin etc.)

REPENTANCE Syn.

Repentance, penitence, remorse, compunction, contrition and *attrition* are sorrow for sin or wrongdoing *Repentance* and *penitence* both denote sorrow for past faults, and a sincere desire to avoid them in the future *Repentance* often stresses a sense of self-condemnation; *patience* points more often to the outward expression to this inward feeling *Remorse*, the stronger word, is a prolonged or recurrent feeling of guilt over something said or done; *compunction* is often no more than a momentary regret for some past, present or contemplated action: to feel *remorse* over past indecisions and failures to act, to ignore a social obligation without *compunction Contrition* and *attrition* are theological terms; *contrition* is repentance arising from the love of **God**, while *attrition* is such repentance arising less worthy motives, such as fear of punishment *Contrition* is also used in a general sense as a close synonym of *penitence* Compare **SORROW**

REPRODUCTION The process by which an animal or plant gives rise to another of its kind

REPROVE To censure, as for a fault; rebuke 2 To express disapproval of (an act) 3 To convince; convict [< OF *reprover* < LL *reprobare* < *re-* again (< L) + *probare* to test < *probus* upright]

REPUTATION The general estimation in which a person or thing is held by others, especially by a community; repute 2 The state of being in high regard or esteem; good repute 3 A particular credit or character ascribed to a person See **FAME**

RESCUE To save or free from danger, captivity, evil, etc.; Deliver [< OF *resourre* < *re-* back (<L) + *escorre* to move, shake < L *excutere* < *ex-* out of + *quatere* to shake]

RESEARCH Diligent, protracted investigation; studious inquiry 2 A systematic investigation of some phenomenon See **SEARCH**

RESERVE To hold back or set aside for special or future use; to store up 2 To keep as one's own; retain 3 Silence or reticence as to one's feelings, opinions, or affairs; also, absence of exaggeration 4 To serve again

RESIST To act against a purpose; oppose; strive 2 Withstand; defeat

RESPECT To have differential regard for; esteem 2 To treat with propriety or consideration 3 To regard as inviolable; avoid intruding upon 4 To have relation or reference to; concern Syn See **ADMIRE~** Regard for and appreciation of worth; honor and esteem 2 Demeanor or deportment indicating deference; courteous regard 3 Expression of consideration or esteem; compliments 4 Conformity to duty or obligation; compliance or observance 5 The condition of being honored or respected 6 A specific aspect or feature; detail

REST To cease from working, exerting oneself, etc., as to refresh oneself 2 To cease from effort or activity 3 o seek or obtain ease or refreshment 4 To be at peace; tranquil 5 To be supported 6 To rely; depend 7 To be placed as a burden or responsibility 8 To be directed; remain 9 To cease presenting evidence in a case 10 The act or state of resting; cessation from labor, exertion, action, or motion; repose; quiet 11 A place of repose; a stopping place; abode

RETURN To come or go back, as to a former condition 2 To come back or revert in thought or speech 3 To answer; respond 4 To yield or produce, as a prophet or interest 5 To report or announce officially 6 The act, process, state, or result of coming back or returning 7 Occurring or presented a second time or again

REVELATION The act or process of making known; making visible and exposing to; view, exhibit and show

RICH Yielding abundant returns; fruitful 2 Abounding in desirable qualities 3 Abundantly supplied, as of knowledge, personality, etc. 4 Exceedingly humorous; amusing

RICHES Abundance of whatever is precious [< OF *richesse* wealth, power < *riche* < Gmc.]

RIGHT Done in accordance with or conformable to moral law or to some standard of rightness; equitable; just; righteous 2 Conformable to Truth or fact; correct; accurate 3 Conformable to a standard of propriety or to the condition of the case; proper; fit; suitable 4 Most desirable or preferable 5 Properly placed, disposed, or adjusted; well-regulated; orderly 6 Sound in mind or body 7 Real or genuine in character; not spurious See **CORRECT~** Natural rights -Rights with which mankind is supposedly endowed by nature -Restore to an upright or normal position -To put in order; set right -To make correct or in accord with facts -Make reparation for

RIGHTEOUS Conforming in disposition and conduct to a standard of right and justice; upright; virtuous 2 Morally right; equitable

RIGHTFUL Characterized by or conforming to a right or just claim; also, owned or held by just claim 2 Consonant with moral right or with justice and Truth 3 Proper 4 Upright; just

RIGHT-HAND Chiefly depended on

RIGHTIST One whose views and policies are right

RIGHTLY Correctly 2 Honestly; uprightly 3 Properly; aptly

RIGHT-MINDED Having right feelings or opinions

RIGHTNESS The quality or condition of being right 2 Rectitude 3 Correctness 4 Straightness

RIVER Large natural streams of (information) usually fed by covering (TRIBUTARY) Persons paying acts, statements and gifts that are intended to show gratitude, respect and admiration (COPIOUS) Super abundant in quantity; excessive in speech and ideas (FULSOME) Complementing and flattering to an excessive degree (DIFFUSE) Lacking clarity and conciseness; pouring and sending out so as to spread and cause to spread among a large number of people; wandering 2 Subject to; impregnating characterized by the excessive use of words

ROCK Ruined; also, destitute or bankrupt

ROD Dominion; power

??? To pass; elaps 2 To wonder about 3 To move ahead; progress 4 To move; push forward 5 To wrap round and round upon itself or on an axis 6 To impel or cause to move onward with a steady, surging motion 7 T wrap or envelop in or as in a covering 8 To emit in a full and swelling manner 9 To rob 10 To return to a previous lower level, as by government direction 1 To arrive, especially in numbers; congregate 12 To wallow; luxuriate 13 To accumulate; amass, as profit

ROOF

ROOT[1] That from which anything derives origin, growth or life and vigor 2 The condition or feeling of belonging to 3 The minimum irreducible base common to all cognate forms 4 To become firmly fixed; established

ROOT[2] To work hard; toil

ROPES To be familiar with all the elements of a sphere of activity 2 To be sophisticated in the ways of the world

ROTE Mechanical routine 2 Repetition of words as a means of learning them, with slight attention to the sense

ROUND Altered for convenience of expression 2 Used to show that a figure has been completely and exactly reached 3 Considerable 4 (Of a person or their manner of speaking) not omitting or disguising anything; frank and Truthful 5 An act of visiting each of a number of people or places; a tour of inspection, typically repeated regularly, in which the safety or well-being of those visited is checked 6 One of a sequence of sessions or groups of related actions or events, typically such that development or progress can be seen between one group and another 7 Located or situated on every side; throughout, all over, everywhere -To surround someone; so as to give support and companionship -To cover or take in the whole area surrounding a particular center -To reach everyone in a particular group or area 8 To lead in another direction 9 Near at hand 10 (Of something abstract) having (the thing mentioned) as a focal point 11 As to encircle or embrace 12 Partially encircling (another person) as part of a gesture of affection 13 Used to convey an ability to navigate or orient oneself 14 In existence, in the vicinity, or in active use

RUDIMENT A first principal, step stage or condition 2 That which is yet undeveloped; *rudimentary* knowledge 3 Being or remaining in an imperfectly developed state

RULE One of a set of explicit or understood regulations or principles governing conduct within a particular activity or sphere 2 A principle that operates within a particular sphere of knowledge, describing or prescribing what is possible or allowable Syn. Precept, principle, standard, axiom, Truth, maxim 3 Control of or dominion over an area or people 4 Exercise ultimate power or authority over (an area and its people) 5 (Of a feeling) have a powerful and restricting influence on (a person's life) 6 Be a dominant or powerful factor or force

RULER One who rules or governs, as a sovereign 2 One who rules lines, as orders
RUSTIC Unculturtured; rude; awkward 2 Unaffected; artless 3 Plain; simple; homely 4 Of or pertaining to any irregular style of work or life style of work

S

SABBATH The seventh day of the week; no burden should come upon the mind 2 All things should be without thought, hesitation, grief etc. 3 All things should be done with joy of heart; all that is done out of joy of heart; not burdensome; easy; happily See **GRACEFUL** [Fusion of OE *sabat* and OF *sabbat, sabat*, both < L *sabbatum* < Gk. *sabbaton* < Hebrew *sabbath* < *sabath* to rest]

	Remember the
Sabbath	Seventh day of the week; no burden should come upon the mind All things should be without <u>thought</u>, <u>hesitation</u>, <u>grief</u> etc. All things should be done with <u>joy of heart</u>; all that is done out of joy of heart; not burdensome Happily and easy day, to keep it
Holy	Regarded with reverence because association with and derived from God; having a divine nature and origin Completely devoted to the service of God; having great Spiritual and moral worth; saintly Designated and set apart for studying Scripture and observance; consecration Characterized by Spiritual exaltation, reverence, etc.; Spiritually pure Evoking, meriting reverence and awe." — Exodus 20:8

Remember the which seventh day of the week? Saturday? Sunday? Wednesday? Why would God care about a manmade day? But on the seventh day God rested And now you have an accurate understanding of how to exercise and perform His rest (and not your own)

SABE To understand; know; savvy [< Sp. *saber* to know < L *sapere]*

SACKCLOTH Any state of sorrow, penance or self-abasement

SACRIFICE A giving up of some cherished or desired Concept, also that which is given up 2 Loss incurred or suffered without return 3 To make an offering or sacrifice of propitiation, supplication etc. [< OF < L *sacrificium* < *sacrum* < religious act (<*sacer* sacred) + *facere* to perform, do]

SACRILEGE The act of violating or profaning anything sacred, including sacramental vows [< OF < L *sacrilegium* < *sacrilegus* temple robber < *sacer, sacris* sacred + *legere* to gather, steal]

SACROSANCT Peculiarly and exceedingly sacred; inviolable

SAD Sorrowful or depressed in spirits; expressing or bearing an appearance of grief or sorrow; unhappy; mournful; gloomy 2 Causing sorrow or pity; distressing; unfortunate 3 Pitifully inadequate; bad; contemptible Syn. *dejected, depressed, desolate, despondent, disconsolate, dismal, doleful, downcast, dreary, lugubrious, melancholy, miserable, sorrowful, woebegone, woeful* Ant. happy, joyous

SAFE Free or freed from danger or evil 2 Having escaped injury or damage; unharmed 3 Not hazardous; not involving risk or loss 4 Conferring safety 5 Prudent or trustworthy 6 Not likely to disappoint; free from doubt or error 7 Not likely to cause harm or injury

SAFETY VALVE Any outlet for pent-up energy or emotion

SAGACIOUS Characterized by discernment, shrewdness and wisdom 2 Ready and apt to apprehend and to decide on a course 3 Quick of scent [< L *sagax, sagacis*, Akin to *sagire* to perceive acutely]

SAGE A venerable man of recognized experience, prudence and foresight; a profoundly wise counselor or philosopher 2 Characterized by or proceeding from calm, far-seeing wisdom and prudence 3 Befitting a sage; profound; learned 4 Grave; serious Syn. See **WISE** [< OF, ult. < LL *sapius* prudent, wise < L pleasant tasting < *sapere* to taste, to have good taste, Akin to **SAVORY**]

SAGEBRUSH An aromatic, bitter, typically perennial herb or small shrub of the composite family, widely distributed on the alkali plains of the western US; especially tridentate, the state under Nevada Compare **WORMWOOD**

SAIL Move smoothly and rapidly or in a stately or confident manner 2 Succeed easily at

SAINT Any one of the blessed in heaven 2 A VERY patient, unselfish person

SAINTHOOD The character or condition of being a very patient, unselfish person 2 Saints collectively

SAKE Purpose of obtaining or accomplishing: to speak slowly for the sake of clarity 2 Affectionate or reverent consideration; interest; account; advantage

SALAAM An oriental salutation or obeisance made with a low bow, the palm of the hand being held to the forehead; also, a respectful or ceremonious verbal greeting [< Arabic *salām* peace, a salutation < *aslama* to submit]

SALT Any compound consisting of the cation of a base and the anion of an acid, combined in proportions that give a balance of electropositive and electronegative charges 2 Piquant humor; dry wit; repartee 3 That which preserves, corrects or purifies; seasoning: the salt of criticism

SALTATORIAL Built or adapted for learning

SALUTARY Calculated to bring about a sound condition by correcting evil or promoting good; beneficial 2 Salubrious; wholesome [< F *salutaire* < L *salutaris* < *salus, salutis* health]

SALVABLE Capable of being saved or salvaged [< LL *salvare* See **SAVE**]

SALVAGE A person in whose favor or behalf salvage has been effected

SALVATION The process or state of being saved; preservation from impending evil 2 Deliverance from sin and penalty, realized in a future state; redemption 3 Any means of deliverance from danger, evil or ruin 4 **Life**, **Truth** and **Love** understood and demonstrated as supreme over all [< OF < LL *salvatio, -onis* < L *salvus* **SAFE**]

SALVE Anything that heals, soothes or mollifies 2 Praise or esteem 3 To soothe; appease, as conscience, etc.

SALVO An evasion, reservation or bad excuse

SAMARITAN Good Samaritan (which see)

SANCTIFY To set apart as holy or for holy purposes; consecrate 2 To free from sin; purify or make holy 3 To give religious sanction to; render sacred or inviolable, as a vow 4 To render productive or conducive to holiness or Spiritual blessing [< OF *sanctifier* < LL *sanctificare* < L *sanctus* holy + *facere* to make]

SANCTIMONY Assumed or outward sanctity; a show of holiness or devoutness; exaggerated gravity or solemnity See **HYPOCRISY**

SANCTION To approve authoritatively; confirm; ratify 2 To countenance; allow 3 Final or authoritative confirmation, justification or ratification 4 A formal decree 5 A provision for securing conformity to law, as by the enactment of rewards or penalties or both 6 In international law, coercive measures adopted, usually by several nations at the same time, to force a nation that is violating international law to desist or yield to adjudication 7 That which makes virtue morally obligatory, or which furnishes a motive for man to seek it [< L *sanctio, -oins* decree, sanction < *sancire* to hollow]

SANCTUARY TABERNACLE~ The human body as the dwelling place of the soul

SANCTUM A private room where one is not to be disturbed -A place of great privacy

SAND Moments of time or life 2 Grit; courage

SANE Mentally sound; not deranged 2 Proceeding from a sound mind [< L *sanus* whole, healthy]

SANGUINE Of buoyant disposition; hopeful; confident; cheerful 2 Ruddy; robust [< OF *sanguin* < L *sanguineus* < *sanguis, -inis* **BLOOD**]

SANITY Soundness of mind; mental health 2 Sane moderation or reasonableness [< L *sanitas* health < *sanus* healthy]

SAPIENCE Wisdom; learning [< OF < L *sapientia* < *sapiens, -entis*]

SAPIENT Wise; sagacious [< OF < L *sapiens, -entis*, ppr. of *sapere* to have good taste]

SATAN

SAVE To set aside for future use 2 To treat carefully so as to avoid fatigue, harm etc. 3 To avoid the need or trouble of; prevent by timely action 4 To deliver from spiritual death or the consequences of sin; redeem [< OF *salver, sauver* < LL *salvare* to save < L *salvus* safe]

SAVOIR-FAIRE Ability to say and do the right thing; tact; literally, to know how to act

SAVOIR-VIVRE Good social manners; literally, to know how to live

SAVOR A complete joy to delight in ; specific, distinctive, characteristic; quality and approach to a quality character 2 With the power to excite the interest **REPUTE~** To be computed; considered, held, deemed, reckoned, and accounted to be such To be considered and esteemed as a person to be as specified (in the passive) 2 A reputation in good repute 3 Respectable 4 To give yourself the pleasure

SAW To perceived with the mind

A maxim; adage 2 Something said; utterance See **PROVERB**

SCAB A mean contemptible fellow 2 A workman who will not join or act with a union

SCALE To determine; decide

SCAPE To gather or accumulate with effort or difficulty 2 To manage or get along with difficulty 3 A difficult situation; predicament

SCARLET Unchaste; whorish

SCATTER To throw about in various places; strew; sprinkle 2 To separate and drive away in different directions; disperse; rout 3 To reflect, refract, or deflect (radiant energy) irregularly 4 Dissipate [ME *scateren* to squander? Akin to **SHATTER**]

SCORN A feeling of contempt or loathing, as for someone or something deemed inferior or unworthy of attention; disdain 2 Behavior characterized by such a feeling; derision 3 An expression of contempt or disdain 4 To hold or treat with contempt; despise 5 To reject with scorn; spurn 6 To mock; jeer Syn.

Scorn, disdain and *contempt* denote feelings directed toward that which we regard as base or repellent *Disdain* is the mildest term; it may be shown simply by the avoidance of the unworthy *Scorn* suggests a more overt expression and is often shown by a loud and haughty rejection of that which offends We may show *scorn* or *disdain* toward someone we find repellent or uninteresting; *contempt* always implies the passing of an adverse moral judgment upon another person Ant. regard, approval, appreciation

SCRIPTURAL Pertaining to, contained in, quoted from or in accordance with the Scriptures

SCRIPTURE The Books of the Old and New Testaments, including often the Apocrypha

SCRUPULOUS Caution in action because of wish to do right; nicely conscientious 2 Resulting from the exercise of scruples; exact; careful

SCRUTINY To observe carefully; examine in detail 2 Close examination or investigation

SEA Anything that resembles or suggests the sea, as something vast, boundless or widespread 2 At a loss; bewildered **SEAL** Anything that confirms or ratifies; a pledge; authentication 2 Any instrumentality that keeps something close, secret or unknown 3 To grant or assign under a seal 4 To establish or settle finally; determine 5 To sign with the cross

SEAR To become withered

SEARCH The act of seeking or looking diligently 2 Investigation; inquiry 3 A critical examination or scrutiny 4 To look through or explore thoroughly or in order to find something; go over or through in making a search 5 To examine with close attention; probe 6 To penetrate or pierce

SEAT The place where anything is situated, settled, or established 2 The privilege or right of membership 3 To locate, settle, or center; usually in the passive Akin to **SIT**

SECOND To act as a supporter or assistant of; promote; encourage

·SECRET Keeping separate or hidden from view or knowledge or from all persons except the individuals concerned; concealed; hidden 2 Beyond normal comprehension; obscure; recondite 3 Known or revealed only to the initiated 4 Affording privacy; secluded 5 An underlying reason; that which when known, explains **The KEY** -In privacy; in a hidden place

SECULAR Of or pertaining to this world or the present life; temporal; worldly; distinguished from Spiritual

To lead astray; entice into wrong, disloyalty, etc.; tempt 2 To induce to engage in secular conversation, especially for the first time [< L *seducere* < *se-* apart + *ducere* to lead]

SEDUCE To lead astray; entice into wrong, disloyalty, etc.; tempt 2 To induce to engage in illicit sexual intercourse, especially for the first time [< L seducere < se- apart + ducere to lead]

SEE To perceive with the mind; to understand 2 To find out or ascertain 3 To have experience or knowledge of 4 Take care of; be sure 5 To find out; inquire 6 To understand; comprehend 7 To think; consider 8 To gain certain knowledge, as by awaiting an outcome 9 To inquire into the facts, causes etc., of -To aid or protect, as throughout a period of difficulty or danger -To work or wait until an undertaking, ordeal etc., is finished

SEED That from which anything springs; source 2 To grow to maturity and produce 3 The cause or latent beginning of a feeling, process, or condition 4 To cause to begin to develop or grow 5 Reproduce itself by means of its own seeds

SEEK To go in search of; to look for 2 To strive for; try to get or obtain 3 To endeavor or try 4 To ask or inquire for; request 5 To go to; betake oneself to 6 To search or explore

SEEMING Having the appearance of reality; apparent but not necessarily actual Syn. Appearance; semblance; especially, false show

SEEMLY Befitting the properties; proper; decorous -Becomingly; decently; appropriately [< ON *saemiliger* honorable < *saemr* fitting]

SEETHE To be agitated or excited, as by rage 2 turmoil

SEIZE Take hold suddenly and forcibly; clutch; grasp 2 To grasp mentally; comprehend; understand 3 To take possession of by authority or right 4 To act upon with sudden and powerful effect 5 To take advantage of immediately, as an opportunity

SELF An individual known or considered as the subject of his own consciousness 2 Anything considered as having a distinct personality 3 Personal interests or advantage 4 Anything, class, attribute that, abstractly considered, maintains a distinct and characteristic individuality or identity

SELF-ABNEGATION The complete putting aside of oneself and one's own claims for the sake of some other person; self-sacrifice

Syn. *Self-abnegation*, *self-denial*, *renunciation* and *self-sacrifice* refer to the voluntary giving up of something desired or prized *Self-abnegation* implies the valuation of another's welfare above one's own *Self-denial* emphasizes conscious, deprivation to achieve some purpose or personal advantage Prolonged *self-denial* becomes *renunciation*: to gain inner peace by the *renunciation* of worldly ambitions The strongest of these words is *self-sacrifice*: it implies the surrender of something dearly prized and may extend to the giving up of life itself for another Ant. Self-indulgence, self-gratification

SEND To cause or direct (a person) to go 2 To cause to be taken or directed to another place 3 To cause to come, happen, etc.; grant 4 To bring into a specified state or condition 5 To cause to issue

SENSE That which commends itself to the understanding as being in accordance with reason and good judgment 2 Capacity to perceive or appreciate 3 To comprehend; understand Syn. *Sense*, *discernment*, *judgment*, *discretion*, *sagacity* and *wisdom* relate to the ability to understand situations, to make sound decisions and to anticipate consequences *Sense*, the most general of these words, is the ability to act effectively in any given situation, and may be a characteristic of both men and animals The other words describe human qualities only *Discernment* is analytic *sense*, the ability to see things clearly and to perceive relationships *Judgment* and *discretion* refers to the practical use of *sense Judgment* is *sense* applied to the making of sound and correct decisions and so depends to some degree upon *discernment*; *discretion* adds a note of caution or shrewdness to *judgment* and suggests the making of decisions that are safe as well as sound and correct *Sagacity* and *wisdom* may be considered the highest development of *sense* Both words suggest native ability, enhanced by training and experience *Sagacity* is habitual good *sense* and sound judgment; *wisdom* is a unique quality including all the others here compared, and implying in addition wide learning and experience, a trained intellect, and the capacity for profound thought and insight

SENSE ORGAN A structure specialized to receive sense impressions, as the eyes, nose, ear, etc.

SENSE PERCEPTION Direct knowledge or perception of things through the senses 2 The capability of sensation; power to perceive or feel 3 The capacity of sensation and rational emotion, as distinguished from intellect and will 4 Susceptibility or sensitiveness to outside influences or mental impressions; also abnormal sensitiveness 4 Appreciation accompanying mental apprehension; discerning judgement 5 Responsiveness to pathos or to artistic or esthetic values 6 Sentimentality

SENSUAL Pertaining to the body or to the physical senses; carnal 2 Resembling imagery that appeals to the senses -Sensuous refers not only to the physical senses but to any means of feeling sensitivity, as intellectual or **ESTHETIC**- Relating to perception by the senses' 3 Sensual is generally restricted to bodily sensations and to the satisfaction of the bodily appetites

SEPARATE To set asunder; disunite or disjoin; sever 2 To occupy a position between; serve to keep apart 3 To divide 4 To isolate 5 To consider separately; distinguish between 6 To draw apart 7 To part company; withdraw from association or combination 8 Distinct; individual [< L *separatus*, pp. of *separare* < *se*- apart + *parare* to **PREPARE**]

SEPARATION Division 2 The state of being disconnected or apart 3 Dividing line 4 Relinquishment of cohabitation between thoughts and self

SERAPH A celestial being having three pairs of wings 2 The highest of the nine orders of angels

SERPENT An insinuating and treacherous person

SERVE To work for, especially as a servant 2 To be of service to 3 To promote the interests of; aid; help 4 To obey and give homage to: to serve **God** 5 To satisfy the requirements of; suffice for 6 To furnish or provide, as with a regular supply 7 To be suitable or usable, as for a purpose 8 To be favorable

SERVICE Assistance or benefit afforded another 2 A useful result or product of labor that is not a tangible commodity 3 Devotion to **God**, as demonstrated by obedience and good works 4 A formal and public exercise of worship 5 The state or position of a servant, especially a domestic servant

SET To put in a fixed or immovable position, condition or state 2 To appoint or prescribe 3 To assign for performance, completion etc. 4 To assign to some specific duty or function 5 To present or perform so as to be copied or emulated 6 To give a specific direction to; direct 7 To describe as taking place 8 To begin a journey 9 To have a specified direction 10 To start; begin 11 To found; establish 12 To purpose or put forward 13 To cause -To encourage; exhilarate 14 Established by authority or agreement; prescribe; appoint 15 Deliberately and systematically conceived 16 Formed 17 Permanent change of form 18 A condition, temporary or recurrent, preparing an individual for a particular kind of action or response

SEW To conclude successfully

SEX Either of two divisions, male and female which organisms are distinguished- (the carnal material structure of an individual life form) or soul and spirit (a whole with interdependent parts, likened to a Living Being) [< OF *sexe-* < L *sexus*, prob. Orig. < *secare* **to divide**]

SHADOW Anything unreal or unsubstantial 2 A faint representation or indication 3 A remnant; vestige 4 An insignificant trace or portion 5 Gloom; a saddening influence 6 An inseparable companion 7 To represent or foreshow dimly or vaguely

SHAKE To affect in a specified manner by or as by vigorous action 2 To weaken or disturb; unsettle 3 To agitate or rouse; stir 4 To get rid of or away from 5 To become unsteady 6 To hurry; make haste 7 To shock or jar mentally 8 To receive fair treatment 9 To make weak, unsound, or unreliable

SHAME A painful sense of guilt or degradation caused by consciousness of guilt or anything degrading, unworthy, or immodest 2 Sensitiveness or susceptibility to such feelings 3 One who or that which brings reproach or disgrace 4 To make ashamed 5 To bring shame upon; disgrace 6 To impel by a sense of shame

SHARE ¹ A portion; allotted or equitable part 2 An equitable part of something enjoyed or suffered in common -To partake equally, as in finding out the mysteries of **God** from His Holy Scriptures 3 To enjoy or endure in common 4 Of Atoms, to arrange (valence electrons) with another atom so that the electrons resonate between them, the resulting configuration being more stable than either atom alone 5 To have a part; participate

SHARE ² A plowshare (which see)

SHARP Having a keen edge or an acute point 2 Coming to an acute angle; not obtuse 3 Keen of perception or discernment; also, shrewd in bargaining; artful 4 Ardent; eager; keen, as the appetite; impetuous, or fiery, as a combat or debate; vigilant or attentive 5 Affecting the mind, as if cutting or piercing; poignant; acrimonious 6 Of consonants, voiceless 7 Excellent, as in dress, mental perception, etc. See **ASTUTE** 8 In a sharp manner; sharply 9 Promptly; exactly

SHEEP A meek or timid person 2 A person who is too easily influenced or led

SHEPHERD A pastor, leader or guide -To watch and tend **SHIELD** To avert; forbid

SHINE To be bright with the expression of a particular emotion Syn. Glowing, beaming, radiant, happy 2 To excel or be conspicuous in splendor, beauty, or intellectual brilliance; be preeminent 3 To cause to shine 4 To try to please 5 To become fond of Syn. *Shine, glow, glair, and twinkle* mean to give out Light A body may *shine* with its own reflected bright and steady Light *Glow* usually implies self-luminosity *Glare* suggests a dazzling brightness To *twinkle* is to give out Light intermittently, as distant stars appear to do

SHIRT Remain calm; keep one's temper

SHOD/SHOE To furnish with a guard 2 Protection against wear

SHOULDER To assume as something to be borne; sustain; bear

SHOW To cause or permit to be seen; manifest 2 To give in a marked or open manner; confer; bestow 3 To cause or allow (something) to be understood or known; explain; reveal 4

To cause (someone) to understand, or perceive; convince; teach 5 To make evident by logical process; prove; demonstrate 6 To guide, lead, introduce 7 To indicate 8 To appear; seem 9 To expose or be exposed 10 To be evident or prominent 11 To be better than 12 Anything shown or manifested 14 A pertense or semblance 15 Any public exhibition, contest, etc. 16 A promise or indication

SHORE Support or assist something that would otherwise fail or decline

SHOWER An abundance of (the Word, epiphanies, understanding, etc.) 2 To discharge; pour out 3 To bestow with liberality

SHUNT To shift or transfer one's views or course 2 To be diverted by a course 3 To evade by turning away from

SHUT To close 2 To prevent ingress or egress 3 To close and fasten securely 4 To forbid entrance into or exit from 5 Confine or exclude; bar 6 To hide; suppress

SICK Expressive of or experiencing disgust or unpleasant emotion 2 Impaired or unsound from any cause as thoughts 3 Mentally unsound 4 Depressed and longing; languishing 5 Declined by reason of satiety or disgust 6 Sadistic or macabre in some way; morbid 7 Of soil 8 Exhausted; unable to produce a profitable yield; diseased -Sick people collectively

SIDE An opinion, aspect, or point of view 2 Superciliousness of manner; pretentiousness 3 Not primary; subordinate; incidental

SIEGE The time during which one undergoes difficulty

SIGHT A mental point of view; estimation 2 An opportunity to investigate or study 3 Great quantity or number -Never; not at all -Not nearly

SIGN To mark or consecrate with a sign, especially with a cross

SIGNIFICANT Having or expressing a meaning; bearing or embodying a meaning 2 Conveying or having some covert meaning

SIGNIFY By signs and words making it known 2 To be an indication of 3 A symbol; having as a 4 Meaning; betokening in any way 5 To amount to have some meaning or importance 6 To express; communicate; announce

SILENCE The state or quality of being silent; abstinence from speech or noise 2 Absence of sound or noise; stillness 3 To make silent; take away the **AUTHORITY** to speak or the **POWER** of reply from 4 To stop the motion or activity of; quiet -Be silent [< F < L *silentium* < *silere* to be silent]

SILVER Eloquent; persuasive

SIMILAR Of like characteristics, nature, or degree; of the same scope, order, or purpose 2 Shaped alike as figures that will become congruently the alteration of linear dimensions, the angels remaining unchanged

SIMPLE Consisting of one thing; single; uncombined 2 Not complex or complicated; easy 3 Without embellishment; plain; unadorned 4 Free from affectation; sincere; artless 5 Of humble rank or condition; lowly 6 Of weak intellect; silly; feebleminded 7 Insignificant; trifling 8 Lacking luxury; frugal 9 Having nothing added; mere 10 That cannot be or has not been decomposed; elementary; also, unmixed 11 Not divided or subdivided; entire 12

That which is simple; an unartificial, uncomplex, or natural (persons character) 13 A person of humble position

SIN A transgression, especially when deliberate, of a law having divine authority 2 Any fault or error; as an offence 3 To violate any requirement of right, duty or propriety; do wrong 4 To effect, cause to have a specified result etc.

SINCERE Being in reality as it is in appearance; real genuine 2 Free from hypocrisy; honest; faithful 3 Being without admixture; pure 4 Sound; whole [< L *sincerus* uncorrupted < *sin-* without + stem of *caries* decay]

SINNER One who transgresses against moral principles

SIT To remain passive, inactive, or in a position of idleness or rest 2 To assume an attitude or take a position for a special purpose 3 To occupy or be entitled to a seat in a deliberative body 4 To have or exercise judicial authority 5 To fit or be adjusted; suit 6 To be suffered or born, as a burden 7 **To keep a good seat upon** 8 To belong to, as a member 9 To join or take part 10 To hold discussions about and look into carefully, as Scripture and His Key

SKIN One's life, as the matters at hand and far off 2 **In a close but not apparent figurative relationship**

SKIRT To evade or avoid (a subject, issue) by **CIRCUMVENTION** To avoid (defeat, failure, unpleasantness, etc.) by artfulness or deception; avoid by anticipating or outwitting 2 To surround or encompass, as by stratagem; entrap: to circumvent a body of enemy troops

SLANDER An oral statement of a false, malicious, or defamatory nature, tending to damage another's reputation, means of livelihood, etc. See **ASPERSE** Doublet of **SCANDAL**

SLAVE A person in mental or moral subjection to a habit, vise or influence

SLAY To smite; strike See **KILL**

SLEEP A state of reduced physical nervous activity and partial unconsciousness 2 **REPOSE**- Situated, or kept in a particular place See **COGNATE**- Allied in characteristics; having the same nature or quality

SLOUGH ¹ A state of moral depravity or despair

SLOUGH ² To discard; shed, as a habit

SLOUGH OF DESPOND Deep despair or dejection; despondency [after the Slough of Despond in John Bunyan's Pilgrim's progress

SMALL Being of slight moment, weight, or importance 2 Lacking in moral or mental breadth; narrow; ignoble; mean; paltry 3 Lacking in the qualities of greatness; not largely gifted 4 Weak in characteristic properties 5 Of low degree; obscure 6 Lacking in power or strength 7 In a small way; trivially; also, timidly

SMILE A pleasant aspect 2 Propitious or favorable disposition; favor; blessing 3 To give a smile; wear a cheerful aspect 4 To show approval or favor 5 To express by means of a smile; effect as by a smile [ME *smilen*, prob. > LG]

Syn. *Smile*, *grin* and *simper* denote an expression of pleasure or amusement made by winding the mouth. In a *smile*, the mouth is closed or slightly opened; in a *grin* it is open wide, displaying the teeth Otherwise, the words differ chiefly in the state of mind inferred from the expression of the face A *smile* suggests pleasure, satisfaction, good humor, approval or smity A *grin* may denote amusement, triumph, or sudden joy Self-consciousness, coyness or affectation are expressed by a *simper*

SMITE To affect powerfully with sudden feeling; in the passive 2 To affect as if by a blow; come upon suddenly: The thought *smote* him

SNOW To make an overwhelming impression on 2 To persuade 3 To overwhelm with a larger amount of something than can be conveniently dealt with 4 To defeat overwhelmingly 5 Entirely pure

SNUFFLE/SNIFF To express contempt 2 Meeting the usual standard, as in quality 3 Not easily deceived; sharp-witted Rare Cant; hypocrisy

SOCIAL Disposed to hold friendly intercourse with others; also, devoted to or promoting friendly intercourse 2 Of, pertaining to or characteristic of persons considered aristocratic, fashionable etc. 4 Venereal; social disease

SOCIETY The system of community life in which individuals form a continuous and regulatory association for their mutual benefit and protection 2 The body of persons composing such a community; also, all people collectively, regarded as having certain common characteristics and relationships 3 A body of persons associated for a common purpose or object

SON Characterized or influenced by some quality or representing the quality or character of (a person, animal, or object)

SORE Grieved; distressed 2 Arousing painful feelings; irritating 3 Extreme or severe 4 Offended; aggrieved 5 Painful memory

SOUL The rational, emotional, and volitional faculties in man, conceived of as forming an entity distinct from the body The emotional faculty of man as distinguished from the intellect 2 A person considered as the embodiment of a quality or attribute The disembodied Spirit of one who has expired -The Divine principle; God **NOTE:** The intellect which is the mind is the Spirit- **THUS:** Without the Spirit man cannot understand and soon will forget all he has known Becoming another man altogether, what benefit was his former life?

SOUND 1 To test or examine by

SOUND 2 **Founded in Truth**; valid; legal 2 **Correct in views or process of thought** 3 Profound as rest; deep; unbroken 4 Complete; effectual; thorough 5 Solid; stable; firm; safe; also, Trustworthy 6 Based on good judgement ~To test the depth of 7 **To discover or try to discover the views and attitudes of (a person) by means of conversation and roundabout questions** 8 To try to ascertain or determine (beliefs, attitudes etc.) in such a manner 9 To search or examine, as with sound Isaiah 1:6

SOVEREIGN Free, independent and in no way limited by external authority or influences

SOW To spread abroad; disseminate; implant: to sow the seed of distrust

SPACE That which is characterized by dimensions extending indefinitely in all directions from any given point, and within which all material bodies are located 2 An occasion; opportunity

SPATE A sudden or vigorous outpouring, as of words, feelings, etc.

SPEAK Express and convey ideas, opinions, etc. 2 To use and be capable of using in conversation

SPIRIT State of mind; mood; temper; the aspect regarded as the intrinsic and central constituent of its character 2 The part of a human being that is incorporeal and invisible and is characterized by intelligence, personality, self-consciousness, and will; the mind 3 The universal aspect of reality, regarded as independent of and opposed to matter 4 The creative animating power or divine influence of God 5 A person regarded with reference to any particular characteristic or temper 6 The vital essence or animating force, especially in man 7 Vivacity, energy; adore 8 Ardent loyalty and devotion 9 True intent or meaning as opposed to outward, formal observance 10 The emotional faculty of man; the heart 11 Having a special kind of nature of 12 Divine substance [< OF *espirit* < L *Spiritus* breath, Spirit < *spirare* to breath Doublet of **SPRITE**] Isaiah 10:18

marrow n. *late 14c [< OE marrow < *mærh* < Proto-Grm *mazga, merg* < OHGrm *margm* Grm *mark* marrow < PIE *mozgo* marrow < Skrit. *majjan Avestan mazga* marrow < Old Church Slav *mozgu* < Lithuanian *smagenės* brain] Fig., Inmost or central part c. 1400 *myelo* v. Before vowels *myel*, word-forming element meaning marrow, spinal cord [< Gk. *myelos* marrow, the **BRAIN-** The enlarged and greatly modified part of the central nervous system 2 Mind; intellect 3 To be obsessed by]*late 14c from marrow + bone n. A poetic [< OE *mearhcofa* marrow-chamber] *1853 [< Gk *myelos* marrow + -oma **PIT-** An abyss so deep that one cannot return from it, as the grave or hell 2 To match as antagonists; set in opposition 3 To set someone or something in conflict or competition with 4 A low or wretched psychological state] *hard seed 1841 [< Du pit, kernel, seed, marrow < MDu pitte, ult., Pro-Grm *pithan* source of **PITH-** The essence of something 2 Concentrated force; vigor; substance 2 The essential part; quintessence; gist heart, substance, nub, core, crux, gist, **meat**, kernel, marrow, **burden**] *also *myeline* soft material found in nerve tissues 1867 [< Gtmn *myelin* 1854 < Gk *myelos* Marrow; the brain; innermost part] *mad, moist, wet, also used of various qualities of food [< Sansk *madati* it bubbles, gladdens, *medah* fat, marrow] ***MEDULLA** n. Hindmost segment of the brain 1650s [< L *medulla* lit., marrow] perhaps related to or influenced by *medius* middle" but compare also Old Irish *smiur*, Welsh *mer* marrow The word was used in the Latin senses in Middle English Related: *Medular; medullary*

SPIRITUAL Of, pertaining to, having the nature of, consisting of Spirit, as distinguished from matter; incorporeal 2 Pertaining to or affecting the immaterial nature or soul of man 3 Of or pertaining to God 4 Sacred; not lay or temporal -*Spiritual* authorities, distinguished from secular 5 Marked or characterized by the highest qualities of the human mind; intellectualized 6 That which pertains to sacred matters or to the Spirit

SPLEEN The organ regarded as the seat of various emotions 2 Ill temper; spitefulness 3 Low spirits; melancholy

SPOIL To impair or destroy the value, beauty, or usefulness of 2 To weaken or impair the character or personality of, especially by overindulgence 3 To lose normal or useful qualities, especially to become tainted or decayed 4 Ruin; destruction 5 Damage; waste

SPREAD To make more widely known, active, etc. 2 To force apart or further apart 3 To set forth or record in full

SPRINKLE A small quantity [ME *sprenkelen* Akin to LG *sprinklen* to scatter]

STAIN Dishonor; disgrace

STAND To remain unimpaired, unchanged, or valid 2 To have or be in a specified state, condition or relation 3 To be consistent; accord; agree 4 To collect and remain -To have a chance or as of success 5 To stay near and ready to help; support 7 To abide by; make good 8 To remain passive and watch, as when help is needed 9 To wait, as for the completion of an uninterrupted message 10 To put up with -To conform to reason 11 Remain upright and entire rather than fall into ruin or be destroyed 12 Rest without disturbance 14 Remain on a specified course 15 Act in a specified capacity 16 Withstand (an experience or test) without being damaged

STAR Classes of self luminous celestial beings, exclusive of certain knowledge, including the Son They are classified according to their orders Collateral adjective: **ASTRAL** relating to a supposed non physical realm of existence to which various psychic and paranormal phenomena are ascribed, and in which the human body is said to have a counterpart 2 Anyone who shines prominently in their calling 3 A heavenly body considered as influencing (someone's) disposition 4 To transform 5 Be prominent or brilliant

STELLAR Exceptionally good; outstanding

STEAL ss

STEER a piece of advice or information concerning the development of a situation

STEM To be descended or derived 2 To resist or make progress against (any opposing force) 3 To stand firm 4 To stop, hold back or damn up, as information [< ON *stemma* to stop]

STILL Making no sound; silent 2 Free from disturbance or agitation; peaceful; tranquil; calm 3 Increasing degree; even more 4 Always; constantly

STOCK A quantity of good acquired or kept on hand for future use in proportion relative to the magnitude existing between parts (ourselves), a part (the Word) and the whole (**God**); to adjust properly as to relative magnitude, amount or degree to think + **REASON**, formed with a harmonious relation of parts, having trust and belief in 2 Livestock 3 To make a careful estimation or appraisal -To give credence to -To have trust or belief in 4 Kept continually ready or constantly brought forth, like old goods 5 The shares that entitle the holder to interest and to part ownership ["Ancient Goods" < for + share with]

STONE To make hard or unyielding, as the heart 2 To turn away; disregard

STOREHOUSE A large or inexhaustible fund; reservoir: a *storehouse* of ideas

STRANGE Unaccountable 2 Distant in manner 3 Inexperienced; unskilled, unaccustomed [< OF *estrange* < L *extraneus* foreign < extra on the outside] Doublet of **EXTRANEOUS**

STRANGLE To repress; suppress 2 To inhibit the action or development of

STRANGER One unversed in or unacquainted or unfamiliar with something specified

STRAY To wander from the proper course 2 To fail to concentrate; digress 3 To deviate from right or goodness 4 Irregular; occasional; casual; unrelated [< OF *estraier* to wander about, ult. < L *extra vagare* to wander outside]

STRENGTH Vigor or force of intellect; moral power, style, etc. 2 The degree of intensity or concentration 3 Binding force or validity, as of Truth 4 One regarded as an embodiment of sustaining or protecting power 5 Potency, as the understanding

STRENGTHEN To encourage; hearten; animate

STRIFE Any contest for advantage or superiority; rivalry

STRIKE To arrive at; come upon 2 To discover; find 3 To affect suddenly or in a specified manner 4 To come to the mind of; occur to 5 To impress in a specified manner 6 To attract the attention of; impress 7 To cause to enter or penetrate deeply or suddenly 8 To arrive at by reckoning 9 To take a course; start and proceed 10 To affect; amaze 11 To have telling effect 12 To originate; hit upon 13 To start up; begin as a friendship 14 A new or unexpected discovery 15 Any unexpected or complete success

STRIPE A decoration of interestthat is added to reveal plainness 2 Distinctive quality or character; kind; sort

STUDY To apply the mind in acquiring a knowledge of 2 To examine; search into 3 To look at attentively; scrutinize 4 To endeavor to memorize 5 To give thought and attention to, as something to be done or devised 6 To follow a regular course of instruction; be a student; disciple 7 To muse; meditate 8 To acquire more complete information concerning; as by investigation 9 A particular instance or form of mental work 10 Something to be studied 11 A specific product of or work resulting from studious application 12 A careful elaborated literary treatment of a subject 13 A state of deep thought or absent-mindedness 14 Earnest endeavour; thoughtful attention or care 15 Something worthy of close attention [< Of *estudier* < *estudie* study < L *studium* zeal < *studere* to apply oneself, be diligent]

STUMBLING

SUBDUE To gain dominion over; subjugate; vanquish 2 To overcome by training, influences or persuasion; tame 3 To repress 4 to reduce the intensity of; soften 5 To bring (man) under cultivation [< OF *soduire* to deceive < L *subducere* to withdraw; infl. in meaning by L *subdere* to overcome] Syn. Conquer 2 Master; control; bridle 3 Check; restrain 4 Moderate; temper

SUBJECT Liable to be affected by; exposed to the influence of 2 Likely to bring about or incur

SUBJECTIVE Relating to, proceeding from or taking place within an individual's mind, emotions etc.: Opposed to *objective* 2 Originating from or influenced by one's own personal interests, prejudices, emotions etc. 3 Of the mind or emotions only; fanciful; illusory

SUBJECTIVISM The doctrine that knowledge is merely subjective and relative and is derived from one's own consciousness 2 The doctrine that we know directly no external object 3 The doctrine that there is no objective standard, test or measure of Truth; relativism 4 The doctrine that the individual feeling is the standard by which to judge right and wrong

SUBJUGATE To bring under dominion; conquer; subdue 2 To make subservient in any way 3 To captivate

SUBLIMATE To refine, purify 2 To convert the energy of (instinctual drives) unconsciously into acceptable social manifestations 3 To undergo sublimation [< L *sublimatus*, pp. of *sublimare* < *sublimis* See **SUBLIME**]

SUBMIT To place under or yield to the authority, will or power of another; surrender 2 To present for the consideration, decision, approval of others; refer 3 To give up 4 To be obedient or submissive; be acquiescent See **DEFER** [< L *submittere*, var. of *summittere* < *sub-* underneath + *mittere* to send]

*__SUBSTANCE__ A substantial quality; solidity 2 The essential part of anything said or written; the gist or purport 3 The essential nature that underlines phenomena; that in which qualities or attributes inhere 4 **That which is eternal** [< OF < L *substantia* < *substare* to be present < *sub-* under + *stare* to stand]

SUBSTRATUM That which forms the foundation or groundwork 2 Matter or mind considered as the basis of qualities and groundwork and phenomena; the substance possessing attributes 3 The substance in which something takes root 4 A displaced language that influences the form of an adopted language by way of bilingual speakers [< NL < L, pp. neut. of *substernere* to spread underneath + *sternere* to strew]

SUBTLE Delicate or tenuous in form, character, etc.; ethereal 2 Pertaining to **PERVASIVE** To pass through [< OF *subtil*, alter. of *soutil* subtle; refashioned after L]

SUBTLE Characterized by cunning, craft or artifice; wily; crafty 2 Keen; penetrative; discriminating 3 Apt; skillful 4 Executed with nice art; ingenious; clever; refined 5 Insidious; secretly active 6 Hard to understand; abstruse [< OF *soutil* < L *subtilis* fine, org., closely woven < *sub-* under + *tela* web]

SUFFER To tolerate or endure 2 To sustain as injury or loss 3 To undergo; pass through, as change 4 To bear; endure 5 To allow; permit Syn. See **ALLOW** [< AF *suffrir*, OF *sofrir*, ult. < L *sufferre* < *sub-* up from under + *ferre* to bear]

SULLY To mar the brightness or purity of; soil; defile; tarnish 2 Anything that tarnishes; a stain; spot; blemish [< MF *souiller*, See **SOIL**]

SUMMER A year of Life, especially of early or happy Life 2 A bright and prosperous period

SUN A person regarded as a source of glory or inspiration or understanding 2 Used with reference to someone's success or prosperity 3 Anything brilliant or magnificent or that is a source of splender 4 A position in the spotlight; publicity 5 To shine

SUP Take into the mouth 2 Small amounts 3 A little at a time

SUPPLE Flexible; pliant 2 Yielding to the humor or wishes of others; especially servilely compliant; obsequious 3 Showing adaptability of mind [< OF *supple*, *sople* < L *supplex*, *-icis* submissive, lit., bending under < *sub-* under + stem of *plicare* to fold]

SUPPLIANT Entreating earnestly and humbly; beseeching 2 Manifesting entreaty or submissive supplication

SUPPLICATE To ask for humbly or by earnest prayer 2 To beg something of 3 To beg or pray humbly; make an earnest request

SUPPLY To provide with adequately; satisfy 2 To make good or compensate for, as a loss or deficiency; make up for 3 An amount sufficient for a given use [< OF *sopleer*, *soupleier* < L *supplere* < *sub-* up from under + *ple-*, root of *plenus* full]

SUPREME Highest in power or authority; dominant 2 Highest in degree, importance, quality etc.; utmost: Supreme devotion 3 Ultimate; last; final See **ABSOLUTE** Abbr. *sup.*, *supr.* [< L *supremus* highest, *superl.* of *superus* that is above < *super* above]

SUPREME BEING God

SUPREME SACRIFICE The sacrifice of one's life

SURPLUS Being in excess of what is used or needed 2 That which remains over and above what has been used or required; excess

SURRENDER To yield possession of or power over to another; give up because of demand or compulsion 2 To give up or abandon, as thoughts 3 To give up or relinquish, especially in favor of (something) beneficial; resign

SURVEY To look at in its entirety 2 To look at carefully and minutely; scrutinize; inspect 3 To determine accurately Syn. See **SEE** The operation, act, process or results of examining a (person) to ascertain the condition, quality, character, depth, etc. See **SOUND**

SUSTAIN To keep from sinking or falling, especially by bearing up from below; uphold; support 2 To endure without yielding; withstand 3 To undergo or suffer, as loss or injury 4 To keep up or maintain; keep in effect or being 5 To uphold or support as being True or just 6 To prove the Truth or correctness of; corroborate; confirm [< OF *sustein-*, stem of *sustenir*, *sostiner* < L *sustinere* < *sub-* up from under + *tenere* to hold]

SWALLOW To put up with or endure; submit to 2 To believe credulously 3 To refrain from expressing or giving vent to; suppress

SWEAT To work hard; toil; drudge 2 To suffer 3 To force to work under unfavorible conditions 4 To heat so as to extract an element that is easily fusible 5 To subject to torture or rigorous interrogation for the purpose of extracting information 6 Fuming impatience; worry; hurry

SWEET Agreeable or delightful to the mind; arousing gentle, pleasant emotions 2 Having gentle, pleasing, and winning qualities; marked by kindness and amiability; dear; beloved 3 Sound; rich productive: said of soil 4 Feeling of something agreeable to the ear, pleasant in disposition and manners, speech and facial expressions 5 Become a delight to the mind, arousing gentle, pleasant emotions 6 It is likened unto ballroom dance music performed with a regular beat, moderate tempo and an emphasis on a warm tone, clearly outlined melody 7 Without lack of improvisation; infatuated; in love

SWIIFT Coming without warning; unexpected 2 Acting with readiness; prompt 3 Quickly 4 Possessing extraordinary powers of flight

SWINE A low, greedy, stupid or vicious person

SWORD Power; authority; sovereignty 2 Power, violence, or destruction -The sword symbolizes power, protection, authority, strength, and courage; metaphysically, it represents discrimination and the penetrating power of the intellect - "The sword of a mouth" metaphorically means: The power, authority, and sovereignty, in the spoken words (because the Truth of it cuts like a knife: the deeper the realization, the deeper the wound, sometimes dividing bone and marrow, also soul and Spirit

SYMBOLIC Conveying a relation or connection

SYNAGOGUE A place for worship and religious instruction 2 A congregation or assemblage for religious instruction and observances [< OF *synagoge* < LL *synagoga* < Gk. *synagōgē* assembly < *synagein* to bring together < *syn-* together + *agein* to lead, bring]

SYSTEM Orderly combination or arrangement of parts, elements, etc., into a whole; especially, such combination according to some rational principle; 2 A group of facts, concepts, and phenomena regarded as constituting a natural whole for purposes of philosophic or scientific investigation and construction 3 The connection or manner of connection of parts as related to a whole, or the parts collectively so related; a whole as made up of constitutive parts 4 The state or quality of being in order or orderly; method

T

TABERNACLE The human body as the dwelling place of the soul

TABLE A SYNOPTICAL~ Presenting the same or similar point of view: said of the first three Gospels (**synoptic Gospels**) as distinguished from the fourth; [< NL *synopticus* < Gk. *synoptikos* < *synopsis* synopsis] statement 2 To postpone discussion of (a resolution etc.) until a future time, or an indefinite period [Fusion OF *table* and OE *tabule*, both < L *tabula* board]

TACIT (tas'it) Existing, inferred or implied without being stated; implied by silence or silent **ACQUIESCENCE~** Quiet submission; passive consent; disposed to yield; **ASSENT~** To express agreement, as with an abstract proposition 2 Not expressed but understood by provisions or operation of the (person) 3 Making no sound, silent; noiseless within, and without [< F *tacite* < L *tacitus*, pp. of *tacere* to be silent]

TAKE To assume occupancy of 2 To assume the responsibilities or duties of 3 To bring or except into some relation to oneself 4 To assume as a symbol or badge 5 To impose upon oneself; subject oneself to; undergo 6 To submit to; accept passively 7 To conduct oneself in response to; react to 8 To undertake to; deal with; contend with; handle 9 To understand; comprehend 10 To carry with one; transport; convey 11 To receive into the body as understanding; a breath etc. 12 To accept as something offered, due or given; have conferred on one 13 To let in; admit 14 To indulge oneself in; enjoy 15 To perform, as an action 16 To avail oneself of (an opportunity etc.) 17 To put into effect; adopt 18 To use up or consume; require as necessary 19 To make use of; apply 20 To ascertain or obtain by measuring; computing 21 To obtain or derive from source; adopt or copy 22 To obtain by writing, write down or copy 23 To obtain a likeness or representation of 24 To experience 25 To conceive 26 To BECOME **IMPREGNATED WITH;** absorb 27 To require by construction or usage 28 To begin to grow; germinate 29 To have the intended effect 30 To make one's way; go 31 To resemble 32 To follow as an example -To gain courage or confidence 33 To include; embrace 34 To understand; comprehend 35 To acquire an interest in or devotion to [OE *tacan* < ON *taka]*

TALISMAN Something supposed to produce extraordinary effects 2 An astrological charm or symbol supposed to benefit or protect the possessor [< F < Sp. < Arabic *tilsam, tilasm* magic figure < Gk. *teleein* to initiate < *telos* end, completion]

TALK To confer; consult 2 To be effective or influential 3 To bring into a specified condition or state by talking 4 To discuss, especially so as to promote; praise; extol [ME *talken*, prob. freq. of *talen*, OE *talian* to recon, speak]

TALL Inordinate; extravagant; boastful: also, unbelievable; remarkable 2 Large; excellent; grand 3 Handsome; fine; proud 4 Brave; sturdy; Spirited

TASTE To prove or try as by touch 2 To have experience; to become acquainted through experience 3 A special fondness and aptitude for a pursuit; bent; inclination 4 The faculty of discerning and appreciating what is appropriate or what is peculiarly correct for a given situation 5 Style or form with respect to the rules of propriety or etiquette 6 The act of examining or testing [< OF *taster* to taste, try, feel, prob. ult. < L *laxare* to touch, handle, appraise]

TATTOO A continuous beating or drumming

TAX A heavy demand on one's powers or resources; any onerous duty or requirement; a burden -To subject to severe demand; impose a burden or load upon 2 To make an accusation against; charge; also, to blame; censure [< OF *taxer* < L *taxare* to estimate, appraise. Akin to **TASK**] Syn. assessment, custom, duty, excise, impost, levy, rate, tithe, toil, tribute

TEACH To train by practice or exercise

TEETH See **TOOTH**

TEMPER Frame of mind; mood; self-command; calmness 2 Something mixed with a substance to alter its properties or qualities 3 A middle course 4 To bring to a state of moderation or suitability, as by addition of another quality; moderate 5 To adjust the tone by temperament; tune 6 To adjust 7 To be or become tempered [Fusion of OE *temprian* to mingle, regulate and < OF *temprer*, *tremper* to soak, temper (character), both < L *temperare* to combine in due proportion]

TEMPERAMENT The characteristics physical and mental peculiarities of an individual as manifested in his reactions 2 Mental constitution; makeup; disposition [< L *temperamentum* proper mixture < *temperare* to mix in due proportions]

TEMPERANCE The state or quality of being temperate; habitual moderation 2 The principle or practice of total abstinence of anger 3 Calmness; reserved; self-control [< OF < L *temperantia*, org. neut. pl. of *temperans*, *-antis*, ppr. of *temperare* to mix in due proportions]

TEMPLE Any place considered as occupied by **God**; especially, a sanctified human body [OE *tempel* or OF *temple*, both < L *templum* temple]

TEMPORAL [1] Pertaining to the affairs of the present life; earthly 2 Pertaining to time 3 Temporary; transitory 4 Pertaining to civil law or authority; lay; secular 5 Expressing or denoting time [< L *temporalis* < *tempus*, *temporis* time]

TEMPORAL [2] Of, pertaining to or situated at the temple or temples: the temporal bone [< L *temporalis* < *tempora*]

TEMPORAL BONE A compound bone situated at either side of the head in man and other vertebrates, and containing the organ of hearing

TEMPORALITY A temporal or material matter, interest, revenue etc.; especially, an ecclesiastical possession or revenue 2 The state of being temporal or temporary

TEMPT To be attracted to; invite 2 To provoke or risk provoking 3 To test; prove [< OF *tempter, tenter* < L *temptare, tentare* to test, try, prob. intens. of *tendere* to stretch]

TEMPTATION The act of tempting or the state of being tempted 2 That which tempts Syn. Alluring; attractive; seductive

TEND To tend to the needs or requirements of; take care of; minister to 2 To watch over; look after 3 To be in attendance; serve or wait 4 To give attention or care

TENDENCY The state of being directed toward some purpose, end or result; inclination; bent; aptitude 2 That which tends to produce some specified effect [< Med. L *tendentia*, org. neut. pl. of *tendens, -entis*, ppr. of *tendere* to extend, tend]

TENDER [1] Characterized by or expressive of a delicate sensibility; kind affectionate; gentle 2 Susceptible to Spiritual or moral feelings 3 Of delicate effect or quality; soft 4 Requiring deft or delicate treatment: A tender subject [< OF *tendre* < L *tener, teneris]*

TENDER [2] To present for acceptance 2 A formal offer of satisfaction

TENOR Course of thought; general purport 2 A settled course or manner of progress 3 General character and tendency; nature

TENT To pay attention to; observe 2 To tend upon; look after 3 Attention; note; heed

TERSE Short and to the point; concise 2 Rubbed to a polish; clean; polished; refined [< L *tersus*, pp. of *tergere* to rub off, rub down]

TEST To subject to a test or trial; try 2a To assay or refine (the character), as in the process of **CUPELLATION**- A refining process in metallurgy, where ores or alloyed metals are treated under very high temperatures and have controlled operations to separate noble metals, like gold and silver, from base metals like lead, copper, zinc, arsenic, antimony or bismuth, present in the ore 2b To examine by some means of reagent 3a To undergo testing 3b To show specified qualities or properties under testing 4 Subject to conditions that disclose the true character of a person in relation to some particular quality 5 An examination made for the purpose of proving or disproving some matter in doubt 6 A series of questions, problems etc., intended to measure the extent of knowledge, aptitudes, intelligence and other mental traits 7 A criterion or standard of judgment 8 An oath or other confirmatory evidence of principles or belief 9a A reaction by means of which the presence and identity of a compound or one of its constituents may be determined 9b The agent or result of such a reaction [< OF, *cupel*, pot < L *testum* earthen vessel < *testa* potsherd, shell]

TESTIMONY The evidence or proof provided by the existence or appearance of 2 A solemn protest or declaration

THANK To express gratitude to; give thanks to 2 To hold responsible for the good done to another [< OE *thancian* < *thane* thanks, thought]

THANKSGIVING The act of giving thanks, as to **God**; an expression of gratitude 2 A public celebration in recognition of divine favor; also, a day set apart for such celebration

THEANTHROPIC Being both divine and human 2 Having or pertaining to a nature both divine and human [< Gk. *theanthropos* < *theos* **God** + *anthropos* man]

UNKNOWN AUTHOR

THEANTHROPISM The doctrine of the manifestation of **God** in man, or the union of the divine and human in Christ 2 The ascription of human characteristics to a deity 3 Belief in the possibility of the combination in one being of a nature both human and divine

THEM [ME *thiem* < ON, to them]

THEN Granting or assigning 2 Imperative work to be performed; being and acting in; belonging to

THEOCENTRIC Centering on or primarily concerned with **God**

THEOCRASY The mingling of several deities or divine attributes in one personality 2 The mystical intimacy or union of the soul with **God** [< LGk. *theokrasia* < Gk. *theos* **God** + *krasis* a mingling]

THEODICY A reconciling the existence of evil with the goodness and sovereignty of **God** [< F *theodicee* < Gk. *theos* **God** + *dike* justice]

THEOMORPHIC Having the form or likeness of **God**

THEOPATHY Religious emotion aroused by meditation on **God** [< Gk. *theopathia* the suffering of **God** < *theos* **God** + *path-*, stem of *paschein* to suffer]

THERE To, toward or into the place

THESAURUS A book containing a storehouse of words, especially of synonyms and antonyms arranged in categories 2 A storehouse; treasury [< L < Gk. *thesauros* treasure house Doublet of **TREASURE**]

THEURGY Divine or supernatural intervention in human affairs 2 The working of miracles through divine or supernatural aid [< Gk. *theourgia* < *theourgos* divine worker < *Theos* **God** + *ergon* work]

THIEF That which causes loss

THING-IN-ITSELF The ultimate, metaphysical reality behind the physical phenomena perceived by the senses

THINK To seem; appear

THINKER A person of a powerful mind who devotes himself to abstract thought

THIRST Any longing or craving 2 To have an eager desire 3 Eagerly desirous

THOUGHTFUL Deliberated; meditate; cognating 2 Attentive; careful consideration, especially manifesting regard for others 3 Intellectual activity of a specific kind 4 Cogitation; meditation

THORN Anyone that causes discomfort, pain, or annoyance; a vexation

THREAD Anything conceived of as serving to give sequence to the whole 2 To make one's way through or over 3 To make one's way carefully 4 To be present throughout; pervade

THRESHOLD The minimum degree of stimulation necessary for the conscious perception: The *threshold* of consciousness; also called *limen* [iminal OE *therscold]* -The pains of childbirth or death

THROAT The passage leading to the **STOMACH** Any desire or inclination 2 Temper; Spirit 3 Pride; haughtiness 4 To take into and retain

THRONE The third of nine orders of angels 2 Royal estate or dignity; sovereign power 3 Exalted state

158

THROW To cast off or shed; lose; discard 2 To give birth to 3 To waste; squander 4 To revert to ancestral characteristics

THUNDER To take for one's own use anything especially popular or effective originated by another: said especially of an argument or cliche 2 To utter vehement denunciations or threats

THUNDERING Usually great or extreme; superlative

Amazed, astonished, or confounded, as with fear, surprise, etc.

THWART To prevent the accomplishment of, as by interposing an obstacle; foil; frustrate; balk

TIGER A fierce, cruel person

TIMBER Personal character, talent, potentiality

TIME Duration with reference to this world and all finite existence as distinguished from eternity or infinity **GESTATION~ (in the Spiritual sense)** The development of an idea, plan, etc., in the mind (in the carnal sense)

TITHE The tenth part of anything

TOGETHER Into contact and union with each other

TONE A predominating disposition; frame or condition of mind; mood 2 Characteristic style or tendency 3 To blend; harmonize

TONGUE Mere speech, as contrasted with fact or deed 2 A people regarded as having its own language: a Biblical use 3 To reproach; chide 4 To talk; prattle 5 A universal knowledge divided by segregated languages

TOOTH To become interlocked as gear wheels 2 Genuine effectiveness of an agreement

TOUCH To attain to; equal 2 To affect the emotions of; move, especially to pity, gratitude, sympathy etc. 3 To be pertinent to; relate to; concern 4 To treat or discuss in passing; deal with 5 To have to do with, use or partake of 6 To cause to happen or occur 7 To prod gently; rouse 8 A test; trial

TRAIT A distinguishing feature or quality of character See **CHARACTERISTIC**

TRAMMEL A passageway That which limits freedom or activity; an impediment; hindrance

TRAMPLE To tread heavily; injure; violate or ruthlessly

TRANCE [1] A condition intermediate between sleep and wakefulness, characterized by dissolution, involuntary movements, and **AUTOMATISMS~** The performance of actions without conscious thought or intention {cont. trample} of behavior, as in hypnosis 2 A dreamlike state marked by bewilderment and an insensibility to ordinary surroundings

TRANCE [2] A passageway

TRANS Across; beyond; through; on the other side of

TRANSCEND To rise above in excellence or degree 2 To overstep or exceed as a limit 3 To be independent of or go beyond (the universe, experience, etc.) 4 To be transcendent; excel

TRANSCENDENT Of very high and remarkable degree; surpassing; excelling 2 Lying beyond the bounds of all possible human experience and knowledge

TRANSCENDENTAL Beyond or contrary to common sense 2 Not formed by the fundamental operations of algebra

TRANSCENDENTALISM Any of several doctrines holding that reality is essentially mental or Spo\iritual in nature, and that knowledge of it can be obtained by intuitive or a priori, rather than empirical, principles

TRANSCENDENTAL NUMBER A number that cannot be formed by the fundamental operations of algebra

TRANSFORM To change the character, nature, condition etc., of 2 To be or become changed in form or character 3 To change (one's expression or operation) into another equivalent to it or having similar properties 4 Any of a group of constructions that can be considered rewritings or rephrasing of one another [< L *transformare* < *trans-* over + *formare* to form < *forma* form] Gen 35:2; Rom 12:2; 2 Corinth. 3:18; 11:13-14; :15; Philip 3:21

TRANSFORMATION A change from one construction to another construction considered more or less equivalent according to the syntactic laws of a language, as in English, from active to passive or from statement to question

TRANSFORMATIONAL Of or pertaining to linguistic transformations

TRANSFORMATIONAL GRAMMAR A grammar that uses transformations as well as phrase structure to account for the derivation of the sentences of a language

TRANSGRESS To break (an oath, promise, word, etc.); violate 2 To pass beyond or over (limits); exceed 3 To be at fault[Across; to step]

TRANSHUMANCE The movement of cattle or other animals to more suitable places as the seasons change, especially of livestock to and from mountain pastures [< F < *transhumer* < Sp. *trashumar* < L *trans* across + *humare* to cover with earth < *humus* earth]

TRANSLATE To give the sense or equivalent of into another language 2 To explain in other words 3 To change into another form; transform 4 To convey or remove from earth to heaven without experiencing natural death To subject (a body) to translation 2 To transport; enrapture

TRANSMIGRATE The act of transmigrating 2 The assumed passing of the soul after death, from one body to another form visible or invisible

TRANSMIT To send from one person to another; forward; or convey; dispatch 2 To communicate 3 To cause to pass through

TRANSMUTE To change in nature, form, quality, etc.

TRANSPORT To carry or convey from one place to another 2 To carry away with emotion 3 To carry into banishment, especially beyond the sea 4 To kill 5 The state of being transported with rapture; ecstasy

TRAP Personal effects, as luggage ; also, household goods

TRAVERSE To examine carefully; survey; scrutinize

TREASURE Of that which is regarded as valuable, precious or rare 2 To lay up in store; storehouse; accumulate 3 To retain carefully in the mind [< OF *tresor* < L thesaurus < Gk. *thesauros* Doublet of **THESAURUS**]

TREE The characteristic of (someones) mental ability, authority, competency, power, etc.

TREE OF KNOWLEDGE OF GOOD AND EVIL

TREE OF LIFE~ ARBORVITAE An evergreen shrub or tree (genus *Thuya* or *Thuja*) of the pine family, especially *T. occidentalis*: also called *white cedar, tree of life* 2 The branching appearance of the white matter shown in a section of the cerebellum [< L *arbor vitae* tree of life] 3 In the Bible 4a A tree in the garden of Eden whose fruit conferred immortality *Gen.* iii 22 4b A similar tree in heaven *Rev.* xxii 22

TRESPASS To pass the bounds of PROPRIETY or RECTITUDE, to the injury of another; intrude offensively; encroach 2 Any offense done to another 3 Any wrongful act accompanied with force, either actual or implied 4 Any offensive thought or scheme

TRIAL The act of testing or proving by experience or use 2 The state of being tried or tested by suffering 3 An experience, person or thing that puts strength, patience or faith to the test [< AF < *trier* See **TRY**]

TRIBE A number of persons of any class or profession taken together

TRIBUTE A speech, compliment, gift, etc., given in acknowledgement of submission or as the price of peace

TRIBULATION A condition of affliction and distress; suffering; also, that which causes it [< OF *tribulacion* < LL *tribulatio, -onis* < L *tribulatus*, pp. of *tribulare* to thrash < *tribulum* threshing floor < *tri-*, root of *terere* to rub, grInd]

TRIM To act so as to appear to appear to favor both sides in a controversy 2 State of adjustment or preperation; fitting condition; orderly disposition 3 Particular character or nature; kind 4 To cheat; victimize

TROUBLE The state of being distressed, annoyed, upset, afflicted or confused 2 Difficulty, perplexity, annoyance, disturbance etc. 3 Toilsome exertion; pains 4 Enmeshed in threatening difficulties 5 Pregnant and unmarried 6 To cause mental agitation to; distress; worry 7 To agitate or disturb; stir up or roil, as water 8 To inconvenience or incommode 9 To annoy or pester; bother 10 To cause physical pain or discomfort to; afflict [< OF *truble, turble* < *turbler* < L *turbula* mob, dim. of *turba* crowd]

TRUE Faithful to fact or reality; not false or erroneous 2 Faithful to friends, promises or principles; loyal; steadfast 3 Conformable to an existing standard, type or pattern; exact 4 Faithful to Truth; Truthful; honest 5 Faithful to the promise or predicted event; your words; correctly indicative 6 Corresponding to the axis of the earth 7 Truth; covenant; pledge [OE *treowe*. Akin to **TRUCE, TRUST**]

TRUMPET A powerful or decisive stroke, resource, etc. 2 A good fellow 3 To surpass; excell 4 To publish abroad; proclaim

TRUST A confident reliance on the integrity, honesty, veracity or justice of another -Confidence; faith 2 Something committed to one's care for use or safe keeping; a charge; responsibility 3 A confidence in the reliability of persons or things without careful investigation 4 One who is trusted 5 Confident expectation, belief; hope 6 Trustworthiness 7 To allow to do something without fear of consequences 8 To expect with confidence or with hope 9 To believe

Syn. *Trust, faith, confidence* and *reliance* denote the feeling that a person will not fail in duty, service or the like *Trust* implies that this feeling has no reservation, and that it rests upon an estimate of character more than upon evidence *Faith* suggests that this feeling is emotional to a large degree; *faith* does not seek evidence, and so may verge upon credulity *Confidence* suggests a more rational *trust* based upon good evidence *Reliance* is distinguished from the other synonyms in that it is more often used for the act of giving trust: thus, reliance may be considered as the outward expression of trust, faith or confidence Ant. mistrust, suspicion, doubt

TRUTH The state or character of being true in relation to being, knowledge or speech 2 Conformity to fact or reality 3 Conformity to rule, standard, model, pattern or ideal 4 Conformity to the requirements of one's being or nature; steadfastness; sincerity 5 That which is True; a statement or belief that corresponds to the reality 6 A fact as the object of correct belief; reality 7 Tendency or disposition to speak or tell only what is True; veracity 8 The quality of being True; fidelity; constancy 9 Right, according to divine law Syn. See **FACT** [OE *treowth* < *treowe* True]

TRY To make an attempt to do or accomplish 2 To subject to a test; put to proof -To attempt to qualify making inferences from them 3 An arrangement or settlement of differences, or of disputed points 4 Possessing comprehension and good sense 5 Tolerant or sympathetic [< OF *trier* to sift, pick out, prob. < LL *tritare* to thresh < L *tritus*, See **TRITE**] Syn. reason, intelligence, intuition, judgment, perception Compare **INTELLECT**

TURN To revolve mentally; ponder 2 To give graceful or finished form to 3 To change or transform; convert 4 To translate 5 To adapt to some use or purpose; apply 6 To cause to become as specified 7 To change the direction or focus of (thought, attention, etc.) 8 To pass or go beyond 9 To cause or compel to go 10 To take a new direction 11 To become transformed; change 12 To deliver; hand over 13 To set in operation; flow, etc. 14 To set free; release from restraint; imprisonment 15 To bend or incline inward 16 To prove (to be); be found 17 To come or go out, as for duty or service 18 To equipt for 19 To bend or incline upward 20 To refer or apply to 21 To bring or be brought to view by plowing 22 To put in appearance; arrive 23 A knack or special ability 24 A deed performed, regarded as aiding another 25 An advantage proposed or gained

TWELFTH-DAY Epiphany

TWELFTH-NIGHT The evening (Jan. 5th) before Epiphany; sometimes evening (Jan. 6th) of Epiphany - adj. Of or pertaining to Twelfth-night

TWELFTH-TIDE The season of Epiphany

TWO Two equal parts of one whole; a division; a subdivision; a variation

U

UGLY Repulsive to the moral sentiments; revolting 2 Bad in character or consequences 3 Ill-tempered; quarrelsome [< ON *uggligr* dreadful < *uggr* fear]

UN-AMERICAN Not American in character, style etc. 2 Not consistent with the ideals, objectives, Spirit etc., of the United States; lacking patriotism or national feeling

UNBODIED Immaterial 2 Released from the body; disembodied

UNBOSOM To reveal, as one's thoughts or secrets; disclose or give vent to 2 To say what is troubling one; tell one's thoughts, feelings, etc.

UNCLEAN Not clean; foul 2 Characterized by impure thoughts; unchaste; depraved

UNDER Beneath, so as to have something directly above; covered by 2 In a place lower than 3 Beneath the concealment, guise, or assumption of 4 Beneath the shelter of 5 Less than in number, degree, age, value, or amount 6 Inferior to in quality, character, or rank 7 Dominated by; owing allegiance to; subordinate to; subservient to 8 Subject to the guidance, tutorship, or direction of 9 Subject to the moral obligation or sanction of 10 With the liability or certainty of incurring 11 Subject to the influence or pressure of; swayed or impelled by 12 Driven or propelled by 13 In the group or class of; within the matter titled or headed 14 Being the subject of 15 During the period of; in the reign of; pending the administration of 16 By virtue of; authorized, substantiated, attested, or warranted by 17 In conformity to; in accordance with; having regard to 18 Planted or sowed with 19 In or into an inferior or subordinate degree or rank Syn.

Under, *below*, and *beneath* all mean in a lower or inferior position, masked or covered by *Under* is the most general of these words, and may also be used to denote subordination *Below* usually denotes a physically lower position, while *beneath* emphasizes a moral inferiority

UNDERSTAND To come to know the meaning or import of; apprehend 2 To comprehend the nature or character of 3 To have comprehension or mastery of 4 To be aware of; realize 5 To have been told; believe 6 To accept as a condition or stipulation 7 To be in agreement with; be privately in sympathy with 8 To have understanding; comprehend 9 To be informed; believe Syn. **See APPREHEND** [OE *understandan* < *under-* under + *standan* to stand]

UNDERSTANDING The power by which one understands 2 The sum of the mental powers by which knowledge is acquired, retained and extended; the power of apprehending relations and making inferences from them 3 An arrangement or settlement of differences, or of disputed points 4 Possessing comprehension and good sense 5 Tolerant or sympathetic Syn. reason, intelligence, intuition, judgment, perception Compare **INTELLECT**

UNDYING Immortal; everlasting

UNEARTH To dig or root up from the earth 2 To reveal by or as by searching

UNEQUIVOCAL Understandable in only one way

UNFAITHFUL Unworthy of trust; faithless 2 Not true to a standard or to an original; not accurate or exact 3 Unbelieving; infidel

UNGODLY Unreasonable; extreme 2 Impious.

UNION The act of uniting, or the state of being united; also, that which is so formed 2 combining or joining of nations, states, parties etc., for some mutual interest or purpose 3 The harmony, agreement or concord that results from such a combining or joining 4 A uniting of several or more perishes for administration or relief for the poor; also, a workhouse administered by such a union Syn. **ALLIANCE**

UNIVERSE The aggregate of all existing things; the whole creation embracing all celestial bodies and all of space; the cosmos 2 In restricted sense, the earth 3 Human beings collectively; mankind

UNSOUND Not logically valid; erroneous 2 Disturbed; not profound

UP To a source, center, conclusion, etc. 2 So as to be secure 3 To or into view or existance 4 In or into a place of safekeeping 5 To an end or close 6 In or into prominence 7 Completely;

totally; wholly 8 To be equal to; be capable of 9 Acquainted with, equal to, or prepared for 10 Ready for use, operation, etc. 11 From the mouth toward the Source of 12 A period of prosperity, elation, etc. 13 To be honest 14 Rising and improving 15 To do or begin to do quickly

UPON Into complete contact with, on, at, or immediately after the important and pressing occasions (in certain various senses)

UTTER Being or done without conditions or qualifications; final; absolute

UXORIOUS Fatuously or foolishly devoted to one's wife; showing extreme or foolish fondness for one's wife

V

VAIL To let fall; lower, as the countenance, in seriousness or submission 2 To take off, as a grin in respect or submission[Aphetic form of obs. *avale* < F *avaler* to lower < '*a val* down < L *ad vallem*, lit., **to the valley**

VAIN Unproductive; worthless; fruitless; useless 2 Having no real basis or worth; frivolous; empty; unreal 3 Ostentatious; showy -To no purpose; without effect [< F < L *vanus* empty]

VALLEY A depression in a man, as one through which a stream flows

VANITY Excessive personal pride; conceit 2 Ambitious displaying; ostentatious; showing off 3 The quality or state of being fruitless, useless, and destitute of reality, etc., of that which is unsubstantial **EGOTISM, PRIDE**

VANQUISH To defeat in battle; overcome; conquer 2 To suppress or overcome (a feeling or emotion) 3 To defeat, as in argument; confute

VAPOR That which is fleeting and unsubstantial 2 Depression of spirits 3 To make idle boasts Psalm 39:5; :11; ***62:9; ***135:7; ***Jer 10:13; ***51:16; Acts 2:19; James 4:14

VEIL PRETEXT A fictitious reason or motive advanced to conceal a real one A specious excuse or explanation [to weave]

VENERATE To look upon or regard with respect and deference; revere [< L *veneratus*, pp. of *venerari* to revere]

VERACITY The habitual regard for Truth; Truthfulness; honesty 2 Agreement with Truth; accuracy 3 That which is Truth [< F *veracite* < L *verax, veracis*]

VERBATIM In the exact words; word for word [< LL < L *verbum* word]

VERIDICAL Telling or expressing the Truth; Truthful; accurate [< L *veridicus* speaking the Truth < *verus* true + *dicere* to say]

VERIFY To prove to be True or accurate; substantiate; confirm 2 To test or ascertain the accuracy or Truth of Syn. See **CONFIRM**

VERITAS *Latin* Truth

VESSEL One who is viewed, chiefly in a religious sense, as having capacity or fitness to receive or contain something (non material)

VESTIGE Visible trace, impression, or sensible evidence or sign of something absent, lost, or gone; trace 2 A part, small or degenerate, but well developed and functional in ancestral forms of organisms [< F < L *vestigium* footprint]

VEX To provoke to anger or displeasure by small irritations; annoy 2 To trouble or afflict 3 To throw into commotions; agitate 4 To make subject of dispute [< OF *vexer* < L *vexare* to shake]

VICARIOUS Made or performed by substitution; suffered or done in place of another 2 Enjoyed, felt, etc., by a person as a result of his imagined participation in an experience not his own 3 Filling the office of or acting for another 4 Performing as an organ, the functions of another; also, occurring in an abnormal situation

VIEW The act of seeing; survey; inspection 2 Mental examination or inspection 3 Power or range of vision 4 That which is seen; outlook; prospect 5 Manner of looking at things; opinion; judgement; belief 6 To look at; see; behold 7 To look at carefully; scrutinize; examine 8 To survey mentally; consider

VILE Morally base; shamefully wicked 2 Despicable; vicious 3 Loathsome; disgusting 4 Degrading; ignominious *vile* treatment 5 Flagrantly bad or inferior 6 Unpleasant or disagreeable 7 Of little worth or account [< AF or OF, fem. of *vil* < L *vilis* cheap]

VIM Force or vigor; energy; Spirit [< L accusative of *vis* power]

VINDICATE To clear of accusation, censure, suspicion, etc. 2 To support or maintain as a right or a claim 3 To serve to justify 4 To lay claim to 5 To set free; rescue

VINDICTIVE Having a revengeful spirit 2 Revengeful or spiteful in quality, character

VINE A plant having a flexible stem that may twine or cling to a support as it grows; also, the stem itself

VINEYARD A field of activity, especially one of Spiritual labor

VINEGAR Sourness of manner, speech, temperament, disposition, etc.

VIOLENCE Perversion or distortion of meaning or intent, etc.

VIOLENT Caused by or exhibiting intense emotional or mental excitement; passionate; impetuous; fierce 2 Characterized by intensity of any kind; extreme 3 Tending to pervert the meaning or sense of

VIOLET One who is modest or self-effacing

VIRGIN Uncorrupted; pure; undefiled 2 Not hitherto used, touched, tilled or worked upon by man 3 Not previously processed 4 Unmixed 5 Lacking experience or contact with; unaccustomed

VIRGINITY The state of being unsullied, unused, untouched, etc.

VIRTU Rare, curious, or beautiful in quality

VIRTUE The quality of moral righteousness or excellence; rectitude 2 The practice of moral duties and the abstinence immorality and vice 3 Sexual purity; chastity, especially in women 4 A particular type of moral excellence, especially one of those considered to be of special importance in philosophical or religious doctrine 5 Any admirable quality or trait 6 Inherent or essential quality, power etc. 7 Efficacy; potency 8 The fifth of the nine orders of angels -By or through the fact, quality, force or authority of -To seem to **do freely or from principle what is or must be done necessarily** [< OF *vertu* < L *virtus* strength, bravery < *vir* man] Syn.

Virtue, goodness, morality, rectitude, and righteousness are compared as they denote the disposition to be good, moral, honest, upright etc. We regard virtue as acquired through self-discipline, and predicate it of human beings only Goodness is an innate quality, and so may be ascribed to God as well as to man Morality involves conformity to an accepted code of right conduct; it is less elevated but more concrete than virtue Rectitude also implies conformity to a moral code, but stresses intention or disposition; hence, a man's morality may arise from fear of punishment or of censure, but his rectitude can come only from a love of the right and a conscious desire to follow it The rectitude of an action is to be found more in its purpose than in its consequences Righteousness is a very close synonym of rectitude, but suggests somewhat more strongly coming from the point of view others

VISAGE The face or facial expression of a person; countenance; distinctive aspect [< OF < *vis* face < L *visus* look, appearance < *videre* to see]

VISIT To comfort or bless 2 To chat or converse sociably 3 A talk or friendly chat 4 An authoritative personal call for inspection and examination, or discharge of an official or professional duty

VITAL FORCE A form of energy regarded as acting independently of all physical and chemical forces in the causation and development of living phenomena

VITALITY Vital or life giving force; principle 2 Power in continuing in force or effect

VITALIZE Endow with Life or energy

VIVACIOUS Full of life and Spirits; lively; active [< L *vivax, vivacis* < *vivere* to live]

VOCABLE A spoken word considered only as a sequence of sounds, **without regard to its meaning** 2 A written word considered only as a sequence of letters

VOCABULARY A list of words or of words and phrases, especially one arranged in alphabetical order and defined or translated; a glossary 2 All the words of a language 3 A sum or aggregate of the words used or understood by a particular person, class etc., or employed in some specialized field of knowledge 4 An aggregate or range of things, qualities or techniques that form the basis of a means of expression [< LL *vocabularius* < L *vocabulum*]

VOICE Opinion or choice expressed; also, the right of expressing a preference or judgement 2 Instruction; teaching; admonition 3 A part, especially as considered abstractly

VOID Without contents; useless and ineffectual, **UNOCCUPIED~** idle, without improvement; (incumbent) resting, leaning, and weighing wholly upon a burden 2 Holding an indicated position like a dependant, **IMPEDIMENT~** Connected by marriage, but having a disability that affects the validity of a marriage 1b Disability that makes it impossible for a person to contract a valid marriage 1c A disability that does not make the marriage null and void, but subjects the parties to a punishment; because of that which bars persons within the specified degrees of **CONSANGUINITY-** Any close connection or **AFFINITY~** natural attraction, liking or inclination between opposite natures with similarities; any close relationship or agreement; Spiritual attraction thought to exist between certain persons; also the person exerting such attraction 3 The force by which atoms are held together in chemical compounds 4 The property or attraction by which differing chemical elements or groups of elements when brought into contact, unite to form a new basic part of a complex whole; a primary, integral part; essential; fundamental rudimental and the surrounding conditions best suited for a person atmospheric forces and powers 5 A principle factual item essential to the solution of some problem or to proper calculation 6 Obligated as a moral obligation, or as necessary under the circumstance, but producing no effect; useless, and empty condition

VOLUNTARY Proceeding from the will or from one's own free choice; unconstrained; intentional; volitional 2 Endowed with, possessing, or exercising will or free choice 3 Effected by choice or volition; acting without constraint 4 Subject to or directed by the will, as a muscle or movement 5a Unconstrained of will; done without compulsion 5b Performed without legal obligation 5c Done without valuable consideration; gratuitous 6 Any work or performance not compelled or imposed by another [< OF *voluntaire* < L *voluntarius* < *voluntas* will]

VOMIT To issue with violence from any hollow place; be ejected 2 To discharge or send forth copiously or forcibly

VOW A solemn promise to God or to a deity or saint to perform some act or make some gift or sacrifice 2 A solemn engagement to adopt a certain course of life, pursue some end, etc.; also, a pledge of faithfulness 3 A solemn and emphatic affirmation 4 To declare with assurance

VULGATE Common; popular; generally accepted 2 Everyday speech 3 Any commonly accepted text [< L *vulgatus* common, orig. pp. of *vulgare* to make common < *vulgus* the common people]

VULGAR Lacking in refinement, good taste, sensitivity, etc.; coarse; crude, boorish; also obscene; indecent 2 The common people

VULGARISM Vulgarity 2 A word or phrase that is in nonstandard or unrefined usage, though not necessarily coarse or gross, as distinguished from those in formal standard use

VULGATE Common; popular; generally accepted text

W

WAGE To engage in and maintain vigorously; carry on 2 To attempt; risk 3 Recompense or yield See **A LIVING WAGE**

WAIL Manifest or feel deep sorrow for; lament

WAIT To stay or remain in expectation, as of an anticipated action or event 2 To remain in readiness 3 To perform duties of personal service or attendance 4 To attend; escort 5 To act as a servant 6 To go to see; call upon; visit 7 A watchman or guard

WAIVE To give up or relinquish a claim to 2 To refrain from insisting upon or taking advantage of; forgo 3 To put off To surrender, abandon, or relinquish voluntarily, either expressly or by implication, as a claim, privilege, or right To reject; cast off; abandon; desert See **WAIF**

WAIF Anything found and unclaimed, the owner being unknown

WAKE To rouse or stir up; excite Akin to **WATCH**

WALK To proceed or advance slowly 2 To return to earth and appear as a ghost 3 To be in continual motion 4 To depart, especially abruptly or without warning 5 To forsake; desert 6 To defeat easily; overwhelm 7 Chosen profession or habitual sphere of action 8 To act or live in some manner

WALL Something suggestive of a wall or barrier 2 To force (one) or be forced to an extremity 3 To provide, surround, protect, etc., as with a wall: a wall to protect her heart

WAN Indicating illness, unhappiness, etc. 2 Sad; mournful 3 Having a gloomy aspect; dismal; dark

WANDER To deviate in conduct or opinion; go astray 2 To think or speak deliriously or irrationally

WANE To diminish in size and brilliance 2 To decline or decrease gradually; draw to an end 3 Decrease, as of power, prosperity; or reputation

WANGLE To obtain or accomplish by indirect or irregular methods 2 To manipulate or adjust, especially dishonestly 3 To resort to indirect, irregular or dishonest methods

WANT To feel a desire or wish for 2 To be deficient in; lack; be without 3 To be needy or destitute 4 To be lacking or absent 5 Privation, poverty; destitution; need 6 A conscious or felt need of something

WANTON Dissolute; licentious, lustful 2 Unjust; malicious; savagery; also, unprovoked 3 Of vigorous and abundant growth 4 Extravagant; running to excess; unrestrained, as in speech 5 Not bound, tied or restrained; loose: *loose* lips sink ships 6 Frolicsome; prankish 7 Refractory; rebellious 8 To grow luxuriantly 9 To waste wantonly 10 A trifler; dallier 11 A person who has been much indulged [ME *wanton* < OE *wan* deficient + ME *towen*, OE *togen*, pp. Of *teon* to bring up, educate]

WAR To be in any state of active opposition: the wage of war is death [OE *wyrre*, *werre* <AF *werre* < OHG *werra* strife, confusion]

WARD A defensive attitude or movement, as in fencing; guard 2 A projection inside a lock, designed to obstruct the turning of any key other than the proper one 3 To guard; protect

WARD Going, developing, facing or directed toward 2 In or toward a specific area, place, point, or direction

WARFARE The waging or carrying on of war; conflict 2 Struggle; strife

WARLIKE Belligerent 2 Pugnacious; hostile

WARLOCK A demon [OE *wǣrloga* traitor, foe, devil < *wǣr* covenant + *leogan* to lie, deny]

WARM Having an affectionate disposition; loving; warm hearted 2 Possessing or marked by ardor, liveliness, cordiality, etc. 3 Excited; agitated; also, vehement; passionate 4 United by affection 5 Uncomfortable by reason of annoyance or danger 6 To make ardent or enthusiastic interest 7 To fill with kindly feeling 8 To become kindly disposed or friendly

WARMTH Ardor or fervid disposition or feeling; excitement of temper or mind

WARNING That which admonishes

WARP To turn from a correct or proper course; give a twist or bias to; corrupt; pervert 2 To go astray 3 A mental or moral deviation or aberration; bias

WARRANT Something that assures or attests; evidence; guarantee 2 That which gives authority for some course or act; sanction; justification 3 To assure or guarantee the quality, accuracy, certainty, or sufficiency of 4 To assure or guarantee the character or fidelity of; pledge oneself for 5 To say confidently; feel sure of

WASH To purify from pollution, defilement, or guilt 2 To undergo testing successfully 3 To wash the interior of (a conscious) by confession 4 To clean without injury

WATCH To look at attentively; observe carefully 2 To wait expectantly; be in a state of expectation 3 To be constantly on the alert; be observant, vigilant, or attentive 4 To be an onlooker or spectator 5 To look at steadily and attentively 6 To follow the course of mentally;

keep informed concerning 7 To keep watch over; guard; tend 8 To be on one's guard; take care 9 Close and continuous attention; careful observation Akin to **WAKE**

WATER Excellence; quality 2 Of the highest degree 3 To be valid or effective 4 The degree of transparency and brilliancy 5 Out of danger and secure 6 To be very free or quick; to provide Life as rivers do water

WAVE A sudden occurrence of or increase in a specified phenomenon, feeling, or emotion

WAY A manner or method of doing something; procedure 2 Space or room to advance 3 A customary or habitual manner or style 4 The range of one's notice or observation

WAYWARD Wanting its way; willful; forward 2 Without definite way or course; unsteady; capricious 3 Unexpected or unwished for

WEAK Lacking in will or stability of character; yielding easily to temptation; pliable 2 Ineffectual 3 Lacking in mental or moral strength; liable to err or fail through feebleness of conception or vacillation of judgement 4 Showing or resulting from poor judgement or a want of discretion or firmness 5 Unable to persuade or convince 5 Lacking in influence or authority 6 Wanting in impressiveness or interest

WEAN To estrange from former habits or associations [OE *wenian* to accustom]

WEAR To have or bear on the person habitually or as a practice 2 To have in one's appearance or aspect; exhibit 3 To impair, waste, or consume by use or constant action 4 To exhaust the strength or patients of; weary 5 To become as specified from use or attrition 6 To tire or exhaust 7 Capacity for resistance to use or impairment; endurance; durability

WEARY Worn with exertion, suffering, etc.; tired; fatigued 2 Discontented or vexed by continued endurance, as something disagreeable, tedious, etc. 3 Indicating, characteristic of, or resulting from fatigue, boredom

WEASEL WORD A word that weakens a statement by rendering it ambiguous or **EQUIVOCAl-** Open to more than one interpretation

WEATHER A prevailing condition, or atmosphere; mental or moral climate 2 To pass through and survive, as a crisis

WEAVE To produce by combining details or elements 2 To bring together so as to form a whole: fancies into theories 3 To twist or introduce into, about, or through something else

WEB Anything artfully contrived or elaborated into a trap or snare; entangle

WEEN To suppose; guess; fancy [OE *wēnan* to think]

WEEP To manifest grief or other strong emotion by shedding tears

WEIGH To consider carefully; estimate the worth of or advantages of 2 To press or force down by burden; oppress 3 To think well of; esteem; regard 4 To have influence or importance 5 To be burdensome or oppressive 6 To consider one's words carefully before speaking

WEIGHT Any quantity of heaviness expressed indefinitely 2 Burden; pressure; oppressiveness 3 The relative tendency of any mass toward a center of Superior mass 4 consequence; importance; Influence 5 To be of importance or significance 6 To exercise one's authority more than is necessary or proper; make unwarranted use of position or power 7 To oppress or burden

WEIGHTY Having great weight; ponderous 2 Having power to move the mind; cogent 3 Of great importance 4 Burdensome

WELCOME Admitted gladly to a place; received cordially 2 Producing satisfaction or pleasure; pleasing 3 Made free to use or enjoy -You are under no obligation 4 The act of bidding or making welcome 5 Greet gladly or hospitably 6 To receive with pleasure [OE *wilcuma* < *will-* will, pleasure + *cuma* guest; infl. in form by WELL and COME, on analogy with [< OF *bien venu*]

WELFARE The condition of faring well; exemption from pain or discomfort; prosperity 2 Organized efforts by a community to improve the social condition of a group or class [ME *wel fare* < *wel* well + *fare* a going < OE *faran* to go]

WELFARE WORK Organized efforts carried on by private organizations to improve the conditions of needy persons

WELKIN The vault of the sky; the heavens [OE *woleen, wolen* cloud]

WELL A source of continued supply, or that which issues forth continuously; a wellspring 2 Satisfactorily, favorably; according to one's wishes 3 In a good or correct manner; properly; expertly 4 Suitably; befittingly; with reason or propriety 5 In a successful manner; prosperously; also, agreeably 6 Intimately 7 To a considerable extent or degree 8 Wholly; thoroughly; completely 9 Graciously, generously; kindly 10 Also; in addition 11 With equal effect or consequence 12 Having good health; free from ailment of the mind or body 13 Right

WELL-APPOINTED Properly equipped; excellently furnished

WELL-FAVORED Of attractive appearance; comely; handsome

WET Quiet wrong; crazy Inexperienced or unsophisticated

WHEEL A turning; revolution 2 An intricate series of motives or influences, acting and reacting on or to one another 3 To take a new direction or course of action; change attitudes, opinions, etc. 4 To act free and independently without restrictions

WHIP To attack with withering scornful criticism; berate; flay

WHIRL A state of confusion; turmoil

WHIRLWIND Violent activity -Extremely swift or impetuous activity

WHISPER Secret communication; hint; insinuation 2 To talk cautiously or furtively; plot or gossip

WHITE Not intentionally wicked or evil; not malicious or harmful 2 Free from spot or stain; innocent 3 Fair and honorable; straightforward; honest 4 Propitious; auspicious

WHITE LIE See under **LIE**

*WHOLE Containing all the parts necessary to make up a total; undivided and undiminished; entire; complete 2 Constituting the full extent, amount, etc., total; entire 3 Having the same parents full brother as opposed the half brother -Integral -Completely; altogether -Taking everything into consideration [Akin to **HALE**]

*WHOLEHEARTED Done or experienced with earnestness, sincerity, etc.

*WHOLESOME Favorable to virtue (an order of angels) and well being; salutary; sound; beneficial 2 Safe; free from danger or risk [See **DANGER, RISK**]

*WHOLE-SOULED Feeling or acting with one's whole heart; devoted; generous

WHORE In the Bible, idolatry

WICKED Evil in principle or **practice**; vicious; sinful; depraved 2 Mischievous; roguish 3 Noxious; pernicious 4 Troublesome; painful -Done with great skill -All that is below good, love, kindness, long suffering, honor, esteem, etc.,

WIDOW To deprive of something desirable

WIELD To exercise authority, power, influence, etc.

WIFE The original meaning of wife in many languages is simply

WOMAN- [OE *wifmann* < *wif* wife + *mann* human being] Shares your beliefs; equally yoked; makes you a better man Trustworthy; ambitious; selfless; attractive; smart; loves (yourself) unconditionally See **WOMAN**
Gen. 2:24; 3:20; 6:18; 7:7; 12:19; 17:19; 20:2; 20:12; 24:7; 39:9; Exodus 20:17; 21:3; 22:16; # 30:16; Deut. 22:19; * 24:5; 27:20; Judges 4:4; 13:2; :11; :13; :19; :21; :22; :23; Ruth 1:1; 1 Sam 1:4; 1:19; 19:11; 25:3; :14; :37; :39; :40; :42; 1 Kings 21:5; :7; :25; 2 Kings 22:14; 1 Chron 7:23; 2 Chron 8:11; Esther 5:10; Job 2:9; 19:17; 31:9-10; Psalm 128:3; Proverbs 5:18; :20; 6:24; :26; :29; 12:4; 18:22; 19:13-:14; 21:9; :19; 23:27; 25:24; 27:15; 31:10; Ecc. 9:9;

WILD Growing or produced without care; not cultivated 2 Boisterous; unruly; unrestrained 3 Immoral; dissolute 4 Affected with or originating violent disturbances; stormy; turbulent 5 Showing reckless want of judgement; rashly; imprudent; extravagant 6 Fantastically irregular or disordered; odd in arrangement or effect 7 Eager and excited, as by reason of joy, fear, desire, etc. 8 Excited to a frenzy or distraction; roused to fury or desperation 9 Being or going far from the proper course or from the course aimed at; erratic -Untamed; reckless -An uninhabited or uncultivated mind; a waste; wilderness -Without control

WILDERNESS A multitudinous and confusing collection: a wilderness of curiosities

WILE An act or means of cunning deception; also, any beguiling trick or artifice 2 Craftiness; cunning, beguile, or mislead 3 Clever or cunning devices or expedients, especially as used to trick or deceive others

WILL [1] The faculty by which the mind makes choices and acts to carry them out 2 The act of experience or exercising this faculty 3 Strong determination; practical enthusiasm; also, self-control 4 That which has been resolved or determined upon; a purpose 5 Power to dispose of a matter arbitrarily; discretion 6 Conscious inclination toward

WILL [2] Willingness or disposition 2 Capability or capacity 3 Custom or habit **SHALL**

WILLING Having the mind favorably inclined or disposed 2 Answering to demand or requirement; complaint 3 Gladly proffered or done; hearty 4 Of or pertaining to the faculty or power of choice; volitional

WIND [1] Breath as expended in words, especially as having more sound than sense; idle chatter; also, vanity; conceit 2 Used to suggest something very fast, unrestrained 3 An irresistible influence 4 An impending situation; coming; about to happen; approaching, brewing 5 Empty, pompous, or boastful talk; meaningless; rhetoric

WIND [2] Move in or take a twisting or spiral course 2 Pass through the mind so as to encircle or enfold; wrap, snake, loop entwine 3 Turn (the Truth) repeatedly around and around [< G lit., to wander]

WINE To entertain or treat with, or as with something tasteful

WING A group within a **POLITICAL** (Relating to the **ideas** or strategies of a particular party or group) party or other organization that holds particular views or has a particular function 2 Speak or act without preparation; improvise 3 Invent a way on the spot (on the fly):

deal with a situation you haven't prepared for 4 Ease and swiftness of movement 5 A person or activity associated with the main situation in particular

WINNOW To examine so as to separate good from bad; analyze minutely; sift 2 To separate (what is valuable) from what is valueless [OE *windwian* < *wind* the wind]

WINTER A time of hibernation 2 A period of time marked by cheerlessness and coldness

WISDOM The power of true and right discernment; also, conformity to the course of action dictated by such discernment 2 Good practical judgment; common sense 3 A high degree of knowledge 4 A wise saying Syn. See **SENSE** [OE *wisdom* < *wise* wise]

WISE [1] Possessed of wisdom; seeing clearly what is right and just; having sound judgment 2 Sagacious; shrewd; calculating 3 Marked by wisdom; prudent; sensible 4 Having great learning; erudite; sage 5 Having practical knowledge of the arts or science 6 Versed in mysterious things 7 Aware of 8 Arrogant or sarcastic in manner; also, offensively bold; impudent, -To know the true facts -To make cognizant of; inform -To make or become aware, informed or sophisticated [OE *wis*]

WISE [2] Way of doing; manner; method [OE *wise* manner]

WISE [3] To incline; turn [OE *wisian*]

WIT The power of knowing or perceiving; intelligence; ingenuity; sagacity; keen or good sense 2 The power or faculty of rapid and accurate observation; the power of comprehending and judging 3 The faculties of perception and understanding 4 The mental faculties with regard to their state of balance 5 Ready perception and happy expression of unexpected or amusing analogies or other relations between apparently congruous ideas; sudden and ingenious association of ideas or words 6 One who has a keen perception of the incongruous or ludicrous and makes skillful use of it in writing or speaking; also, clever conversationalist 7 Significance; meaning; import 8 Mental activity [OE]

WITCHCRAFT Extraordinary influence or fascination

WITH As a member or associate 2 Characterized or marked by; characteristically possessed of 3 In charge of 4 At the same time as 5 In the same direction as 6 In proportion to 7 Having received or been granted [OE]

WITHAL In addition; as a further factor or consideration 2 All the same; nevertheless (used when adding something that contrasts with a previous comment)

WITHIN In the inner part; interiorly 2 Inside the body, heart, or mind 3 In the inner or interior part or parts of; inside 4 In the limits, range or compass of 5 In the reach, limit, or scope of 6 An inner part or place

WITNESS To see the execution of (Bible contradictions & mysteries) and subscribe to it for the purpose of establishing its authenticity

WOMAN Literally wo-man See **MAN** It is notable that it was thought necessary to mention woman is the definition of the word wife and address the Spirit in man as opposed to the soul which is a man, to man which represents either a male or female person, to form a word denoting a female person exclusively (it was only a "thought") This noble word *woman*, Spirit-stirring as it passes over English ears, is in America banished, and 'ladies' and 'females' substituted; the one to English taste mawkish and vulgar; the other indistinctive and gross

WOOD To act like a maniac; frantic; raging; mad [OE *wod* insane]

WOOL Perfect in quality and quantity; one hundred percent genuine [OE *wull*]

WORD A linguistic form that can meaningfully be spoken in isolation 2 A command, signal or direction 3 A promise; avowed intention 4 The Logos; the Son of **God** 5 The Scriptures as an embodiment of divine revelation -To understand or deal with One literally in accordance with His own statement

WORK Continued mental exertion or activity, directed to some purpose or end; labor 2 The acts, obligations, etc., that one does or undertakes in return for something of value; especially, the activities by which one earns one's livelihood 3 Any prolonged effort 4 That upon which labor is expended; an undertaking; task 5 Exhausting effort; toil 6 The matter at hand; the business that remains to be undone 7 The product of mental labor 8 Manner of working, or style of treatment; workmanship 9 The whole of anything 10 Moral duties considered as external acts, especially as meritorious 11 To prove effective or influential; succeed 12 To become as specified 13 To cause or bring about; effect; accomplish 14 To cause to be as specified, usually with effort 15 To influence; lead 16 To break up the fallow ground 17 To plow

WORLD The ancient root of world meant age or life of man The first part is the same as **WERE-** it means **MAN 2** The second part is related to **OLD** The Anglo-Saxons first used **WORLD** meaning- human existence and life on earth, as opposed to a conscience state of being and happiness which is defined as heaven

WORMWOOD That which embitters or makes bitter; bitterness [Alter. of obs. *wermod* < OE; infl. in form by **WORM** and **WOOD**]

WORSHIP Excessive or ardent devotion or admiration 2 The object of such devotion or admiration 3 A title of honor in addressing persons of rank or station 4 To have an intense or exaggerated admiration 5 To honor 6 To perform acts or have sentiments of worship [OE *weorthscipe* < *weorth* value] Gen 24:26; :48; :52; Exod 4:31; 12:27; 24:1; 32:8; 33:10; 34:8; :14; Deut 4:19; 8:19; 11:16; 12:1; ***:4; :31; ***17:3; 26:10; 29:26; 30:17; Josh. 5:14; Judge 7:15; 1 Sam 1:19; 15::30; 2 Sam 12:20; 1 Kings 9:6; :9; 12:30; 2 Kings 5:18; 17:36; 18:22; 21:21; 1 Chron 16:29; 2 Chron 7:3; :22; 20:18; 29:30; ***Ezra 3:1; Neh 8:6; ****9:3; :6; Job 1:20; ****Psalm 5:7- the fear of the Lord is the beginning of knowledge; 22:27; :29; 29:2; 45:11; 66:4; 81:9; 86:9; ***95:6; 96:9; 138:2; Isa 2:8; :20; 27:13; 36:7; 44:15; **46:6; 49:7; 66:1; Jer 8:2; ***13:10; ***25:6; ***26:2; Ezek 46:2; :9; Dan 3:12; :18; :28; Hosea 13:1; Micah 5:13; Zeph 2:11; 3:10

WORTHY Possessing worth or value; deserving of respect or honor; having valuable or useful qualities 2 Having such qualities as to be deserving of or adapted to some specified thing; fit; suitable 3 Well deserving -Trustworthy; valuable; worthy; necessary; beneficial; exemplary [ME *wurthi, worthi*] Gen 32:10; 2 Sam 22:4; 1 Kings 1:52; Psalm 18:3; Matt 3:8; :11; 8:8; 10:10-11; :13; :37-38; 22:8; Mark 1:7; Luke 3:8; :16; 7:6-7; 10:7; 15:19; :21; 20:35; 21:36; John 1:27; Acts 5:41; 13:25; Romans 8:18; 16:2; 1 Corin 15:9; Eph 4:1; Phili. 1:27; Col 1:10; 1 Thes 2:12; 2 Thes 1:5; :11; 1 Tim 1:15; 4:9; 5:17-18; 6:1; Heb 3:3; 10:29; 11:38; 3 John 1:6; Rev 3:4; 4:11; 5:2; :4; 5:9; :12

WRETCHED Sunk in dejection; profoundly unhappy 2 Causing misery or grief 3 Unsatisfactory or worthlessness in ability or quality 4 Despicable; contemptuous [OE *wrecca* outcast < *wrecan* to drive]

WRINKLE Producing the appearance of ageing, as by **excessive exposure to the elements** (inside, not out) 2 To be or become contracted into wrinkles or ridges [OE *gewrinclod*, pp. Of *gewrinclian* to **wind**]

WRITE To show or make visible to the mind for understanding, as by letters

WRONG Not correct; mistaken; erroneous 2 Not suitable; inappropriate; improper 3 Not according to the right, proper or correct method, standard, intention, etc. 4 Not working or acting properly or satisfactory; amiss 5 Intended or made to be turned under, inward or so as not to be seen 6 Not desired or intended 7 Not favored by conventional social standards 8 Not morally right, proper, or just; immoral 9 Unsatisfactory 10 To lapse from the strict path of rectitude 11 To turn out badly; go astray -In a wrong direction, place or manner; awry See **INJUSTICE, OFFENCE** -To impute evil to unjustly; misrepresent; malign 2 To seduce or dishonor (a Spirit/ woman) [OE *wrang* twisted < ON *rangr* awry, unjust] Gen 16:5; Exod 2:13; # 5:7-8; Deut 19:16; Judg 11:27; 2 Sam 19:19; 1 Kings 8:47; 2 Kings 18:14; *** 1 Chron 12:17; 16:21; 2 Chron 6:37; Job 1:22; 19:3; :6-7; 21:27; 24:12; 36:23; Psalm 35:19; 38:19; 69:4; 105:14; 119:78; :86; Prov 8:36; Jer 22:3; 40:4; Lam 3:59; Ezek 22:29; Dan 6:22; Matt 20:13; Luke 23:41; Acts 7:24; :26-27; Acts 18:14; 24:20; 25:10; 1 Corin 6:7-8; 2 Corin 7:2; :12; 12:13; Col 3:25; Phile. 1:18; 1 Peter 2:19; 3:13

WYCLIFFE John 1324?-84 English religious reformer; first translator of the entire Bible into English Also spelled *Wiclif, Wickliffe* Also **Wyc'lif**

X

XAVIER Saint Francis, 1506-52, Spanish Jesuit missionary in the Orient; One of the founders of the Society of Jesus: called **the Apostles of the Indies**

XP Chi and rho the first two letters of X, P, I, Z, T. O, Z, the Greek word for Christ, introduced by Constantine the Great as an emblem of Christ

Y

YAHWEH In the Old Testament, the national **God** of Israel: **God**: a modern translation of the Tetragramation See **JEHOVAH** Also *Jahveh, Jahwe, Jahweh* Also *Yahve Yahveh* [< *Hebrew* Y H W H]

YAHWIST The author of those portions of the Hexateuch in which **God** is mentioned as *Yahweh*, or *Jehovah* Compare **ELOHIST** Also spelled *Jahvist, Jahwist, Jehovist* Also **Yah'vist**

YEAST Subject to scorn; scorner 2 To be stirred up or inflamed 3 To be turbulent and stormy 4 Mental or moral **FERMENT~** To excite with emotions or passion; agitate; stir up; instigate [Thoroughly] [Old English, of Germanic origin; related to Dutch gist and German *Gischt* froth yeast < Gk *zein* to boil]

YES MAN One who agrees without criticism; a servile, acquiescent assistant; today

YET In addition; beside 2 Before or at some future time 3 In continuance of a previous state or condition; still 4 Up to the present time; before 5 Than that which has been previously affirmed 6 Nevertheless 7 As much as [OE *giet, gieta]*

YIELD To give forth by a natural process, or as a result of labor or cultivation 2 To give in return, as investment 3 To give up, as to superior power; surrender; relinquish 4 To concede or grant 5 To pay, repay or reward 6 To provide a return; produce; bear 7 To give up; submit 8 To give away assent or comply 9 To give place, as through inferiority or meekness Syn. See **DEFER, RELINQUISH~** The amount yielded; product; result, as from study, exercising the Spirit [OE *gieldon, geldan* to pay] Disposed to yield; feasible; obedient Gen 1:11-12; 49:20; Lev 19:25; 25:19; 26:4; :20; # 11:4; :34; 20:8; Deut 11:17; ****22:9; ****2 Chron 30:8; Neh 9:37; Job 6:29; 24:5; 40:20; Psalm 67:6; 85:12; 107:37; Prov 7:21; 12:12; Jer 17:8; Ezek 34:27; 36:8; Dan 3:28; Joel 2:22; Hab 3:17; Hag 2:19; Matt 13:8; 27:50; Mark 4:7-8; :28; Luke 8:8; 12:16; Acts 23:21; Gal 2:5; Heb 12:11; James 3:12; :17; ***Rev 22:2

YOGA Hindu system of mystical and ascetic philosophy that involves certain physical and mental disciplines together with a withdrawal from the world and abstract meditation upon some Spiritual principle or complete mind; peace; rest; silence; soundness of mind 2 A related system of exercise, the purpose of which is to achieve both physical and Spiritual well-being [< Hind. < Skt., lit., union]

YOKE An oppressive force or influence; a crushing burden or weight 2 That which binds or connects 3 Servitude, or some visible sign of it -To; bring into bondage [OE *geosc*]
Gen 27:40; Deut 28:48; 1 Kings 12:4; 19:19; Isaiah 9:4; Isa 10:27; 47:6; 58:6; :9; Jer 2:20; 5:5; 27:2; :8; :11-12; 28:2; :4; :10-11; :13-14; 30:8; 51:23; Lam 1:14; 3:27; Ezek 30:18; 34:27; Hosea 11:4; Nahum 1:13; Matt 11:29-30; Luke 14:19; Acts 15:10; *2 Corin 6:14; Gal 5:1; 1 Tim 6:1

YOUTH The period of being or development; fresh; vigerous

Z

ZEAL Enthusiastic devotion; adore, especially for a cause
11:29; 25:11; :13; Psalm 69:9; 119:139; Prov 23:17; Isa 42:13; 59:17; John 2:17; Acts 21:20; 22:3; Rom 10:2; 1 Corin 14:12; 2 Corin 7:7; :11; 9:2; Gala 1:14; 4:17-18; 2 Tim 1:17; Titus 2:14; ***Revelation 3:19

ZEITGEIST The spirit of the time; the intellectual and moral tendencies that characterize any age or epoch

ZION Any place or community considered to be especially under God's rule 2 The heavenly Jerusalem; heaven 2 Kings 19:21; :31; Psalm 2:6; 9:11; 14:7; 20:2; 48:2; 50:2; 65:1; 74:2; 76:2; 84:7; 87:2; :5; 102:13; 110:2; 125:1; 126:1; 129:5; 132:1; 132:13; ***133:3; 137:1; Song of Solomon 3:11; Isa 1:8; ***2:3; ***4:2-3; ***8:18; **14:32; ***28:16; 29:8; 30:19; 31:4; 40:9; 41:27; *51:1; ***:3; :11; **:16; ***52:7; :8; 59:15; 61:3; *66:5; Jer 3:14; *4:6; **6:2; 31:12; 50:28; Lamen 1:4; 2:4; *:10; *:18; Amos *6:1; Micah 4:1-2; :6-7; :10; :13; Zeph 3:14; :16; Zech 1:14; 2:7; :10; 8:3; 9:9; :13; Matt 21:5; John 12:15; Rom 9:33; ****Heb 12:22; 1 Peter 2:6

DISPOSITION

THE EARTHLY MAN

As opposed to the Spiritual One

You will eat the flesh of mighty men and drink the blood of the
princes of the earth as if they were rams and lambs, goats and
bulls—all of them fattened animals from Bashan Ezekiel 39:18
And Adam gave names to all cattle, and to the fowl of the air,
and to every beast of the field Genesis 2:20

NOTE: This is a list of animals from the Bible, which all describe the dispositions
of mankind. This list will include names such as beast, bird, ram and lamb
which, though generally applied to fabulous beings, have nevertheless, because of
misunderstandings or educational prejudices of the Greek and Latin translators,
crept into the versions, and have been applied to real animals *wiki*

Addax-	Characteristics of a very savage, hard to catch man
Ant-	Accustomed to laying up stores of things for use at later times
Antelope-	A man on account of his lustre and soft expression of the eye

Ape-	Characteristics include tool using behavior, social group dynamics, capacity for language and comprehension, and levels of aggression (They show Possibile capacity for friendship)
Asp-	A spiteful or treacherous person
	And they
Laded	loaded with a burden their
Asses-	Femine and masculine foolish and stupid
	People with the
Corn	things regarded as trite and overly sentimental, and departed thence Genesis 42:26
Badger-	One who ask repeatedly and annoyingly for something; pester. Synonyms: harass, bother, plague, torment, hound, nag, bug, harry, tease, go on at; informal, hassle
Bat-	A crabby, sarcastic old woman
Bear-	A rough, unmannerly, or uncouth person a large, heavy, cumbersome man
Beast-	An objectionable or unpleasant person a person's brutish or untamed characteristics having a mundane and unspiritual life
Boar-	To exhibit actions and/or behaviors of ignorance, self-centeredness, selfishness and a belief of superiority to others
	Those who exhibit this type of behavior are often spoiled and embellish their own worth to gain attention, as well as suppress their own internal self consciousness of being substandard or worthless
Bones-	The basic structural framework of the soul
Bone marrow-	The spirit
Bull-	One who pushes or drives others powerfully or violently stupid or untrue talk; nonsense
Bullock-	Unaccustomed to fulfilling the necessities of relationships insubordinate mind set
Calf-	A gawky witless young man
Camel-	One who transports an abundance of knowledge in the deserts of disillusion and ignorance A dromedary Also...
Milch Camel	Someone who milks others for Information Takes advantage and exploits others (in addition to camel definition)
Caterpillar-	A plunderer
Colt-	A young or inexperienced person
Cow-	One who overawes; intimidates or daunts
	Tyrannizer

Creep- One for whom it is impossible to perceive uneasy apprehension a repugnant person; extremely distasteful; unacceptable abhorrent, revolting, repulsive, repellent, disgusting, offensive, objectionable, cringeworthy, vile, foul, nasty, loathsome, sickening, nauseating, hateful, detestable, execrable, abominable, monstrous, appalling, insufferable, intolerable, unacceptable, contemptible, unsavory, unpalatable; gross, horrible, horrid; noisome

Deer- A totem representing sensitivity, intuition and gentleness a symbol of harmony, happiness, peace and longevity

Dingo- One who propagates warlike ideas (warmonger). One who or that which is Considered uncivilized or wild (warrigal)

Dog- A person regarded as unpleasant, contemptible, or wicked referring to someone who is abject or miserable, esp., because they have been treated harshly a failure one who causes continual trouble to act lazy; fail to try one's hardest voracious instincts and fierceness, loathsomeness; it was regarded as the emblem of lust, and of uncleanness in general

Dove- One having peace of the deepest kind

One who soothes and quiets worried or troubled thoughts, able to find renewal in the silence of the mind

Dragon- One who speaks to others about the need for strength, courage, and fortitude

Dromedary- Creative, self-sufficient, healer, replenisher

Eagle- One having the characteristics of the importance of honesty and Truthful Principles

Ewe A meek bashful timid femenin person

Ewe Lamb A beloved or an only child

Fiery flying serpent- Eagar or fierce in spirit; passionate; impetuous swiftly moving Insinuating person

Fish- One who subtly or deviously tries to elicit a response or some information from someone, searching typically by groping or feeling for something concealed One who connects with purposeful movement and mindful independence, but for the rough currents that sometimes hinder goals A person considered as having characteristic, such as lack of emotion or intelligence ~Out of one's usual environment; not comfortable or at ease ~Neither one thing or the other; without definite convictions, opinions etc.; nondescript To try to get something in an artful or an indirect manner "Why do You make men like fish of the sea, Like creeping things that have no ruler over them?" Habakkuk 1:14

Flea- One causes others to feel unsettled with rebukes or rebuffs

Fly-	one known to represent lies, gossip, excuses, and anything that's dirty or impure, hateful, spiteful, malice, or blameful, also to pass swiftly be circulated among many people one who Is successful knowing and clever alert, wide awake in the day time
Foal	The young of...
Fox-	One who is a cunning sly person who baffles or deceives
Goat-	a femanine or masculine lecherous man one who is the butt of a joke or on whom blame is placed; scapegoat to move one to anger or annoyance lustful
Hawk-	one who preys on others; swindler; shark
Jackal-	One who lies or keep in hiding, as for some evil reason
Kine-	A flock of (see **COW**)
Kite-	A person who exploits or preys on others quickly one who is fraudulent towards others
Leopard-	Cunning, having a habit of lying in wait, and has the fierceness of a conqueror
Lice/louse-	A contemptible; foul; a mean person; stinker; rat; worthless; inferior having plenty or too much (of)
Locust-	One who destroys the necessities which sustain the life of man
Mole-	
Pigeon-	One who is easily swindled
Ram-	One who drives or forces another down or into something
Swine-	Of, pertaining to, or characteristic of a low, greedy, stupid, or vicious person
Weasel-	A sneaky treacherous person worn with exertion, suffering, etc.; tired; fatigued, discontented, **or** vexed by continued endurance, as of something disagreeable, tedious, etc.
Whelp-	A young fellow; a contemptuous term One of the young of a dog, wolf, lion, or other beast
Wildcat-	An aggressive quick-tempered unsound person; risky running wild or without control
Viper-	A treacherous or spiteful person

TREASURE

STOREHOUSE

The word **treasure** originated between 80 BC- AD 200; derived from Latin **THESAURUS** In the 1400's, the French adopted **TRESOR** from **thesarurus**, meaning~ One who or that which is regarded as valuable; precious; rare; (the Way those who know God, who is in every man, regard Christ) Also, to retain carefully, as in the mind **Thesauros** originated in Greek as **THESAUROS** from Homer, A.D. 200, meaning **TREASURE HOUSE** In English, **TREASURE** and **THESAURUS** are books containing a *STOREHOUSE of words, especially synonyms and antonyms arranged in categories ~**Storehouse; treasury** ~Doublet of **THESAURUS**

"Bring all the tithes into the **STOREHOUSE** that there maybe food in My house" Malachi 3:10

"The **Tree** of **Life** was also in the midst of the garden, and the tree of the knowledge of good and evil" Genesis 2:9

For example see: Translation under **CONTRADICTION**

STOREHOUSE: Deut. 28:8; 1 Chron. 26:15 :17, 27:25; 2 Chron. 32:28; Neh. 10:38, 12:44, 13:12-:13; Psalm 33:7; Jer. 50:26; Joel 1:17; Luke 12:24

<u>GENESIS 1</u>

:2   The

(earth)   unrefined, coarse mortal body; also, those who inhabit it, and The worldly and Temporal affairs, as contrasted with spiritual ones (was/were) without

(form)   Proper arrangement or order in the manner in which something is done Constructed, devised, and developed as acquiring in the mind; as habit and liking, to give specific exemplified character to that which makes up an ELEMENT Shaped by discipline and training; to mold and Begin to exist With fitness of mind for performance with An intrinsic nature as distinguished from the matter that embodies its essence, and

(void)   Without contents; useless, ineffectual, (UNOCCUPIED) idle, without improvement; (INCUMBENT) resting, leaning, and weighing wholly upon a burden Holding an indicated position like a dependant, (IMPEDIMENT) Connected by marriage, but having a disability that affects the validity of a marriage; a disability that makes it impossible for God to contract a valid marriage A disability that does not make the marriage null and void, but subjects the man to a punishment; because of that which bars him within the specified degrees of (CONSANGUINITY) Any close connection or (AFFINITY) natural attraction, liking and inclination between opposite natures with similarities A Spiritual attraction thought to exist between certain persons; also the one exerting such attraction The force by which atoms are held together in chemical compounds The property and attraction by which differing chemical elements or groups of elements when brought into contact, united to form a new basic part of a complex whole; primary, integral part; essential; fundamental, rudimentary, and the surrounding conditions best suited for a person's atmospheric forces and Powers A principle factual item essential to the solution of the problem and to proper calculation Obligated as a moral obligation, and necessary under the circumstance, but producing no effect; useless, and empty condition and

(darkness)   Ignorance, wickedness; lack of clarity; obscurity; concealment, secrecy absence of Light; (which is) the lack of knowledge, with cheerless, disheartening, dismal things of concealed evil, sinister, atrocious, ignorant, unenlightened mind of the spirit was on the

(face)   Awareness of the literal and most evident meaning which is apparently most important and designed to fulfill a purpose To see to completion and endure, as by the preserving Manner To meet with courage and confront <u>To</u> become and <u>be</u> <u>made</u> <u>aware</u> of, and ` <u>realize</u> impudence, impertinence, insolence, cockiness, audacity, nerve, gall, shamelessness, impoliteness, disrespect, bad manners and presumptions In each others immediate presence; confronting, notwithstanding Judging by all appearances To act in open defiance, in His presence, with plain words; and frankly To save himself from embarrassment and disgrace; preserving his own dignity and reputation By disconcerting and prevailing over by a bold, audacious denial An assertion of the (deep)   Most profound and intense part Difficult to understand; and obscure Grave; serious Heartfelt; sincere absorbing; engrossing Sound; heavy and profound Having penetrating intellectual powers Profoundly cunning and artful Sagacious, wise, profound, and shrewd Mysteriously involved In difficult, serious circumstances; in trouble In a vast extent, as of space, time, etc. Part of greatest intensity; in a way that is impossible to disentangle or separate And the

(Spirit)   vital essence and animating force, especially in man Part of a human being that is incorporeal and invisible, and is characterized by intelligence, personality, self-consciousness, and will; the mind; mood; temper Vivacity, energy; adore Ardent loyalty and devotion True intent and meaning as opposed to outward, formal observance The emotional faculty of man; the heart The breath Having a special kind of nature Divine substance; infused with the Spirit and encouragement of God was

(hovering) Remaining in an uncertain and irresolute state HOW? In what way? To what degree, extent and amount? In what state and condition? For what reason and purpose? To what effect? With what meaning! over the

(face)   Awareness of the literal and most evident meaning of what is apparent that is most important and designed to fulfill a purpose To meet with courage and confront To become and be made aware of, realizing In each others immediate presence of the

(waters)   Excellence and quality Of the highest degree The degree of transparency and brilliancy Out of danger and secure To be very free and quick To be valid and effective; to provide Life as rivers do water

The mortal body; also, those who inhabit it, and The worldly and Temporal affairs, as contrasted with spiritual ones were without discipline and training Without contents; useless, ineffectual, and the lack of knowledge, with cheerless, disheartening, dismal things of the ignorant, unenlightened mind of the spirit was on the literal and most evident meaning which is apparently most important and designed to fulfill a purpose of the way that is impossible to disentangle or separate And the part of a human being that is incorporeal and invisible, and is characterized by intelligence, personality, self-consciousness, and will of God was Remaining in an uncertain and irresolute state over the literal and most evident meaning of what is apparent, that is most important and designed to fulfill a purpose of the valid and effective; provision of Life

---

:3   Then God said, "Let there be

(Light)   No burdensome or oppression, but easily borne Not difficult; Arduous, but easily done Not great in degree or concentration Intended and enjoyed as entertainment; not lofty or heroic Designating the less massive types of weapons and equipment, as with an enLightened exhortation", and there was Light.

Then God said, "Let there be No burden or oppression, but easily borne enLightened exhortation", and there was Light

---

:4   And God saw the

(Light)   Not burdensome or oppressive, but easily borne Not difficult;

Arduous, but easily done Not great in degree or concentration Intended and enjoyed as entertainment; not lofty or heroic Designating less massive types of weapons and equipment, as with an enLightened exhortation, that *it* was

(good)   Morally excellent; virtuous Honorable; worthy Generous; loving; kind Well behaved; tractable Proper; desirable Favorable; approving Pleasant; agreeable Having beneficial effects; (SALUTARY) Calculated to bring about a sound condition by correcting evil and promoting good; wholesome Reliable; Safe Suitable; qualified Skillful; expert Genuine; valid Excellent in quality, degree and kind (ORTHODOX) Correct; conforming in sound doctrine Of sufficient quality and extent; ample Unspoiled; fresh Being in sound condition Satisfactory and appropriate for specific action, purpose, etc. -Altogether; completely; very Capable of lasting, surviving, and remaining valid and in operation for (an indicated period of time) Able and willing to pray, give produce (inspiration) Entitling Used to show approval of that which is desirable, serviceable, fitting, etc. Beneficial advantage; profitable That which is morally and ethically desirable -For the last time; permanently and forever To be successful To compensate; replace; repay To fulfill (the promise and agreement, etc.) To prove; substantiate -To credit Dutiful, obedient Able, competent Adequate and Wholesome and God divided the Light from the darkness

And God saw the less massive types of weapons and equipment, as with an enLightened exhortation, that it was Having beneficial effects; (SALUTARY) Calculated to bring about a sound condition by correcting evil and promoting good and God divided the Light from the darkness

---

:5   God called the Light

(Day)   A point in time marked by the beginning of a <u>new</u> development; an interval of time memorable for extraordinary events, important influences, and unusual circumstances Conflict and its result A time considered as propitious and opportune A day of contest and the contest itself A period of success, influence, accomplishment; etc., and the

(Darkness)   Ignorance, wickedness; evil; lack of clarity; obscurity; secrecy; concealment; absence of Light (which is) lack of knowledge Cheerless, disheartening, dismal things of concealed evil, sinister, wicked, atrocious, ignorant, unenlightened mind of the spirit He called

(Night)   A condition of ignorance, gloom, painful confusion of the soul

The dark Mental and moral darkness; sorrow; grief Anything unknown The state of not knowing; obscurity; hidden; mysterious -Unrevealed, unlearned, and Unknown information So the evening and the morning were the first day

God called the Light A point in time marked by the beginning of a new development A day of contest and the contest itself A period of success And the lack of knowledge He called painful confusion of the soul So the evening and the morning were the first day

:6 Then God said, "Let there be a

(firmament) sphere or world viewed as a collection of people To support and make firm; in the midst of the

(waters) Excellence; of quality Of the highest degree To be valid and effective The degree of transparency and brilliancy, and let it divide the Spiritual waters from the carnal waters

Then God said, "Let there be a collection of people in the midst of the highest degree To be valid and effective, and let it divide the Spiritual (understanding) from the carnal (knowledge)

NOTE: remember Jesus saying, "This water makes you thirst again, but I will give you Life giving rivers of water, which when you drink you will never thirst again""

:7 Thus God

(made) brought about the existence By shaping and combining of materials He produced; built; constructed and fashioned To bring about and cause To bring to a state and condition To form and create in the mind, as a plan, conclusion, and Judgment To entertain mentally To understand the meaning and significance To utter and express, as for the record To represent as being and appearing To put forward and proffer To carry on and engage in To earn and acquire To act in such a way as to win and gain To amount to; add up to Draw up, enact, and frame, as laws, wills, treaties, etc. To affect and form as characteristics and personalities To estimate to be and be reckoned To prepare and arrange for use To induce and compel To be the essential element and determinant of (mankind) To afford and provide To become through development; having the essential qualities To cause the success To complete To win a place and position To have sexual intercourse with (God) To cause (man) to assume a specified condition To act and behave in a certain manner To start and appear to start to do something To be made To get along with what is available, especially with an inferior substitute To bring about the success of To see; discern To comprehend and understand To establish by evidence To succeed To be the parts of; constitute To settle differences and become friendly again To supply what is lacking Eager for amorous conquest To atone and compensate for the

(firmament) expanse of the heavens A sphere and world viewed as a collection of people To support, to make firm and

(divided) To subject to the process of division To cause to be apart To split into opposed sides; cause dissent in; disunite To separate into sections To separate into groups; and classify To separate into pieces and portions To distribute the pieces and portions To share the

(waters) preparation holding a gaseous and volatile substances in the Solution which were

(under)   Beneath, so as to have something directly above; covered by A place lower than Beneath the concealment, guise, and assumption rank Inferior to in quality, character, and understanding Dominated by; owing allegiance to; a subordinate; a subservient Subject to the guidance, tutorship, and direction of Being the subject to the moral obligation and sanction With the liability and certainty of incurring The group and class; within the matter titled and Headed Subject to the influence and pressure; swayed and impelled Driven and propelled During the period and reign; pending the administration in Planting and sowing with conformity; in accordance with and having regard for Virtue of; authorized, substantiated, attested, and warranted by the

(firmament)   expanse of the heavens., A sphere and world viewed as a collection of people To support and to make firm from the

(waters)   Excellence and quality Of the highest degree The degree of transparency and brilliancy Out of danger and secure To be valid and effective To be very free and quick; to provide Life as rivers do water which were

(above)   happiness in heaven, the

(firmament)   expanse of the heavens and A sphere and world viewed as a collection of people To support and make firm and it was so

Thus God brought about the existence He produced To cause (man) To understand the meaning and significance To see and discern To supply what is lacking To atone and compensate for the expanse of the heavens and To share the volatile substances in the Solution which were Subject to the guidance, tutorship, and direction of Being the subject to the moral obligation Planting and sowing with conformity the sphere and world viewed as a collection of people from the Excellence and quality Of the highest degree which were in heaven, the expanse of the heavens To support and make firm and it was so

---

:9

(Then)   Granting and assigning imperative work to be performed; being and acting in, even belonging to

(God)   the divine, creative Principle; Life, Truth, Love; Mind; and
Spirit said,

(let)   exhort and command to be willing to refrain from disturbing and tampering with the pressure or tension Discharge, dismiss and excuse, as from work and obligation, allowing to escape punishment and penalty to make known; reveal and reduced tension Deal more gently with the

(waters)   preparation holding a gaseous and volatile substances in the solution under the

(heaven's)   condition of great happiness, full of beautiful peace; and general expressions of approval Be

(gathered)   come aware of it through deduction or observation To summon up and muster, as One's energies, for an effort

(together)   into contact and union with each other

186

(into)   To and toward the inside from the outside Passing through the outer boundary and limit of the form, state, and condition of

(one)   being and designating an unspecified

(place)   particular point, part, passage; right and proper position in its natural and original position, and

(let)   exhort and command the

(dry)   Plain; unadorned, devoid of interest and life; dull; boring

Devoid of emotion; cold and stiff Quietly shrewd, impersonal Unproductive Talking stop

(land)   To cause someone to Come to rest after falling or being thrown from A conceptual realm and domain Any (HEREDITAMENT)- (CORPOREAL)- Of, or of the nature of, the body; bodily; mortal 2 Of a material nature; physical 2 Tangible (INCORPOREAL-) Not having material existence To bring to a point, condition, and state To succeed in obtaining and achieving especially in the face of strong competition <u>Denoting</u> a <u>particular</u> <u>sphere</u> of <u>activity</u> and <u>group</u> of <u>people</u>

(appear)   to be clear to the mind and obvious To come before the public; and to be published And it was so

Granting and assigning imperative work to be performed, even belonging to the divine Spirit said, "Deal more gently with the volatile substances in the solution under the condition of great happiness Become aware of it through deduction and observation for an effort into contact and union with each other Passing through the outer boundary and limit of the form, state, and condition of being, and designating an unspecified, particular, natural, and original position, and exhort and command the Plain; unadorned, devoid of interest and life; dull; boring Devoid of emotion; cold and stiff Quietly shrewd, impersonal, Unproductives Talking to stop To cause (someone) to Come to rest after falling or being thrown from A conceptual realm To bring to a condition To succeed in obtaining and achieving especially in the face of strong competition; to be clear to the mind and obvious To come before the public; and to be published And it was so

---

:10   And God called the

(dry)   Plain; unadorned, devoid of interest and life; dull; boring

Devoid of emotion; cold and stiff Quietly shrewd, impersonal Unproduction

(land)   A conceptual realm and domain Any (HEREDITAMENT)- (CORPOREAL)- Of, or of the nature of, the body; bodily; mortal Of a material nature; physical Tangible and (INCORPOREAL-) Not having material existence

(Earth)   The unrefined, coarse mortal body; also, the those who inhabit it Worldly and temporal affairs, as contrasted with spiritual ones, and the gathering together of the waters He called

(seas)   Something vast, boundless, and widespread

And God called the Plain; unadorned, devoid of interest and life; dull; boring Devoid of emotion; cold and stiff Quietly shrewd, impersonal Unproductive A conceptual realm and domain; mortal, also the those who inhabit it Worldly and temporal affairs, as contrasted with spiritual ones, and the gathering together of the waters He called Something vast, boundless, and widespread

LEVITICUS 1

:1   Now the Lord

(called)   Summoned and Aroused To draw out To make a brief visit Designate and invoke from heaven into action Characterized in any way To remember; recollect To bring to consideration To bring up for discussion An inward urge to this specific work To solemnly (INVOKE) call on in prayer, as a witness, for Inspiration He supplicated, entreated, solicited, begged, Beseeched; and implored to Moses, and

(spoke)   Expressed and conveyed ideas, opinions, etc. To use and be capable of using in conversation to him from the

(tabernacle)   The human body as the dwelling place of the soul of

(meeting)   Observation, perception, and recognition; also, face to face,

saying,

Now the Lord Summoned An inward urge to this specific work to Moses, and conveyed ideas to him from the dwelling place of the soul of Observation, perception, and recognition; also, face to face, saying,

---

:2   "Speak to the children of Israel, and say to them: When any one of you

(brings)   conveys and causes a person to come with you toward the place

I AM To cause him to appear and introduce into his mind as a persuading course of action, To set forth giving rise as evidence to The Truth To cause to have reference, application and influence To rear; and educate To reveal Revive; and accomplish restoration to consciousness To give birth and produce fully A cause to be evident To suggest calling to attention an

(offering)   Act of presenting or suggesting for acceptance or rejection; proffer; gentleness; concern and sympathy To suggest for consideration; a purpose, idea or ideal kept before the mind as an end of effort or action To present himself with solemnity in worship To show readiness to do or attempt; to purpose To present; and appear as a token of devotion; A plan; or design; aiming at a particular characteristic to be effective and attained with a practical result; settled resolution; with determination in constancy; in proposition Having the intention of doing and accomplishing, and a clear exercising will with determination to the Lord, you shall

(bring)   Convey or cause a person to come with oneself to or toward a place To cause to come about 3 To introduce into the mind; cause to appear To cause to adopt or admit, as a persuasion, course of action, etc. To set forth as evidence To accomplish; to cause to happen To revive; restore to consciousness To give birth or produce fully To give rise to To reveal; cause to be evident, as the Truth To cause to have reference, application, or influence To rear; educate To suggest or call attention to your offering of the

(live)	characteristic pertaining to, or abounding in Life Present interest and importance; currently valid Vivid and brilliant ready and retained for use, Life, not to be destroyed or disregarded
(stock)	A quantity of good acquired or kept on hand for future use in proportion relative to the magnitude existing between parts (the Word), a part (ourselves) and the whole (Spirit); to adjust properly as to relative magnitude, amount and degree [to think + **REASON**] formed with a harmonious relation of parts, having trust and belief in To make a careful estimation and appraisal -To give credence to Kept continually ready and constantly brought forth, like old goods The shares that entitle the holder to interest and to part ownership of the
(herd)	Large crowd of people, a contemptuous term -The common people; the masses To bring or group together and to care for and drive as a Shepherd (sheep/ cattle) and of the
(flock)	Groups of persons who are members of the same church or congregation; also the whole body of Christians Any group of persons under the care of or supervision of someone Like bands of people traveling or otherwise grouped together, coming or going into crowds

"Speak to the children of Israel, and say to them: When any one of you causes a person to come with you toward the place I AM To suggest calling to attention an intention of accomplishing a clear exercising will with determination to the Lord, you shall bring your offering of the characteristic pertaining to, or abounding in Life formed with a harmonious relation of parts, of the common people and of the the whole body of Christians

---

	:3 If his offering is a
(burnt)	strong emotion and passion undergoing (FISSION) the act of (CLEAVING) splitting and dividing along the natural line of division, as that of bone and marrow Penetrate and advancing through the water, adhering closely; stuck; and clung remaining faithful to the principles in spite of prosecution (FISSION) by exposing the one part to more Light by masking the other parts
(sacrifice)	cherished and desired objects, persons, and ideas etc., also that which is given up Loss incurred and suffered without return To make an offering and sacrifice of propitiation, supplication, etc., of the
(herd)	Large crowd of people, a contemptuous term -The common people; the masses 2 To bring or group together and to care for and drive as a Shepherd (sheep/ cattle), let him offer a male without
(blemish)	A moral fault or (TAINT) Pervading or spreading through Being perceived in every part with emotions; ideas, etc., imbued with an offensive, noxious, or deteriorating quality or principle Defect, as an error or lack of something needed for completion Having a dim luster; he shall offer it of his own free

(will) Faculty by which the mind makes choices and acts to carry them out The act of experience and exercising this faculty Strong determination; practical enthusiasm; also, self-control That which has been resolved or determined upon; a purpose Power to dispose of a matter arbitrarily; with Conscious Inclination and discretion at the

(door) Any means of entrance, exit, approach and access of the

(tabernacle) dwelling place of the soul of meeting

(before) Under the consideration or perception of knowing the Lord

If his offering is a strong emotion and passion undergoing FISSION of cherished and desired objects, persons, and ideas, etc., of the Large crowd of people, let him offer a male without A moral fault he shall offer it of his own free Faculty by which the mind makes choices and acts to carry them out at the approach and access of the dwelling place of the soul of meeting Under the perception of knowing the Lord

---

:4 Then he shall

(put) Bring into a specified state, condition and relation To ascribe and attribute To bring forward for consideration, debate, answer, etc. To express in words To write down; record To humble and deflate To grow To exert To enter in and To give a representation To accomplish successfully To bring to successful completion To cause to undergo To provide -To endure; tolerate his

(hand) Assistance; cooperation Possession and control; supervisory, care Pledge and promise Source of knowledge, information, etc. Considered as producing something Nearby; readily Available and About to occur By the action of; and directly from innocence; Freedom from guilt -Without thought for the future, or the possibility of saving or planning So as to satisfy all the needs and wishes Each holding the hand of another; in close association In one's possession; available for use Finished and done; immediately; without delay To be engaged in an excessive amount of work To continue an activity and interest so as not to lose skill or knowledge To bless, consecrate, ordain etc. To disclose one's involvement and intentions To engage in; undertake The controlling advantage To give, offer and transmit To assist and lead To give deserved praise and recognition To give to the next in succession To distribute and offer among individuals on the

(head) The front, forward and beginning part of The highest and uppermost part The superior part of The source Mind; intelligence Self-control; self-possession; sanity Progress in the face of opposition; headway A climax, and CULMINATE~ To reach the highest point and degree;and to come to a final result and effect To reach the MERIDIAN~ Midday Pertaining to and at the highest and culminating point of development, eminence, etc. To give men freedom of action and unrestrained authority of the

(burnt) strong emotion and passion undergoing FISSION- the act of

190

CLEAVING- splitting and dividing along the natural line of division, as that of bone and marrow Penetrating and advancing through the water adhering closely; stuck; and clung remaining faithful to the principles in spite of prosecution FISSION- By exposing the one part to more Light by masking the other parts

(offering)   To present or suggest for acceptance or rejection; for consideration; a purpose, idea or ideal kept before the mind as an end of effort and action To present yourself with solemnity and in worship To show readiness to do or attempt; purpose To present; appear as a token of devotion; plan; design; aiming at a particular characteristic to be effective and attained with a practical result; settled resolution; with determination in constancy; in proposition Having the intention of doing and accomplishing, with determination and a clear exercising will, and it will be accepted on his behalf to make atonement for him

Then he shall bring forward for consideration, To enter in and To give his Assistance; cooperation, and control To continue an activity and interest so as not to lose skill or knowledge Without thought for the future To give deserved praise and recognition on the superior part of the highest and culminating point of development and to come to a final result and effect (from) the principles in spite of prosecution To present and appear as a token of devotion A plan, a design with determination and a clear exercising will, and it will be accepted on his behalf to make atonement for him

SAMUEL 24

:13   As the

(proverb)   PITHY- Concise and forcefully expressive saying, in a clever and amusing way, having a witty and ingenious ending, especially one condensing the wisdom of experience; ADAGE- A statement expressing a general Truth; APHORISM- A concise statement of a scientific principle, typically by an ancient classical author; MAXIM- A statement expressing a general Truth or rule of conduct ENIGMATIC- Difficult to interpret or understand; mysterious saying A typical example; deliberately obscure of the

(ancients)   characters collectively of ancient times VENERATE- Syn. Adore, revere, venerate, worship, mean to regard with absolute respect salted with soundness of character Characterized by and proceeding from calm, far seeing wisdom and prudence Profound; learned, Greve; serious WISE SAGE say's,

(Wickedness)   "All that is below good, love, kindness, long suffering, honor, esteem, etc., proceeds from the

(wicked)   All that is below" But My

(hand)   Assistance; cooperation Supervisory care Pledge and promise
Source of knowledge, information etc. Considered as Producing Nearby; readily available About to occur By the action of; and directly from innocence; Freedom from guilt -Without thought for the future, or the possibility of saving or planning So as to satisfy all the needs and wishes -Each holding the hand

of another; in close association In one's possession; available for use Finished and done; Immediately; without delay To be engaged in an excessive amount of work Continue an activity or interest so as not to lose skill or knowledge To bless, consecrate, ordain etc. To disclose one's involvement and intentions To engage in; undertake The controlling advantage To give, offer and transmit To assist and lead To give deserved praise and recognition To give to the next in succession To distribute and offer among individuals shall not be

(against) In contact with or pressing upon; in opposition In hostility or resistance In contrast or comparison with or Directly opposite you

As the ingenious ending, especially one condensing the wisdom of experience A concise statement of a scientific principle A statement expressing a general Truth or rule of conduct A typical example of the characters collectively to regard with absolute respect salted with soundness of character say's, "All that is below good, love, kindness, long suffering, honor, esteem, etc., proceeds from All that is below" But My Assistance; cooperation, Supervisory, care, Pledge, and promise, Source of knowledge To be engaged in an excessive amount of work To assist and lead To give deserved praise and recognition shall not be In hostility or resistance In contrast or comparison with or Directly opposite you

ECCLESIASTES
Also referred to as
The PREACHER
And Appropriately styled as
The Confession of King Solomon
1

1   The

(words) Logos (cosmic reason giving order, purpose, and intelligibility to the world) and Son of God To understand and deal with God literally in accordance with His own statements Divine revelation To keep the promise The self-same Scriptures as an embodiment of the Preacher, the

(son) characterized, and influenced by representing the quality and character of David, king in Jerusalem

The cosmic reason giving order, purpose, and intelligibility to the world To understand and deal with God literally in accordance with His own statements the divine revelation To keep the promise of the Preacher, the characterized, and influenced by representing the quality and character of David, king in Jerusalem

---

2   Vanity of

(Vanities) Excessive personal pride; conceit Ambitious displaying; ostentatious; showing off The quality and state of being fruitless, useless, and destitute of reality, etc., of that which is unsubstantial in EGOTISM of PRIDE saith the Preacher, vanity of vanities; all is

(vanity) Excessive personal pride; conceit Ambitious displaying; ostentatious; showing off and the quality and state of being fruitless, useless, and destitute of reality, etc., of that which is unsubstantial in EGOTISM of PRIDE

3   What

(profit) to go forward hath a man of all his

(labor) Arduous mental exertion and toil Heavy rolling and pitching of his vessel Exerting himself for a cause or purpose Progressing with great efforts and painful exertion Being oppressed and hampered Working laboriously; over working and over elaborating To till; plow and cultivate In toil and in distress which he taketh under the sun?

What to go forward hath a man of all his Arduous mental exertion and toil Exerting himself for a cause or purpose Progressing with great efforts and painful exertion which he taketh under the sun?

---

4   One

(generation) of such a group regarded as having similar opinions, behaviors, etc., and a bringing of them into being; by production and origination

(pass) To succeed in meeting the requirements of (a test, trial etc.) To go beyond or surpass; exceed; transcend: It passes all comprehensions To cause to allow (a specified period of time) to elapse; spend To cause or allow to move, go past, proceed, advance etc. To approve or sanction; ratify; enact To be approved or sanctioned by To cause or allow to get through (a test, trial etc.) To convey or transfer from one to another; circulate; transmit: to pass the Word To permit to go unnoticed or unmentioned To pledge or promise To obtain a way; secure a passage To lead or extend; run To come to an end; draw to a close To go about or circulate; be current To change or move from one condition, state, etc., to another; to be altered and translated To be mutually exchanged To take place; happen; occur To be allowed or permitted without challenge, pressure etc. To undergo a test etc., successfully; fulfill the requirements To be approved, sanctioned To come to an end; disappear To give out or circulate as genuine; palm off A permit, order or license giving the bearer authority to enter, move about, depart etc., without the usual restrictions A state of affairs; situation -To cause to be fulfilled, accomplished, and realized

(away) On and on continuously From one's keeping, attention, or possession At once; without hesitation, and another generation

(cometh) Exist as an effect or result Turn out or proved to give and do what is requested To return, revive; attain and attract To regain former status by presenting and offering service To be brought into use to be eligible to receive, acquire, and inherit entrance into and join those who acquitted themselves and became the descendants of those emerging from trial, making progress and developing to be made public; to be published and declared openly Taking possession to change sides, and be successful To survive, giving and doing what is required -To recover, revive, and amount to and result in being an equal 8 To purpose and produce a cause to emerge: but the

(earth) the mortal body; the worldly and temporal affairs, as contrasted with Spiritual ones abideth forever

One of such a group regarded as having similar opinions nd behaviors and a bringing of them into being To cause and allow (a specified period of time) to elapse To succeed in meeting the requirements of (a test, trial, etc.) To obtain a way; secure a passage To change or move from one condition, state, etc., to another; to be altered or translated To cause to be fulfilled, accomplished and realized On and on continuously Existing as an effect or result and another generation To be brought into use to be eligible to receive, acquire, and inherit entrance into and join those who acquitted themselves and became the descendants of those emerging from trial, making progress and developing to be made public: Taking possession to change sides, and be successful, but the the mortal body abideth forever

5   The

(sun) brilliant magnificence, and that of a source of splendor also

(arise) come into being; originate; issue forth; to results; and proceed, and the

(sun) brilliant magnificence, and that of a source of splendor goeth

(down) with earnestness; completely and fully from an earlier time and Individual, and hasteth to His

(place) right, privilege and duty A particular point, part, passage, etc., At the right and proper position Right and suitable Way: One thing giving place to another In its natural and original position Rise to success To happen; and occur To be arranged in a particular position and sequence To find a place; situation and a home To appoint to a post and office To identify and classify To arrange for the satisfaction, handling, and disposition To bestow and entrust: Life in your hands To invest To emphasize and resonate tones of (the voice) consciously resulting from His role and position that causes Him to be in His particular situation where He arose

The brilliant magnificence, and that of a source of splendor also came into being and the brilliant magnificence, and that of a source of splendor goeth with earnestness, and hasteth to His Rise to success To find a place; situation and a home To arrange for the satisfaction, handling, and disposition To bestow and entrust: Life in your hands where He arose

6   The

(wind) way one makes by a turning and twisting course To introduce and proceed carefully and deviously; insinuating To gain an end by indirect and subtle methods To warp; twist To bring to conclusion and settlement To put into readiness for action; excite; and arouse

(goeth) Having a regularly scheduled route and a specific destination To pass from one person to another To move and act in a specific way To pass into someone's possession To pass (himself) into a state and condition To be, continue, and appear in a specified state and condition To be sold or bid for To be abolished, relinquished and give up To die toward the (south) Alliance of people and groups formed for a (**ILLICIT**) purpose; forbidden by law, rules, and custom Illegal, unlawful, illegitimate, criminal, felonious; outlawed, banned, prohibited, unauthorized, unsanctioned; malfeasance, taboo, forbidden, impermissible, unacceptable, adulterous; secret, clandestine, furtive, and

(turneth) To move so that the upper side becomes the under To reverse the order and arrangement; causing to be upside down

Causing and compelling to go; driven To change the flow and direction of one's thoughts about unto the

(north) Free state The maryland; it

(whirleth) turns away and aside quickly Into a state of confusion; turmoil A rapid succession of events, social activities, etc., about continually, and the

(wind) way one makes by a turning and twisting course To introduce and proceed carefully and deviously; Insinuating carefully and deviously; to gain an end by indirect and subtle methods To warp; twist To bring to conclusion and settlement To put into readiness for action Excited and aroused, it

(returneth) comes and reverts back in thought and speech toward a former condition again according to his

(circuits) route that starts and finishes at the same place

The way one makes by a turning and twisting course To gain an end by indirect and subtle methods Having a regularly scheduled route and a specific destination To pass from one person to another To pass into someone's possession To pass (himself) into a state and condition forbidden, unacceptable, furtive, and reversing the order and arrangement; To change the flow and direction of one's thoughts about unto the Free state; it turns away and aside quickly Into a state of confusion; turmoil about continually, and the Insinuating carefully and deviously; to gain an end by indirect and subtle methods, it comes and reverts back in thought and speech toward a former condition again according to his route that starts and finishes at the same place

---

7   All the

(rivers) large natural streams (of information) usually fed by covering

(tributary) persons paying acts, statements and gifts that are intended to show gratitude, respect and admiration (copious) super abundant in quantity; excessive in speech and ideas (fulsome) complementing and flattering to an excessive degree (diffuse) lacking clarity and conciseness; pouring and sending out so as to spread and cause to spread among a large number of people; wandering Subject to; impregnating Characterized by the excessive use of words (run)   to continue and proceed without restraint Moving and passing into a specified state and condition (suppurate) (maturate) fully developing To occur and return, to the mind To incline and tend in continuous succession To drive and force To mold Maintain and control the operation Allowing to continue and mount up Suffering from exhaust, damage; lesson in worth, vigor, etc., as by overworking An unusually large number of demands Great sustained demands To spend wastefully and squander To stab, pierce, and to come to an end into the

(sea)   vast expanse and quantity (profusion) expressed in the sense of extravagance, squandering and waste of (host) the flock; herd and congration yet the

(sea)   vast expanse and quantity (profusion) expressed in the sense of extravagance, squandering and waste of (host) the flock; herd and congregation is not

(full)   engrossed and preoccupied Overflowing with ideas and information, etc. To the maximum development, power and strength [back formation] unto the

(place)   Particular part, point and passage To identify, classify and arrange for the satisfaction, handling and disposition whence the

(rivers)   large natural streams of (information) usually fed by covering

(tributary) persons paying acts, statements and gifts that are intended to show gratitude, respect and admiration (copious) super abundant in quantity; excessive in speech and ideas (fulsome) complementing and flattering to an excessive degree (diffuse) lacking clarity and conciseness; pouring and sending out so as to spread and cause to spread among a large number of people; wandering subject to; impregnating characterized by the excessive use of words

(come)   to advance, move into view and become perceptible Existing as an effect arriving at a state and condition To emanate and proceed; be derived To become Turn out and prove to be offered, obtained and produced thither they

(return)   To come or go back, as to a former condition The act, process, state, or result of coming back or returning again

All the persons paying acts, statements and gifts that are intended to show gratitude, respect and admiration super abundant in quantity; excessive in speech and ideas complementing and flattering to an excessive degree lacking clarity and conciseness; pouring and sending out so as to spread and cause to spread among a large number of people; wandering Subject to; impregnating Characterized by the excessive use of words to continue and proceed without restraint To occur and return, to the mind To drive and force To mold Maintain and control the operation Suffering from exhaust, damage; lesson in worth, vigor, etc., as by overworking Great sustained demands To spend wastefully and squander To stab, pierce, and to come to an end into the vast expanse expressed in the sense of extravagance, squandering and waste of (host) the flock; herd and congregation is not engrossed and preoccupied Overflowing with ideas and information, etc. To the maximum development, power, and strength unto the Particular part, point and passage To identify, classify and arrange for the satisfaction, handling and disposition whence the large natural streams of (information) usually fed by persons paying acts, statements and gifts that are intended to show gratitude, respect and admiration pouring and sending out so as to spread and cause to spread among a large number of people; wandering subject to; impregnating characterized by the excessive use of words to become perceptible Existing as an effect arriving at a state and condition thither they come or go back, as to a former condition The act, process, state, or result of coming back or returning again

---

It is written in the Quran, 3:45 The Angels said, "O Mary, God gives you good news of a Word from Him His name is the Messiah, Jesus, son of Mary, well-esteemed in this world and the next, and one of the nearest 3:46 He will speak to the people from the crib, and in adulthood, and will be one of the righteous" 3:47 She said, "My Lord, how can I have a child, when no man has touched me?" He said, "It will be so God creates whatever He wills To have anything done, He only says to it, 'Be,' and it is" 3:48 And He will teach him the Scripture and wisdom, and the Torah and the Gospel 3:49 A messenger to the Children of Israel: "I have come to you with a sign from your Lord I make for you out of clay the figure of a bird; then I breathe into it, and it becomes a bird by God's leave And I heal the blind and the leprous, and I revive the dead, by God's leave And I inform you concerning what you eat, and what you store in your homes In that is a sign for you, if you are believers"

ISAIAH 29

	:8 It shall even be as when an
(hungry)	Not fertile; poor or barren Eagerly desirous; craving man
(Dreameth)	Has an unreal, beautiful, charming experience, so perfect and wonderful that it can hardly be accepted as real To imagine or envision To consider as possible or to be able to imagine, and, behold, he
(Eateth)	gain knowledge; learn; study; find out; research; look in to To absorb; pay full attention ; but he
(Awaketh)	stir up; excite [< to watch] An arousing of attention and interest; revival, and his soul is
(Empty)	Without value, substance or significance; unsubstantial
	Destitute and devoid: or as when a
(thirsty)	Any longing or craving To have an eager desire of An eagerly desirous man
(Dreameth)	Having an unreal, beautiful, charming experience, so perfect and wonderful that it can hardly be accepted as real To imagine or envision To consider as possible to be able to imagine, and, behold, he
(Drinketh)	receives and absorbs eagerly through the senses and the mind; but he
(Awaketh)	stir up; excite [< to watch] An arousing of attention or interest; revival, and, behold, he is
(Faint)	Lost consciousness; swoon failed in courage and hope To grow weak Lacking in distinctness, brightness, etc. Without enthusiasm, purpose, or energy; feeble; weak - A temporary loss of consciousness, and his soul hath
(Appetite)	A strong liking or inclination: so shall the multitude of all the nations be, that fight against mount Zion

UNKNOWN AUTHOR

It shall even be as when an Not fertile; poor or barren Eagerly desirous; craving man Has an unreal, beautiful, charming experience, so perfect and wonderful that it can hardly be accepted as real To imagine or envision To consider as possible or to be able to imagine (epiphany), and, behold, he researches and looks into it To pay full attention and absorb, but he stir up interest, and his soul is Without, substance, significance or value ; unsubstantial Destitute and devoid: or as when a ny longing or craving An eagerly desirous man Having an unreal, beautiful, charming experience, so perfect and wonderful that it can hardly be accepted as real To imagine or envision, and, behold, he receives and absorbs eagerly through the senses and the mind; but he excites An arousing of attention or interest, and, behold, he is Lost consciousness, failed in courage and hope Lacking in distinctness Without enthusiasm, purpose, or energy; feeble; weak, and his soul hath A strong liking or inclination: : so shall the multitude of all the nations be that fight against mount Zion

MATTHEW 1

:18   Now the

(birth)   Beginning; origin 2 PARTURITION- Archaic CONFINEMENT- Archaic LYING-IN- Of an earnest request for aid, support, sympathy, mercy, etc. A request and reference for a decision, corroboration, judgment, etc. Evoking and attracting the interest, desire, curiosity, sympathy, and the like To make a serious, urgent, and heartfelt request, applying to the higher court of

(Jesus)   The highest human corporeal concept of the divine

(Christ)   manifestation of God was as

(follows)   Holding to the course To conform To use and take as a model; imitate To watch and observe closely To have an active interest in To understand the course, sequence and meaning, as an explanation To come after as a consequence and result To move and act in the cause To accompany; attend To pay attention To follow to the end To comply with, as orders and instructions To perform fully; completely To bring to full completion To increase the effectiveness of by further action:

After His mother Mary was

(betrothed)   To pledge, especially of faith With confidence to

(Joseph)   God, "may He add, may He increase"

(before)   Under the consideration and perception of knowing, they came

(together)   Into contact and union with each other, she was

(found)   To give origin to; set up; establish and lay the foundation on the basis; (of a) PREMISE- Proposition that serves as a ground for reasoning, and conclusions "if the premise is True, then the conclusion must be True" An assertion; proposition which forms the basis for a work with

(Child)   A specific quality Considered as a result or product of a specified condition of the Holy Spirit

Now the Beginning Of an earnest request for aid To make a serious, urgent, and heartfelt request, of applying to the higher court The highest human corporeal concept of the divine the manifestation of God was as Holding to the course To conform To watch and observe closely, To understand the course, sequence, and meaning, as an explanation To bring to full completion After His mother Mary was To pledge, especially of faith to God, Under the consideration and perception of knowing, they came Into contact and union with each other, she was To give origin to An assertion; proposition which forms the basis for a work with A specific quality Considered as a result or product of a specified condition of the Holy Spirit

:19   Then

(Joseph)   God, added and increased her

(husband)   Process and result of joining two or more things together to form a single entity A combination or mixture of two or more elements BETROTH- Truth (expressing TRANSITIVITY-)] Being or relating to a relation with the property that if the relation holds between a first element and a second and between the second element and a third, it holds between the first and third elements equality, it is a transitive relation

(being)   Essential nature; SUBSTANCE- The essential part of anything which qualities and attributes inhere to That which is eternal To be present To be understanding BEING- A thing LIVING- To remain operative; last To have one's home; dwell To lead and regulate one's life, as in accordance with rules, principles, etc. To enjoy a varied and satisfying life; be joyously and enthusiastically alive To escape destruction; stay afloat and in flight despite danger, as a vessel To exemplify and put into practice in one's life; to be forbearing in regard to the conduct, characteristics, etc., of others; to live and behave so as to expiate and expunge the memory of an error, crime, inflicting pain on others, putting oneself before others, esteeming oneself above another, showing partiality, selfishness, concealing what should be known, table-bearing, cheating, being without justice, speaking without benefit, being ungrateful, unmerciful, falsifying, misleading, denying, self-projecting, etc. To fulfill a bargain; obligation, and all in all that proceeds out of thy mouth!! To put up with; endure; tolerate To live and reside as a domestic servant a

(just)   Fair, even handed, and impartial in acting or judging Adhering to high moral standards; upright; honest Morally right; equitable Legally valid; legitimate Rightly given; merited; deserved Well founded; substantial True; correct; accurate Fitting; proper Righteousness in the sight of God To the exact point; precise Really; very; Simple

(man)   One having virtues [Akin to L < men's mind] and not wanting to make her a

(public)   Well known; open to all; without concealment For the use of the people at large and those that may be grouped together for any given purpose Participated by the people as

(example)   Something deserving to be imitated and copied; model; exemplar A design to serve as a warning and deterrent to others by way of illustration; as a typical instance -To act in such a way as to arouse others to imitation; now only in the passive, was

(minded)   Having and characterized by a (specific kind of) mind Disposed of; having an inclination to

(put)   Bring into a specified state, condition and relation To attribute
To bring forward for debate, answer, ascribe, consideration, etc. To express in words To write down; record To humble and deflate To grow To exert To enter To bring to successful completion To cause to undergo To provide To give a representation of her

(away)   At once; without hesitation On and on continuously In another direction

(secretly)   Keeping separate and hidden from view and knowledge and from all persons except the individuals concerned; concealed; hidden Beyond normal comprehension; obscure; recondite Making known and revealing only to the initiated Affording privacy; secluded An underlying reason; of which when known, explains; The KEY -In privacy; in a hidden place

Then God, added and increased her Process and result of joining two or more things together to form a single entity The essential part of which qualities and attributes inhere That which is eternal To be understanding To escape destruction and all in all that proceeds out of the mouth!! a fair True; correct; accurate Fitting, and proper Righteousness in the sight of God Really; very; Simple One having virtues and not wanting to make her a model A design to serve as a warning and deterrent to others by way of illustration was characterized by a (specific kind of) mind Disposed of; having an inclination to Bring to successful completion To give a representation of her In another direction Keeping separate and hidden from view and knowledge and from all persons except the individuals concerned Beyond normal comprehension Making known and revealing only to the initiated

---

      :20   But while He

(thought)   Deliberated; meditated; cognated Attentive; careful; consideration, especially manifesting regard for others Intellectual activity of a specific kind Characterized by premeditated thought about these things, behold, an angel of the Lord

(appeared)   came into view; to seem likely Being clear to the mind and obvious to him in a

(dream)   Unreal, beautiful, charming experience, so wonderful and perfect that it could hardly be accepted as real To imagine or envision To consider as possible to be able to imagine, saying, "Joseph,

(son)   Characterized or influenced by some quality or representing some quality and character of Christ, do not be

(afraid)   Filled with fear and apprehension to

(take)   Assume occupancy of The responsibilities and duties To bring and except into relation to yourself To assume as a symbol and badge To impose upon yourself; subject yourself to; undergo Submit to and accept passively To conduct yourself in response To undertake; deal with; contend with; handle To understand and comprehend To carry with you; transport; convey To receive into the body as understanding; a breath, etc. To let in and admit To indulge yourself in; enjoy To perform, as an action To avail yourself of (an opportunity, etc.) To put into effect; adopt To use up and consume; require as necessary To make use of and apply To ascertain and obtain by measuring; computing To obtain and derive from the Source; adopt and copy To obtain by writing down and copying To obtain a likeness and representation To experience To conceive TO BECOME IMPREGNATED WITH To begin to grow To have the intended effect To make your Way To resemble To follow as an example -To gain courage and confidence To include; embrace To acquire an interest in and devotion to A quantity collected at one time To accept as something offered, due, and given to you Mary your

(wife)   Spirit, for that which is

(conceived)   To form in the mind ; develop mentally To understand; grasp To express in a particular way To become pregnant To believe To form a concept in her is of the Holy Spirit

But while He meditated Intellectual activity of a specific kind Characterized by premeditated thought about these things, behold, an angel of the Lord came into view Being clear to the mind and obvious to him in an epiphany saying, "Joseph, Characterized or influenced by some quality or representing some quality and character of Christ, do not be Filled with fear and apprehension to Bring and except into relation to yourself To receive into the body as understanding To obtain by writing down and copying To acquire an interest in and devotion to To accept as something offered, due, and given to you Mary your Spirit, for that which is To form in the mind and believe To form a concept in her is of the Holy Spirit

---

    :21   And she will

(bring)   convey and cause a person to come to and toward a place To cause to come about To introduce into the mind and cause to appear To cause to adopt and admit, as a persuasion, course of action, etc. To accomplish; cause To revive; restore to consciousness To GIVE BIRTH and produce fully To give rise to To reveal; cause to be evident, as the Truth To cause to have reference, application and influence To rear; educate To suggest and call attention to A coming to be; as evidence, to set forth a

(Son)   Characteristic influenced by a quality and representing a quality and character, and you shall (call) summon; draw out Arouse To designate and characterize in any way To bring to action and consideration To make a brief visit To invoke from heaven into action To remember; recollect To bring up for action and discussion An inward urge to some specific work To solemnly INVOKE- call on (a deity or Spirit) in prayer, as a witness, and for inspiration; supplicate, entreat, solicit, beg, implore; beseech His

(name) Word by which a concept etc., is known and referred to; especially the appellation of a person Semblance and form, as essence and actuality The sacred and powerful appellation of God Distinction To designate; assign for a particular job, duty To achieve To entitle To identify To specify; determine

(Jesus) The highest human corporeal concept of the divine (idea), for He will

(save) Set aside for future use To treat carefully so as to avoid fatigue, harm, etc. To avoid the need and trouble of; prevent by timely action To deliver from spiritual death and the consequences of sin; redeeming His people from their

(sins) Transgression, especially when deliberate, of a law having divine authority Any fault and error; as an offence To violate any requirement of right, duty and propriety; and wrong To effect, cause to have a specified result etc.

And she will reveal; cause to be evident, as the Truth, reference, application and influence To educate A coming to be; as evidence, to set forth a Characteristic influenced by a quality and representing a quality and character, and you shall invoke from heaven into action calling on in prayer, as a witness, and for inspiration of His Word by which a concept etc., is known and referred to To deliver from spiritual death and the consequences of sin; redeeming His people from their wrong To cause to have a specified result etc.

:22 So all this was done that it might be fulfilled which was spoken by the Lord through the prophet, saying:

:23 "Behold, the

(virgin) Uncorrupted; pure; undefiled Not hitherto used, touched, tilled, or worked upon by man Not previously processed Unmixed Lacking experience and contact with; the unaccustomed shall be with

(child) A specific quality Considered as a result and product of a specified condition, and bear a

(Son) representation Characterized by a quality regarded as the product of a particular person's influence and characteristics, and they shall call His

(name) Sacred and powerful appellation of God

(Immanuel) , God with us, which is translated,

(God with us) "Immanuel"

"Behold, the Uncorrupted Not hitherto worked upon by man shall be with A specific quality and of a specified condition, and bear a quality regarded as the product of a particular person's influence and characteristics, and they shall call His Sacred and powerful appellation of God God with us, which is translated, "Immanuel"

:24   Then Joseph, being

(aroused)   stirred up To excitement, as to a state of high emotion; from

(sleep)   A state of reduced physical nervous activity and partial unconsciousness REPOSE- situated, and kept in a particular place with those COGNATE- related to and descended from a common ancestor Allied in characteristics; having the same nature and quality, did as the angel of the Lord commanded him and

(took)   Received into his body as understanding; a breath, etc. To assume the responsibilities and duties To assume as a symbol and badge To impose upon himself To undergo To submit to; accept passively and conduct himself in response To bringing and excepting into relation, (etc.) to him his wife

:25   And did not

(know)   have conversation with her till she brought forth her firstborn Son And he called His name

(Jesus)   the highest human corporeal concept of the divine (idea)

MATTHEW 2

:11   And when they had

(come)   To exist as an effect and result Turn out and proved to and do what is requested To return, revive; attain, and attract To regain former status by presenting and offering service To be brought into use, to be eligible to receive, acquire and inherit entrance into and join those who acquitted themselves and became the descendants of those emerging from trial, making progress and developing to be made public; to be published and declared openly Taking possession to change sides, and be successful To survive, giving and doing what is required to recover, amount to and result in being an equal To purpose and produce a cause to emerge into the

(house)   The body as a dwelling place for the Spirit and soul, they saw the

(young)   Early period of being and development Newly formed

(Child)   specific quality Considered as a result and product of a specified condition with Mary His

(mother)   Divine Principle; God To bring forth; produce and create

To care for and protect To admit and claim authorship, and

(fell)   The skin of a human being

(down)   to and at a lower level of intensity, volume, and activity

In and into a weaker and worse position, mood, and condition Out of action and unavailable for use (especially temporarily) typically because forward progress has been stopped Throughout Supporting or going along with someone else Directing and moving toward a lower place and position (etc.) and

(worshiped) Possessing worth and value; well deserving of respect and honor; having valuable and useful qualities Having such qualities as to be deserving of and adapted to some specified thing; fit; suitable Trustworthy; valuable; necessary; beneficial; exemplary of Him And when they had

(opened) Passage and access because of the absence and removal of barriers, restrictions, etc. Became receptive and enlightened Frank and communicative; not given to deception or concealment Manifest Accessible to new ideas; unprejudiced Receptive with no restrictions on those allowed to attend and participate To improve and make possible access to and passage through To make available and more widely known To become more communicative and confiding To begin and be formally established in their

(treasures) Riches, accumulated and possessed Of that which is regarded as valuable, precious and rare To lay up in store; accumulate To retain carefully in the mind (Doublet of THESAURUS), they

(presented) Put forward for consideration and action; submitting, as a petition To exhibit, to view and notice To suggest to the mind For the time being To nominate to a BENEFICE- A permanent Church APPOINTMENT To make a priest and minister; confer holy orders on

(gifts) A natural endowment; aptitude Of a right and power of giving GENIUS- Extraordinary intelligence that of most intellectually superior individuals: also, one who posses such intelligence A aptitude for doing and achieving a particular thing: especially, an outstanding gift for some specialized activity The essential Spirit and distinguishing characteristic of a particular individual A supernatural being appointed to guide a person throughout life: a guardian Spirit A person who exerts a strong, formative influence over another for good [**Spirit to beget**] Syn. Genius, talent, gift, aptitude, and faculty refer to superior mental ability Genius, the strongest word, is conceived as a mental power far beyond explanation in terms of heritage and education and manifests itself by exceptional originality Talent is a natural readiness in learning and doing in a particular field; it is conceived of as an inborn resource that may or may not be developed Gift is akin to genius on a lower plane; it is also an innate quality and ability that manifests itself without cultivation Aptitude is special ability to learn and become proficient, while a faculty is a particular, inborn and acquired mental skill and knack to Him:

(gold) A characteristic considered to be precious, beautiful, and of the most superior quality, frankincense, and myrrh

And when they had to be eligible to receive entrance into the The body as a dwelling place for the Spirit and soul, they saw the Newly formed specific quality with Mary His

MATTHEW 10

:7   And as you go,

(preach)   Advocate and recommend urgently: to preach patience

To proclaim and expound upon: to preach one must possess his soul by patience To minister; administer saying, "The

(king*dom)   One who is PREEMINENT~ Distinguished above all others; outstanding; CONSPICUOUS~ clearly visible; easily seen Readily attracting attention DOM- Denoting a state and condition; a class of people and the attitudes associated with them, regarded collectively as of

(heaven)   Any condition of great happiness; God, and the Supreme

Being; the celestial powers Full of the beauty and peace befitting heaven Having general expressions of approval is at

(hand)   Assistance; cooperation Supervisory care Pledge and promise Source of knowledge, information etc. Considered as Producing Nearby; readily available About to occur By the action of; and directly from innocence Freedom from guilt -Without thought for the future, or the possibility of saving or planning So as to satisfy all the needs and wishes -Each holding the hand of another; in close association In one's possession; available for use Finished and done Immediately; without delay To be engaged in an excessive amount of work Continue an activity or interest so as not to lose skill or knowledge To bless, consecrate, ordain, etc. To disclose one's involvement and intentions To engage in; undertake The controlling advantage To give, offer, and transmit To assist and lead To give deserved praise and recognition To give to the next in succession To distribute and offer among individuals"

And as you go recommend urgently to preach one must possess his soul by patience saying, "The clearly visible of Having general expressions of approval is at The controlling advantage To distribute and offer among individuals"

JUDE

:17   But you, beloved, remember the words which were spoken before by the apostles of our Lord Jesus Christ:

:18   How they told you that there would be

(mockers) imitators; counterfeiters To defy; make futile and meaningless To deceive and disappoint; delude Merely imitating and resembling the reality A deceitful, impudent, and contemptible imitation Something ludicrously futile, inadequate, and unstable in the last time who would

(walk) proceed and advance slowly In a continual motion; habitual sphere of action To defeat easily; overwhelm To forsake; desert To depart, especially abruptly and without warning To return to earth and appear as a ghost according to their own ungodly lusts These are

(sensual) Pertaining to the body and to the physical senses; carnal Resembling imagery that appeals to the senses -Sensuous refers not only to the physical senses but to any means of feeling sensitivity, as intellectual or ESTHETIC- Relating to perception by the senses' Sensual is generally restricted to bodily sensations and to the satisfaction of the bodily appetites of persons, who cause

(divisions) to think, and feel The state of being at variance, as in opinion, agreement, discord, not having the

(Spirit) State of mind; mood; temper; the aspect regarded as the intrinsic and central constituent of its character The part of a human being that is incorporeal and invisible and is characterized by intelligence, personality, self-consciousness, and will; the mind The universal aspect of reality, regarded as independent of and opposed to (the sensual appetite which comes through the senses, also known as) matter because it is carnal The creative animating power and divine influence of God A person regarded with reference to any particular activity, characteristic, and temper (which are invisible) The vital essence and animating force, especially in man Vivacity, energy; ador Ardent loyalty and devotion True intent and meaning as opposed to outward, formal observance which is sensual The emotional faculty of man; his heart The breath -The ability to articulate Having a special kind of nature Divine substance; God To infuse with Spirit and animation; inspirit; encourage

But you, beloved, remember the words which were spoken before by the apostles of our Lord Jesus Christ: How they told you that there would be imitators Merely imitating and resembling the reality in the last time who would To return to earth and appear as a ghost according to their own ungodly lusts These are Sensuous refers not only to the physical senses but to any means of feeling sensitivity persons, who cause The state of being at variance not having the The universal aspect of reality, regarded as independent of and opposed to (the sensual appetite which comes through the senses, also known as) matter

---

REVELATIONS 1

:1   The

(Revelation) act and process of making known; making visible exposing to view; show; and exhibition of

(Jesus) The highest HUMAN- compound made up of many individuals, functioning as a whole, of that which is established in the mind as a result of conscious thinking with INFINITE-boundless limits; without end and perfect SPIRIT state of mind; mood; temper and disposition Characterized by intelligence, personality, self-consciousness and will **corporeal** (CONCEPT) In the sense, thought, frame of mind; conceived of as the (DIVINE) Supreme Being addressed, appropriated, heavenly, celestial, extremely good, Spiritual aspects of man, devoted in like character in attributes and qualities to that of Christ, to discover and declare (obscure things in the future) by divination and prophecy, by perception of epiphanies, intuition, and insight, through the constant practice and exercise of the Word through

(Christ) The manifestation of God which

(God) The divine creative Principle; Life, Truth, & Love; Mind; Spirit

(gave) transfers freely without asking anything in return; to be the source performance and do the action indicated To devote free gifts making donations; to furnish a view and passage To conduct ourselves creditably, as in difficult situations; to exchange on equal terms; and hand over the Bride (our Spirit) to the Bridegroom (God our Husband); making known the secret of Him to show His servants–things which must shortly take place And He sent and

(signified) By signs and words made it known To be an indication of A symbol; having as a Meaning; betokening in every way To amount to have meaning and importance To express; communicate; and announce it by His angel to His servant John

The making known of The highest compound made up of many individuals, functioning as a whole without end and perfect SPIRIT state of mind devoted in like character in attributes and qualities to that of Christ, to discover and declare (obscure things in the future) by divination and prophecy, by perception of epiphanies, intuition, and insight, through the constant practice and exercise of the Word through The manifestation of God which The divine creative Principle; Life, Truth, & Love; Mind; Spirit transfers freely without asking anything in return making known the secret of Him to show His servants–things which must shortly take place And He sent and By signs and words made it known To express; communicate; and announce it by His angel to His servant John

---

:2 Who

(Bare) Not clothed or covered Without addition; basic and simple plainly, essentially, fundamentally, straightforwardly, purely Uncovered and exposed it to view Really; very Giving record of the

(word) Linguistic form that can meaningfully be spoken in isolation A command, signal, and direction A promise; avowed intention The Logos; the Son of God The Scriptures as an embodiment of divine revelation -To understand and deal with One literally in accordance with His own statement of

(God)   The divine, creative Principle; Life, Truth and Love; Mind; Spirit This Being regarded as the source and embodiment of some specific attribute, principle, virtue, etc. The self-existent and eternal Creator, Sustainer and Ruler of the universe, and of the

(testimony)   solemn protest and declaration of

(Jesus Christ)   The highest human corporeal concept of the divine Manifestation of God, and of all things that he

(saw)   Perceived with the mind; to understand To find out and ascertain To have experience and knowledge of Take care of; be sure To find out; inquire To comprehend To think; consider To gain certain knowledge, as by awaiting an outcome To inquire into the facts, causes, etc., of -To aid and protect, as throughout a period of difficulty and danger -To work and wait until an undertaking, ordeal, etc., is finished -To penetrate, as a disguise or deception -To be responsible for and give Attention

Who Uncovered and exposed to view a record of the Scriptures as an embodiment of divine revelation of The divine, creative Principle; Life, Truth and Love; Mind; Spirit -To understand and deal with One literally in accordance with His own statement, and of the solemn protest and declaration of The highest human corporeal concept of the divine Manifestation of God, and of all things that he Perceived with the mind; To gain certain knowledge, as by awaiting an outcome To inquire into the facts, causes, etc.

:3

(Blessed)   Honored and exalted; glorified invoking God's favor To bestow happiness and prosperity; making happy Endowed, as with a gift Guarded and protected is he that

(readeth)   Apprehends the meaning by perceiving the meaning of the printed and written characters To understand the significance, intent, etc. To apprehend the meanings of things written To make a study of; also, to obtain the knowledge Discovers the true nature by observation and scrutiny To interpret in a specified manner To have as its wording: the passage reads "principle", not "principal" To bring you into a specified condition by reading, perceive, and infer what is not expressed or obvious, as a hidden or true meaning, implication, and motives and they that

(hear)   Listen officially or judicially To respond to; acced to Be informed and made aware; perceive and understand the meaning LISTEN Be attentive in order to hear Give attention; give heed To be influenced and persuaded of the

(words)   Linguistic form that can meaningfully be spoken in isolation
The command, signal and direction The promise; avowed and intention The Logos; the Son of God The Scriptures as an embodiment of divine revelation -To understand and deal with One literally in accordance with His own statement of this

(prophecy) Prediction made under divine influence and direction Any prediction Discourse delivered by a prophet under divine inspiration, also The Book of prophecies and

(keep) Hold and continue to hold in a specified state, condition, relation, place, etc. To continue and cause to continue; maintain To be faithful to and abide by (a promise, vow, one's word etc.) To do the required work; manage and conduct To defend from harm To care for; be in charge of; tend to To observe, as by discerning To be the support To write down and preserve in good order To stay in or on To maintain for use To preserve in good condition To persist in; continue with To remain good for a later time -To remain in the graces To maintain good condition To cause to continue Means of subsistence Guard and custody; care Very seriously; not for mere amusement Permanently those

(things) The ultimate, metaphysical reality behind the physical phenomena perceived by the senses which are

(written) To show and make visible to the mind for understanding, as by letters therein: for the

(time) Duration with reference to this world and all finite existence as distinguished from eternity and infinity GESTATION~ (in the Spiritual sense) The development of an idea, plan, etc., in the mind is at

(hand) Assistance; cooperation Possession and control; supervisory care A source of knowledge, information, etc. Considered as producing something Nearby and readily available About to occur By the action of; directly from innocence -Freedom from guilt -Without thought for the future, or the possibility of saving or planning So as to satisfy all the needs and wishes -Each holding the hand of another; in close association; one's possession; available for use Finished and done; Immediately; without delay To be engaged in an excessive amount of work -To continue an activity and interest so as not to lose skill or knowledge To bless, consecrate, ordain, etc. -To disclose one's involvement and intentions -To engage in; undertake -The controlling advantage To give, offer, and transmit To assist and lead -To give deserved praise and recognition -To give to the next in succession -To distribute and offer among individuals
:5   And from

Jesus The highest human corporeal concept of the divine
Christ manifestation of God, who is the
faithful Truth and trustworthy in the performance of duty, the fulfillment of promises and obligations, etc.; constant; loyal Worthy of belief and confidence Truth in detail and accurate in description With honorable intentions
Witness To see the execution and subscribe to it for the purpose of establishing its authenticity, and the first begotten of the
Dead Exhausted; worn out Barren Without Spiritual life or vitality

Lacking activity, excitement, and interest Without luster, without resonance; muffled Without resilience Tasteless; flat Complete; absolute Having full and unrelieved force Having no certain outlet or opening Incapable of being moved emotionally Utterly tired; exhausted, infertile; barren; without resilience, without vitality, Spirit, enthusiasm, or the like Not fruitful; unproductive The period of greatest darkness, coldness, and the

prince   The son of the Sovereign One of a high order of nobility
A Chief, leader, and One of the highest rank of any class of the

kings   One who is PREEMINENT~ Distinguished above all others; outstanding; CONSPICUOUS~ Clearly visible; easily seen Readily attracting attention [together + to look at] Denoting a state and condition of being Denoting a class of people and the attitudes associated with them, regarded collectively Domestic Dominion The totality of those having a certain state of mind and condition of disposition of the

Earth   Unrefined, coarse mortal body; also, those who inhabit it
Unto Him that loved us, and

washed   Purified from pollution, defilement, and guilt To undergo testing successfully To wash the interior of (the conscious) by confession and without injury, to clean us from our

sins   Transgressions, especially when deliberate, of a law having divine authority Any fault or error; as an offence Violations of any requirement of right, duty or propriety; wrongdoing To effect and cause to have a specified result etc. in his own

Blood   Disposition of mind; temperament; mood Everything that one can obtain The vital PRINCIPLE~ An accepted rule of conduct An axiom and doctrine Guiding sense of the requirements and obligations of right conduct Composition and organization, method of operation Originating and actuating agency and force Constituent element, material, etc., serving to pose and make up a thing, :6 And hath

made   Produced by fabrication, invention and skill; not occurring naturally The time from the beginning to be sure of success Admirable, and well situated us

Kings   One who is PREEMINENT~ Distinguished above all others; outstanding; CONSPICUOUS~ Clearly visible; easily seen Readily attracting attention [together + to look at] Denoting a state and condition of being Denoting a class of people and the attitudes associated with them, regarded collectively Domain Domestic Dominion The totality of those having a certain state of mind and condition of disposition and

Priests   unto God and his Father; to him be

Glory   The state of being invested with glory A glorified state

Distinguished honor and praise; exalted reputation Something bringing praise and renown; an object of special distinction Worshipful praise; adoration To give glory to God Magnificence; splendor The bliss of heaven The state of exaltation, extreme well being, prosperity etc. A nimbus halo and

Dominion   Sovereign and supreme AUTHORITY; the POWER of ruling and governing; domination for

Ever   Any time; on any occasion By any possible chance Any possible and convincing way At all times; invariably Throughout the entire course of time; always; forever To an extremely great extent and degree; extraordinarily; exceedingly Extremely often; repeatedly and ever. Amen

:7   Behold, he cometh with

Clouds   A state and cause of gloom, suspicion, trouble, and worry

A frowning and depressed look (Of such an emotion such as worry, sorrow, and anger) showing in (someone's face) That which darkens, obscures, and threatens Overshadowed by reproach To render gloomy and troubled To cover with calamity and disgrace; sully, as a reputation; and every

Eye   Look; gaze Attentive observation; watchful care

Capacity to discern with discrimination A particular expression; MEIN- The outward manifestation of personality or attitude Interest; desire A manner of viewing; judgment; opinion To get the attention To look at admiringly or invitingly To look at amorously and covetously To agree in all respects With a view to One's own interests To look at carefully and scrutinize shall see Him, and they also which

Pierced   Being affected sharply and deeply, as with emotion, pain etc. To penetrate to the source and meaning; solve; understand Him: and all

Kindreds   Those similar in one or more ways; alike of the

Earth   The unrefined, coarse mortal body; also, those who inhabit it Worldly and temporal affairs, as contrasted with Spiritual ones shall

Wail   Manifest, feeling deep sorrow and lament because of Him

Even So, Amen

:8   I am

Alpha   The beginning and first of everything Designating in order of importance and discovery and

Omega   Is translated as the end; the Last, the

beginning   Initial circumstances and Earliest stage and the

Ending   The Purpose of an action; aim An Inevitable and natural consequence Ultimate state To bring to a finish and conclude, saith the Lord, which

Is   Has existence, Truth, and actual Light To take place and happen To stay and continue To belong To express purpose, duty, possibility, futurity, etc. Respectively Near, by, and which was, and which is to

Come   Exist as an effect and result Turn out and proved to give and do what is requested To return, revive; attain and attract To regain former status by presenting and offering service To be brought into use to be eligible to receive, acquire, and inherit entrance into and join those who acquitted themselves and became the descendants of those emerging from trial, making progress and developing to be made public; to be published and declared openly Taking possession to change sides, and be successful To survive, giving and doing what is required -To recover, revive, and amount to and result in being an equal To purpose and produce a cause to emerge into, the Almighty

I AM Designating in order of importance and discovery and translated as the end the Initial circumstances and the Ultimate state To bring to a finish and conclude, saith the Lord, which Has existence, Truth, and actual Light To express purpose, duty, possibility, futurity, etc., and which was, and which is to offer service To be brought into use to be eligible to receive, acquire, and inherit entrance into and join those who acquitted themselves and became the descendants of those emerging from trial To purpose and produce a cause to emerge into, the Almighty

---

:15   And His

(feet)   Condition of stability; well-established In and into the condition of restored health like unto

(fine)   Superior in quality and excellent Highly satisfactory; very good Possessing superior ability and skilled Keen; sharp Trained to the highest efficiency Subtle; nice Delicate of perception; discriminating Elegant; polished; fastidious: fine manners Cloudless; clear Free from impurities; pure

(brass)   People in authority and of high rank A person's hardness And effrontery, as if they

(burn)   Being of strong emotion and passion undergoing

FISSION- The act of **CLEAVING**- splitting and dividing along the natural line of division, as that of bone and marrow Penetrate and advance through the water adhering closely; stuck; clung Remaining faithful to the principles in spite of prosecution FISSION by exposing the one part to more Light by masking the other parts in a

(furnace)   A grueling test or trial; and His voice as the sound of many waters

And His Condition of stability; well-established like unto Possessing superior ability and skilled People in authority and of high rank as if they Clung; Remaining faithful to the principles in spite of prosecution in a A grueling test or trial; and His voice as the sound of many waters

---

:16   And He had in His

Accordance with and conformable to moral law and to standards of rightness; equitable; just Conformable to Truth and fact; correct; accurate Conformable to a standard of propriety and to the condition of the case; proper; fit; suitable (right)   Most desirable and preferable Properly placed, disposed, and adjusted; well-regulated; orderly Sound in mind and body; healthy Real and genuine in character; not spurious Correct~ Natural rights -Rights with which mankind is supposedly endowed by nature -To restore to an upright and normal position -To put in order; set right -To make correct and in accord with facts Making reparation for

(Hand)   Assistance; cooperation Possession and control; supervisory care A pledge and promise A source of knowledge, information, etc. Considered as producing something Nearby; readily available About to occur By the action of; and directly from Innocence -Freedom from guilt -Without thought for the future, or the possibility of saving and planning So as to satisfy all the needs and wishes -Each holding the hand of another; in close association In one's possession; available for use Finished and done; Immediately; without delay To be engaged in an excessive amount of work -To continue an activity and interest so as not to lose skill or knowledge To bless, consecrate, ordain, etc. -To disclose one's involvement and intentions -To engage in; undertake -The controlling advantage To give, offer, and transmit To assist and lead -To give deserved praise and recognition -To give to the next in succession -To distribute and offer among individuals seven

(Stars)   Classes of self luminous celestial beings, exclusive of certain knowledge, including the Son They are classified according to their orders ASTRAL relating to a supposed non physical realm of existence to which various psychic and paranormal phenomena are ascribed, and in which the human body is said to have a counterpart Anyone who shines prominently in their calling Heavenly bodies considered as influencing (someone's) disposition To transform Be prominent and brilliant: and

(Out)   Away from specified and usual places From a source among others, so as to remove, deplete, even exhaust as a result and conclusion, unto the end Being an activity; and a state manifeste of His

(Mouth)   Entrance into and exit out from anyone; Having and characterized by a (specified kind of) speech went a

(Sharp)   Keen edge and an acute point Keen perception and discernment; also, shrewd in bargaining; artful Ardent; eagar; keen, as the appetite; impetuous, and fiery, as a combat or debate; vigilant and attentive Affecting the mind, as if cutting or piercing; poignant; acrimonious Of consonants, voiceless Excellent, as in dress, mental perception, etc. See ASTUTE In a sharp manner; sharply Promptly; exactly two

Advantage; superiority Keenly sensitive The point and state immediately before something unpleasant or momentous occurs Intense, sharp, and striking qualities Qualities and factors that give superiority over close rivals and

(Edged)   competitors Moving gradually, carefully, and furtively in a particular direction, as in conversation To defeat by a small margin To give an intense and sharp quality to

(Sword)   Power; authority; sovereignty Violence, and destruction

A symbol of power, protection, authority, strength, and courage; metaphysically, it represents discrimination and the penetrating power of the intellect - "The sword of a mouth" metaphorically means: The power, authority, and sovereignty, in the spoken words because the Truth of it cuts like a knife: the deeper the realization, the deeper the wound, sometimes dividing bone and marrow, also, soul and Spirit: and His

(Countenance)   Innocent appearance of the facial features expression, encouraging look and expression, also, approval; support Self control; composure was as the

(Sun)   Person regarded as a source of glory and inspiration and

An understanding Used with reference to success and prosperity Anything brilliant and magnificent that is a source of splendor A position in the spotlight; publicity To shine in His

(Strength)   Vigor and force of intellect; moral power, style, etc. The degree of intensity and concentration Binding force and validity, as of Truth One regarded as an embodiment of sustaining and protecting power Potency, as the understanding

And He had in His Rights with which mankind is supposedly endowed by nature A source of knowledge, information, etc. To be engaged in an excessive amount of work seven Heavenly bodies considered as influencing (someone's) disposition To transform and Being an activity; and a state manifeste of His Entrance into and exit out from anyone; Having and characterized by a (specified kind of) speech went a Keen perception and discernment Affecting the mind (with) two Intense, sharp, and striking qualities The power, authority, and sovereignty, in the spoken words because the Truth of it cuts like a knife and His encouraging look and expression was as the Person regarded as a source of glory and inspiration and An understanding To shine in His Vigor and force of intellect (and) Potency, as the understanding

---

2:2   I know thy

(Works)   Continued mental exertion and activity, directed to some purpose and end The acts, obligations, etc., that one does and undertakes in return for something of value; especially, the activities by which one earns one's Livelihood (in place of the experience of natural death) Any prolonged effort That upon which labor is expending An exhausting effort The matter at hand; the business that remains to be undone A product of mental labor Manner of working, and style of treatment; workmanship The whole of anything Moral duties considered as external acts, especially as meritorious To prove effective and influential; to succeed To cause and bring about; effect; accomplish To cause to be as specified, usually with effort To influence and lead To break up fallow ground To plow, and thy

Labour   Arduous mental exertion and toil To exert oneself for a cause and purpose Progress with great effort or painful exertion To be oppressed and hampered To work out laboriously; over work; over elaborate To till; plow cultivate, and thy

Patience	Possessing and demonstrating quiet, uncomplaining endurance under distress or annoyance and long suffering Tolerant, tender and forbearing Capable of tranquility awaiting results and outcomes Capable of bearing Preserving; diligently Anything passively affected by external actions and impressions [to suffer], and how thou canst not bear them which are
Evil	Morally bad (and practice) wicked deeds Causing injury, damage, and every other undesirable result; harmful and prejudicial Marked by, full of, and threatening misfortunes and distress; unlucky and disastrous Not highly thought of in public esteem; not well thought of That which is morally bad; wrongdoing and wicked That which causes suffering, misfortune, and disastrous Any particular thing, as an act, condition, or characteristic, that is evil Pernicious, hurtful, destructive, immoral, and ill: and thou hast
(tried)	them which say they are
(apostle)	One sent forth; a messenger, and are not, and hast
Found	To give origin to; set up; establish and lay the foundation on the basis; (of a) PREMISE- A proposition that serves as a ground for reasoning, and conclusions: "If the premise is True, then the conclusion must be True" A assertion or work proposition which forms the basis for them
Liars	
	:3 Hast
Borne,	and hast
Patience	Possessing and demonstrating quiet, uncomplaining endurance under distress and annoyance; long suffering Tolerant, tender and forbearing Capable of tranquility awaiting results and outcomes Capable of bearing Preserving; diligently Anything passively affected by external actions or impressions [to suffer], and for my name's
Sake	Purpose of obtaining and accomplishing: to speak slowly for the sake of clarity Affectionate and reverent consideration; interest; account; advantage hast
Laboured	Arduous mental exertion; toil To exert yourself for a cause and purpose To progress with great effort and painful exertion To be oppressed and hampered To work out laboriously; over work; over elaborate To till; plow cultivate, and hast not
Fainted	Lost consciousness; swooned Failed in courage or hope
	Grown weak Lacked in distinctness, brightness, etc. Without enthusiasm, purpose, and energy; feeble; weak - A temporary loss of consciousness
	:4 Nevertheless I have somewhat
Against	In contact with and pressing upon; in opposition In hostility and resistance Directly opposite In contrast with thee, because thou hast

Left Gone away To relate to a person or group favoring liberal, socialist, and radical views Allowing to remain to be used and dealt with Causing to be in a particular state Let (someone) do and deal with something without offering help or assistance Cause to remain as a trace and record Deposit and entrust to be kept, collected, and attended to Entrust decisions, choices, and actions to (someone else, especially someone considered better qualified) than thy first

Love Deep devotion and affection for One who is beloved A very great interest in, and enjoyment of One, also the One so enjoyed The benevolence and mercifulness of God toward mankind The adoration and devout affection of man toward God The kindness and charitableness man should show toward others As a favor; without compensation For any consideration; under any circumstances For the sake of; in loving consideration To conceive a strong and devoted feeling for One To take pleasure and delight in and like very much

   :9 I know thy

Works Continued mental exertion and activity, directed to some purpose and end; labor The acts, obligations, etc., that one does and undertakes in return for something of value; especially, the activities by which one earns one's Livelihood (in place of the experience of natural death) Any prolonged effort That upon which labor is expended; an undertaking; task Exhausting effort and toil The matter at hand; the business that remains to be undone A product of mental labor Manner of working, or style of treatment; workmanship The whole of anything Moral duties considered as external acts, especially as meritorious To prove effective or influential; succeed To become as specified To cause or bring about; effect; accomplish To cause to be as specified, usually with effort To influence; lead To break up fallow ground To plow, and

Tribulation A condition of affliction and distress; suffering; also, that which causes it, and

Poverty The condition or quality of being poor and without sufficient substance, said of knowledge Absence or scarcity of necessary qualities, characteristics, or understanding, (but thou art

Rich Yielding abundant returns; fruitful Abounding in desirable qualities Abundantly supplied, as of knowledge, personality, etc. Exceedingly humorous; amusing) and I know the

Blasphemy Impious or profane speaking of God, and of a sacred person and things The act of claiming the attributes of God Any irreverent act and utterances of them which say they are Jews, and are not, but are the

Synagogue Place for worship and religious instruction A congregation and assemblage for religious instruction and observances of

Satan Evil which doesn't always appear to be such

I know thy Continued mental exertion and activity, directed to some purpose and end is expended; an undertaking; task Exhausting effort and toil The matter at hand; the business that remains to be undone and condition of affliction and distress; suffering; also, that which causes it, and The condition or quality of being poor and without sufficient substance, said of knowledge (but thou art Abundantly supplied, as of knowledge, personality, etc.,) and I know the irreverent act and utterances of them which say they are (now Christians) and are not, but are the assemblage for religious instruction and observances of Evil which doesn't always appear to be such

---

:10

Fear
: An agitated feeling aroused by awareness of (some thought) or concern To be uneasy; apprehensive over (an unwanted or unpleasant possibility) To have a deep reverential awe of: To feel fear within: I fear invisible soul's near me that I may become a ghost like unto them To feel uneasy: have misgivings To be grieved through understanding one's own darkest error none of those things which thou shalt suffer: behold, the

Devil
: Subordinate evil spirit Evil; a lie; error; opposes Truth A belief in death, sickness and matter A wicked, malicious or ill-natured person A wretched fellow -Between equally bad alternatives; in a dilemma -Exclamation of anger, disgust, etc. -Trouble to be expected as a consequence -To acknowledge the ability or success of a bad or disliked person; antagonist etc. -To annoy or harass -To slander shall

Cast
: To give birth, especially prematurely To arrange by some system or into divisions To revolve something in the mind; deliberate To conjecture; forecast some of you into

Prison
: A place of confinement, that ye may be

Tried
: To make an attempt to do or accomplish; undertake; endeavor To subject to a test; put to proof -To attempt to qualify The act of trying; trial; experiment making inferences from them An arrangement or settlement of differences, or of disputed points ; and ye shall have

Tribulation
: A condition of affliction and distress; suffering; also, that which causes it ten days: be thou

Faithful
: True and trustworthy in the performance of duty, the fulfillment of promises and obligations etc.; constant and loyal Worthy of belief and confidence; Truthful True in detail and accurate in description To betray your own beliefs and principles unto

Death
: The unreal and untrue Absence of Spiritual Life Mortal A matter of time, and I will give thee a

Crown
: The highest part Something that imparts splendor, honor, and finish The most perfect and bcomplete state and type To endow with honor or dignity To surmount; be the topmost part To enthrone To finish and make complete; consummate of

Life   Existence regarded as a desirable condition A Spiritual state regarded as continuation or perfection of animate existence A living being; soul; Spirit; mind The period of an individual's existence between birth and translation The period during which something continues to be effective, useful, etc. Manner of existence; characteristic activities A source and support of existence; essential necessity Energetic force; vitality; animation A source of liveliness; animating Spirit A Living Model; also a representation of such a Model The divine principle, God -As though to save someone's Life; with urgent effort, speed, etc. -Under any circumstances -Any easy and happy Life; the sweet Life To recall vividly to the mind To regain consciousness To become animated To seem to be real and alive

(do not) Be uneasy; apprehensive over (an unwanted or unpleasant possibility) Be grieved through understanding one's own darkest error (fear) none of those things which thou shalt suffer: behold, the Evil; belief in death, sickness and matter -Trouble to be expected as a consequence shall revolve something in the mind; conjecture; forecast some of you into A place of confinement, that ye may be subject to a test; put to proof -To attempt to qualify and ye shall have A condition of affliction and distress; suffering; also, that which causes it ten days: be thou Worthy of belief and confidence; Truthful True in detail and accurate in description To betray your own beliefs and principles unto The unreal and untrue, and I will give thee a finish and honor The most perfect and complete state and type The most perfect and complete state and type of Existence regarded as a desirable condition A Spiritual state regarded as continuation and perfection of animate existence A living being; soul; Spirit; mind The period of an individual's existence between birth and translation The period during which continues to be effective, useful, etc. Manner of existence; characteristic activities The Source and support of existence; essential necessity Energetic force; vitality; animation The Source of liveliness; animating Spirit A Living Model; also a representation of such a Model The divine principle, God -As though to save your Life; with urgent effort, speed, etc. -Under any circumstances -Any easy and happy Life; the sweet Life To recall vividly to the mind To regain consciousness To become animated To seem to be real and alive

---

:13   I know thy

Works   Continued mental exertion and activity, directed to some purpose, end and labor The acts, obligations, etc., that you do and undertake in return for something of value; especially, the activities by which you earns your Livelihood Every prolonged effort That upon which labor is expended Exhausting effort and toil The matter at hand; the business that remains to be undone The product of mental labor Manner of working, and style of treatment The whole of everything Moral duties considered as external acts, especially as meritorious To prove effective and influential; succeeding To become as specified To cause; bring about; effect and accomplish To cause to be as specified, usually with effort Influencing and leading To break up fallow ground To plow, and where thou

Dwellest   Linger as on a subject To continue in a state and place, even where

Satan's   both evil and good are common

Seat   Place where everything situated, settled, and established The privilege and right of membership

Location, settlement, and center is: and thou holdest

Fast   To total self deny Not liable to fade The act and practice of abstaining, as from conversation and the company of others; pleasure To be still (for ten days) then effective Deep and SOUND Not easily moved; Firm in place To keep you back; refrain voluntarily from action and forbear for My name, and hast not

Denied   Declared to be untrue; contradicted Refused to believe; declare to be false or invalid, as doctrine Refused to give; withheld Refuse to acknowledge; disowned; repudiated Refused access Refused to accept nor declined My

Faith   testimonies about Me as recorded in the Scriptures and other religious writings, even in those days wherein Antipas was My

Faithful   Truth and trust, worthy in the performance of duty, the fulfillment of promises and obligations, etc.; constant; loyal Worthy of belief and confidence; Truthful True in detail and accurate in description To betray one's own beliefs and principles With honorable intentions Anything given adherence and credence to

Martyr   One who suffers and sacrifices everything for a principle, cause, etc. To be tortured and prosecuted, who was slain among you, where Satan dwelleth

I know thy Manner of working, and style of treatment The whole of everything and where thou Linger as on a subject To continue in a state and place, even where both evil and good are common A place where everything situated, settled, and established is: and thou holdest To total self denial The act and practice of abstaining, as from conversation and the company of others for My name and has not Declared to be untrue; contradicted or Refuse to acknowledge My testimonies about Me as recorded in the Scriptures and other religious writings, even in those days wherein Antipas was My fulfilling of promises and obligations, etc., and constantly; loyal to anything given adherence and credence to One who suffers and sacrifices everything for a principle, cause, etc.

SACRED TEXTS

http://www.sacred-texts.com/

All Scripture is given by inspiration of God, and is profitable for doctrine,
for reproof, for correction, for instruction in righteousness 1 Tim 3:16

The Book of Tobias
https://www.sacred-texts.com/bib/apo/tob.htm

The Lost Books of the Bible, 1926
http://www.sacred-texts.com/bib/lbob/index.htm

The ACTS of PAUL and THECLA
http://www.sacred-texts.com/bib/lbob/lbob14.htm#img_10500

The GOSPEL of NICODEMUS, FORMERLY CALLED ACTS of PONTIUS PILATE
http://www.sacred-texts.com/bib/lbob/lbob10.htm

13 By these five cubits and a half for the building of the ark of the Old Testament, we perceived and knew that in five thousand years and a half (one thousand) years, Jesus Christ was to come in the ark or tabernacle of a body;

The FORGOTTEN BOOKS of ADAM & EVE
http://www.sacred-texts.com/bib/fbe/

The AQUARIAN GOSPEL of JESUS CHRIST
http://www.sacred-texts.com/chr/agjc/

The CORPUS HERMETICUM
http://www.sacred-texts.com/chr/herm/h-intro.htm

I. POIMANDRES, the SHEPHERD of MEN
http://www.sacred-texts.com/chr/herm/hermes1.htm

16. Thereon, O Mind of me, for I myself as well am amorous of the Word (Logos) 26. Why shouldst thou then delay? Must it not be, since thou hast all received, that thou shouldst to the worthy point the way, in order that through thee the race of mortal kind may by [thy] God be saved?

III. THE SACRED SERMON
http://www.sacred-texts.com/chr/herm/hermes3.htm

IV. THE CUP or MONAD
http://www.sacred-texts.com/chr/herm/hermes4.htm

This short text gives an unusually lucid overview of the foundations of Hermetic thought. The stress on rejection of the body and its pleasures and on the division of humanity into those with Mind and those without. 5. The senses of such men are like irrational creatures'; and as their [whole] make-up is in their feelings and their impulses, they fail in all appreciation of self; they do not wonder at those things which really are worth contemplation

VI. In GOD ALONE is GOOD and ELSEWHERE NOWHERE
http://www.sacred-texts.com/chr/herm/hermes6.htm

"The Good", in Greek thought, is also the self-caused and self-sufficient, and thus has little in common with later conceptions of "goodness," just as the Latin word virtus and the modern Christian concept of "virtue" are very nearly opposites despite their etymological connection. The word "passion" here also needs to be understood in its older sense, as the opposite of "action" 2. For just as naught of bad is to be found in such transcendent Being, so too in no one of the rest will Good be found 2. But seeing that the sharing in all things hath been bestowed on **matter**, so doth it share in Good

VII. The GREATEST Ill AMONG MEN is IGNORANCE of GOD
http://www.sacred-texts.com/chr/herm/hermes7.htm

2. seek ye for one to take you by the hand and lead you unto Gnosis' gates. 2. For that it hath with mass of matter blocked them up and crammed them full of loathsome lust, so

that thou may'st not hear about the things that thou shouldst hear, nor see the things thou shouldst see.

XIII. The SECRET SERMON on the MOUNTAIN
http://www.sacred-texts.com/gno/th2/th227.htm

my son! Withdraw into thyself, and it will come; *will*, and it comes to pass; throw out of work the body's senses, and thy Divinity shall come to birth; purge from thyself the brutish torments—things of matter.

X. The KEY
http://www.sacred-texts.com/chr/herm/hermes10.htm

This longer tractate presents itself explicitly as a summary or abridgement of the General Sermons (CH II-IX), and discusses the Hermetic view of knowledge and its role in the lives and afterlives of human beings.

APOCALYPSE of ADAM
http://gnosis.org/naghamm/adam.html

And the angels of the great Light will dwell with them. No foul deed will dwell in their heart(s), but only the knowledge of God.

The BOOK of ENOCH
http://www.sacred-texts.com/bib/boe/

written during the second century B.C.E., is one of the most important non-canonical apocryphal works, and probably had a huge influence on early Christian, particularly Gnostic, beliefs. Filled with hallucinatory visions of heaven and hell, angels and devils, Enoch introduced concepts such as fallen angels, the appearance of a Messiah, Resurrection, a Final Judgement, and a Heavenly Kingdom on Earth.

The DIVINE PYMANDER of HERMES MERCURIUS TRISMEGISTUS 1650
http://www.sacred-texts.com/eso/pym/index.htm

TAUGHT BY GOD

Job 34:32	Teach me what I do not see
John 6:45	And they shall all be taught by God
Isaiah 54:13	And they shall all be taught by God
Micah 4:2	He shall teach them
John 14:26	But the Helper, the Holy Spirit; He shall teach you all things
2 Tim 3:16	All Scripture is given by inspiration of God, and is profitable for doctrine, for reproof, for correction, for instruction in righteousness
Exod 4:12	Now therefore, go, and I will be with your mouth and teach you what you shall say."
Deut 6:1	Now this is the commandment, and these are the statutes and judgments which the Lord your God has commanded to teach you
Deut 32	Give ear, O heavens, and I will speak; and hear, O earth the words of My mouth
:2	Let My teaching drop as rain...
Job 36:22	Behold, God is exalted by His power; Who teaches like Him?
Psalm 25:8	Good and upright is the Lord; Therefore He teaches sinners in the way
Psalm 32:8	I will instruct you and teach you in the way you should go; I will guide with My eye
Psalm 34:11	Come, you children, listen to me; I will teach you the fear of the Lord.

Prov 1:7	The fear of the Lord is the beginning of knowledge
Psalm 51:13	Then I will teach transgressors Your ways, And sinners shall be converted to You
Psalm 94:10	He who instructs the nations, shall He not correct, He who teaches man knowledge?
Psalm 94:12	Blessed is the man whom You instruct, O Lord, And teach out of Your law
Psalm 132:12	keep My covenant And My testimony which I shall teach them
Isaiah 28:26	For He instructs him in right judgment, His God teaches him
Isaiah 30:20	And though the Lord gives you The bread of adversity and the water of affliction, Yet your teachers will not be moved into a corner anymore, But your eyes shall see your teachers
Isa 48:17	Thus says the Lord, your Redeemer, The Holy One of Israel: "I am the Lord your God, Who teaches you to profit, Who leads you by the way you should go
Jer 31:34	No more shall every man teach his neighbor, and every man his brother, saying, 'Know the Lord
Matt 7:28	And so it was, when Jesus had ended these sayings, that the people were astonished at His teaching
Luke 12:12	For the Holy Spirit will teach you in that very hour what you ought to say"
Act 1:1	The former account I made, O Theophilus, of all that Jesus began both to do and teach
Act 4:18	So they called them and commanded them not to speak at all nor teach in the name of Jesus
1 Corin 14:26	How is it then, brethren? Whenever you come together, each of you has a psalm, has a teaching, has a tongue, has a revelation, has an interpretation. Let all things be done for edification
Colos 1:28	Him we preach, warning every man and teaching every man in all wisdom, that we may present every man perfect in Christ Jesus
Heb 8:11	None of them shall teach his neighbor, and none his brother, saying, 'Know the Lord,' for all shall know Me, from the least of them to the greatest of them.
Matt 23:8	for One is your Teacher, the Christ, and you are all brethren.
Matt 23:10	And do not be called teachers; for One is your Teacher, the Christ
1 John 2:27	But the anointing which you have received from Him abides in you, and you do not need that anyone teach you; but as the same anointing teaches you concerning all things, and is true, and is not a lie, and just as it has taught you, you will abide in Him
1 Cor 14:19	yet in the church I would rather speak five words with my understanding that I may teach others also, then ten thousand words in a tongue.

2 Tim 4:3	For the time will come when they will not endure sound doctrine, but according to their own desires, because they have itching ears, they will heap up for themselves teachers
Rom 2:20	an instructor of the foolish, a teacher of babes, having the form of knowledge and Truth in the law
Rom 2:21	You, therefore, who teach another, do you not teach yourself?
1 Tim 1:7	desiring to be teachers of the law, understanding neither what they say nor the things which they affirm
Jerem 32:33	And they have turned to Me the back, and not the face; though I taught them, rising up early and teaching them, yet they have not listened to receive instruction
Luke 19:47	And He was teaching daily in the temple

AMERICA

James Garfield
THE 29th. PRESIDENT OF THE United States

Now more than ever before, the people are responsible for the character of their Congress. If that body be ignorant, reckless and corrupt, it is because the people tolerate ignorance, recklessness and corruption. If it be intelligent, brave and pure, it is because the people demand these high qualities to represent them in the national legislature…. If the next centennial does not find us a great nation … it will be because those who represent the enterprise, the culture, and the morality of the nation do not aid in controlling the political forces. <u>The Constitution is not an instrument for the government to restrain the people</u>, <u>it is an instrument for the people to restrain the government</u> — lest it come to dominate our lives and interests. It cannot be emphasized too strongly or too often that <u>this great nation was founded, not by religionists, but by Christians; not on religions, but on the Gospel of Jesus Christ</u>. For this very reason peoples of other faiths have been afforded asylum, prosperity, and freedom of worship here

Abraham Lincoln

We have been the recipients of the choicest bounties of heaven. We have been preserved, these many years, in peace and prosperity. We have grown in numbers, wealth and power, as no other nation has ever grown. But we have forgotten God. We have forgotten the gracious hand which preserved us in peace, and multiplied and enriched and strengthened us; and we have vainly imagined, in the deceitfulness of our hearts, that all these blessings were produced by some superior wisdom and virtue of our own. Intoxicated with unbroken success, we have become too self-sufficient to feel the necessity of redeeming and preserving grace, too proud to pray to the God that made us! It behooves us, then to humble ourselves before the offended Power, to confess our national sins, and to pray for clemency and forgiveness. I believe there are more instances of the abridgment of the freedom of the people by the gradual and silent encroachment of those in power, than by violent and sudden usurpation.

We may congratulate ourselves that this cruel war, civil war is nearing its end. It has cost a vast amount of treasure and blood... It has indeed been a trying hour for the Republic; but I see in the near future a crisis approaching that unnerves me and causes me to tremble for the safety of my country. <u>As a result of war, corporations have been enthroned and an era of corruption in high places will follow</u>, and the money power of the country will endeavor to prolong its reign by working upon the prejudices of the people until all wealth is aggregated in a few hands, and the Republic is destroyed. I feel at this moment more anxiety for the safety of my country than ever before, even in the midst of war. God grant that my suspicions may prove groundless. <u>The money powers prey upon the nation in times of peace and conspire against it in times of adversity</u>. <u>The banking powers are more despotic than a monarchy, more insolent than autocracy, more selfish than bureaucracy</u>. <u>They denounce as public enemies all who question their methods or throw light upon their crimes</u>. <u>I have two great enemies, the Southern Army in front of me and the bankers in the rear</u>. Of the two, the one at my rear is my greatest foe. America will never be destroyed from the outside. If we falter and lose our freedoms, it will be because we destroyed ourselves. Shall we expect some transatlantic military giant, to step over the ocean, and crush us at a blow? Never! — All the armies of Europe, Asia and Africa combined, with all the treasure of the earth (our own excepted) in their military chest; with a Bonaparte for a commander, could not by force, take a drink from the Ohio, or make a track on the Blue Ridge, in a trial of a Thousand years. <u>At what point, then is the approach of danger to be expected? I answer, if it ever reach us, it must spring up amongst us</u>. It cannot come from abroad. If destruction be our lot, we must ourselves be its author and finisher. As a nation of freemen, we must live through all time, or die by suicide. <u>We have forgotten God</u>. I have been driven many times upon my knees by the overwhelming conviction that I had nowhere else to go. My own wisdom, and that of all about me, seemed insufficient for the day. To sin by silence when they should protest makes cowards of men. <u>We the People are the rightful masters of both Congress and the Courts–not to overthrow the Constitution, but to overthrow the men who pervert the Constitution</u>. Nearly all men can stand adversity, but if you want to test a man's character, give him power. Many free countries have lost their liberty, and ours may lose hers; but if she shall, be it my proudest plume, not that I was the last to desert, but that I never deserted her. <u>I know that the great volcano at Washington, aroused and directed by the evil spirit that reigns there</u>, is belching forth the lava of political corruption in a current broad and deep, which is sweeping with frightful velocity over the whole length and breadth of the land, bidding fair to leave unscathed no green spot or living thing; while on its bosom are riding, like demons on the waves of hell, the imps of that evil spirit, and fiendishly taunting all those who dare resist it's destroying course with

230

the hopelessness of their effort; and, knowing this, I cannot deny that all may be swept away. Broken by it I, too, may be; bow to it I never will.

The probability that we may fall in the struggle ought not to deter us from the support of a cause we believe to be just; it shall not deter me. If ever I feel the soul within me elevate and expand to those dimensions not wholly unworthy of its almighty Architect, it is when I contemplate the cause of my country deserted by all the world beside, and I standing up boldly and alone, and hurling defiance at her victorious oppressors. Here, without contemplating consequences, before high heaven and in the face of the world, I swear eternal fidelity to the just cause, as I deem it, of the land of my life, my liberty, and my love. And who that thinks with me will not fearlessly adopt the oath that I take? Let none falter who thinks he is right, and we may succeed. But if, after all, we shall fail, be it so. We still shall have the proud consolation of saying to our consciences, and to the departed shade of our country's freedom, that the cause approved of our judgment, and adored of our hearts, in disaster, in chains, in torture, in death, we never faltered in defending

Patrick Henry

The liberties of a people never were, nor ever will be secure when the transactions of their rulers may be concealed from them. If ye love wealth greater than liberty, the tranquility of servitude greater than the animating contest for freedom, go home from us in peace. We seek not your counsel, nor your arms. Crouch down and lick the hand that feeds you; and may posterity forget that ye were our countrymen. He therefore is the truest friend to the liberty of this country who tries most to promote its virtue, and who, so far as his power and influence extend, will not suffer a man to be chosen into any office of power and trust who is not a wise and virtuous man... The sum of all is, if we would most truly enjoy this gift of Heaven, let us become a virtuous people. If ever time should come when vain and aspiring men shall possess the highest seats in Government, our country will stand in need of its experienced patriots to prevent its ruin. The general principles on which the fathers achieved independence were. . . . the general principles of Christianity. "God who gave us life gave us liberty. And can the liberties of a nation be thought secure when we have removed their only firm basis, a conviction in the minds of the people that these liberties are of the Gift of God? That they are not to be violated but with His wrath? Indeed, I tremble for my country when I reflect that God is just; that His justice cannot sleep forever." 1781, Query XVIII of his Notes on that State of Virginia. "My views...are the result of a life of inquiry and reflection, and very different from the anti-christian system imputed to me by those who know nothing of my opinions. To the corruptions of Christianity I am indeed opposed but not to the genuine precepts of Jesus himself. I am a Christian in the only sense in which he wished anyone to be; sincerely attached to his doctrines in preference to all others..."

April 21, 1803 in a letter to Dr. Benjamin. "**The doctrines of Jesus are simple, and tend to all the happiness of man**."

"Of all the systems of morality, ancient or modern which have come under my observation, none appears to me so pure as that of Jesus....I am a real Christian, that is to say, a disciple of the doctrines of Jesus." Thomas Jefferson

John Adams
SIGNER OF THE DECLARATION OF INDEPENDENCE; JUDGE; DIPLOMAT; SIGNER OF THE BILL OF RIGHTS; 2nd. PRESIDENT OF THE UNITED STATES

The general principles on which the fathers achieved independence were the general principles of Christianity. I will avow that I then believed, and now believe, that those general principles of Christianity are as eternal and immutable as the existence and attributes of God. Without religion, this world would be something not fit to be mentioned in polite company: I mean hell. The Christian religion is, above all the religions that ever prevailed or existed in ancient or modern times, the religion of wisdom, virtue, equity and humanity. Suppose a nation in some distant region should take the Bible for their only law book and every member should regulate his conduct by the precepts there exhibited. . . . What a Eutopia – what a Paradise would this region be! I have examined all religions, and the result is that the Bible is the best book in the world. Remember, democracy never lasts long. It soon wastes, exhausts, and murders itself. We have no government armed with power capable of contending with human passions unbridled by morality and religion. Avarice, ambition, revenge, or gallantry, would break the strongest cords of our Constitution as a whale goes through a net. Our Constitution was made only for a moral and religious people. It is wholly inadequate to the government of any other. The Works of John Adams, ed. C. F. Adams, Boston: Little, Brown Co., 1851, 4:31

John Quincy Adams
SIXTH PRESIDENT OF THE UNITED STATES; DIPLOMAT; SECRETARY OF STATE; U. S. SENATOR; U. S. REPRESENTATIVE; "OLD MAN ELOQUENT"

The hope of a Christian is inseparable from his faith. Whoever believes in the Divine inspiration of the Holy Scriptures must hope that the religion of Jesus shall prevail throughout the earth. Never since the foundation of the world have the prospects of mankind been more encouraging to that hope than they appear to be at the present time. And may the associated distribution of the Bible proceed and prosper till the Lord shall have made "bare His holy arm in the eyes of all the nations, and all the ends of the earth shall see the salvation of our God". In the chain of human events, the birthday of the nation is indissolubly linked with the birthday of the Savior. The Declaration of Independence laid the cornerstone of human government upon the first precepts of Christianity.

Elias Boudinot
PRESIDENT OF CONGRESS; SIGNED THE PEACE TREATY TO END THE AMERICAN REVOLUTION; FIRST ATTORNEY ADMITTED TO THE U. S. SUPREME COURT BAR; FRAMER OF THE BILL OF RIGHTS; DIRECTOR OF THE U. S. MINT

Let us enter on this important business under the idea that we are Christians on whom the eyes of the world are now turned... Let us earnestly call and beseech Him, for Christ's sake, to preside in our councils. . . . We can only depend on the all powerful influence of the Spirit of God, Whose Divine aid and assistance it becomes us as a Christian people most devoutly to implore. Therefore <u>I move that some minister of the Gospel be requested to attend this Congress every morning</u> . . . in order to open the meeting with prayer.

A letter to his daughter:

You have been instructed from your childhood in the knowledge of your lost state by nature the absolute necessity of a change of heart and an entire renovation of soul to the image of Jesus Christ – of salvation through His meritorious righteousness only – and the indispensable necessity of personal holiness without which no man shall see the Lord [Hebrews 12:14]. You are well acquainted that the most perfect and consummate doctrinal knowledge is of no avail without it operates on and sincerely affects the heart, changes the practice, and totally influences the will – and that without the almighty power of the Spirit of God enlightening your mind, subduing your will, and continually drawing you to Himself, you can do nothing. . . And may the God of your parents (for many generations past) seal instruction to your soul and lead you to Himself through the blood of His too greatly despised Son, Who notwithstanding, is still reclaiming the world to God through that blood, not imputing to them their sins. To Him be glory forever! For nearly half a century have I anxiously and critically studied that invaluable treasure [the Bible]; and I still scarcely ever take it up that I do not find something new – that I do not receive some valuable addition to my stock of knowledge or perceive some instructive fact never observed before. In short, were you to ask me to recommend the most valuable book in the world, I should fix on the Bible as the most instructive both to the wise and ignorant. Were you to ask me for one affording the most rational and pleasing entertainment to the inquiring mind, I should repeat, it is the Bible; and should you renew the inquiry for the best philosophy or the most interesting history, I should still urge you to look into your Bible. I would make it, in short, the Alpha and Omega of knowledge. Congress, 1854. The great, vital, and conservative element in **our system is the belief of our people in the pure doctrines and the divine Truths of the Gospel of Jesus Christ**

Charles Carroll
SIGNER OF THE DECLARATION OF INDEPENDENCE; SELECTED AS DELEGATE TO THE CONSTITUTIONAL CONVENTION; FRAMER OF THE BILL OF RIGHTS; U. S. SENATOR

On the mercy of my Redeemer I rely for salvation and on His merits, not on the works I have done in obedience to His precepts. Grateful to Almighty God for the blessings which, through Jesus Christ Our Lord, He had conferred on my beloved country in her emancipation and on myself in permitting me, under circumstances of mercy, to live to the age of 89 years, and to survive the fiftieth year of independence, adopted by Congress on the 4th of July 1776, which I originally subscribed on the 2d day of August of the same year and of which I am now the last surviving signer. I, Charles Carroll give and bequeath my soul to God who gave it, my body to the earth, hoping that through and by the merits, sufferings, and mediation of my only Savior and Jesus Christ, I may be admitted into the Kingdom prepared by God for those who love, fear and truly serve Him. Without morals a republic cannot subsist any length of time; they therefore who are decrying the Christian religion, whose morality is so sublime and pure (and) which insures to the good eternal happiness, are undermining the solid foundation of morals, the best security for the duration of free governments

John Dickinson
SIGNER OF THE CONSTITUTION; GOVERNOR OF PENNSYLVANIA; GOVERNOR OF DELAWARE; GENERAL IN THE AMERICAN REVOLUTION

Rendering thanks to my Creator for my existence and station among His works, for my birth in a country enlightened by the Gospel and enjoying freedom, and for all His other kindnesses, to Him I resign myself, humbly confiding in His goodness and in His mercy through Jesus Christ for the events of eternity. Governments could not give the rights essential to happiness… We claim them from a higher source: from the King of kings, and Lord of all the earth

l./I/I.(>. 1/I/I.(>

Printed in the United States
By Bookmasters